Gender, Nationalism, and War

Virginia Woolf famously wrote "as a woman I have no country," suggesting that women had little stake in defending countries where they are considered second-class citizens, and should instead be forces for peace. Yet women have been perpetrators as well as victims of violence in nationalist conflicts. This unique book generates insights into the role of gender in nationalist violence by examining feature films from a range of conflict zones. In *The Battle of Algiers*, female bombers destroy civilians while men dress in women's clothes to prevent the French army from capturing and torturing them. *Prisoner of the Mountains* shows a Chechen girl falling in love with her Russian captive as his mother tries to rescue him. Providing historical and political context to these and other films, Matthew Evangelista identifies the key role that economic decline plays in threatening masculine identity and provoking the misogynistic violence that often accompanies nationalist wars.

MATTHEW EVANGELISTA is President White Professor of History and Political Science and former chair of the Department of Government at Cornell University.

Gender, Nationalism, and War

Conflict on the Movie Screen

Matthew Evangelista

CAMBRIDGE
UNIVERSITY PRESS

CAMBRIDGE UNIVERSITY PRESS
Cambridge, New York, Melbourne, Madrid, Cape Town,
Singapore, São Paulo, Delhi, Tokyo, Mexico City

Cambridge University Press
The Edinburgh Building, Cambridge CB2 8RU, UK

Published in the United States of America by Cambridge University Press, New York

www.cambridge.org
Information on this title: www.cambridge.org/9780521173544

First published 2011

Printed in the United Kingdom at the University Press, Cambridge

A catalog record for this publication is available from the British Library

Library of Congress Cataloging in Publication data
Evangelista, Matthew, 1958–
    Gender, nationalism, and war : conflict on the movie screen / Matthew Evangelista.
        p.   cm.
    Includes bibliographical references and index.
    ISBN 978-0-521-17354-4 (pbk.)
    1. Women in motion pictures.   2. War films–History and criticism.
    3. Sex role in motion pictures.   4. Nationalism in motion pictures.
    5. Political violence in motion pictures.   6. Men in motion pictures.
    7. Women–Political activity.   8. Violence in women.   I. Title.
    PN1995.9.W6E73   2011
    791.42′6581–dc22
    2010051876

ISBN 978-1-107-00194-7 Hardback
ISBN 978-0-521-17354-4 Paperback

To Robert Hennessy, a devoted teacher who encouraged my pursuit of the joys of language and literature, and to the students of my course on Gender, Nationalism, and War who inspired this book.

Contents

List of figures   *page* ix
Preface   xi

1   Virginia Woolf's purse   1
    War as a mostly male activity   4
    Hypotheses on gender, nationalism, and war   11
    Masculinity, femininity, and violence in the American Western   17
    Trailer: gender and nationalist violence on film   21

2   Algeria: a world constructed out of ruins   25
    Colonial exploitation and discrimination   27
    Gender roles before the independence movement   32
    Origins of the Algerian war   35
    Subverting stereotypes in *The Battle of Algiers*   39
    Pontecorvo's neorealism and its limits   58
    Algeria after independence   63
    The proliferation of small (misogynist) men   66
    Legacies of violence   78

3   Yugoslavia: archetype or anomaly?   80
    Yugoslavia's history: conflict and coexistence   82
    What constitutes difference? Bosnia's ephemeral ethnicity   86
    Grievance and greed: economic sources of conflict   90
    Media manipulation: "Television was more important than history"   95
    Women and nationalism in Yugoslavia   98
    Gender and the wars   103
    Pretty Village, Pretty Flame   114

4   Chechnya: virgins, mothers, and terrorists   139
    Two centuries of Russo-Chechen relations   143
    Solidifying stereotypes in Chechnya   145
    Socio-economic change and the demise of the Soviet model   147

Chechnya's bid for independence   149
War after war   151
Women, violence, and Islam   156
Gender between tradition and modernity   159
Sexual violence and the limits of peacemaking   165
Chechnya on screen   169
From romantic realism to crude caricature   177
From "White Stockings" to "Black Widows"   187
Gender role reversal and the promise of redemption   192

5   Québec: *oui*, no, or *femme*   203
Origins of French Canadian nationalism   204
Women and the early nationalist movement   209
The Quiet Revolution   212
Language and sovereignty   214
The FLQ and the October Crisis   218
Nô: "The culture survives because of the mothers"   223
Yvette and the 1980 referendum   236
Choosing not to choose: "So what's the problem?"   242

6   "To live to see better times": gender, nationalism,
      sovereignty, equality   253
Nationalism   255
Sovereignty   259
Equality   263
Sequel: gender and nationalist violence on film   269

Index   272

Figures

1.1	Economic emasculation (*Glengarry Glen Ross*)	*page* 17
1.2	Symbolic emasculation (*High Noon*)	19
1.3	Reconsidering nonviolence (*High Noon*)	20
2.1	Wedding ceremony (*The Battle of Algiers*)	40
2.2	Passing as Muslim (*The Battle of Algiers*)	43
2.3	"Didn't you know?" (*The Battle of Algiers*)	43
2.4	Female shield (*The Battle of Algiers*)	44
2.5	*Soirée* (*The Battle of Algiers*)	45
2.6	"Don't you find it rather cowardly?" (*The Battle of Algiers*)	46
2.7	"Give us your bombers, sir" (*The Battle of Algiers*)	46
2.8	*Boudoir* (*The Battle of Algiers*)	48
2.9	Cutting hair (*The Battle of Algiers*)	48
2.10	Applying lipstick (*The Battle of Algiers*)	49
2.11	Waiting (*The Battle of Algiers*)	49
2.12	Passing as European (*The Battle of Algiers*)	50
2.13	Ice cream (*The Battle of Algiers*)	51
2.14	Second thoughts? (*The Battle of Algiers*)	52
2.15	Passing as women (*The Battle of Algiers*)	55
2.16	Hiding in the well (*The Battle of Algiers*)	55
2.17	"They had to transform themselves into us" (*The Battle of Algiers*)	56
3.1	Cutting the ribbon (*Pretty Village, Pretty Flame*)	119
3.2	"Will there be a war?" (*Pretty Village, Pretty Flame*)	121
3.3	"Fuck the art, just pull the trigger" (*Pretty Village, Pretty Flame*)	123
4.1	Dina guards her prisoners (*Prisoner of the Mountains*)	174
4.2	Dina takes the guns (*Prisoner of the Mountains*)	176
4.3	Abdul returns (*Prisoner of the Mountains*)	176
4.4	Violating "the unwritten rule" (*Checkpoint*)	178
4.5	Madam investigator arrives (*Checkpoint*)	179
4.6	Naked welcome (*Checkpoint*)	180
4.7	Zhanna and Akhmed (*House of Fools*)	197

4.8   "Down with fascism and Russian chauvinism!"
      (*House of Fools*)   198
4.9   Zhanna and the "White Stocking" sniper (*House of Fools*)   199
4.10 "But we are enemies now" (*Prisoner of the Mountains*)   201
4.11 A soldier's mother (*Prisoner of the Mountains*)   201
5.1   A male actor with a female mask (*Nô*)   226
5.2   A female actor with a masculine face (*Nô*)   228
5.3   François-Xavier and Sophie (*Nô*)   229
5.4   Michel (*Nô*)   229
5.5   At the sushi restaurant (*Nô*)   231
5.6   Backstage (*Nô*)   234
5.7   Sophie arrested (*Nô*)   235
5.8   "They've become bourgeois" (*Nô*)   236

Preface

Women make up more than 15 percent of the US armed forces, on active duty and in the reserves and National Guard. They have occupied the office of secretary of state and national security adviser in Democratic and Republican administrations. They have served in Iraq and Afghanistan as heroes and victims, sometimes at the same time, as in the case of Jessica Lynch. At Abu Ghraib prison women held positions ranging from prison commandant, General Janis Karpinski, to rank-and-file torturer, Lynndie England, and as prominent scapegoats for the crimes committed there and by their superiors. From the Tailhook scandal to "don't ask, don't tell," one can hardly avoid the issue of gender and war, and that is only in the US military. Outside the United States, women have played key roles as guerrilla fighters, as peace activists, peacekeepers, mediators, and judges presiding over international tribunals for bringing war criminals to justice. As I put the finishing touches to this book, the headlines report on the situation in the Russian North Caucasus, where human rights abuses connected to the violence in Chechnya have given rise to the phenomenon of female suicide bombers. It is no wonder that the topic of gender and war has increasingly attracted the attention of not only feminist scholars, who have long been interested in it, but a broad range of academics and journalists.

The first course I taught on gender was an undergraduate seminar at the University of Michigan in the early 1990s called "Women under Socialism." Although I offered it in a political science department, the students and I did not read any political science articles. Instead we relied entirely on fiction, biography, and journalistic essays as the raw material for doing what political scientists do – formulate hypotheses and make generalizations based on comparison. The course dealt mainly with comparisons across generations of women, between countries, and between political systems – before, during, and after "socialism." Violence and nationalism received some attention in our discussions of Vietnam and China and our examination of the ongoing disintegration of Yugoslavia. In the intervening fifteen years since I taught that course (only once), ethnic and nationalist violence came to dominate much of the news in our post-Cold War world. When I joined the faculty at Cornell in 1996, I began teaching a seminar on "Gender, Nationalism, and War," and I showed a few feature films relevant to the topic, including Gillo Pontecorvo's 1966 masterpiece, *The Battle of Algiers*. I found the students eager to explore the insights offered in the cinematic treatment of gender and violence in the context of nationalist struggles, and with each iteration of the course, the role of the films grew. The result is this book, an unusual combination of visual and political analysis that draws on conventional historical and social-science sources, as well as the movies.

This project has given me the opportunity to return to one of my first loves, Russian and comparative literature – among the only things I enjoyed about high school and the focus of much of my undergraduate study – and an abiding interest in the cinema that dates from about the same time. I dedicate it to Robert Hennessy, who taught me Russian language and Russian and European literature in high school, and who has continued over the decades to garner rave reviews from his students (as I was able to find out from a certain internet site); and to my own students, who inspired me to bring the tools of literary and visual analysis to the study of politics.

I owe a great debt to many colleagues who helped with this project, including (and I apologize if I have left anyone out): Heidi Arsenault, Anindita Banerjee, Olivier Barsalou, Bettina Bradbury, Raphaëlle Branche, Benjamin Brower, Susan Buck-Morss, Holly Case, Debra Castillo, Michele Chiaruzzi, Nancy Condee, miriam cooke, Chip Gagnon, Danielle Haque, Heather Hendershot, Aida Hozić, Jonathan Kirshner, Mark Kramer, Tafer Mahiedinne, Aleksandra Milićević, Vladimir Padunov, Mark Selden, Michel Seymour, Anna Marie Smith, and Suzanne Boivin Sommerville. Some provided valuable advice for framing the study, others read individual case chapters carefully and saved me from numerous embarrassing mistakes, still others offered suggestions and information, including about reproducing the images captured from the films.

I received excellent comments on some of the chapters and related papers from participants in the workshop on Violence, Gender, and the Cinematic Nation, sponsored by Cornell's Peace Studies Program (now the Judith Reppy Institute for Peace and Conflict Studies), and the members of the Brett de Bary interdisciplinary writing group on Human Rights and Cosmopolitanism, funded by a grant from the Mellon Foundation and organized by Stephanie DeGooyer and Diane Rubenstein. Some of my thinking on this topic benefited from the wonderful experience of co-teaching an undergraduate seminar with my colleague Mary Katzenstein. I am especially grateful to John Haslam of Cambridge University Press for his willingness to consider this project and to Carrie Parkinson, Josephine Lane, Joanna Breeze, and Carol Fellingham Webb for their help.

A word on the book's use of images from the films. All of the images I "captured" myself from DVDs; they are not production or publicity stills from the studios. I am grateful to Michael Tolomeo for enhancing the resolution so that they could be reproduced. My use of these images for a scholarly publication falls well within the bounds of the doctrine of "fair use," under US copyright law. I agree with the view of the US Society for Cinema and Media Studies that reproducing an image is the equivalent of quoting a word or phrase from a novel and that acknowledgment of the source, rather than permission, is required for such use. For this book, I have notified the copyright owners of my intended use, but not requested permission, with two exceptions. Given my extensive use of images from *The Battle of Algiers*, including for the book's cover, I requested and received permission to use them all without charge. I am grateful to Zaphira Yacef and Kevin Durst of Casbah Entertainment for their cooperation. I also appreciate the interest in my project from the representatives of Robert Lepage, the director of *Nô*, and his team at La Caserne and In Extremis Images, and, in particular, Vincent Masson.

The book is the product of work over an extended period, interrupted by various administrative duties at Cornell. I completed first drafts of several chapters while on a Fulbright scholarship in Italy in 2005–2006. Our apartment in Milan was located near the intersection of Via Leone Tolstoi – a fitting location, given the extent to which Tolstoi's writing inspired some of the films at the center of my chapter on Chechnya, and inspired my own interest in language, literature, and culture when I was still a teenager. The project received a big boost from a relaxing and productive week at the home of my mother, Irene Tibert, and her husband, Bill, in Florida. I spent the two hundred thirty-second anniversary of US independence and the forty-sixth anniversary of Algerian independence (the next day) there, revising my chapter on Algeria. I am grateful to the Tiberts and to my in-laws, Maurice and Myril Filler, for their continued interest in and support of my work. I thank Joanie for, among many things, watching movies with me.

1 Virginia Woolf's purse

> "We all came out of Gogol's 'Overcoat,'" the most famous apocryphal saying of Russian literature, is attributed to Dostoevsky. It suggests not only that Gogol was the great source of the Russian novel but that his works lent themselves to a wide enough range of interpretations for his overcoat to shelter, comfortably, future Turgenevs, Chekhovs, Dostoevskys, and Tolstoys.
>
> Alex de Jonge, 1974[1]

Motherland. Mother tongue. The birth of the nation. These common metaphors suggest a link between gender and nationalist movements. Women in general and mothers in particular are responsible for inculcating the key characteristics that define a cultural or ethnic identity, including such basics as language, religion, dress, and cuisine. Women serve as "boundary markers" between different national, ethnic, and religious communities, and thus might be expected to play an important role when such communities come into violent conflict.[2] Yet the relationship between gender, identity, and ethnic or nationalist conflict is only beginning to receive systematic investigation from social scientists.[3] In some major overviews of ethnic conflict, by anthropologists and political scientists alike, one cannot even find *gender* or *women* in the index.[4]

---

[1] Alex de Jonge, "Under the Overcoat," review of Henri Troyat, *Divided Soul: The Life of Gogol*, *New York Review of Books*, 21, 6 (April 18, 1974).

[2] Deniz Kandyoti, "Identity and its Discontents: Women and the Nation," *Millennium: Journal of International Studies*, 20, 3 (1991), pp. 429–443; Anne McClintock, *Imperial Leather: Race, Gender and Sexuality in the Colonial Contest* (New York: Routledge, 1995).

[3] See, for examples of statistical and qualitative case-study approaches, respectively, Mary Caprioli, "Primed for Violence: The Role of Gender Inequality in Predicting Internal Conflict," *International Studies Quarterly*, 49, 2 (June) 2005, pp. 161–178; and Joyce P. Kaufman and Kristen P. Williams, *Women, the State, and War: A Comparative Perspective on Citizenship and Nationalism* (Lexington, MA: Lexington Books, 2007).

[4] Jack David Eller, *From Culture to Ethnicity to Conflict: An Anthropological Perspective on Ethnic Conflict* (Ann Arbor: University of Michigan Press, 1999); Ted Robert Gurr, *Peoples versus States: Minorities at Risk in the New Century* (Washington, DC: United States Institute of Peace Press, 2000). The neglect of gender and women holds true for theories

1

A number of scholars have begun to remedy the situation by addressing the role of women and political violence broadly – a subject made more urgent in the wake of the "war on terror," the Abu Ghraib torture scandal, and incidences of female suicide terrorism.[5] Although few in number, the scholars who have looked specifically at the relationship between gender, nationalism, and conflict have produced some intriguing hypotheses – about men as well as women. They have followed a path blazed by one of the most creative thinkers about these matters – the novelist and essayist Virginia Woolf.

For scholarship is not the only, or even the most effective, way to generate insights about social relations. Few have captured the psychology of a speculative economic bubble and the consequences for society – a timely subject for the first decade of the twenty-first century – as well as the nineteenth-century English novelist Anthony Trollope in *The Way We Live Now* (1875). Russian literature is rich with examples of novelists conveying some of the most profound human emotions and interactions – from the existential anxiety of Gogol's Akakii Akakievich in "The Overcoat" (1842) to the self-absorbed nihilism of Dostoevskii's revolutionaries in *The Devils* (1872). Tolstoi so effectively portrayed the range of human relationships across gender, age, and historical time (not to mention the verisimilitude of his battle scenes) that a later Russian writer, Isaac Babel, observed of *War and Peace* (1869): "If the world could write by itself, it would write like Tolstoi."[6]

In that context it is not surprising that Virginia Woolf, the novelist, should produce such enduring insights into the relationship between gender, nationalism, and war. In *Three Guineas*, she poses the question: how are we to prevent war? She seeks to answer it by responding in a series of

of violence that are not necessarily related to nationalism or ethnicity. For a critique, see Laura Sjoberg and Caron E. Gentry, *Mothers, Monsters, Whores: Women's Violence in Global Politics* (London: Zed Books, 2007), esp. ch. 7. One of the most influential treatments of nationalism, Benedict Anderson's *Imagined Communities* (London: Verso, 1983), has also come in for criticism of its neglect of gender. See, in particular, McClintock, *Imperial Leather*.

5 See Caroline O. N. Moser and Fiona C. Clark, eds., *Victims, Perpetrators or Actors? Gender, Armed Conflict and Political Violence* (London: Zed Books, 2001); Tara McKelvey, ed., *One of the Guys: Women as Aggressors and Torturers* (Emeryville, CA: Seal Press, 2007); Paige Whaley Eager, *From Freedom Fighters to Terrorists: Women and Political Violence* (Aldershot: Ashgate, 2008); Sarala Emmanuel, "The Female Militant Romanticised," *Women in Action*, 1 (2002), www.isiswomen.org/wia/wia102/femmilitant.htm; Sjoberg and Gentry, *Mothers, Monsters, Whores*. Cynthia Enloe, the preeminent theorist of gender, nationalism, and war, whose work is discussed throughout this book, has written on the issues raised by the "global war on terror" as well. See, for example, her *Globalization and Militarism: Feminists Make the Link* (Lanham, MD: Rowman & Littlefield, 2007).

6 Quoted in Richard Pevear's Introduction to *War and Peace*, trans. by Richard Pevear and Larissa Volokhonsky (New York: Random House, 2007), p. vii.

letters to requests for donations (a guinea) from the leaders of an antiwar society, an organization to promote women in the professions, and a fund for building a women's college. She finds the impetus to war in men's competitive behavior, not only in the armed forces, but in higher education, the clergy, and business. She conveys her views in witty, barbed prose, but also in pictures. She makes the point that one sign of men's hierarchical nature is their reliance on dress "to advertise the social, professional, or intellectual standing of the wearer." When women advertise their profession by their dress – at least "in the opinion of St. Paul" – they are considered "immodest."

Yet the tradition, or belief, lingers among us that to express worth of any kind, whether intellectual or moral, by wearing pieces of metal, or ribbon, coloured hoods or gowns, is a barbarity which deserves the ridicule which we bestow upon the rites of savages. A woman who advertised her motherhood by a tuft of horsehair on the left shoulder would scarcely, you will agree, be a venerable object.[7]

In the original edition of *Three Guineas* (but unfortunately not in the subsequent paperback editions), these remarks were followed by several photographs of men in feathers, wigs, furs, gowns, jewelry, and ornate hats – all intended to convey Woolf's point that the symbols of masculine competition make for "a ridiculous, a barbarous, a displeasing spectacle."[8]

If, as the cliché has it, a picture is worth a thousand words, then a moving picture should be worth at least a scholarly article or book. The premise of this book is that we can learn much about the relationship that Virginia Woolf first explored in the 1930s between gender, nationalism, and war by watching movies. In the chapters that follow, I explore the myriad ways that gender stereotypes contribute to the militarization of national movements by examining feature films that treat major nationalist conflicts – in Algeria, former Yugoslavia, Chechnya, and Québec. The project is explicitly interdisciplinary. I employ the tools of visual and textual analysis (but not the jargon, to the extent I can avoid it) to evaluate what social scientists like to call *hypotheses* about relationships between gender, nationalism, and violence. My main inspiration is the essay by Virginia Woolf, a woman known primarily for her fiction, yet it is the causal logic of her arguments about the real world around her

---

[7] Virginia Woolf, *Three Guineas* (New York: Harcourt, Brace, 1938), pp. 29–30. For an exploration of how the theme of St. Paul's teachings figures in *Three Guineas*, see Christine Froula, *Virginia Woolf and the Bloomsbury Avant-Garde: War, Civilization, Modernity* (New York: Columbia University Press, 2005), ch. 8.
[8] Woolf, *Three Guineas*, pp. 30–31.

that invites further inquiry. Political scientists have begun to gather and analyze data to evaluate some of Woolf's hypotheses – even if they seem unaware of their provenance. I discuss some of their findings in the pages that follow. But the bulk of this study is devoted to exploring a potentially richer source of insights – modern cinema. In discussing the films, I provide context for each historical case and connect the findings of social scientists regarding, for example, economic and demographic sources of violence, to the depictions of gender and conflict on screen.

This chapter begins with a summary of the state of the debate about the relationship between gender and war, drawing on the work of two US political scientists who present sharply divergent views. It then turns to *Three Guineas* to draw out the hypotheses Woolf has embedded there. A number of feminist scholars have found inspiration in Woolf's work and have developed or moved beyond her insights in valuable ways.[9] This chapter links their work to the findings of economists and demographers who have related violence to the lack of economic opportunities for young males. The notion of the "proliferation of small men" helps explain why men sometimes resort to violence and why women are often the victims. I summarize the key hypotheses connecting gender and nationalist violence before introducing the main empirical focus of the book – ethnic and nationalist conflict in four countries – and elaborating on my rather unconventional (for a political scientist, at least) decision to explore the relationships between gender, nationalism, and violence through analysis of cinema. The chapter ends with an illustration of my technique, applied to a movie genre that will be familiar to most readers: the American Western.

War as a mostly male activity

In 1998, the journal *Foreign Affairs* published an article called "Women and the Evolution of World Politics." Its author was a public intellectual well known for his contributions to other high-profile debates, but not yet this one: Francis Fukuyama. Drawing upon a cursory reading of the literature in primatology, Fukuyama argued that human males, like their chimpanzee cousins, are by nature aggressive. He suggested that "there is something to the contention of many feminists" (unspecified) who maintain that "aggression, violence, war, and intense competition

---

[9] The most influential work for me has been that of Cynthia Enloe. Particularly rich with insights is her chapter "Nationalism and Masculinity," in *Bananas, Beaches, and Bases: Making Feminist Sense of International Politics* (Berkeley, CA: University of California Press, 1990), where she even draws a bit on Hollywood movies to make some points about gender and colonialism.

for dominance in a status hierarchy are more closely associated with men than women." He parted company with his understanding of "the feminist view" that such behaviors are "wholly the products of a patriarchal culture," because "in fact it appears they are rooted in biology." Moreover, the prospects for resocializing men to be less violent – what he took to be the feminist agenda – are dubious: "What is bred in the bone cannot be altered easily by changes in culture and ideology."[10]

A few years after the *Foreign Affairs* article appeared, the political scientist Joshua Goldstein published a major study, *War and Gender*, in which he sought to address essentially the same question that attracted Fukuyama's attention: "why warfare is virtually an all-male occupation."[11] Goldstein, who worked for a time as a research biologist at Stanford University and knew the specialist literature well, took a very different perspective from Fukuyama on the question of biology versus culture. The difference was apparent from the very outset of his book when he explained why he eschewed the conventional terminological distinction between *sex* as a biological category and *gender* as a cultural one. In sharp contrast to Fukuyama's bred-in-the-bone contention, Goldstein offered almost the opposite of the common wisdom: "Biology provides diverse potentials, and cultures limit, select, and channel them." More strikingly Goldstein claimed that "culture directly influences the expression of genes and hence the biology of our bodies." Thus, "no universal biological essence of 'sex' exists, but rather a complex system of potentials that are activated by various internal *and* external influences."[12]

Goldstein's claim that culture influences genetic expression and our very bodies might seem surprising at first. Some of the evidence seems obvious in retrospect, however. Goldstein pointed out, for example, that cultures that favor boys over girls (most of them) will typically encourage families to give priority to their male offspring in terms of nutrition and education, with measurable impact on the physical and mental development of their bodies. Mothers who nurse male babies for longer periods than female babies, for example, are carrying out a culturally determined practice with clear biological effects. Societies that do not allow girls to engage in sports limit their physical abilities by a cultural decision. Societies that do not allow girls to attend schools do the same for their mental capacities.

---

[10] Francis Fukuyama, "Women and the Evolution of World Politics," *Foreign Affairs*, 77, 5 (September/October 1998), pp. 24–40.

[11] Joshua S. Goldstein, *War and Gender: How Gender Shapes the War System and Vice Versa* (Cambridge University Press, 2001), p. 169.

[12] Ibid., p. 2, original emphasis.

Gender-differentiated play styles contribute to explaining Goldstein's puzzle of male-dominated warfare, but only in combination with key influences that fall under the rubric of socialization or cultural construction. The first is segregation of boys and girls, typically reinforced or engineered by parents and teachers. Goldstein points out that "children's gender segregation is much less pervasive and absolute than is gender segregation in war," where traditionally only males have fought. Nevertheless, he sees it as "a first step in preparing children for war." Rough-and-tumble play among boys becomes "tied directly to the boys' future roles in wartime (play-fighting, dominance, heroic themes, and specific war scripts)."[13]

The most powerful socializing processes are those that associate masculinity with toughness, discipline, and ability to control and hide emotions – traits valuable for engaging in warfare. For, contra Fukuyama, "war does not come naturally to men (from biology), so warriors require intense socialization and training in order to fight effectively. Gender identity becomes a tool with which societies induce men to fight."[14] Women play a key role in this process by shaming boys and men who do not fit the masculine model and by embodying the "opposite" feminine model of the nurturing, emotional mother, lover, or nurse. The practice among male soldiers of feminizing their enemies "to encode domination" also reinforces the militarized masculine stereotype.[15] It is in effect the external variant of, and what often serves to justify, the subordination of women at home.[16]

Neither Fukuyama nor Goldstein dealt much with the sexualization of war, an issue that seems increasingly evident in US military policy. It entails not only the feminization of enemies but the fear of homosexuality.[17] A US marine's memoir of the 1991 Gulf war describes rituals of mock homosexual rape as a tool for building camaraderie within the unit, and accusations of homosexuality and the crudest misogyny as key elements of basic training – features prominent in the second US war against Iraq in 2003 as well.[18] For female soldiers, even as they made up

---

[13] Ibid., pp. 248–249.

[14] Ibid., pp. 252–253. On the extraordinary efforts that armies and societies must undertake to get soldiers to overcome their aversion to killing, see (Lt. Col.) Dave Grossman, *On Killing: The Psychological Cost of Learning to Kill in War and Society* (Boston: Little, Brown, 1995).

[15] Goldstein, *War and Gender*, p. 406.

[16] J. Ann Tickner, *Gender in International Relations* (New York: Columbia University Press, 1992); Tickner, *Gendering World Politics* (New York: Columbia University Press, 2001).

[17] A classic discussion of the Cold War era is Carol Cohn, "Sex and Death in the Rational World of Defense Intellectuals," *Signs*, 12, 4 (Summer 1987), pp. 687–718.

[18] Anthony Swofford, *Jarhead: A Marine's Chronicle of the Gulf War and Other Battles* (New York: Scribner, 2003), pp. 21, 44–45; Tyler Gilbert, interviewed by Sam Diener, "Basic

15 percent of the US force, the sexualization of war plays a major role as well. "Sex is key to any woman soldier's experience in the American military," writes a female veteran of the 2003 Iraq war. She describes two exclusive categories into which male soldiers put females – "slut" or "bitch," depending on the woman's availability for sex. Those in the latter category are often denounced as lesbians and become victims of sexual violence.[19] In some of the cases discussed in this book the feminization and homosexualization of enemies figures prominently as a source of violence and possible explanation for why men join armed groups – to prove that they are "real men," neither women nor gay.[20]

Some six decades before Francis Fukuyama made his foray into feminism, Virginia Woolf, in *Three Guineas*, anticipated many of the hypotheses that he and later Joshua Goldstein put forward, even as they disagreed with each other on basic points. Her small book contained the seeds of many fruitful explorations of the links between gender and war, carried out subsequently by prominent feminist scholars Cynthia Enloe, Cynthia Cockburn, Joane Nagel, and others. If, as this chapter's epigraph suggests, Gogol's "Overcoat" (the short story and the metaphor) could cover a range of Russian writers from Dostoevskii to Turgenev (and, one could add, many others in the Soviet and post-Soviet eras), the purse that holds Woolf's three guineas is equally capacious. She had, in 1938, explored many of the relationships between gender, nationalism, and war that subsequent scholars have rediscovered and investigated.[21] She even captured one of the key issues of contention between Fukuyama and Goldstein – the biological effects of culture, in the form of norms of gender discrimination.

Training: Basic Cruelty, Basic Misogyny," *Peacework* (February 2005), pp. 6–7; Joseph Rocha, "I Didn't Tell. It Didn't Matter," *The Washington Post*, October 11, 2009. These practices obviously predate the Gulf wars; see, e.g., Helen Michalowski, "The Army Will Make a 'Man' Out of You," in Pam McAllister, ed., *Reweaving the Web of Life: Feminism and Nonviolence* (Philadelphia: New Society Publishers, 1982), pp. 326–335.

[19] Kayla Williams, *Love My Rifle More Than You: Young and Female in the US Army* (New York: Norton, 2005), p. 18. On links between fear of lesbianism and misogynistic violence, see Suzanne Pharr, *Homophobia: A Weapon of Sexism*, 2nd edn (Berkeley, CA: Chardon Press, 1997; originally published 1988).

[20] See, for example, John Borneman, "Toward a Theory of Ethnic Cleansing: Territorial Sovereignty, Heterosexuality, and Europe," in his *Subversions of International Order* (Albany, NY: State University of New York Press, 1998), pp. 273–317; Beverly Allen, *Rape Warfare: The Hidden Genocide in Bosnia-Herzegovina and Croatia* (Minneapolis: University of Minnesota Press, 1996); and Dubravka Zarkov, "The Body of the Other Man: Sexual Violence and the Construction of Masculinity, Sexuality and Ethnicity in the Croatian Media," ch. 5 in Moser and Clark, eds., *Victims, Perpetrators or Actors?*

[21] Cynthia Enloe acknowledges the importance of *Three Guineas* to her own work in her collection *The Curious Feminist* (Berkeley, CA: University of California Press, 2004).

Writing in the dark days before the outbreak of World War II, Woolf sought to convey, in an extended response to a fund-raising letter from the treasurer of a peace organization, why her outlook on matters related to war and peace differed so much from his. She made the point that despite the fact that women were legally allowed to earn their own livings in the professions (but only since 1919 in England), they still "differ enormously" from men. In fact, she distinguished between two "classes." In the realm of education, for example, "your class has been educated at public schools and universities for five or six hundred years, ours for sixty." Regarding property, "your class possesses in its own right and not through marriage practically all the capital, all the land, all the valuables, and all the patronage in England. Our class possesses in its own right and not through marriage practically none of the capital, none of the land, none of the valuables, and none of the patronage in England." Perhaps more metaphorically than Goldstein, she nevertheless adduces the same point: "That such differences make for very considerable differences in mind and body, no psychologist or biologist would deny ... Though we see the same world, we see it through different eyes."[22]

Woolf had something to say about Fukuyama's proposals as well. He suggested that status-seeking "alpha" males might pursue the non-military opportunities that a liberal, market economy offers them in the universities, politics, and the stock market, as an alternative outlet for their aggressive proclivities. Woolf, by contrast, maintained that such competitive behavior under capitalism – even in seemingly benign institutions such as the universities of Cambridge and Oxford – is precisely what leads men to engage in wars. For her, aggressive competition for university titles – and their visual representations in gowns, ribbons, and tassels – is a symptom of the same syndrome that induces soldiers to seek higher ranks through their military exploits.

As for women, Woolf proposes two competing explanations for their possible attitudes towards war. Denied education and property, treated as a slave to her father and husband, a woman might reject national sentiment and support for her country's wars by declaring "as a woman I have no country." This slogan, mistakenly taken by some as an adequate summary of Woolf's argument, is in fact only a hypothesis. Woolf offers an alternative possibility as well – that women support war in an attempt to achieve greater equality with men:

How else can we explain that amazing outburst in August 1914, when the daughters of educated men ... rushed into hospitals, some still attended by their

---

[22] Virginia Woolf, *Three Guineas* (New York: Harcourt, Brace, 1966 [1938]), p. 18. Citations hereafter are to the paperback edition.

maids, drove lorries, worked in fields and munitions factories, and used all their immense stores of charm, of sympathy, to persuade young men that to fight was heroic … So profound was her unconscious loathing for the education of the private house with its cruelty, its poverty, its hypocrisy, its immorality, its inanity that she would undertake any task however menial, exercise any fascination however fatal that enabled her to escape. Thus consciously she desired "our splendid Empire"; unconsciously she desired our splendid war.[23]

In preparing *Three Guineas*, Woolf had conducted prodigious research in order to come up with her generalizations. She read widely in "biography and autobiography," as her detailed notes attest, and followed current debates, for example, in the House of Commons, from the daily newspapers, what she called "history in the raw."[24] Ultimately Woolf arrived at a series of hypotheses, some pointing towards women's rejection of war and the hierarchical, competitive institutions that she identified as its main cause, others suggesting the conditions under which women might favor war – primarily in order to better their own positions in a highly discriminatory society. What she did not anticipate, writing in the period before the emergence of anticolonial movements of "national liberation" in the wake of World War II, was the role that women would play in nationalist violence. Under conditions of double discrimination, within their own societies and within the structure of colonial control of their country, women often resorted to violence – in ways that neither Fukuyama's bred-in-the-bone biology nor Goldstein's more sophisticated cultural and sociological account explains. Woolf was attuned to women's potential for *resistance* to oppression (including colonialism or imperialism), but seemed to assume that resistance would take nonviolent form.[25] Neither she, nor many subsequent observers, have sought to understand why under some conditions women (or men, for that matter) resort to violence while under others they pursue nonviolent resistance. During the era of decolonization, dominant expectations about appropriate gender roles – that men would be violent and women nonviolent – often made women more effective than men at carrying out acts of anticolonial violence. The Algerian war of independence against French colonial rule is the most striking example, and Gillo Pontecorvo's film *The Battle of Algiers* (*La Battaglia di Algeri*, 1966), discussed in the

[23] Ibid., p. 39.

[24] Ibid., p. 7. For more background, see Naomi Black, *Virginia Woolf as Feminist* (Ithaca, NY: Cornell University Press, 2003), esp. ch. 3, "The Evolution of *Three Guineas*."

[25] On Woolf's views on imperialism, see Black, *Virginia Woolf as Feminist*, pp. 175–178. On the complicated relationship between British feminism and imperialism, see Antoinette M. Burton, *Burdens of History: British Feminists, Indian Women, and Imperial Culture, 1865–1915* (Chapel Hill, NC: University of North Carolina Press, 1994).

next chapter, remains one of the most powerful portrayals of the effect of gender on that conflict.

Nor could Woolf have anything to say about the role of postcommunist nationalism in eastern Europe or the former Soviet Union. Indeed, in her lifetime, Russia was the world's only communist state. She could not anticipate that the demise of some communist regimes would lead to the outbreak of wars justified on nationalist or ethnic grounds – or the myriad ways that women and gender would be implicated. For example, in former Yugoslavia – the topic of chapter 3 – women played multiple roles, sometimes as leaders of antinationalist and peace movements, often as victims of sexual violence perpetrated under the nationalist banner, and occasionally as promoters of extreme nationalist policies. Although there are few female characters in Srđan Dragojević's *Pretty Village, Pretty Flame* (*Lepa sela, lepo gore*, 1996), the film captures the role of gender in prewar and wartime Yugoslavia in a way that helps us understand how the conflict became so infused with misogynist violence.

Chapter 4 is devoted to Chechnya, Russia's rebellious republic, which has suffered two devastating wars since declaring its independence in the early 1990s. Following the Russian military incursion into Chechnya in late 1994, some Chechen mothers worked with their Russian counterparts to free Russian soldiers taken prisoner by the Chechen fighters. Other Chechen women became supporters of the violent resistance to Russian occupation, even to the point of undertaking suicide terrorism – out of some combination of desperation, desire to avenge the loss of their relatives at the hands of Russian soldiers, or the political motive of expelling the occupiers. Over a period of more than a dozen years, as violence raged in Chechnya, Russian directors produced a wide range of films treating the conflict, from Sergei Bodrov's *Prisoner of the Mountains* (*Kavkazskii plennik*, literally "Caucasian Prisoner," 1996) to Aleksandr Sokurov's *Aleksandra* (2007). This chapter covers several of them, offering insights into the strikingly different ways the conflict itself and the role of gender have been portrayed.

That women could identify with nationalism by supporting nationalist or separatist movements that did not pose the risk of violent conflict was another possibility that Woolf failed to consider. Yet the experience of modern Québec nationalism, at least since the mid-1970s, constitutes precisely such a phenomenon. It is the topic of chapter 5, the centerpiece of which is an analysis of Robert Lepage's 1998 film, *Nô*. Following a brief period of political violence modeled on Third World national liberation movements, and suppressed by the federal government, Québec nationalists – or sovereigntists (*souverainistes*) as they often prefer to be called – confined their struggle to peaceful means. Battles were now fought at the ballot box and in peaceful demonstrations in support of referenda seeking to define Québec's status vis-à-vis the Canadian federation. Lepage's film, set in 1970 and in 1980, captures both the peaceful and violent elements of Québec nationalism with revealing insights into the role of gender.

These four cases – Algeria, former Yugoslavia, Chechnya, and Québec – provide ample material for exploring the various ways that gender relates to nationalism, violence, and war. In each chapter, my analysis draws on the work of historians and political scientists, as well as primary source materials, and it relies on examination of major feature films depicting each nationalist conflict to illustrate generalizations about gender, nationalism, and war. The next section reviews those generalizations, most of which find antecedents in *Three Guineas*, and thus, one might say, come out of Virginia Woolf's purse.

Hypotheses on gender, nationalism, and war

Several sets of hypotheses link gender identities to nationalism and conflict. One set concerns beliefs that men and women hold about the attributes of masculinity and femininity as they relate to ethnic/nationalist conflict and violence. One common conception about *men's* beliefs is that in order for nationalist movements to become militarized, men must embrace an identity that defines their masculinity as directly linked to the armed protection of their society's women.[26] Curious about men's understanding of their own roles, scholars such as Cynthia Enloe and Joane Nagel offered a challenge to conventional ways of looking at war and nationalism. They questioned standard accounts that take men's resort to violence in support of national defense or liberation for granted, as natural and expected.

The traditional means for defending territory from external attack or expelling colonial occupiers has always entailed violence, wielded primarily by men. That is why Woolf's critique in *Three Guineas* was so unsettling to many readers in the 1930s, including close friends who supported violent defense of the revolution in Spain or rearmament throughout Europe to face the threat of Nazi Germany. They accepted that men would join guerrilla or state armies and that women would support them. Only in the twenty-first century did a man in the field of political science identify the overwhelming predominance of men in armies as

---

[26] Cynthia Enloe, *The Morning After: Sexual Politics at the End of the Cold* War (Berkeley: University of California Press, 1993); Joane Nagel, "Masculinity and Nationalism: Gender and Sexuality in the Making of Nations," *Ethnic and Racial Studies*, 21, 2 (March 1998), pp. 242–269.

a *puzzle* worth trying to explain in a book-length study. Goldstein summarized a substantial literature by feminist scholars who had highlighted the processes by which boys are socialized into associating masculinity with violence. But he did not have much to say about why that violence would be channeled towards nationalist goals.

Often we neglect to seek explanations for phenomena until they seem puzzling to us. Thus, much theorizing about gender, nationalism, and war was stimulated by the violent breakup of Yugoslavia. This was a country, after all, in its communist iteration founded on principles of internationalism and ethnic tolerance ("brotherhood and unity"), where the only theoretically meaningful divides were supposed to be based on class, and the common project was to eliminate them. If nationalism nevertheless was reasserting itself, the puzzle remained why it had to take violent form. By the time the Yugoslav wars broke out, the world had already witnessed the mainly peaceful disintegration of the Soviet Union, a much larger multinational communist state, founded on similar ideological precepts, and would soon see Slovakia and the Czech Republic go their separate ways as Czechoslovakia broke up without violence.[27]

Cynthia Enloe has suggested what is necessary to engender nationalist violence on a large scale, and, in particular, what it takes to get men to fight:

> Militarization of ethnic nationalism often depends on persuading individual men that their own manhood will be fully validated only if they perform as soldiers, either in the state's military or in insurgent autonomous or quasi-autonomous forces. But although the most persuasive socialization strategies succeed because they manage to portray soldiering as a "naturally" manly activity, in reality socialization requires explicit and artificial construction, sometimes backed by coercion. Large advertising budgets allocated to defense ministries in countries that rely on volunteer militaries, and harsh penalties assigned by the state to draft-dodgers in countries dependent on conscription, both signal a degree of deliberateness in sustaining militarized notions of masculinity.[28]

What roles do women have to play if violent defense or promotion of nationalism or ethnic difference is to become accepted as natural? Here there are several possibly contradictory hypotheses. The first holds that women would have to assume their role as the passive, protected segment of society in order for men to identify successfully with a militarized masculinity. Thus in seeking to anticipate, for example, which ethnic

---

[27] For an attempt to explain the divergent paths of these three cases, see Valerie Bunce, "Peaceful versus Violent State Dismemberment: A Comparison of the Soviet Union, Yugoslavia, and Czechoslovakia," *Politics and Society*, 27, 2 (June 1999), pp. 217–237.

[28] Enloe, "All the Men Are in the Militias, All the Women Are Victims: The Politics of Masculinity and Femininity in Nationalist Wars," ch. 7 in *The Curious Feminist*.

groups might adopt methods of violent secession, one would look to those groups where women are culturally predisposed to accept submissive roles. But we know from the case of former Yugoslavia that "modern" societies with high levels of nominal gender equality (in education, employment, etc.) can also fall prey to ethnic violence. The Yugoslav case gives rise to a set of hypotheses that identifies *changes* in gender relations as a possible early-warning sign of impending ethnicized violence. Pressures on women to produce more babies, and consequent limitations on women's reproductive rights, were a significant component of the nationalist mobilization in Serbia and Croatia, for example. The goals were generally to increase the population of one's ethnic group vis-à-vis the others, and in the most militarized versions, to provide future soldiers for ethnic conflict.[29] That gender played a role in the nationalisms of former Yugoslavia seemed apparent also in the conduct of the wars themselves and the extent to which they entailed organized campaigns of mass rape and other sexual atrocities.[30]

Contrary to hypotheses associating militarized nationalism with increasing gender inequality are those that see nationalist movements as a vehicle for *improving* women's status. With rare exceptions nationalism did not play such a positive role in its original nineteenth-century European guise.[31] The (male) nationalist's appeal to tradition usually included patriarchal practices that prescribed women's subordinate role. Moreover, as J. Ann Tickner pointed out, even though in nationalist ideologies "family metaphors are used to evoke a safe space or sense of belonging, families are not always considered a safe space for women. In most societies, families, frequently beyond the reach of law, have often been the site of unsanctioned violence against women and children."[32]

Beliefs about the emancipatory potential of nationalism were more widespread in the anticolonial movements of the second half of the twentieth century.[33] As Deniz Kandiyoti argues, "nationalist aspirations for popular sovereignty stimulate an extension of citizenship rights, clearly

---

[29] Patricia Albanese, "Leaders and Breeders: The Archaization of Gender Relations in Croatia," in B. Wejnert, M. Spencer, and S. Drakulic, eds., *Women in Post-Communism,* Research on Russia and Eastern Europe 2 (Greenwich, CT: JAI Press, 1996), pp. 185–200.

[30] Borneman, "Toward a Theory of Ethnic Cleansing;" Allen, *Rape Warfare*; Alexandra Stiglmayer, ed., *Mass Rape: The War against Women in Bosnia-Herzegovina,* trans. by Marion Faber (Lincoln: University of Nebraska Press, 1994).

[31] Gisela Kaplan, "Comparative Europe: Feminism and Nationalism: The European Case," in Lois A. West, ed., *Feminist Nationalism* (New York: Routledge, 1997), pp. 3–40.

[32] Tickner, *Gender in International Relations,* p. 63.

[33] Frantz Fanon, "Algeria Unveiled," in *A Dying Colonialism* (New York: Grove Press, 1965; originally published in Paris in 1959 as *L'an cinq de la révolution algérienne*); Anne McClintock, "'No Longer in a Future Heaven': Nationalism, Gender, and Race," in

benefiting women."[34] Yet, she points out, there are contradictions in the "gender agenda of some nationalist projects," whereby "women can, at the same time, participate actively in, and become hostages to, such projects." She highlights three portrayals of women that underline the contradictory nature of the relationship between gender and nationalism: women as (1) victims of social backwardness; (2) icons of modernity; or (3) privileged bearers of cultural authenticity.[35] Several of the cases in this book attest to the value of these categories.

Much of the literature on gender and nationalism focuses on questions of identity and shared ("intersubjective") understandings of appropriate gender norms. The best work on these topics links them to material factors. Much promising research highlights the role of economic and demographic conditions and how they might influence whether a nationalist movement becomes militarized and how a militarized movement might affect gender relations.

Demographers have identified a phenomenon known as the "youth bulge," which they associate with male violence – often in the service of nationalist or ethnic causes, and frequently with a strong misogynistic bent.[36] Chris Dolan, in a study of conflict in northern Uganda, has linked this phenomenon directly to gender norms. He found that when young men were unable to meet the cultural norm of masculinity, as expressed, for example, in ability to obtain a job adequate to attract a wife and support a family, they tended to turn to alcohol, to engage in violence, to commit suicide, or to join militias. He dubs the phenomenon the "proliferation of small men."[37] It is hardly limited to impoverished Third World countries. Drawing on public opinion data, Julie Brown describes a similar set of gender values for post-Soviet Russia: "Women's self-esteem tends to be linked to work and family more or less independently of each other. For men, family responsibilities are directly linked to work-related success. A 'real man' is one who provides for the material needs of his family. An unemployed woman can still be a good wife and mother, but

---

Geoff Eley and Ronald Grigor Suny, eds., *Becoming National: A Reader* (New York: Oxford University Press, 1996), pp. 259–284.

[34] Kandiyoti, "Identity and its Discontents," p. 429.

[35] Ibid., p. 431; Enloe, *Bananas, Beaches, and Bases*, ch. 3.

[36] Richard P. Cincotta, Robert Engelman, and Danielle Anastasion, *The Security Demographic: Population and Civil Conflict after the Cold War* (Washington, DC: Population Action International, 2003), esp. ch. 3 on the youth bulge.

[37] Chris Dolan, "Collapsing Masculinities and Weak States – A Case Study of Northern Uganda" in Frances Cleaver, ed., *Masculinities Matter!* (London: Zed Books, 2003), pp. 57–83; see also the consideration of economic factors in Cynthia Cockburn, "The Gendered Dynamics of Armed Conflict and Political Violence," ch. 2 in Moser and Clark, eds., *Victims, Perpetrators or Actors?* pp. 17–18.

for a man, failing to earn a living also means failure as husband and father."[38] The link between economic conditions and recruitment of soldiers is also evident in the United States, where joining the armed forces is often a last resort for men (and women) who lack other options. Given that military service, or generally the use of violence in support of the nation or group, offers an alternative means to validate masculine identity, we should not be surprised to find violence associated with poor economic prospects for young men of military age.

Cynthia Enloe, writing on Yugoslavia in the late 1980s, has explored the implications for women of these challenges to masculine identity – what some have called "economic emasculation."[39] Enloe and others hypothesize that high unemployment among men could be linked to pressures for women to stay out of the workforce and have babies instead, with attendant limitations on their control over reproduction: restrictions on availability of abortion and contraceptives. I address this issue in the chapter on Yugoslavia, but it seems relevant elsewhere as well. In my examination of Algeria, for example, I link the "proliferation of small men" to the violent war for independence, in which many men in the "youth bulge" age cohort perished. The phenomenon may also have been a contributing factor to the often misogynistic violence that erupted in the late 1980s and led to Algeria's bloody civil war in the 1990s. Around the same time, a large cohort of unemployed men provided recruits for the nationalist militias that fought for independence in Chechnya, as I discuss in chapter 4. Even in relatively peaceful Québec, one can identify the potential for misogynistic violence among some young men who resent the successes that women have achieved in education and the traditionally male-dominated professions.

Although in the chapters that follow I explore a number of hypotheses – many originating with Virginia Woolf's work – two major themes emerge: (1) improving women's relative status vis-à-vis men tends to reduce conflict between political communities; and (2) a decline in men's economic prospects, to the extent it challenges their masculine identity, can create a backlash against women, resulting in violence both in and outside their own community. The first theme is consistent with the expectations of Woolf and feminist scholars who followed her lead and suggests a positive relationship between women's equality and peace.

[38] Julie V. Brown, "The Second Sex," *Transitions Online*, www.tol.cz, October 24, 2006, copy archived with the author. The article is a review of Rebecca Kay, *Men in Contemporary Russia: The Fallen Heroes of Post-Soviet Change?* (London: Ashgate, 2006), from which Brown develops her analysis.

[39] Enloe, "All the Men;" Marko Zivkovic, "Ex-Yugoslav Masculinities under Female Gaze, or Why Men Skin Cats, Beat up Gays and Go to War," *Nationalities Papers*, 34, 3 (July 2006), p. 259.

The second theme, however, sounds a cautious note. In 1963, Betty Friedan predicted in *The Feminine Mystique* that men would not feel threatened when their wives found fulfillment in professions and work outside the home. "When women do not need to live through their husbands and children," she wrote, "men will not fear the love and strength of women, nor need another's weakness to prove their own masculinity." During the 1980s, survey research challenged Friedan's prediction. Studying the mental health of men relative to women, for example, Ronald Kessler and his colleagues at the University of Michigan found that "the increase in distress among men can be attributed, in part, to depression and loss of self-esteem related to the increasing tendency of women to take a job outside the home."[40] By the 1990s, in the context of a steady loss of high-paying traditional "male" jobs, for some American men that distress turned into violence, directed against women – not on the scale of ex-Yugoslavia or Algeria, to be sure, but worrying nonetheless. I return to this theme in the concluding chapter.

The main premise of this book is that cinema conveys the relationships between gender, violence, and nationalism in powerful ways. Consider Dolan's concept of the "proliferation of small men," the challenge that economic failure poses to a man's very identity. Susan Faludi has identified the theme in the 1957 science-fiction film, appropriately titled *The Incredible Shrinking Man*. Scott Carey, the "hero" played by Grant Williams, loses his job after being doused by radiation from a US nuclear-weapon test (much as happened to Japanese fishermen in 1954). He is fired from his job when he becomes too small to work. His wife Louise seeks to protect him, until she loses track of him in the basement. As Faludi describes, Scott "is left with only feminine defenses – to hide in a dollhouse, to fight a giant spider with a sewing pin...The tinier he gets, the greater his combativeness becomes – and his desire for a combatant to defeat." He takes his frustration out on his wife. "Every day I became more tyrannical, more monstrous in my domination of Louise," Scott reports.[41]

One can hardly imagine a more vivid portrayal of the humiliation of the "small man" than James Foley's 1992 film, *Glengarry Glen Ross*. The movie is based on a play by David Mamet about real estate agents trying to peddle condominium developments for speculative investments in 1980s Los Angeles. The pivotal scene comes when Blake, the character played by Alec Baldwin, arrives from headquarters to "motivate" the

---

[40] Susan Faludi, *Backlash: The Undeclared War against American Women* (New York: Three Rivers Press, 2006; originally published 1991); she quotes Friedan on p. 73 and Kessler *et al.* on p. 55.

[41] Susan Faludi, *Stiffed: The Betrayal of the American Man* (New York: Perennial, 2003; originally published 1999), pp. 30–31.

Figure 1.1 Economic emasculation. *Glengarry Glen Ross* (1992)

unsuccessful salesmen by challenging their masculinity in a torrent of violent, sexualized abuse. The men have been unable to close any deals, based
on the "leads" – names of potentially interested customers – the company
has provided them. One of the older men, with the androgynous name
Shelley, complains that the leads are weak. Blake explodes: "'The leads
are weak.' The fucking leads are weak? You're weak." As the camera zooms
in on the intimidated face of his victim, Blake makes the sexual challenge
increasingly explicit: "Your name is 'you're wanting,' and you can't play
in the man's game, you can't close them, then go home and tell your wife
your troubles. 'Cause only one thing counts in this world: get them to
sign on the line which is dotted. You hear me you fuckin' faggots?" If the
prospect of losing his job in 1980s Los Angeles can put a man in such a
state of anxiety about his masculinity, one can appreciate the effect it has
in more traditional societies, where marriage is explicitly contingent on a
man's securing adequate employment. Unemployed young men become
fodder for nationalist violence and ethnic scapegoating.

Masculinity, femininity, and violence in the American Western

Before proceeding with the discussion of gender, violence, and nationalism in the movies, I want to illustrate the value of using cinematic analysis
by considering just the first two elements – gender and violence – in a
genre familiar to most readers: the American Western. Fred Zinnemann's

High Noon (1952), with Gary Cooper and Grace Kelly, illustrates especially well the insights that Woolf conveyed in *Three Guineas*, while at the same time challenging the gender stereotypes she describes.

For Virginia Woolf a main cause of war was men's perceived need to compete for status, whether in business, education, the clergy, or the armed forces. She viewed women as a force for peace because, denied the opportunities available to men, they were not (yet) implicated in the status hierarchies that characterized male life. Her prescription for peace required that women remain apart from that life, that they create a Society of Outsiders. The members would commit themselves "not to fight with arms" – easy enough, given that women were not welcome in the armed forces. They would also "refuse in the event of war to make munitions or nurse the wounded." In dealing with men, members of the Outsiders' Society would agree "not to incite their brothers to fight, or to dissuade them, but to maintain an attitude of complete indifference."[42] Some readers have wondered why Woolf would not want women to try to dissuade men from fighting, why she advocated indifference rather than opposition to men's taking up arms. Herein lies one of her most compelling insights. If masculine identity is tied to violent defense of the nation, then it seems only natural that feminine identity – its presumed opposite – be associated with nonviolence. The more women betray their feminine nature by opposing violence and fearing war, the more it falls to men to fulfill their masculine duty to fight.

High Noon offers an iconic portrayal of these paired binary relationships – male/female, violent/nonviolent. An early scene shows a wedding in a frontier town. Marshal Will Kane is marrying Amy Fowler, a Quaker, who has convinced him to accede to her pacifist convictions by giving up his career in law enforcement to manage a store back east. Following the marriage ceremony, the town judge reminds Will of a second ceremonial obligation: he has to give up his gun and remove his marshal's badge. "Alright, it's coming off," he says, "but I've got to be paid first." At that point he lifts up his new bride to kiss her. Then he unpins the badge and places it on the holster holding his gun. He gives up a key symbol of his masculinity, only after having confirmed that he is still a man by publicly kissing his wife. The scene is interrupted by a new challenge to the now former marshal's masculinity. The news arrives that Frank Miller, a notorious killer whom Marshal Kane had arrested and sent to a distant prison, has been released and is returning on the noon train to seek his revenge.

Kane's friends urge him to flee before Miller arrives. "Think of Amy," says Mark, an elderly, retired marshal. He slaps the horse to send the carriage with the newlyweds off to the train station, then nurses his sore

---

[42] Woolf, *Three Guineas*, pp. 106–107.

Figure 1.2 Symbolic emasculation. *High Noon* (1952)

hand. In a later scene, when Kane tries unsuccessfully to recruit deputies to help him face the returning killer, Mark sits feebly in his chair, offering his "busted knuckles" as an excuse for not joining the violent resistance. Mark symbolizes impotence, thereby reinforcing Kane's masculine identity. The starkest contrast is between Kane and his Quaker wife. The more Amy resists Kane's taking up arms again, the more he feels it his duty. If women, weak half-men, and cowards refuse to defend the town, then true men must do so. The lyrics of the movie's theme song, penned by Ned Washington, complement the visual images and leave no doubt about the relationship between gender and violence:

> *Do not forsake me O my darlin'*
> *On this our wedding day.*
> *Do not forsake me O my darlin'*
> *Wait, wait along.*
>
> *The noonday train will bring Frank Miller.*
> *If I'm a man I must be brave*
> *And I must face that deadly killer*
> *Or lie a coward, a craven coward,*
> *Or lie a coward in my grave.*[43]

---

[43] Quoted in Deborah Allison, "'Do Not Forsake Me: The Ballad of High Noon' and the Rise of the Movie Theme Song," *Senses of Cinema*, Issue 28 (September-October 2003), http://archive.sensesofcinema.com/contents/03/28/ballad_of_high_noon.html.

Figure 1.3 Reconsidering nonviolence. *High Noon* (1952)

High Noon was considered an unusual Western, dismissed as "un-American" by some critics, such as John Wayne. Gary Cooper was too old for a typical hero. His character spent much of the film walking around in desperation, showing obvious fear, and even crying as he wrote his will. But ultimately he summons his masculine courage in counterpoint to his wife's feminine pacifism – which she, in turn, abandons at the last minute to save the day. Thus, the movie reinforces the basic binary between peaceful women and violent men, but it also defies common gender and even ethnic stereotypes, as with its portrayal of Helen Ramirez (Katy Jurado), the strong, independent Mexican-American saloon owner. In this respect, too, *High Noon* serves as a good example of the sort of movies I discuss in the book – ones that illustrate traditional gender relationships, but also suggest unusual, alternative possibilities.[44]

[44] A more typical Western that illustrates the binary relationships between gender and violence would be George Stevens' *Shane* (1953), with Alan Ladd, Jean Arthur, and Jack Palance. Male identity is at stake as a brave stranger helps defend homesteaders from cattlemen who want to drive them away. The wife of the man whose farm the stranger helps to defend is obviously attracted to the stranger, as is their son. The husband and the stranger come to blows over who gets to risk death by confronting the cattleman's

Trailer: gender and nationalist violence on film

Rather than *test* the hypotheses that come out of the rich tradition of gender analysis that Virginia Woolf pioneered, I seek to *illustrate* the range of possible relationships between gender and nationalist violence across time and space as depicted in several major films. Although this is not a conventional work of political science, my selection of "cases" does reflect a certain approach to "research design" that borrows from that discipline.[45] The films' settings span five decades, from the mid-1950s to the early years of the twenty-first century, and cover four countries – Algeria, Yugoslavia, Russia, and Canada – and separatist republics or provinces within them: Bosnia and Herzegovina, Chechnya, and Québec.

The countries vary a great deal in terms of location and character, and that variation should help us in considering how far certain generalizations "travel." Algeria had been an impoverished French territory for more than a century before the movement for independence erupted into violence in the wake of World War II. For a Muslim society, the participation of women in violence – joining guerrilla forces in the countryside and engaging in urban terrorism – was particularly striking. When war broke out between and within the constituent republics of the Yugoslav federation in 1991, the role of women was very different. Many women were active politically in the movements for democratization and social justice. Yet, regardless of ethnic or religious affiliation (or nonaffiliation), few women participated in violent activities. Many instead became victims of violence. Nationalist conflict took on a particularly misogynist cast and included campaigns of systematic, mass rape. The Algerian war against the French did not witness violence against women on such a vast scale, but post-independence Algeria did – during the civil conflict that erupted in the early 1990s, a topic taken up in chapter 2. The war in Russia's breakaway republic of Chechnya differs from the other cases not least in the fact that the violence there has persisted since the Russian incursion into Chechen territory in 1994, but has varied in form and intensity, with the role of women – on both the Russian and Chechen sides – changing over time. Québec diverges significantly from the other examples in several respects. Among our cases it is the only one of a

---

hired gun, while the wife pleads for them to stop, and the young son receives a lesson in what constitutes the essence of masculinity – violence.

[45] Although I employ historical material that most social scientists would recognize as evidence, I also draw insights from an unconventional source: feature films. These insights do not constitute "data" that a social scientist would normally accept. Even the status of documentary film as a source of "objective" evidence is hard to sustain. See Paula Rabinowitz, *They Must Be Represented: The Politics of Documentary* (London: Verso, 1994).

stable democratic political system and the only case where a nationalist movement, which for a brief time self-consciously posed the threat of revolutionary violence on the model of Algeria or Vietnam, was successfully suppressed and channeled into peaceful political activity. Québec is also the least patriarchal of the four societies, which some observers attribute to the traditional role of matriarchy in the native populations and among the early French settlers who interacted with them.

The films themselves represent a range of styles. Gillo Pontecorvo filmed *The Battle of Algiers* on location to resemble a documentary, intentionally using grainy black-and-white film, local nonprofessional actors, and a *cinéma vérité* style of camera work and editing that paid homage to the Italian neorealist tradition. Three decades later, Srđan Dragojević made a very different film, *Pretty Village, Pretty Flame*, for which he employed some of the leading stars of Yugoslav cinema, use of brilliant color, and a surrealist or magic realist style reminiscent of the revolutionary work of his predecessor Dušan Makavejev. Both films use a fragmented narrative that jumps forward and back in time, but whereas Pontecorvo is careful to indicate with subtitles the date and even the hour when the action takes place, Dragojević's editing produces a much faster, even frenetic pace that leaves the viewer unsure of time or place until well into or even after a given scene. These artistic differences reflect well the different natures of the two wars. The Algerian war of independence was a classic "national liberation" struggle, with clear enemies on each side, even when civilians were the targets of violence (and despite considerable internecine conflict among the Algerians). The wars of Yugoslav succession were what Mary Kaldor calls "new wars" – a postmodern mix of organized crime and senseless violence carried out by often drunk or drug-addled gangs of militia and regular army troops.[46] Such conditions seem particularly conducive to the "proliferation of small men" and the misogynist violence they wreak. Dragojević's cinematic techniques of jump cuts and ambiguous chronology are well suited to the "new wars."

The chapter on Russia's war in Chechnya, unlike the other three which treat only one film each, examines several. The duration of post-Soviet Russia's violent confrontation with the Chechens justifies this decision: from the 1994 invasion, through the retreat of Russian forces and the uneasy and chaotic truce of 1997–1999, to the resumption of war in 1999 and the "Chechenization" of the conflict following the end of major military operations in the early years of the new millennium. Russian popular attitudes towards the war as well as the character of the

---

[46] Mary Kaldor, *New and Old Wars: Organized Violence in a Global Era*, 2nd edn (Cambridge, UK: Polity Press, 2006).

conflict itself have changed over the course of a decade and more. The changes were reflected in the movies made about the war over the years and in the changing dynamics of gender relations revealed in them. There are many films from which to choose. I have focused on ones that reflect a high level of artistic quality and recognition (if not widespread distribution) outside Russia. Almost all have received awards, at home and abroad. The films include the rather romanticized portrayal of the conflict in Sergei Bodrov's *Prisoner of the Mountains* – a beautiful work filmed in the mountains of Dagestan that incorporates elements of magical realism in an otherwise conventional narrative. Aleksandr Rogozhkin's *Checkpoint* (*Blokpost*, 1998) reflects the senselessness of the first war and makes apparent why it ended with Russia's ignominious withdrawal. Its depiction of Chechen women as both victims and perpetrators of violence marks a stark change from Bodrov's portrait of Chechen female innocence. Aleksei Balabanov's *War* (*Voina*, 2002) portrays the brutalization of the second Russian invasion of Chechnya, the Islamicization of the Chechen resistance, and the naiveté of the international community in a series of binary oppositions based on gender stereotypes. Andrei Konchalovskii's *House of Fools* (*Dom durakov*, 2002) and Aleksandr Sokurov's *Aleksandra* (2007) offer strikingly different ways to think about the Russo-Chechen conflict. Each in its own way holds out hope of reconciliation through love and redemption – in the former case through a subversion of gender stereotypes, and in the latter through an appeal to a particularly enduring one: the pacific nature of women and the promise of female solidarity, themes that recall Woolf's *Three Guineas*.

Québec filmmaker and playwright Robert Lepage incorporates a range of styles in his 1998 film, *Nô*. He films both in black and white and in color to distinguish between his two locations, Montréal and Osaka, Japan in October 1970, as well as between Montréal 1970 and Montréal 1980. The film is a comedy, a farce within a farce, as the actors of Lepage's real-life Québec City theater troupe play Québécois actors performing in Japan as well as terrorists *manqués* back in Montréal. The issues he addresses, however, are quite serious, on both the political and personal level, with gender as the main theme that connects them. The film allows us to pose the question: what kind of gender relations contribute to the militarization of nationalist conflict, and what kind might serve to resolve such conflicts peacefully?

In choosing the films to analyze, I have not deliberately sought to represent national film industries or indigenous filmmakers or to draw equally on male and female directors. My goal is not to portray gender relations as seen from the perspective of either the victim or the victimizer in situations of nationalist violence, but to identify common ways that gender norms figure in popular cinematic representations, regardless of who produced them. Thus the film that represents the Algerian–French conflict was made by an Italian filmmaker (in collaboration with an Algerian writer and political figure); the film on the war in Bosnia was made by a Belgrade-based director, sometimes accused of a pro-Serb bias (as I discuss in chapter 3); the films about the Chechen conflict were, with one exception, made by Russian men, but with active participation from male and female actors and film industry personnel from the North Caucasus region. The film about Québec was made by a man with publicly acknowledged sovereigntist sympathies and an openly gay sexual orientation that may or may not influence his portrayal of gender.

The relevant question for me is whether these film representations of gender, nationalism, and war encompass an adequately broad range of possible ways of relating these factors. In my view, they do. Such variation in a social-science research design would be considered important, especially if the study yielded generalizations that seem to hold across the different cases. Although I do not claim that the films I examine constitute *evidence* useful for testing hypotheses, I do argue that using visual and cultural analysis of the relationships between gender, nationalism, and violence as revealed in the films yields meaningful insights. If social scientists choose to follow up with more systematic research, as I suggest in the concluding chapter, all the better.

2   Algeria: a world constructed out of ruins

> Do you know something Ali? Starting a revolution is hard, and it's even harder to continue it. Winning is hardest of all. But only afterward, when we have won, will the real hardships begin.
>
> Larbi Ben M'hidi, in Gillo Pontecorvo's *The Battle of Algiers* (1966)

> Perhaps a new world is being constructed out of ruins, a world where women will be wearing pants, literally and figuratively, a world where what remains of the old traditions that adhere to the inviolability of women, both literally and figuratively, will be viewed as a nuisance and swept away.
>
> Mouloud Feraoun, journal entry, April 3, 1958[1]

In *Three Guineas*, Virginia Woolf identified many reasons for women to opt out of the traditionally male pursuit of warfare. She attributed war to the status-seeking behavior of men, whether in the business world, in higher education, or in the clergy, and she hoped that peace would come when women rejected the hierarchical, competitive, masculine world, and formed a community of Outsiders. Having faced discrimination at home, in the ownership of property, in educational opportunities, and in the workplace, women would appear to have no reason to value their country over any other one and thus to share none of the nationalist sentiment that seemed to drive men to fight. This line of argument produces the slogan by which the book is probably best known: "As a woman I have no country."

Joshua Goldstein, in *War and Gender*, follows Woolf by taking as his starting point the observation that warfare has traditionally been gendered male. Throughout history, with seemingly rare exceptions, men have fought and women have either supported their efforts or, as in Woolf's case, criticized their resort to violence in favor of peaceful alternatives. Goldstein summons vast empirical evidence to support this finding, but he neglects a key subcategory of warfare where women have played quite prominent roles: struggles of "national liberation."

[1] Mouloud Feraoun, *Journal, 1955–1962: Reflections on the French–Algerian War* (Lincoln: University of Nebraska Press, 2000), p. 242.

The role of women in national liberation movements predates the era of decolonization that followed World War II. The anti-Nazi resistance during the war, for example, included prominent roles for women. The subject of women in resistance movements became the focus of much scholarly research during the 1990s, with important studies of female French, Greek, and Italian partisans, among others, and a considerable memoir literature. Among the topics that attracted attention were the role of gender identity in relations between men and women and how gender affected their attitudes towards violence and resistance.[2]

With the emergence of anticolonial wars following World War II, a further element was added to the mix of gender, nationalism, and violence. Women in the colonies became the objects of struggle between the men of the colonial administration and the men in the independence movements.[3] The phenomenon was already familiar to historians of the Soviet Union, who examined the way the Bolsheviks (and their opponents) in the Muslim regions of central Asia invoked the status of women and employed symbols such as the veil to promote (or oppose) modernization and undermine (or bolster) the forces of tradition.[4] In the struggles against European colonial rule, many women rejected the passive role of object of male–male conflict. They joined the national liberation effort themselves, sometimes embracing or supporting violence, and became, or tried to become, agents of their own destiny. Paradoxically, among the sources of their strength, especially in Muslim societies, were the stereotypes held by the men of the colonial administration and armed forces.

Gillo Pontecorvo's *The Battle of Algiers* (*La Battaglia di Algeri*, 1966) is the first and most important film to capture this phenomenon. The impact of gender stereotypes on nationalist violence and terrorism figures

---

[2] For prominent examples, see Jane Slaughter, *Women and the Italian Resistance, 1943–45* (Denver, CO: Arden Press, 1997); Margaret Collins Weitz, *Sisters in the Resistance: How Women Fought to Free France, 1940–1945* (New York: Wiley, 1995); Janet Hart, *New Voices in the Nation: Women and the Greek Resistance, 1941–1964* (Ithaca, NY: Cornell University Press, 1996). The memoir literature on women in the Italian resistance is particularly extensive. See the online bibliography: www.url.it/donnestoria/bibliografia/femminismob. htm#fascismo. Beyond Europe and World War II there are rich examples from Asia, particularly the Chinese revolutionary movement. See, e.g., Ono Kazuko, *Chinese Women in a Century of Revolution, 1850–1950* (Stanford University Press, 1989); Christina Kelley Gilmartin, *Engendering the Chinese Revolution: Radical Women, Communist Politics, and Mass Movements in the 1920s* (Berkeley, CA: University of California Press, 1995). I am grateful to Mark Selden for calling these works to my attention.

[3] Cynthia Enloe, *Bananas, Beaches, and Bases: Making Feminist Sense of International Politics* (Berkeley, CA: University of California Press, 1990), ch. 3.

[4] Gregory J. Massell, *The Surrogate Proletariat: Moslem Women and Revolutionary Strategies in Soviet Central Asia, 1919–1929* (Princeton University Press, 1974); Douglas Northrop, *Veiled Empire: Gender and Power in Stalinist Central Asia* (Ithaca, NY: Cornell University Press, 2004).

prominently in it, although most observers have focused on other aspects of this multifaceted masterpiece – and, technically speaking, women only appear on screen for about fifteen minutes of a film that lasts more than two hours.[5] In this chapter I examine how Pontecorvo depicts the use of gender and national stereotypes – by traditional and "Europeanized" Algerian women – to accomplish their acts of anticolonial violence and terrorism, and his portrayals of male French soldiers and women and men of European origin, who became known as *pieds noirs*. I analyze how Pontecorvo uses his camera lens to capture the attitudes of Algerian women who are planting bombs that they know will destroy innocents, including children. I compare the history of women's roles in the Algerian national liberation struggle, 1954–1962, as depicted by Pontecorvo, with the revelations that have come out recently in memoirs of female Algerian militants and French military officials and in the impressive archival work and interviews of French and Algerian historians.

The chapter begins with a summary history of the French presence in Algeria, including its impact on traditional gender roles, and provides background on the origins of the Algerian war. It then turns to Pontecorvo's *Battle of Algiers*, analyzes its depiction of the subversion of gender stereotypes, and compares it with the recent revelations about the behavior and treatment of women during the war. Next the chapter examines Algeria in the wake of victory over the French, the status of women in the post-independence era, and the economic and political crises that gave rise to the violence of the 1990s civil war, with its prominent misogynist elements. This violence, I suggest, was one of the war's most enduring legacies and helped to undermine the gains that Algerian women had achieved by taking up arms in support of independence.

Colonial exploitation and discrimination

France first claimed Algeria as a colony in 1830, wresting it from the control of the Ottoman Empire at about the same time as the Russian Empire was expanding into the Caucasus. Indeed, as chapter 4 describes, the French experience in Algeria resembles in many ways Russian involvement in Chechnya, including the brutal nature of the initial invasion and subsequent occupation.[6] As Anthony Toth writes, "French

---

[5] Danièle Djamila Amrane-Minne, "Women at War: The Representation of Women in *The Battle of Algiers*," trans. by Alistair Clarke, *Interventions*, 9, 3 (2007), p. 342.

[6] For work that takes up this comparison, see Maïrbek Vatchagaev, *L'aigle et le loup: La Tchétchénie dans la guerre du Caucase au XIXe siècle* (Paris: Buchet-Chastel, 2008); Matthew Evangelista, "Is Putin the New de Gaulle? A Comparison of the Chechen and Algerian Wars," *Post-Soviet Affairs*, 21, 4 (October–December 2005), pp. 360–377.

troops raped, looted (taking 50 million francs from the treasury in the Casbah), desecrated mosques, and destroyed cemeteries. It was an inauspicious beginning to France's self-described 'civilizing mission,' whose character on the whole was cynical, arrogant, and cruel." With the fall of Algiers, European settlers embarked on "a bargain-hunting frenzy to take over or buy at low prices all manner of property – homes, shops, farms and factories."[7] Despite the failure of the initial military resistance, the indigenous Arabic- and Berber-speaking populations (known as the Imazighen, or Amazigh in the singular) resisted French occupation, and, like the mountain peoples of Chechnya and Dagestan during the same years, heeded a call to holy war.

The French, like the Russians, reacted with brutality, destroying entire villages, driving peasants from their land, and "smoking out" rebels in caves. In one instance of June 1845, known as the "enfumades du Dahra," the whole tribe of the Ouled Riah, including women and children, hid themselves in caves to escape the violence. The French commander ordered the army to "smoke them out like foxes," even after they had agreed to demands to pay a fine and to submit to French authority.[8] The soldiers built fires at the entrance to the caves and killed between five hundred and a thousand people by asphyxiation. As one French observer declared, "We have surpassed in barbarism the barbarians we came to civilize" – a sentiment similar to those expressed by Lev Tolstoi, a contemporary Russian observer of the Caucasus wars.[9]

The cruelty of the French was not limited to the initial conquest and subsequent repression of revolts. The system of colonial domination was fundamentally destructive of native life and welfare. Algeria endured an initial period of French military rule – the so-called *régime du sabre* – from 1830 until the 1848 revolution in France, when the new government of the Second Republic temporarily ended the Algerians' colonial

---

[7] Anthony Toth, sections on the Invasion of Algiers and The Land and the Colonizers. In Helen Chapan Metz, ed., *Algeria: A Country Study* (Washington, DC: US Government Printing Office for the Library of Congress, 1994), http://countrystudies.us/algeria/. The online version of this study is not paginated, so I refer to the sections (usually a few paragraphs each) from which I have drawn material or quotations. The colonization of the Sahara region of Algeria, which differed in some respects from the northern and Berber areas, is treated in Benjamin Claude Brower, *A Desert Named Peace: The Violence of France's Empire in the Algerian Sahara, 1844–1902* (New York: Columbia University Press, 2009).

[8] Jacques Morel, *Calendrier des crimes de la France outre-mer* (Calendar of the Crimes of Overseas France), website, Version 0.51, April 11, 2005, http://pagesperso-orange.fr/jacques.morel67/ccfo/crimcol/node58.html.

[9] Benjamin Stora, *Algeria, 1830–2000: A Short History*, trans. by Jane Marie Todd (Ithaca, NY: Cornell University Press, 2001), p. 5; Alistair Horne, *A Savage War of Peace, Algeria 1954–1962* (New York: Viking, 1977), p. 30.

status. It declared Algeria an integral part of France and organized the
territory into three *départements* (Algiers, Oran, and Constantine) under
civilian government. But with the overthrow of the republic in 1852 and
the establishment of the Second Empire, Napoleon III returned Algeria
to military control. He did, however, provide a way for its Muslim inhabitants to become French citizens – under very restrictive conditions. As
Toth explains, "they had to accept the full jurisdiction of the French legal
code, including laws affecting marriage and inheritance, and reject the
competence of the religious courts. In effect, this meant that a Muslim
had to renounce his religion in order to become a French citizen."[10] By
1936 only 2,500 native Algerians had obtained French nationality in that
fashion.[11]

Most destructive of traditional Algerian society was the mass emigration from Europe that followed in the decades after the initial conquest.
As Toth summarizes,

the European settlers were largely of peasant farmer or working-class origin
from the poor southern areas of Italy, Spain, and France. Others were criminal
and political deportees from France, transported under sentence in large numbers to Algeria. In the 1840s and 1850s, to encourage settlement in rural areas
official policy was to offer grants of land for a fee and a promise that improvements would be made. A distinction soon developed between the *grands colons*
(great colonists) at one end of the scale, often self-made men who had accumulated large estates or built successful businesses, and the *petits blancs* (little
whites), smallholders and workers at the other end, whose lot was often not
much better than that of their Muslim counterparts. [12]

According to John Ruedy, although by 1848 only 15,000 of the 109,000
European settlers were in rural areas, their colonization contributed significantly to destroying traditional society "by systematically expropriat-
ing both pastoralists and farmers."[13] The situation for Algerians worsened
with France's defeat in the Franco-Prussian war. In 1871, under pressure
to resettle refugees from Alsace-Lorraine, the French government sent
five thousand of them to Algeria, providing them land at the expense
of native farmers. During the 1870s, the settler population of Algeria
continued to expand, as tens of thousands of Muslims were forced off
their land.

The European population of Algeria more than quadrupled from
about 35,000 in the early 1840s to more than 159,000 in 1856, and

[10] Anthony Toth, section on Colonization and Military Control in Metz, *Algeria*.
[11] Martin Evans and John Phillips, *Algeria: Anger of the Dispossessed* (New Haven, CT: Yale
University Press, 2007), p. 31.
[12] Toth, section on The Land and Colonizers in Metz, *Algeria*.
[13] Quoted in ibid.

reached almost 633,000 by the turn of the century.[14] To add insult to injury, in their new Muslim homeland the new settlers typically used the expropriated agricultural land to plant vineyards to grow wine that the natives were forbidden by their religion to drink. In subsequent years, immigrants from Italy, Spain, and Malta would come to Algeria seeking work. These Europeans – the people who came to be called *pieds noirs* in the 1950s – received land, jobs, citizen rights, and other opportunities that were denied to native-born Algerians.

The inequalities in land distribution that came with European immigration were particularly damaging to Algeria's rural population. In subsequent chapters we will observe the impact of international economic conditions on the prospects for nationalist violence – in particular, the effect of integration into the world economy, neoliberal policies of "structural adjustment," and indebtedness to foreign banks on socialist economies' systems of full employment in Yugoslavia and the former Soviet Union. We can already glimpse a similar dynamic at work in Algeria in the second half of the nineteenth century. Thanks to the territory's integration into the international agricultural market, the dramatic increases in world grain prices in the period after the Crimean war led to pressure on the grain supply and mass starvation in the countryside. Some 20 percent of the population of Constantine perished in the course of three years. In 1871, when the military government reneged on promises to provide loans to replenish the supply of seeds, natives of the Kabylie region rebelled. After putting down the insurrection, the "French authorities imposed stern measures to punish and control the whole Muslim population." They confiscated "more than 500,000 hectares of tribal land and placed the Kabylie under a *régime d'exception* (extraordinary rule), which denied the due process guaranteed French nationals."[15]

In the last decades of the nineteenth century the French authorities introduced a *Code de l'indigénat* that governed the behavior of its colonial subjects. The precedent had been set already in Algeria in the mid-1860s when a number of measures reinforced inequalities between the native population and the Europeans. Colonial rule imposed particularly discriminatory policies in the economic sphere. In the first decade of the twentieth century, for example, Algeria's Muslims made up nearly 90 percent of the population, but earned only 20 percent of the country's income. Nevertheless they were obliged to pay 70 percent of direct taxes and 45 percent of the total taxes collected.[16] The introduction of

---

[14] Kamel Kateb, *Européens, "indigènes" et juifs en Algérie (1830–1962): Représentations et réalités des populations* (Paris: L'Institut national d'études démographiques, 2001), p. 187.

[15] Anthony Toth, section on Colonization and Military Control in Metz, *Algeria*.

[16] Anthony Toth, section on Hegemony of the Colons in Metz, *Algeria*.

the modern market and wage employment had a disorienting effect on those who were able neither to maintain their traditional village ways nor to integrate fully into the wage economy, for lack of full-time jobs. This "class," which persisted well into the postcolonial period, Pierre Bourdieu has termed the Algerian *subproletariat*, "the aberrant by-product of an economic and social order that does not offer everyone the possibility of achieving the goal it imposes as an absolute necessity – a money income."[17]

A common image of colonialism pictures it as combining repression and exploitation with the introduction of elements of a more advanced European civilization, such as education. In the case of Algeria, the French began by destroying the existing rather successful education system. Mary-Jane Deeb points out that a French report written on the eve of the conquest "noted that in 1830 the literacy rate in Algeria was 40 percent, a remarkable rate even by modern standards."[18] Religious schools were mainly responsible for this achievement, as students were taught to read Arabic in order to study the Qur'an. Within twenty years of the French invasion, the colonial authorities had closed half of them. The system they introduced in place of the original one heavily favored the European colonizers. In 1892, for example, the French government earmarked 2.5 million francs for the education of European settlers' children, but only 450,000 francs for the vastly more numerous Muslim Algerians. Indeed at a time when the school-age population of Muslim Algerians was five times that of Europeans, the government was spending more than five times as much on the *European* schools as on the Muslim ones. A half-century later, the situation still heavily favored the Europeans. By 1945, the 200,000 European children were educated at 1,400 primary schools, whereas the 1.25 million Algerian children were crowded into fewer than half as many schools (699).[19] In 1949 the authorities ended segregated schooling of colonial and Algerian children. They planned to increase Muslim enrollments as part of the 1954 reforms known as the Constantine Plan, intended to improve living conditions overall. "On the eve of independence, however," as Deeb writes, "the European-oriented curricula were still taught exclusively in French, and less than one-third of school-age Muslim children were enrolled in schools at the primary level. At the secondary and university levels, only 30 percent and 10 percent of the students, respectively, were Algerians." As a consequence of

---

[17] Pierre Bourdieu, "The Algerian Subproletariat," in I. William Zartman, ed., *Man, State, and Society in the Contemporary Maghrib* (New York: Praeger, 1973), p. 84.
[18] Mary-Jane Deeb, sections on Arabization and Education in Metz, *Algeria*.
[19] Horne, *Savage War of Peace*, pp. 60–61.

such discriminatory policies, when the French finally left Algeria in 1962 adult literacy among Algerian Muslims had fallen from the 40 percent reported in 1830 to about 10 percent.[20]

Such blatant discrimination sowed the seeds of the uprisings that culminated in the war for liberation. Another element contributing to the violence – not a cause per se, but a permissive factor – was a demographic one: the "youth bulge" that emerged between 1948 and 1954, the product of unusual growth in the population aged 15–24 years. According to Ali Kouaouci, these age cohorts "formed the bulk of combatants in the Algerian revolution when they were 15–24 years old" and "sustained a heavy price in human lives during the 1954–66 period."[21]

Among the young people who joined the revolution were many women. What inspired them to embrace violence in the cause of national liberation? To ask why women resorted to violence is not to take for granted or "naturalize" the fact that men resorted to violence as well.[22] Even though men have played the dominant role historically in political violence, we want to understand their motivations in specific cases as well. Looking to gender relations provides insights into behavior of both men and women confronting choices about violence in nationalist movements.

Gender roles before the independence movement

Before the arrival of the French, Algerian society was patriarchal and patrilineal. The basic kinship unit was the *ayla*, through which males recognized common descent back to a grandfather or great-grandfather. Extended families consisted of mother and father, their married sons and their families, their unmarried sons and daughters, their divorced or widowed daughters with their children. Senior male members made all major family decisions, administered common pastoral and cultivated territory, distributed work assignments, and represented the family in dealing with outsiders.[23] Islamic tradition governing marriage viewed it as "a civil contract rather than a sacrament, and consequently, representatives of the bride's interests negotiate[d] a marriage agreement with representatives of the bridegroom."[24]

---

[20] Deeb, section on Education in Metz, *Algeria*.
[21] Ali Kouaouci, "Population Transitions, Youth Unemployment, Postponement of Marriage and Violence in Algeria," *The Journal of North African Studies*, 9, 2 (Summer 2004), pp. 28–45.
[22] Paige Whaley Eager, *From Freedom Fighters to Terrorists: Women and Political Violence* (Aldershot: Ashgate, 2008), p. 110.
[23] Mary-Jane Deeb, section on Preindependence Society in Metz, *Algeria*.
[24] Deeb, section on Family and Household in Metz, *Algeria*.

Gender figured into French colonial attitudes towards Algeria right from the start, as it did in most colonial relationships. As one history of Algeria suggests, "there is no better vantage point for understanding the assumptions that underpinned colonialism than Eugène Delacroix's 1834 painting Women of Algiers," the result of the painter's trip to Algeria and Morocco two years earlier. "In portraying the Algerian women as submissive, sensual and inviting, he is implicitly saying that the country is a place of fertile riches and therefore ripe for colonization."[25]

Gender played a role not only in imagining but also in carrying out the French colonization of Algeria. Frantz Fanon, in "Algeria Unveiled" and in other essays, has made a convincing case that the French colonial authorities deliberately sought to undermine traditional Algerian institutions, with a particular focus on the family, in order to secure control over the new territory. Fanon, born in colonial Martinique, had served in the French army in World War II, studied psychiatry in France, and then worked in a hospital in Algeria. He became a leading supporter of Algeria's independence and a spokesperson for the Algerian revolution and the organization that claimed to lead it, the Front de Libération Nationale (FLN).[26]

According to Fanon, "beneath the patrilineal pattern of Algerian society," French specialists had identified "a structure of matrilineal essence." "Behind the visible, manifest patriarchy," they claimed to find a "more significant existence of a basic matriarchy." He describes the implications of their analysis as follows:

This enabled the colonial administration to define a precise political doctrine: "If we want to destroy the structure of Algerian society, its capacity for resistance, we must first of all conquer the women; we must go and find them behind the veil where they hide themselves and in the houses where the men keep them out of sight." It is the situation of woman that was accordingly taken as the theme of action. The dominant administration solemnly undertook to defend this woman, pictured as humiliated, sequestered, cloistered … It described the immense possibilities of woman, unfortunately transformed by the Algerian man into an inert, demonetized, indeed dehumanized object. The behavior of the Algerian was very firmly denounced and described as medieval and barbaric. With infinite science, a blanket indictment against the "sadistic and vampirish" Algerian attitude toward women was prepared and drawn up. Around the family life of the Algerian, the occupier piled up a whole mass of

---

[25] Evans and Phillips, *Algeria*, p. 4. For a fuller discussion of these and other images, see Ranjana Khanna, *Algeria Cuts: Women and Representation, 1830 to the Present* (Stanford University Press, 2008).
[26] For consideration of Fanon's continuing relevance, see Immanuel Wallerstein, "Reading Fanon in the 21st Century," *New Left Review*, 57 (May–June 2009), pp. 1–9.

judgments, appraisals, reasons, accumulated anecdotes and edifying examples, thus attempting to confine the Algerian [man] within a circle of guilt.[27]

Upon its publication in Paris in 1959, the French government immediately banned the collection of Fanon's essays in which he offered this analysis, which suggests that he was on to something. Marnia Lazreg's impressive research in French military archives has since corroborated Fanon's argument that the French army was more interested in undermining the nationalist movement than in liberating Algerian women per se. As she puts it, "the army's strategic interest in women stemmed from its assessment that the FLN was having a positive impact on the Algerian family, especially in matters of marriage, and was thus changing gender relations in the right direction for women, but not with France as a sponsor."[28] A detailed study of the Equipes Médico-sociales Itinérantes (EMSI), teams of French-directed Muslim women working with the female population in the countryside, comes to a similar conclusion. Ryme Seferdjeli quotes a French military document from March 1959 justifying the creation of the EMSI "solely as part of the response to the revolutionary war" waged by the Algerian nationalists.[29]

The program of undermining Algerian society by targeting its women is familiar from the Soviet experience in central Asia. By making women's liberation an achievement of the colonial authorities, the French, like the Bolsheviks before them, sought to recruit new female allies while humiliating their male relatives. Years later, a similar if more brutal attempt to undermine the solidarity of Muslim communities led to campaigns of mass rape in Bosnia, as the next chapter describes.

Whatever the French military's motives, the strategy of targeting women failed – creating resentment among the males and provoking anti-French sentiment even among the females who were the ostensible beneficiaries of the "enlightened" colonial policies favoring women's liberation. As we shall see, the strategy also sowed the seeds of misogynistic violence in post-independence Algeria, as Islamist militants pursued a delayed vengeance against the legacy of French colonialism, using women as their objects, much as the French had done.

In 1960, a French conscript soldier named Marc Garanger recognized the counterproductive nature of the colonial regime's modernizing

[27] Frantz Fanon, "Algeria Unveiled," in *A Dying Colonialism* (New York: Grove Press, 1965; originally published in Paris in 1959 as *L'an cinq de la révolution algérienne*), pp. 37–38.
[28] Marnia Lazreg, *Torture and the Twilight of Empire: From Algiers to Baghdad* (Princeton University Press, 2008), p. 146.
[29] Ryme Seferdjeli, "The French Army and Muslim Women during the Algerian War (1954–62)," *Hawwa: Journal of Women of the Middle East and the Islamic World*, 3, 1 (2005), p. 49.

techniques – such as providing identification cards to women. He was assigned the task of photographing indigenous Algerians, some two thousand of them over the course of two hundred days, in order to provide them the identity cards which would serve to restrict their movement and engagement in collective activities. Garanger was obliged to photograph women's faces, which in turn required that they lift their veils. Thus, Garanger was "the first to witness the protest apparent on the women's faces," as Ranjana Khanna explains.

It is as if they break out of the constraints of the frame offered to them by the official photographic genre and provide something that could never be predicted by the formal element of the repetitive task in which the photograph represents identity. Instead, the face, by the slightest indication of individuation, marks its own parameters of being as potential defiance. The photograph is, however, the constitution of the subject and being: it is as if prior to the moment Garanger took the photograph, the face, attached to individuated identity such as that revealed in the production of identity cards, did not exist.[30]

Contrary to the expectations of the French authorities that they could win over Algerian women by means of such forced "liberation," they instead created many more enemies – ones who would prove particularly effective in supporting the violent resistance to French occupation.[31]

Origins of the Algerian war

Always treated as second-class citizens, Algerians took advantage of France's humiliating capitulation to Nazi power during World War II to press for independence, much as Chechen activists would later pursue their goal of autonomy from a disintegrating Soviet Union after the Cold War. At the end of World War II, the Algerians' attempt to gain independence centered initially on mass demonstrations. When these were met with force the independence movement eventually turned to a campaign of guerrilla warfare, combined with acts of terrorism. On May 8, 1945, the day of the armistice ending the war in Europe, thousands of Algerians paraded in the streets with banners proclaiming "Down with fascism and colonialism." In an incident at Sétif, the police fired on the demonstrators, provoking a spontaneous uprising during which more than a hundred European residents of Algeria were killed. In response,

---

[30] Khanna, *Algeria Cuts*, pp. 21–22.
[31] Khaoula Taleb Ibrahimi, "Les Algériennes et la guerre de libération nationale. L'émergence des femmes dans l'espace public et politique au cours de la guerre et l'après-guerre," in Mohammed Harbi and Benjamin Stora, eds., *La Guerre d'Algérie, 1954–2004: la fin de l'amnésie* (Paris: Editions Robert Laffont, 2004), pp. 197–226.

the French air force attacked villages, the navy bombarded the coast, and the army rounded up and shot people. The death toll of the civilian population ranged from 15,000 (official French estimates) to 45,000 (Algerian claims).[32]

For many Algerian political activists who had sought to reform French policy through peaceful means, the events of May 1945 marked a turning point. As Evans and Phillips describe, "confronted with the continued intransigence of the French authorities, they saw violence and direct action as the only way forward." Yet this was not the only possible response. One of the leading reformers, Ferhat Abbas, "drew a very different lesson from Sétif. The French response led him to the conclusion that violence was futile" in the face of superior French force and willingness to use it indiscriminately. He founded a movement "seeking to bring together those Muslims who were still committed to evolutionary change."[33]

Yet the political space for nonviolent change diminished with the rebellion launched on November 1, 1954 by the newly formed Front de Libération Nationale and the brutal French response. As its name implied, the FLN sought national independence. It broadcast a manifesto by radio, highlighting two main goals: "(1) restoration of the Algerian state, sovereign, democratic, and social [sic], within the framework of the principles of Islam; and (2) preservation of all fundamental freedoms, without distinction of race or religion."[34]

The initial FLN insurrection was concentrated in the Aurès region, but with scattered attacks throughout the country creating the impression of an organization much larger and more widespread than it was. The army reacted by carrying out sweep operations – known in French as *ratissages*, from "comb" or "rake" – and establishing settlement camps for populations driven from the combat zones. Joined by French paratroopers and the Foreign Legion – including many veterans of the German SS – the armed forces engaged in torture and summary execution. In a memoir published in 2001, a French officer who participated directly in the system of torture in Algeria acknowledged that thousands of those who were imprisoned never returned: after being tortured, they were simply killed and buried in secret graves.[35] These practices were common in colonial wars against insurgent forces dating back to the middle of the nineteenth century, and in chapter 4 we encounter them again in the Chechen wars,

---

[32] Horne, *Savage War of Peace*, pp. 16–20. Evans and Phillips, *Algeria*, suggest even lower official figures, between 1,020 and 1,300, p. 52.

[33] Evans and Phillips, *Algeria*, pp. 52–53.   [34] Ibid., p. 57.

[35] Paul Aussaresses, *Services spéciaux Algérie 1955–1957* (Paris: Perrin, 2001), pp. 34–35.

with Russia's indiscriminate bombing, sweep campaigns (*zachistki*), torture, and extrajudicial murders.[36]

In both Algeria and Chechnya, the policies of the central governments alienated potential supporters of compromise solutions, such as Ferhat Abbas, and drove them into the arms of the rebels. In both cases a further source of violence was internecine fighting between the indigenous forces. In Algeria, the FLN sought to lead the movement for independence and to undermine its main rival, the Mouvement National Algérien or MNA, founded by Ahmed Ben Messali Hadj – whose arrest by the French authorities had helped provoke the demonstrations of May 1945. The MNA was particularly popular among immigrant Algerian workers in France, which became the battleground for violent conflict between the FLN and MNA. Some five thousand Algerians are estimated to have died in these so-called café wars.[37]

Powerful psychological barriers prevented the French from accepting the Algerians' claims to independence. From the French perspective Algeria had been part of France for longer than some of its European territories, such as the province of Savoie and the city of Nice (ceded by Italy in 1860 in return for France's support for Italian unification). Despite its overseas status, French political figures across the spectrum insisted that Algeria was no less part of France than Brittany or Provence (to take two regions with distinct traditions and languages, assimilated rather late into the dominant culture) – although their commitment to this claim wavered from time to time.[38] A popular expression claimed that the Mediterranean Sea divided France as the River Seine divided Paris.[39] Certainly in November 1954, half a year after the fall of Dien Bien Phu had set in train a process of decolonization (as the French left Vietnam), Interior Minister François Mitterrand was only expressing a widely held view when he asserted that "Algeria is France" and must remain so. In response to offers by the FLN to negotiate Mitterrand responded: "The only possible negotiation is war."[40] Psychological attachment to the territory was undoubtedly bolstered by the discovery of oil in the Sahara in 1952, some seventy years after Chechnya's oil

---

[36] Human Rights Watch, "Human Rights Situation in Chechnya: Human Rights Watch Briefing Paper to the 59th Session of the UN Commission on Human Rights," April 2003, www.hrw.org/backgrounder/eca/chechnya/unchr-chechnya-04.htm.

[37] Anthony Toth, section on Polarization and Politicization in Metz, *Algeria*.

[38] Ian S. Lustick, *Unsettled States, Disputed Lands: Britain and Ireland, France and Algeria, Israel and the West Bank-Gaza* (Ithaca, NY: Cornell University Press, 1995).

[39] Raphaëlle Branche, "Entre droit humanitaire et intérêts politiques: les missions algériennes du CICR," *Revue historique*, 609 (January–March 1999), p. 103, n. 4.

[40] For the first quote: Yves Marc Ajchenbaum, ed., *La guerre d'Algérie, 1954–1962* (Paris: Librio, 2003), p. 94; for the second: Horne, *Savage War of Peace*, p. 99.

industry contributed to the industrialization of the region under Russian sponsorship. The Sahara also became France's preferred test range as it developed its nuclear arsenal, making Paris all the more reluctant to give up control.

The leadership of the FLN decided that only an escalation of the violence could force France to cede control of Algeria. Its policy initially limited attacks to military and government targets, but in August 1955 the FLN political authorities for the Constantine region ordered indiscriminate attacks on civilians near the town of Philippeville. Armed fighters and civilian supporters massacred 123 people, including elderly women and babies. As the FLN intended, the French authorities called for further repressive measures. As Toth describes, "the government claimed it killed 1,273 guerrillas in retaliation; according to the FLN, 12,000 Muslims perished in an orgy of bloodletting by the armed forces and police, as well as *colon* gangs." Vigilantes from the *pieds noirs* community became an increasingly explosive factor in provoking further violence. The local police were often complicit in these formally unauthorized activities, as a key scene in *The Battle of Algiers* depicts. Particularly notorious were the so-called *ratonnades* (from the word *raton*, or "little rat"), campaigns of murder of suspected FLN members and sympathizers.[41] The FLN sought to polarize Algerian society into occupiers and liberators, with no room for a neutral position, and to position itself as the only force capable of saving the Algerian people from the escalating colonial violence. The French army, police, and *pieds noirs* vigilantes all played their parts according to the script.

The conflict in Algeria, as later in former Yugoslavia and in Chechnya, wreaked devastation on the civilian population. As with the US war in Iraq and the Soviet and US-led wars in Afghanistan, the governments prosecuting the conflicts claim not to have counted how many civilians their soldiers were killing. Thus the estimates for the Algerian war (1954–1962) cover a wide range, with several hundreds of thousands of deaths likely, and some claims of up to 1.5 million, on the Algerian side.[42] French military authorities reported 18,000 soldiers dead (a third from causes unrelated to combat) and 65,000 wounded. Some 3,000 European civilians died, typically victims of terrorist attacks (of which 42,000 were recorded). The French acknowledge killing 141,000 Algerian rebels and

---

[41] Toth, sections on Philippeville and FLN in Metz, *Algeria*.

[42] Guy Pervillé, "La guerre d'Algérie: combien de morts?" in Harbi and Stora, *La guerre d'Algérie*, pp. 477–493; on the problems associated with documenting deaths, see Raphaëlle Branche, *La guerre d'Algérie: une histoire apaisée?* (Paris: Editions du Seuil, 2005), pp. 204–217.

French sources estimate the FLN killed (or abducted and presumably killed) 70,000 Muslim civilians.[43]

In Algeria, contrary to generalizations about gender roles in warfare, women played an active part in the violence – not only as victims, as in Yugoslavia for example, but as perpetrators as well. In the Algerian war, women engaged directly in violence as accomplices to male assassins, by joining guerrilla forces (although usually not bearing arms) in the countryside known as the *maquis*, and, ultimately, as *poseuses de bombes*, staging terrorist attacks against civilians.[44] The role of Algerian women in terrorist violence is probably best known from Pontecorvo's film. Although not a documentary, *The Battle of Algiers* provides a rather faithful depiction of the activities of FLN women in carrying out bombings of civilian targets in the European quarter of Algiers. They played on gender stereotypes to accomplish what their male counterparts were unable to do.

Subverting stereotypes in *The Battle of Algiers*

As Cynthia Enloe and other feminist theorists have argued, "the militarization of any nationalist movement occurs through the gendered workings of power," as masculinity becomes associated with the use of violence in the service of the nation. Such "changes in ideas about masculinity," argues Enloe, "do not occur without complementary transformations in ideas about what it means to be a woman." Thus we can expect the militarization of a nationalist movement "when a community's politicized sense of its own identity becomes threaded through with pressures for its men to take up arms, for its women to loyally support brothers, husbands, sons, and lovers to become soldiers."[45] In the Algerian case, women played such supportive roles, but their direct engagement in violence was the most striking aspect of the conflict.

The film anticipates a subversion of the traditional roles in an early scene depicting a wedding. The marriage ceremony for Mahmud and Fathia is held in secret, as it represents an assertion of the FLN's civil authority over a sovereign Algeria, and in particular what the revolutionaries called the *Zone Autonome d'Alger*, in violation of France's exclusive claims to govern. Although he recites a short introductory prayer, the middle-aged man in a European-style suit who presides over the ceremony is not an imam, but an official of the FLN underground government. The

[43] Anthony Toth, section on The Generals' Putsch in Metz, *Algeria*.
[44] Ibrahimi, "Les Algériennes et la guerre de libération nationale."
[45] Cynthia Enloe, *The Morning After: Sexual Politics at the End of the Cold War* (Berkeley, CA: University of California Press, 1993), pp. 246–247.

Figure 2.1 Wedding ceremony. *The Battle of Algiers* (1966)

book he carries is not the Qur'an, but an FLN registry of civil marriages. Although a few of the participants at the wedding wear traditional clothing (djebellas, kaftans, fez), and even though men and women assemble separately – the men downstairs and the women upstairs, preparing the bride – that is about the extent of anything recognizably traditional or Islamic in this scene. Mahmud sports a western suit jacket, white shirt, and necktie. Most strikingly, Fathia wears a short, sleeveless, white patterned dress, and her thick, black hair loose on an uncovered head. She confidently shakes the hand of the FLN official at the close of the ceremony. Pontecorvo signals the viewer that the Algerian revolution is not an atavistic, religiously inspired rebellion, but a modern, secular challenge to colonial domination, whose program includes gender equality.

The FLN did appeal to Islam at various points in its propaganda. It was a natural response to embrace an Islamic identity, given that French discrimination was explicitly directed at the Muslim character of Algerian society. The French created the Muslim as the Other in colonial Algeria. Only by renouncing Islam could an Algerian hope to achieve the benefits of French citizenship. As with many nationalist and anticolonial conflicts, the identity of the Algerian nationalist was forged in reaction to the character of the colonial oppression.

Pontecorvo's film subtly portrays the links between Islam and a liberation movement that in its most basic elements was inspired by (French) enlightenment values of secular egalitarianism and democracy. One section of the film depicts the FLN's campaign to eradicate prostitution, drug abuse, and alcoholism from the Muslim community of the Casbah.

The FLN's main leader responsible for the organization's activities in Algiers was Saadi Yacef, who subsequently directed the bombing campaign that provides much of the dramatic tension in *The Battle of Algiers*. In the film, the character who plays that role is named El-hadi Jaffar, and the "actor" who plays Jaffar is Saadi Yacef, whose memoir formed the basis for the screenplay and whose contacts in the Algerian government helped provide funding for the film.[46] One scene shows Ali la Pointe (Ali Amara), the petty criminal who became chief deputy to Jaffar/Yacef, visiting a brothel, where the madam and her Algerian employees seem to know him well. Ali is looking for a local gangster and pimp, named Hacène. When he finds him, Ali verbally conveys the FLN's death sentence and then mows Hacène down with a machine gun hidden in his cloak. In the background, as Ali fires, one hears the Muslim call to prayer.

Clearly Pontecorvo wants to invoke an Islamic element in the FLN's campaign to clean up the Casbah – to save the honor of Algerian women (really the honor of their fathers and brothers) by ending prostitution, and by abolishing habits that violate the Qur'an, such as consumption of alcohol. But this is not primarily a religiously inspired campaign. It is a political one – to assert the FLN's control over the community and to expel or eliminate unreliable elements. That discipline and political control were the main objectives is suggested by an observation that the historian Raphaëlle Branche makes, when she points out that the FLN added tobacco to the list of banned substances, in effect requiring people to give up "their everyday activities" such as cigarette smoking to prove their loyalty to the movement – even though there was nothing in Islam that forbade tobacco. The sanctions for breaking the rules were severe – in this case, mutilation of an offender's nose or lips.[47] The film portrays an equally cruel punishment for violating the rule against alcohol con- sumption, when a crowd of young children chases a drunk and stumbling man, clearly an alcoholic, beating him and eventually pushing him down a set of concrete stairs. The scene gives us a glimpse of the brutalizing effects of colonialism and war on children – effects that persisted long into the post-independence period.

The actual Algerian war, as well as Pontecorvo's cinematic recreation of the Battle of Algiers, challenged several prevailing stereotypes about women and violence. Most obviously, an essentialist feminist perspec- tive of gender violence and warfare as predominantly male runs into

---

[46] Nicholas Harrison, "An Interview with Saadi Yacef," *Interventions*, 9, 3 (2007), pp. 405–413.

[47] Raphaëlle Branche, "La masculinité à l'épreuve de la guerre sans nom," *CLIO*, 20 (2004), http://clio.revues.org/document1408.html.

trouble right from the start. Women play a key role in the urban guerrilla warfare in Algiers (and other cities). In one of the early scenes of *The Battle of Algiers*, Ali la Pointe is released from Barberousse prison (also known as *Serkadji*) where he has received a political education from FLN militants who were his fellow prisoners. There he witnessed the execution by guillotine of an FLN prisoner, an actual event that many have described as triggering the wave of Algerian violence that launched the Battle of Algiers – and inspiring some of the women who carried it out.[48] Upon his release Ali is given an assignment to assassinate a French police officer. His accomplice is Djamila, a young woman dressed in traditional head-to-toe *haik*. She hides a pistol in her basket and hands it to Ali at the last moment. This was a very common role played by Algerian women during the war. Because the French had sealed off the European quarter of Algiers from the Muslim Casbah, it would have been impossible for men to carry out their attacks if women had not first smuggled the weapons through the French checkpoints.

In one scene, at a checkpoint controlling entrance to the European quarter from the Casbah, a soldier begins to search a woman and demand her identity papers. As she yells at him to take his hands off, another soldier admonishes him, "Didn't you know that you're never supposed to touch one of their women?" As in the scene with Ali, the woman passes through the checkpoint to a café, where she hands a revolver to a young man who uses it to shoot a police officer sitting at a table.

In response to the series of attacks on mainly military and police targets, French vigilantes retaliate by blowing up an apartment complex on Rue de Thèbes. Again, Pontecorvo's take on this real event highlights the role of gender, and, in particular, a certain gendered "division of labor" in the violence carried out by the European colonial population, in contrast to the more egalitarian Algerian approach. Historians describe the Rue de Thèbes bombing as a collaboration between the police and an "ultra" group of *pieds noirs* whose subsequent rampage of "counterterrorism" would yield thousands of deaths in the last days of French occupation in 1962.[49] Pontecorvo sets the scene for the late-night bombing by showing the vice-commissioner of the police and his *pieds noirs* accomplice, Henri Arnaud, at an evening party with their families in a wealthy neighborhood of European Algiers. The young French women, in short, sleeveless dresses and jewelry, laugh and drink on the outdoor

---

[48] Michel Veuthey, *Guérilla et droit humanitaire*, 2nd edn (Geneva: Institut Henry-Dunant, 1983), p. 146, for the relationship between executions and terrorist reprisals; and the testimony of Baya Hocine on Algiers in 1957, in Danièle Djamila Amrane-Minne, *Des femmes dans la guerre d'Algérie* (Paris: Editions Karthala, 1994), p. 146.

[49] Horne, *Savage War of Peace*, ch. 9.

Figure 2.2 Passing as Muslim. *The Battle of Algiers* (1966)

Figure 2.3 "Didn't you know that you're never supposed to touch one of their women?" *The Battle of Algiers* (1966)

patio, as Bernadette Arnaud calls up to her Algerian nanny Fatma to have the children say their prayers and go to bed.[50] Then the men get in a car and depart, ostensibly to participate in a male-only game of cards.

[50] The irony of the situation is even clearer in Franco Solinas' original script, as the (Muslim) Algerian nanny corrects the children in the recital of their (Christian) prayers. See PierNico Solinas, ed., *The Battle of Algiers* (New York: Charles Scribner's Sons, 1973), pp. 56–57.

Figure 2.4 Female shield. *The Battle of Algiers* (1966)

"Why can't you play cards here?" ask the wives. As viewers learn the real reason for the men's early departure, they may think of the traditional gendered division of labor in a wartime situation – with the men heading off to the front and the women staying home with the children. In this case, rather than engage in combat, the men cross through a checkpoint into the dark streets of the Casbah, deserted under curfew, to carry out an atrocity: they set a bomb to blow up a civilian apartment complex. Pontecorvo contrasts the superficially peaceful family life of the bourgeois European population, as represented by the women, with the violence wielded by the men, at the expense of Algerian families.

In the mythology of the Algerian revolution, the Rue de Thèbes explosion serves to justify the subsequent terror bombing campaign against civilian European targets, as if civilians had heretofore been immune to FLN attack. In fact, the violation of the civilian–combatant distinction – what Michael Walzer has called "the political code" of revolutionaries, "analogous to the laws of war" – had long preceded the Battle of Algiers.[51] Although it may be true that the FLN had not previously used bombs to attack civilians in Algiers, it had not by any means limited its previous attacks to soldiers and police. As we saw earlier, in August 1955 the FLN had launched massacres against European civilians (and Algerian political rivals) in the port town of Philippeville, with weapons ranging from knives to grenades. The FLN justified the attacks in turn as a response to the longstanding French policy of "collective

[51] Michael Walzer, *Just and Unjust Wars* (New York: Basic Books, 1977), ch. 12.

Figure 2.5 *Soirée. The Battle of Algiers* (1966)

responsibility," which resulted in aerial bombardment of villages, with thousands of civilian casualties.[52] Thus the remark attributed to Saadi Yacef upon his arrest in 1957: "I had my bombs placed by hand because I did not have any airplanes like you to transport them. But they made fewer victims than the aviation or artillery [attacks] on our villages and *djebels* [mountains]."[53]

The film renders this argument about terrorism as a "weapon of the weak" in a somewhat more dramatic fashion. In this case, Yacef's point is made by Larbi Ben M'hidi, an FLN leader captured by Colonel Mathieu's troops and put before French and foreign journalists at a press conference. An earnest young journalist demands, "Mr. Ben M'hidi, don't you find it rather cowardly to transport bombs in women's baskets and use them to kill innocent people?" He responds, "And you, don't you find it much more cowardly to drop napalm bombs on defenseless villages and kill a thousand times more innocents? Give us your bombers, sir, and you can have our baskets."

In any event, the French bombed villages in the countryside and their *ultra* supporters bombed civilian homes in Algiers. The film faithfully depicts both the sorrow of the survivors of Rue de Thèbes as they remove the dead and wounded from the wreckage of the apartment building and the anger and will for revenge that surged through the Casbah in the aftermath of the attack. Pontecorvo shows Jaffar/Yacef recruiting

[52] Horne, *Savage War of Peace*, esp. pp. 119–123, 184.
[53] Quoted in Veuthy, *Guérilla et droit humanitaire*, p. 145.

Figure 2.6 "Mr. Ben M'hidi, don't you find it rather cowardly to transport bombs in women's baskets and use them to kill innocent people?" *The Battle of Algiers* (1966)

Figure 2.7 "Give us your bombers, sir, and you can have our baskets." *The Battle of Algiers* (1966)

young Algerian women to carry bombs into the European quarter. As Yacef recalled in his memoirs, he sought to overcome any reluctance on the part of his *poseuses de bombes* by telling them that they would be avenging the deaths of Muslim children killed at Rue de Thèbes.[54] At

---

[54] Saadi Yacef, *Souvenirs de la Bataille d'Alger* (Julliard: Paris, 1962).

least one of them, however, claims not to have needed the additional per-
suasion. Zohra Drif, a first-year law student in 1954–1955, was already
determined to fight. "I wanted to join a terrorist group," she recalls. The
FLN had offered her the task of sheltering fighters in town, or even serving with the guerrilla forces in the *maquis*. "But this is not what I wanted
to do. I wanted to participate in armed action. I thought in the *maquis* I
would only be used as a nurse or secretary, so I wanted to join a terrorist
group, here in town."[55] She got her chance.

A central episode in the film is the transformation of "Saadi's girls,"
as they exchange their traditional dress for European fashions, cutting
and dyeing their hair, and applying make-up. The original scenario had
them talking among themselves, but Pontecorvo decided to eliminate the
dialogue, in favor of the rhythmic leitmotif that returns during a pivotal
bombing scene. Despite the regrets of his scriptwriter Franco Solinas,
it was an inspired artistic choice on Pontecorvo's part. In this case art
trumped real life, as Danièle Djamila Amrane-Minne observes in an article comparing the movie with the actual situation of female militants
during the war: "Women are almost totally silent throughout the whole
film. This is all the more striking because, in fact, the atmosphere within
resistance groups was usually characterized by a close camaraderie
between men and women, sustained by lively debates."[56]

The overall atmosphere in the *boudoir* is solemn and almost melan-
choly. These Algerian women, however liberated in their professional
aspirations and personal strengths, are evidently reluctant to transform
themselves into the European ideal of feminine beauty. They cut their
hair with regret, apply cosmetics with the utmost seriousness and no sign
of pleasure or self-satisfaction.

It is uncertain whether Pontecorvo intended anything like this, but the
scene can be read as a complicated metaphor about the relationship of
the women to their voluntary but still resented task and to the man who
oversees them. The room, in effect, resembles a brothel, with its mir-
rors, toiletries, and women in various states of undress. Jaffar enters and
surveys the scene, inspecting his protégées. In the only light moment,
Zohra Drif switches from the local dialect of Arabic in which they had
exchanged greetings. Casting Jaffar a mock coquettish look, she seeks
his approval by inquiring in French, "Ça va, Monsieur?" (In real life,
Zohra Drif was Yacef's unmarried partner.) Do the women feel that they

---

[55] From her interview with Amrane-Minne, *Des femmes*, pp. 137–138. In her interview
in the film, "Remembering History" (2004), included with the US DVD, Zohra Drif
expressed no remorse over the civilians killed in her bombing of the Milk Bar. Nor did
she in an interview conducted in September 2006. See William Maclean, "50 Years On,
Algiers Bomber Sees US 'Error' in Iraq," Reuters, September 28, 2006.

[56] Amrane-Minne, "Women at War," p. 347.

Figure 2.8 *Boudoir*. *The Battle of Algiers* (1966)

Figure 2.9 Cutting hair. *The Battle of Algiers* (1966)

are prostituting themselves, denying their Muslim heritage, by passing as Europeans? Or is the analogy found in their anticipated acts of violence? Perhaps these acts represent the ends-justify-the-means thinking of a prostitute who has no other recourse for survival but to sell herself for sex.

Once transformed into Europeans, the FLN women set out on their mission. They cross the checkpoint from the Casbah into the European quarter, this time subverting stereotypes of the peaceful, apolitical

Figure 2.10 Applying lipstick. *The Battle of Algiers* (1966)

Figure 2.11 Waiting. *The Battle of Algiers* (1966)

European woman in Algiers. Zohra Drif, with beach bag in hand, flirts with the French soldier who just waves her through with a request to join her at the beach on his next day off.

The other two women, whose names in real life were Hassiba Ben Bouali and Djamila Bouhired, have no trouble crossing either, with Djamila playing on a maternal stereotype, bringing her young son along with her, only to leave him temporarily when she later sets her bomb. The favoritism of the French soldiers is apparent in how they speak to the people waiting in line to cross. Using formal language to a European

Figure 2.12 Passing as European. *The Battle of Algiers* (1966)

woman, a soldier calls "Passez, Madame," and lets her through. To the Algerian woman next in line, a brusque command in the informal: "Toi, avance!" ("You, come forward!").

One of the most effective and affecting scenes in the film comes when Hassiba places her bomb in a café. The camera scans the crowded room, focusing on one face at a time. The viewer is drawn particularly to a young child licking an ice-cream cone. The camera then returns to Hassiba's face, completely impassive, as she sees the child and the others she is about to kill.[57]

The scene with Hassiba in the bar shows Pontecorvo's use of something close to the Kuleshov effect, a technique named after the Russian director, L. V. Kuleshov, a major theorist of montage. In his original experiment, Kuleshov took a clip of the Russian movie idol Ivan Mozzhukhin, juxtaposed it to three different scenes (in his collaborator Vsevolod Pudovkin's recollection, a bowl of soup, a dead woman in a coffin, and a child playing with a toy bear), and showed it to an audience. The audience was convinced that Mozzhukhin was portraying different emotional reactions, depending on the scene with which he was juxtaposed, when in fact the clip of the actor was identical in

---

[57] In reality, Hassiba Ben Bouali, a social worker by profession, was not one of the three bombers who carried out the attacks of September 30, 1956, although she was a member of Yacef's group. Instead it was Zohra Drif's fellow law student Samia Lakhdari, accompanied by her mother, who blew up the Cafétéria on Rue Michelet. Djamila Bouhired's bomb, placed at the Air France terminal, failed to detonate. Horne, *Savage War of Peace*, p. 186. See also Amrane-Minne, "Women at War," p. 346.

Figure 2.13 Ice cream. *The Battle of Algiers* (1966)

each instance.[58] In the case of Pontecorvo's montage, his actor, Fusia El Kader, is expressionless after each cut to a future victim of her bomb, but viewers read into her face whatever emotion they deem most appropriate to the situation. When I have asked my students how they interpret the character's reactions, some see hesitation and the anticipation of remorse, even expecting that she will change her mind and not carry out the attack. Others see cold determination and the absence of concern for the victims.

Pontecorvo's soundtrack reinforces the tension in the scene, but does not resolve the question of Hassiba's feelings. As she approaches the café to enter, we hear only street sounds. They stop abruptly as Hassiba steps into the café, replaced by a rhythmic pounding. Created by an instrument that evokes native Algerian music, the sound resembles a cross between a heartbeat and a train rumbling down the track. Its meaning is as ambiguous as the image it accompanies. Does it represent Hassiba's heart, and if so what about it? Fear of committing murder, fear of getting caught, or simply the pressure of knowing that she has little time before the bomb goes off? She glances repeatedly at the clock, much as the characters do in *High Noon*, as they await the midday train. Is it indeed a train sound, representing Pontecorvo's view, once expressed in an interview, that the violence of revolutionary anticolonial movements was somehow historically

[58] S. I. Iutkevich, general editor, *Kino: Entsiklopedicheskii slovar'* (Moscow: Sovetskaia Entsiklopediia, 1986), pp. 220–221; Geoffrey Nowell-Smith, *The Oxford History of World Cinema* (New York: Oxford University Press, 1996), pp. 166–167.

Figure 2.14 Second thoughts? *The Battle of Algiers* (1966)

necessary and inevitable, driven by the engine of history?[59] Fanon, in "Algeria Unveiled," averred that "no one takes the step of placing a bomb in a public place without a battle of conscience."[60] Yet Pontecorvo's direction remains agnostic on the question, and, as we shall see, one of his real-life models has repeatedly challenged Fanon's interpretation.

The scene shocks with its violation of the viewer's expectations about the maternal instinct. Here a mother murders some other mother's (and father's) child. The fact that some women do engage in such violent acts in the course of nationalist conflicts might call into question some of the assumptions underlying a "maternalist" approach to gender and war. According to this approach, women as mothers are expected to be peaceful and nurturing. If they resort to violence in defense of their own families, they are still expected to avoid harming children.

Despite the prominent role played by women in Pontecorvo's film, and the director's deliberate effort to challenge easy stereotypes, none of the movie critics who hailed the film's debut made any mention of gender.[61] One is tempted to explain this oversight as a product of the times. Perhaps 1966 was too early to expect reviewers to see movies through a

---

[59] "Marxist Poetry: The Making of *The Battle of Algiers*," documentary film (2004).

[60] Fanon, "Algeria Unveiled," p. 55.

[61] This claim is based on my reading of all the major reviews provided as part of the Italian DVD version of *La Battaglia di Algeri* and the fact that one of the leading students of the film makes no reference to the topic of gender in her summary of the reviews. See Joan Mellen, *Filmguide to* The Battle of Algiers (Bloomington, IN: Indiana University Press, 1973), ch. 6.

feminist lens, or as Enloe puts it, with "feminist curiosity." In this case, that explanation would be wrong. As we have seen, six years before the filming of *The Battle of Algiers*, Fanon had published "Algeria Unveiled." The essay contained a sophisticated analysis of the techniques employed by the FLN women, and his observations on gender and violence in the Algerian revolution are particularly insightful. Not only does the analysis predate Pontecorvo's treatment, it most likely was the main inspiration for it. We know that Pontecorvo and Solinas read Fanon's work and interviewed many participants in the Algerian events in the course of their extensive research in Paris. Fanon's influence on their film is readily apparent. And, of course, their collaborator Saadi Yacef knew first-hand the importance of the women's activities.

Fanon's work was based on his familiarity with the actual practices of his fellow revolutionaries. Consider this passage, and how it evokes the scene of Zohra Drif crossing the checkpoint:

> Carrying revolvers, grenades, hundreds of false identity cards or bombs, the unveiled Algerian woman moves like a fish in the Western waters. The soldiers, the French patrols, smile to her as she passes, compliments on her looks are heard here and there, but no one suspects that her suitcases contain the automatic pistol which will presently mow down four or five members of one of the patrols.[62]

An interesting difference between Fanon's analysis and Pontecorvo's depiction is a reversal of the order by which Algerian women deceived the French about their intentions. Pontecorvo's women start by wearing traditional dress and then switch to European styles. According to Fanon, it happened the other way around: "The Algerian woman's body, which in an initial phase was pared down, now swelled. Whereas in the previous period the body had to be made slim and disciplined to make it attractive and seductive, it now had to be squashed, made shapeless and even ridiculous. This, as we have seen, is the phase during which she undertook to carry bombs, grenades, machine-gun clips." Once the French wised up to the women's practice of carrying bombs concealed in the *haik*, "every veiled woman, every Algerian woman became suspect."[63] In chapter 4 we see a similar process at work in the Russian forces' approach to Chechen women.

The order in which Algerian women sought to subvert French expectations of their gender roles is not so important. Indeed there were cases when women deployed both sets of stereotypes – traditional and European – in the course of the same operation. Malika Ighilhariz tells her remarkable story of serving as a driver and courier for the FLN.

---

[62] Fanon, "Algeria Unveiled," p. 58.   [63] Fanon, "Algeria Unveiled," p. 62.

The organization gave her false identity papers – she posed as a French woman named Martine – and a big American De Soto to drive.

My hair blowing in the wind, I passed through all the cordons with big smiles. To reenter the Casbah, I parked on Boulevard de la Victoire, just next to Barberousse, near the police station. They would see me get out of the car, *à la française*, I would enter a building where I would put on my cloak and my veil, I would come back out veiled and go down to the Casbah. I dropped off what I had to deliver and took what had to be gotten out of the Casbah – messages, weapons. And I replayed the same game. In the corridor of a building I took off the cloak, put back on my lip rouge, my glasses, I went out and got back in my beautiful car.[64]

Ighilhariz evinces none of the hesitation at transforming herself into a *française* that we glimpsed in the scene of the three women changing their clothes. We hear no complaints about her having to apply lipstick or the fact that driving her beautiful car made her hair blow in the wind.

Ighilhariz achieved a certain freedom by posing as the French woman, Martine. Other Algerian women enjoyed *relative* freedom because of the constraints placed on men. Under the special circumstances of French military occupation of the Casbah, women from a traditional society that typically restricted their movements and their opportunities became in this case freer than the men. Pontecorvo captures this change well in a scene where Jaffar (Yacef) and Ali la Pointe are forced to don cloaks and veils in order to move around the Casbah. Less skilled than the women at walking in such a costume, they are detected and are forced to resort to firing their weapons as they flee. To escape, they must rely on the goodwill of two women whose house they enter. The women help them descend into a dry well in the middle of the apartment, the men still wearing skirts and looking sheepish and rather ridiculous.

The vulnerable position of the FLN men seems to have strengthened the women in the movement and given them a sense of purpose and pride. Zohra Drif evokes these feelings as she sums up the effect of the war on Algerian men and women.

At first I simply carried out orders, but the conditions became more and more difficult. The Casbah was blocked off, the brothers would have been immobilized if we were not there. We lived the same life, but as far as the activity was concerned we had a more intense life than they did, because we could move around veiled. It was they who found themselves confined (*cloîtrés*). At one point, they would veil themselves to be able to go out; they had to transform themselves into us in order to stick their noses outside.[65]

---

[64] Interview with Malika Ighilhariz, in Amrane-Minne, *Des femmes*, esp. p. 149.
[65] Interview with Zohra Drif, in Amrane-Minne, *Des femmes*, p. 138.

Figure 2.15 (Almost) passing as women. *The Battle of Algiers* (1966)

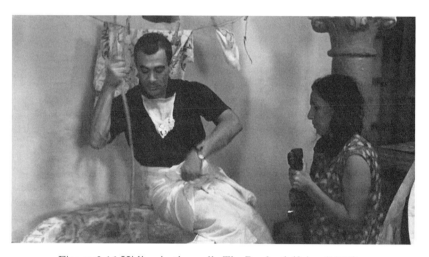

Figure 2.16 Hiding in the well. *The Battle of Algiers* (1966)

Contrast Zohra Drif's recollection with that of Saadi Yacef:

Normally women took the back seat. But when war broke out, we needed them. They fed us. They were lookouts on the terraces. The women were indispensable and totally implicated. Among the women who gave me cover were law students who threw off the yashmak [veil]. They wanted to participate directly in the struggle – plant bombs, hide weapons, do liaison work. They were exactly like the men. Sometimes better. A woman who plants a

Figure 2.17 "They had to transform themselves into us in order to stick their noses outside." *The Battle of Algiers* (1966)

bomb is better than a man who does nothing or just hands out flyers. They played a key role.[66]

Yacef clearly appreciates the role that women played and he makes an unmistakable reference to Drif and her female law-student friend (Samia Lakhdari) who joined the movement with her. Yet he equally clearly genders Algerian nationalists as *male*: "*We* needed *them*." Fanon's work, for all its insight into gender dynamics, takes it for granted that the Algerian revolutionary is gendered male. He struggles with his French colonial counterpart to determine the proper role for women in Algeria. The men on each side want to take credit for liberating women, protecting women. In this rendering, the women have no agency of their own.[67] For Saadi Yacef's part, he makes a point of praising the women of the FLN, but uses that praise to question the masculinity of men who did not engage in violence. Finally, Yacef implicitly downplays the women's contribution when he fails to mention the point that Drif highlights – that she came to lead the resistance in Algiers when he could no longer move around for fear of arrest.

[66] Liza Bear, "On the Frontlines of 'The Battle of Algiers,'" n.d. (2004?) www.indiewire. com/people/people_040112algiers.html.
[67] Fanon, "Algeria Unveiled." See also the discussion in Anne McClintock, "'No Longer in a Future Heaven': Nationalism, Gender, and Race," in Geoff Eley and Ronald Grigor Suny, eds., *Becoming National: A Reader* (New York: Oxford University Press, 1996), pp. 259–284.

Neither does the film acknowledge the leadership role that Drif played. It portrays her and Yacef being arrested together, thereby giving the audience the impression that for each of them the end of their activity coincided with their arrest. Although they were, indeed, captured at the same time, Saadi Yacef had in effect been long immobilized by the heavy French military presence, whereas Drif had been free to take over the active leadership in Algiers. Drif was engaged in other spheres besides running operations in Algiers. She was, for example, author of a plan to organize an underground women's network, with a goal, among others, of documenting incidences of torture.[68]

Zohra Drif seems to be one of those women about whom both Virginia Woolf and Cynthia Enloe hypothesize. Whatever her commitment to the cause of Algerian independence – and it was undoubtedly a strong one – she was also driven to assert her *individual* independence, and to do so by engaging in violence: "I wanted to join a terrorist group ... I wanted to participate in armed action." Many Algerian women reacted in a similar way to the prospect of violent revolution. As Deeb writes, "women, accustomed to a sheltered and segregated life, found themselves suddenly thrust into revolutionary militancy. For many, the war offered the first opportunity for independent activity in the world beyond the home."[69] This explanation echoes Woolf's account of English women's "loathing for the education of the private house with its cruelty, its poverty, its hypocrisy, its immorality, its inanity," all of which could drive them to support war and empire as (in Woolf's view) a kind of false consciousness.[70]

Yet Zohra Drif, for one, did not fit Woolf's category of "daughters of educated men," with the implication that they themselves would not be allowed an education. On the contrary, she was a law student and presumably headed towards an independent professional career. Woolf did not anticipate that a woman like Zohra Drif would be driven by more than the selfish pursuit of her own career, that she would embrace violence and war in the interest of a cause – the national liberation of her country. Indeed, the militant and sometimes murderous actions of a Zohra Drif or a Malika Ighilhariz, to the extent they were motivated by nationalist sentiment, seem to defy Virginia Woolf's most famous claim, which I proposed in the introduction to interpret as one of her many hypotheses: "As a woman I have no country." Women of the FLN clearly felt an allegiance to an Algerian nation for which they were willing to kill and die.

---

[68] Lazreg, *Torture*, p. 146; Amrane-Minne, *Des femmes*, p. 141.
[69] Deeb, section on The Revolution and Social Change in Metz, *Algeria*.
[70] Virginia Woolf, *Three Guineas* (New York: Harcourt, Brace, 1966 [1938]), p. 39.

The final scene of the film shows an ebullient crowd of mainly women facing down the French riot police and soldiers. Pontecorvo expresses their diversity by showing women veiled and unveiled, in European and traditional dress. The camera lingers on individual faces. The director creates a sensation of movement by repeatedly returning to the same figures, making them move (sometimes literally) two steps forward, one step back, as they jeer at the soldiers, shout slogans, issue a chorus of ululations, and wave home-crafted national flags. The scene is full of hope and celebration.

Yet the end of the war, and the full French withdrawal, were still many years and untold thousands of deaths away. The violence continued even after the Évian Accords of March 1962 declared a cease-fire. The *pieds noirs* extremists did not want an independent Algeria to succeed. Their Organisation de l'Armée Secrète (OAS) embarked on a "scorched earth" policy and campaign of terror that reached into metropolitan France as well. Anthony Toth describes it as "the most wanton carnage that Algeria had witnessed in eight years of savage warfare."[71] In March OAS operatives were setting off on average 120 bombs daily. In May, in one Algerian city, the paramilitary forces of the *pieds noirs* killed between ten and fifty Algerians every day. They blew up forty schools in the last four days of that month. In June the "Delta commandos" burned down the library of Algiers, destroying some sixty thousand books – echoes of Stalin's genocidal policies in Chechnya during the 1940s, when he sought to erase the existence of the Chechen people after deporting them en masse to the east.

Anticipating reprisals for such outrages, the European residents of Algeria fled to France, leaving Algeria to its unhappy fate. In April 1962, the French electorate approved the Évian Accords by referendum, with a vote of 91 percent in favor. By the end of the month 350,000 *colons* had immigrated to France. Within a year, some 1.4 million refugees left the country, including most of the Jewish community and the Algerian *harkis* who had served the French. The provisional executive of the newly independent Algeria declared as the national day of independence July 5, 1962 – the 132nd anniversary of the French army's first entry into Algeria.[72]

Pontecorvo's neorealism and its limits

The Battle of Algiers has the look and feel of a documentary, so much so that the director made a point of issuing a disclaimer at the outset (in the

---

[71] Toth, section on The Generals' Putsch in Metz, *Algeria*.
[72] Horne, *Savage War of Peace*, chs. 23–24 ; Stora, *Algeria*, ch. 8.

initial US release) that the film contained no newsreel footage. This was apparently a point of pride for Pontecorvo, as he had clearly modeled his film on the neorealist classic *Open City* (*Roma, città aperta*, 1945) by Roberto Rossellini – and was apparently inspired to pursue a filmmaking career by Rossellini's next film, *Paisan* (*Paisà*, 1946). As Joan Mellen points out, "perhaps the true originator of Pontecorvo's film style is Eisenstein, as it was for Rossellini. Pontecorvo derives his conception of political filmmaking, in which individual personalities interact with and are subordinated to a historical outlook, from the Eisenstein of *Strike*, *Potemkin*, and *October*."[73] Another similarity is Pontecorvo's use of the crowd as a collective actor, so that even though he has *visually* striking individual characters, he does not seek to develop their personalities to any great extent. "Our intention was to create a 'choral protagonist,' not a single person but the whole people of Algeria as our hero," Pontecorvo explained to an interviewer in 2004.[74] Pontecorvo seems to make an exception not for his heroes, but for his "villain." Colonel Mathieu, the commander of the paratroopers (*les paras*) is presented as intelligent and subtle, and has some of the best lines. The character is apparently a composite of several French officers, including Marcel Bigeard and Jacques Massu, and is played by the only professional actor in the film – Jean Martin, an early opponent of the war.

Both *Open City* and *The Battle of Algiers* prominently feature an apartment complex with an open courtyard, where the police conduct raids, running up and down stairs, to round up suspects who are later subjected to torture. In Rossellini's film the German Gestapo carry out the raids and torture, whereas in Pontecorvo's it is the French paratroopers and Foreign Legionnaires (whose ranks included many Germans). For fans of French cinema, viewing *The Battle of Algiers* in the mid-1960s, Pontecorvo's film likely evoked another early classic – Julien Duvivier's *Pépé le Moko* (1937), about a gangster from Marseilles, played by Jean Gabin. That film also takes place in Algiers, with much of the action unfolding in the Casbah, where *Pépé*, like the FLN two decades later, hides out from the authorities. The film opens with a sweeping panorama of the city, similar to some of Pontecorvo's shots, and follows its characters to locales that resemble some of the ones in *The Battle of Algiers*. It is possible that Pontecorvo received some inspiration from this example of "poetic realism," a style that influenced the Italian neorealists and shares some elements in common with *film noir*. Pontecorvo's opening scene

---

[73] Mellen, *Filmguide*, pp. 8–9.
[74] Emory Holmes II, "A War Film with Striking Relevance," *Los Angeles Times*, January 4, 2004; Saadi Yacef makes the same point in Harrison, "An Interview with Saadi Yacef," pp. 407–408.

of Ali la Pointe fleeing the police through the streets of the European quarter, to the sound of suspenseful, rhythmic music, certainly evokes a *noir* atmosphere.

A focus of particular dramatic tension in the film is the ultimatum to Ali la Pointe, the sole remaining leader of the revolt in Algiers, after the French paratroopers have engaged in widespread torture in order to locate and eliminate the rest of the organization's leadership. Ali is hidden in a tiny space behind a false wall, with three others: Mahmud, the twelve-year-old Petit Omar, and Hassiba. After evacuating residents from the building, a French captain urges Ali to surrender and spare the lives of his young companions. Adopting the women-and-children-first convention, he calls "Let the boy and woman out first, then you and the other man." According to the memoir of Paul Aussaresses, a former military officer involved in the Algerian campaign, there was in reality no ultimatum. The French forces, once they had located Ali's hiding place, simply detonated an explosion that killed Ali and the others and destroyed six surrounding houses.[75] There was no warning for the residents to evacuate. As harshly realistic as Pontecorvo's film seems, it does in fact soften somewhat the actual brutality of the war – whatever the truth about this particular incident.

The same is true of the film's treatment of torture. The torture scenes in *The Battle of Algiers*, like those in *Open City*, are grim. But we know from the historical record that the reality was far worse. For all its apparent verisimilitude, *The Battle of Algiers* risks misleading viewers who might rely on it as their only source for the French practices.

In the opening scene, for example, a torture victim named Sadek has just divulged the hiding place of Ali la Pointe. Colonel Mathieu arrives and tells the poor man that he will be let go after accomplishing one task, that nothing further will be done to him.[76] Sadek is then dressed in a French uniform and brought to the apartment where Ali and his fellow militants are hiding. The scene conveys the impression that after he does this job, Sadek will go free. In the real Battle of Algiers, the

---

[75] Aussaresses, *Services spéciaux*, p. 124. In his own memoir, one of the top military leaders of the Algerian war offers an account consistent with what Pontecorvo shows: Jacques Massu, *La vraie bataille d'Alger* (Paris: Librairie Plon, 1971), caption of the photo showing the destroyed building, between pp. 124 and 125.

[76] There is apparently no published script that reflects the actual dialogue in the film. The DVD that comes with the Italian version of *La Battaglia di Algeri*, released in 2003, contains a scenario identified as revisions of the Italian version of October 19, 1966. It is closer than the version published in English as Solinas, *The Battle of Algiers*, but still differs a great deal. In general, the script contains much more dialogue than Pontecorvo ultimately used, as he would often trim back his actors' lines or even replace them altogether with music.

torture victims were not so lucky. In many cases the French tortured
them to death. If they did not die under torture, they were often killed
after revealing information to their torturers and buried in mass graves. If
they were set free, they were usually assassinated by the FLN as traitors.
As Aussaresses, a direct participant in the torture, explained, "it was rare
that prisoners interrogated [i.e., tortured] at night would be found still
alive the next morning. Whether or not they talked, they were generally
neutralized." He acknowledged carrying out torture and summary executions himself.[77] During the Battle of Algiers, from January to October
1957, some 25,000 people were arrested. According to some sources,
3,024 were left unaccounted for, presumably killed and "disappeared."
Others suggest much higher figures.[78]

More germane to the topic of gender roles in the Algerian war, *The
Battle of Algiers* shows only men being rounded up and tortured. In fact
women were equally subject to such violence, from all sides. Algerian
female militants regularly suffered torture, in which rape played a significant part.[79] In the countryside French forces and the FLN alike were
implicated in massacres that included killing pregnant women. French
troops engaged in mass rapes of village women.[80] Threats of rape reflected
the belief – among both the French and the Algerians – that women constituted the most vulnerable members of the target population, as when
the FLN sought to extort money from a shopkeeper with the ultimatum
that otherwise "your daughter will be abducted and will serve as the mat-
tress for the army of liberation … we have our eyes on her."[81]

It is not surprising that a film produced in cooperation with the
Algerian government should neglect to cover the FLN's violence against
women (aside from the random violence of the bombing campaign).
Why Pontecorvo would choose not even to hint at the French practices
of sexual violence is less clear. Maybe he wanted to preserve a chance
that the film would actually be shown in France. Despite loud calls to do
so, the film was not technically banned, but when one cinema sought to

[77] Aussaresses, *Services spéciaux*, p. 153.
[78] Ibid., p. 195, citing Paul Teitgen who oversaw the police forces as head of the Algiers
prefecture. On this point and for a consideration of the overall death toll, see Pervillé,
"La guerre d'Algérie: combien de morts?" esp. p. 489; and Branche, *La guerre d'Algérie*,
pp. 204–217.
[79] Amrane-Minne, *Des femmes*.
[80] Lazreg, *Torture*, especially the section Rape as a Military Strategy, pp. 154–160;
Raphaëlle Branche argues that the extent to which rape served as a deliberate strategy
(as opposed to simply being permitted or encouraged) varied from region to region and
unit to unit. See her "Sexual Violence in the Algerian War," ch. 9 in Dagmar Herzog, ed.,
Brutality and Desire: War and Sexuality in Europe's Twentieth Century (New York: Palgrave
Macmillan, 2009).
[81] Quoted in Horne, *Savage War of Peace*, p. 410.

show *The Battle of Algiers* in the Latin Quarter in 1971 it had to reverse the decision when extremists smashed the theater's windows at every showing.[82] Other significant works that described French use of torture in Algeria also were poorly received at the time, if not banned outright. These include Alain Resnais' 1963 film *Muriel: The Time of Return* (*Muriel ou le temps d'un retour*), which explores the psychological consequences for a former French soldier who was involved in the torture of a young Algerian woman, and Pierre Vidal-Naquet's *La torture dans la République*, published in English and Italian translations in 1963, but not released in France until 1972.[83]

Presumably the research that Pontecorvo and Solinas conducted in Paris brought them into contact with Simone de Beauvoir's published account of the torture and abuse of Djamila Boupacha, who became something of a *cause célèbre* when her treatment at the hands of French authorities became known. As Ranjana Khanna summarizes, Boupacha was "kicked in the chest by a group of soldiers and had a rib permanently displaced; had electrodes affixed with transparent tape to her nipples, legs, face, anus, and vagina and was given electrical shocks; was burned with cigarettes; and was 'deflowered' by a beer bottle."[84]

Khanna suggests that men – both French and Algerian – have tended to downplay, or not even to notice, the sexual violence carried out against women. She describes the case of an Algerian woman named Kheira. In 1959 a group of thirty or forty French soldiers had systematically gang-raped her at an internment camp over a period of several months – a practice that we will encounter again in the next chapter's discussion of the Yugoslav wars. Kheira was fourteen or fifteen years old at the time. She became pregnant and bore a son who later emigrated to France. Kheira's case became known only because in 2001 her son, Mohamed Garne, won compensation from the French government for the violence inflicted against him during the Algerian war: "as a fetus, when his mother was beaten during pregnancy; as an infant abandoned by his mother; and as a man of thirty being told by his mother that he was a product of war rape." Garne's lawyer, Jean-Yves Halimi, was the son of Gisèle Halimi, Djamila Boupacha's lawyer of four decades earlier. According to

---

[82] Benjamin Stora, "Still Fighting: *The Battle of Algiers*: Censorship and the 'Memory Wars,'" *Interventions*, trans. by Mary Stevens, 9, 3 (2007), p. 369.

[83] For a discussion, see Branche, *La guerre d'Algérie*, pp. 22–23.

[84] Khanna, *Algeria Cuts*, p. 83, citing Simone de Beauvoir and Gisèle Halimi, *Djamila Boupacha* (Paris: Gallimard, 1962). A thorough discussion of the competing reports of physicians and psychiatrists who evaluated Boupacha is found in Raphaëlle Branche, *La torture et l'Armée pendant la guerre d'Algérie, 1954–1962* (Paris: Gallimard, 2001), pp. 340–342.

Khanna, even he failed to make clear that Garne was a victim precisely owing to the violence inflicted on his mother. As she concludes:

Even though it was implicitly acknowledged that Kheira was violated, she was acknowledged only because of her son's trauma, and because, unlike Mohamed, she had no claim to French citizenship, she had no rights to a case such as her son's. The case demonstrates how the shadow figures of the war are violently cut from this pathbreaking legal finding in which the father nation, France, belatedly acknowledges its bastard son – by skipping a generation of women silenced through amnesty or madness. In the awarding of reparation from father to son, Kheira herself became incidental, the instrument of the violent reproduction of the masculinist state.[85]

From this perspective, the French state, gendered as male, commits the ultimate misogynist act – by negating a woman who has been raped and denying her trauma – even while acknowledging and compensating the trauma of her son. A similar dynamic seems to be at work in post-colonial Algeria, where women who symbolically gave birth to the nation amid horrendous violence continue to suffer at the hands of their male offspring.

Algeria after independence

No one viewing Pontecorvo's *Battle of Algiers* can fail to be moved by the film's uplifting final scenes, with their hypnotic images of smiling, defiant, and triumphant women. But anyone with knowledge of late twentieth-century Algeria must also feel a sense of regret at lost opportunities and shattered dreams – especially for women. More prescient are the views expressed in the epigraphs that open this chapter. The first – that the real hardships will come after the revolution has succeeded – come from a movie character representing the real-life FLN leader, Larbi Ben M'hidi. His surviving comrade Saadi Yacef, whose memoir formed the basis for the film script, claimed at one point to have voiced the original insight: "Those were my lines," he told an interviewer. "It doesn't matter. I give them to everybody!"[86] Indeed, we have already encountered Yacef giving away his line (also to Ben M'hidi in the film) about exchanging Algerian women's baskets for French airplanes. The second epigraph – that in gaining equality ("wearing pants") women will lose their traditional inviolability – comes from the diary of Mouloud Feraoun. An Algerian-Berber writer and teacher, educated in French schools, he

---

[85] Khanna, *Algeria Cuts*, pp. 1–4.
[86] Bear, "On the Frontlines." In another interview Yacef gives Ben M'hidi credit for the point. See Harrison, "An Interview with Saadi Yacef," p. 406.

published several novels in French about his native Kabylie and was a correspondent of Albert Camus.[87] Feraoun tried to steer a moderate course between the violence of French colonialism and the extremism of the FLN, and he kept a diary recounting how difficult – and ultimately impossible – that task proved to be. He was assassinated by the OAS on March 15, 1962, just three days before the Évian Accords ended the war. Feraoun's diaries, published posthumously in Paris in 1962, are one of the early sources of description of the French army's practice of mass rape in the villages of Kabylie, one of the most violent areas of the country.[88]

According to Saadi Yacef, Larbi Ben M'hidi was so concerned about the factional infighting that he expected to dominate post-independence Algeria that he would rather die than experience it.[89] The French torture squads obliged him in his wish. Although the French authorities reported that he had committed suicide in his cell, we know now from the admission of Paul Aussaresses that the army murdered Ben M'hidi.[90]

The first few years after independence were indeed characterized by violent conflict in the upper echelons of the FLN. The situation stabilized when Colonel Houari Boumediène staged a military coup in 1965 and established a military-backed Council of the Revolution to run the country. Boumediène suspended the constitution and the National Assembly and appointed himself both president and prime minister. Algeria embraced a form of militarized socialism, with an economy that some would characterize as closer to state capitalism. The FLN leadership emphasized heavy industrialization, funded by the sale of oil and gas as its main exports.[91]

In 1978 Boumediène died suddenly from a rare blood disease at the age of fifty-three. As Hugh Roberts describes, "the political primacy of the armed forces was immediately reaffirmed in the choice of the senior army officer, Colonel Chadli Bendjedid, as Boumediène's successor."[92] Yet Bendjedid's ideologically rigid, military-dominated government was ill-suited to handle the serious economic crisis Algeria faced in the 1980s, a crisis exacerbated by a heavy external debt.

---

[87] Aïcha Kassoul and Mohamed Lakhdar Maougal, *The Algerian Destiny of Albert Camus*, trans. by Philip Beitchman (Bethesda, MD: Academica, 2006), ch. 7.

[88] Feraoun, *Journal, 1955–1962*, p. 262.   [89] Bear, "On the Frontlines."

[90] Aussaresses, *Services spéciaux*, pp. 161–171. Again, Massu's account, in *La vraie bataille*, remains consistent with the story that M'hidi committed suicide.

[91] On the early years of independence, see Evans and Phillips, *Algeria*, ch. 3.

[92] Hugh Roberts, *The Battlefield Algeria, 1988–2002: Studies in a Broken Polity* (London: Verso, 2003), p. 20.

In two other cases we examine in this book – former Yugoslavia and Chechnya – similar conditions contributed to the outbreak of violent nationalist conflict. In Algeria's case, the violence, when it broke out in the early 1990s, took on religious overtones and pitted armed Islamist groups against the army and the ruling elites at first, and then against broad segments of the society, as the country erupted into full civil war. The features that the Algerian case shares in common with the Yugoslav and Chechen ones include dramatic economic decline, and particularly widespread unemployment among young men, coupled with a failure of the existing governmental institutions to cope with the problem and a loss of credibility in the dominant ideology. In all three cases, the wars involved corruption and racketeering, with motives of greed and revenge often blurring political and ideological divides. In the Algerian case, and many others, the economic decline is associated with "globalization" – the country's integration into the international economy and its pursuit of liberalizing reforms dictated by the major lending institutions, the World Bank and International Monetary Fund. Programs of "structural adjustment," with major reductions in fiscal spending, limit the abilities of the government to respond to the crisis in unemployment, as the burden of foreign debt overwhelms the country's finances.

For Algeria, the crisis was forestalled for many years by the country's abundance of natural gas, its main export. But in the second half of the 1980s, with the decline of energy revenues triggered by a drop in the price of oil, the Algerian economy lost its safety net. As Anthony Toth explains, "the country's economic crisis deepened in the mid-1980s, resulting in, among other things, increased unemployment, a lack of consumer goods, and shortages in cooking oil, semolina, coffee, and tea. Women waited in long lines for scarce and expensive food; young men milled in frustration on street corners unable to find work. An already bad situation was aggravated by the huge drop in world oil prices in 1986."[93]

In short, the Algerian economic crisis was exacerbated by demographic and political-religious factors. Algeria in the late 1980s was experiencing what demographers call a "youth bulge," when a sizeable proportion of the working-age population (usually 40 percent) falls between the ages of fifteen and twenty-nine. Statistical studies of countries with youth bulges have indicated higher incidences of internal armed conflict and strife than in countries with relatively fewer youths.[94] To understand

---

[93] Anthony Toth, section on Chadli Bendjedid and Afterward in Metz, *Algeria*.
[94] Henrik Urdal, "The Devil in the Demographics: The Effect of Youth Bulges on Domestic Armed Conflict, 1950–2000," World Bank, Social Development Papers, Conflict Prevention and Reconstruction, paper no. 14 (July 2004).

why young men might be susceptible to appeals to violence, and particularly misogynist violence, we need to consider other factors. Chris Dolan's notions of "collapsing masculinities" and the "proliferation of small men" are a good place to start.[95] In the Algerian case, political Islam added further fuel to the fire. Algerian Islamists had rejected from the start the revolution's commitment to gender equality and had been chipping away at it for years.

The proliferation of small (misogynist) men

As the Algerian revolution brought women formal equal rights, many became educated and pursued professional careers, and some rose to positions of prominence, including, for example, Zohra Drif, who became a leading member of the Algerian Senate. But when civil war broke out in 1992, women became some of its main victims. The perpetrators were gangs of roving young men, many associated with the Islamist opposition forces, who had long been denied political power. Women were kidnapped and raped, sometimes en masse, then murdered or abandoned. Professional women who expressed feminist beliefs, or even simply dared to work outside the home, were murdered in the hundreds.[96] How can one explain the catastrophic course of events that followed such a hopeful liberation?

One important consideration is the rise of Islamist sentiment and its relationship to the former French regime and the first generation of FLN leaders. Political Islam made its way into Algerian politics owing largely to the FLN's monopolization of public life, its corruption, and its failure, through mismanagement of the economy, to provide an adequate standard of living. Islamist groups in Algeria, as in many countries of the Middle East and North Africa, sought to fill the void by offering social services and promoting an alternative ideology to the stale socialist variant espoused by the FLN. The more the FLN's economic policies became discredited by unemployment, lack of consumer goods, and government corruption, the stronger the position of the Islamist opposition to advocate changes in social policy – with women as their main target.

One should bear in mind that despite the egalitarian ideology of the Algerian revolution, Islamists had begun their campaign against women already in the first years of independence. They criticized the behavior of the liberated women "who had fought in the FLN ranks and now refused

---

[95] Chris Dolan, "Collapsing Masculinities and Weak States – A Case Study of Northern Uganda," in Frances Cleaver, ed., *Masculinities Matter!* (London: Zed Books, 2003), pp. 57–83.
[96] Evans and Phillips, *Algeria*, p. 193.

to wear the veil." An official visit to Kuwait by Djamila Bouhired, one of the bombers of the Battle of Algiers, caused a scandal when she emerged from her plane with her head uncovered to meet a welcoming delegation of veiled female teachers and an embarrassed minister of education.[97] In 1964, the founding of Al Qiyam ("Values"), the first mass organization promoting traditional Islamic values, threatened to undermine the position of women and their newly achieved rights. Already the status of women in independent Algeria was considered worse than in neighboring Tunisia or Morocco. Government-sponsored organizations, such as the National Union of Algerian Women, had few adherents and did little to protect women's rights. Rural workers, in particular, remained unorganized and susceptible to patriarchal traditions.

In the mid-1970s, with the infighting behind them and state authority consolidated, Algeria's rulers introduced major reforms into the political system. A new constitution was drafted which revived the National Assembly as a functioning parliament. Despite the revolutionary regime's egalitarian rhetoric, the aura of militarized masculinity surrounding the FLN and the army boded ill for the status of women. Some women were elected to the parliament and women continued to serve in communal assemblies, but overall political representation of women was low. In 1967, for example, 99 female candidates were elected to communal assemblies (out of 10,852 positions nationwide). By the late 1980s, the number was still below 300.[98]

The army, as self-proclaimed defender of the values of the revolution, should have been at the forefront of defense of women's rights against the assault of the Islamists. Instead, certain aspects of the legacy of the war of independence appear to have contributed to the gendered nature of the violence that broke out in the 1990s. Particularly ominous was the effect on a key segment of the officer corps of their apparent insecurity about their own masculinity. In consolidating his power in the mid-1960s, Boumediène had removed potential competitors from the high command – particularly veterans of the war who enjoyed independent bases of support. He replaced them with a group of officers known as the Déserteurs de l'Armée Française or DAF – latecomers to the revolution who had been trained by and had served in the French army. As Evans and Phillips explain,

Most of these officers had been promoted by the Governor General Robert Lacoste in 1956 in an effort to combat discrimination in the French army. Ever sensitive to status, upon defecting they had exploited this promotion as

[97] Ibid., *Algeria*, p. 78.
[98] John P. Entelis with Lisa Arone, section on the Women's Movement in Metz, *Algeria*.

a lever to enjoy a higher command than they would ever have dreamed of in the French force. The Lacoste reforms became the butt of many jokes within military circles because in effect they had turned corporals and sergeants into generals, and the role of the DAFs in the post-independence state has been controversial ever since. Writing in 2002 the journalist Hichem Aboud, himself a former army officer, saw a straight line between the DAF and the violence of the 1990s.[99]

Already insecure about their status, and subjected to scorn by the Islamists who criticized anyone with a francophone education, the DAFs were primed to respond with violence against the extremists. It would not be surprising if they viewed the violence that characterized the civil war as a way to bolster their masculinity, by appealing to *redjla* – the Algerian notion of masculine toughness.

Something like *redjla* presumably exists in most cultures. It is part of what makes warfare a traditionally male domain. *Redjla* became particularly militarized in the Algeria of the mid-1960s with the eclipse of the political wing of the FLN in favor of the armed forces. Following the military coup of 1965, Boumediène emphasized *redjla* as a source of popular support, especially in Algeria's international orientation. Policies such as a strong position against Israel and in favor of the Palestinian cause, an antagonistic approach to the United States and France, nationalization of the oil industry and participation in the embargo sponsored by the Organization of Petroleum Exporting Countries (OPEC) were particularly popular. "Algerians responded to Boumediène's message that there would be no more toadying to the West and *redjla*, symbolizing Algeria's new-found power in the world, became the cornerstone of his foreign policy."[100]

Boumediène's untimely death in 1978 coincided with the economic downturn, corruption at the highest levels, and the rise of the Islamist challenge. Male pride in Boumediène's *redjla* gave way to despair and frustration, and a crisis in masculinity that portended grave consequences for women. As Toth describes, "Islamists gained increasing influence in part because the government was unable to keep its economic promises. In the late 1970s, Muslim activists engaged in isolated and relatively small-scale assertions of their will: harassing women who they felt were inappropriately dressed, smashing establishments that served alcohol, and evicting official imams from their mosques."[101] Their attempts at influencing government policy to reduce women's rights were not always successful, even as the FLN regime sought to bolster its

---

[99] Evans and Phillips, *Algeria*, pp. 83–84, 208–209.
[100] Ibid., *Algeria*, pp. 82–83.
[101] Anthony Toth, section on Chadli Bendjedid and Afterward in Metz, *Algeria*.

sagging legitimacy by accommodating some Islamist demands. In 1980, for example, under pressure from Islamists, the government issued a decree forbidding women from leaving the country without a male chaperone. In the face of widespread protests by women, including graduate students studying in France, the decree was rescinded as a violation of the 1976 Constitution's guarantees of gender equality and freedom of movement.[102]

As far as the impact on women is concerned, the FLN's biggest concession to the Islamists came in 1984 when President Chadli Bendjedid allowed for changes in the Family Code. Mary-Jane Deeb explains that the code was "debated between those who wanted family life organized along Western secularist lines and those who favored a family structure conforming to Islamic principles and ethics," at least as Islamists chose to understand them. It was "proposed, discussed, and shelved at least three times over a period of two decades before being adopted into law in 1984."[103] In 1981, the code's provisions provoked street demonstrations by women in Algiers, with marches led by veteran resistance fighters including Zohra Drif. Algerian feminists took to calling the Code of the Family (Code de la famille) the "Code of Infamy" (Code de l'infamie) instead.[104] Deeb points out that although "some of the 1984 code's provisions are more liberal than those of the 1981 version, the code essentially reflects the influence of Islamic conservatives. The family unit is 'the basic unit of society'; the head of the family is the husband, to whom the wife owes obedience."[105] In Khanna's view, some elements of the code, particularly in their impact on women, echo the French colonial-era Code de l'indigénat.[106] In effect, women became deprived of their autonomy and relegated to the status of children: as legal minors they were wards of their fathers or other male relatives before marriage and wards of their husbands afterwards. "In the Code, women did not exist as individuals in their own right but only as 'daughters of,' 'mothers of,' 'sisters of,' or 'wives of.'"[107] Divorce became nearly impossible for women to initiate. Women were not allowed to work outside the home without the permission of their male guardians.

The first major crisis for the Bendjedid regime came in October 1988, when thousands of young men rioted in central Algiers. The riots of "Black October," which soon spread to the rest of the country, were "essentially

[102] Evans and Phillips, *Algeria*, p. 137.
[103] Deeb, section on Family Code in Metz, *Algeria*.
[104] Hélène Cixous, "Letter to Zohra Drif," *College Literature*, 30, 1 (Winter 2003), pp. 82–90; Evans and Phillips, *Algeria*, pp. 137–138.
[105] Deeb, section on Family Code in Metz, *Algeria*.
[106] Khanna, *Algeria Cuts*, p. 9.   [107] Evans and Phillips, *Algeria*, p. 126.

male events," carried out by secondary students and the unemployed. In the words of Evans and Phillips, the popular violence "represented a world turned upside down, a moment of inversion which, no matter how transitory, no matter how fleeting, allowed the young male rioters to recover a sense of honour, dignity and manhood." As they waved banners proclaiming "We are men," they directed their hostility towards President Chadli Bendjedid. "In the minds of the young men behind the violence, the contrast between Chadli – weak and effete – and Boumediène – tough and upright – was ever present." The rioters accused Bendjedid of lacking Boumediène's attribute of *redjla* – and not only that: "Slogans, taking the form of rhyming couplets in colloquial Arabic, ridiculed Chadli as a eunuch. He was a laughing stock, they claimed, and dominated by his wife Halima, the real power behind the throne."[108] *Boumedien, ardja' lina. Hlima wellet tehkoum fina*, they yelled: "Boumediène, come back to us. Halima has come to dominate us."[109]

The Bendjedid regime reacted harshly to the riots of Black October. Mass arrests and repression were the order of the day. The army engaged in widespread and well-documented torture – employing many of the techniques made notorious by the French during the war of independence. "If large swathes of young men were drawn into the web of Islamist terrorism during the nineties it was partly because they saw such violence as revenge for the killings of their brothers and sisters in October 1988."[110]

Despite the charges of feminine influence, Bendjedid was no friend to Algerian women. According to Roberts, his "regime showed itself to be sympathetic to the grievances of the Arabists and unremittingly hostile to the Berberists," who sought to have their language granted official status, "and the feminists." It "quietly encouraged the Islamists as a means of reducing the Left."[111] Paradoxically, Bendjedid's liberalization of the Algerian political system opened the way for further discrimination against women. Pressure from many sectors of society – not only from the Islamists – pushed the FLN to liberalize both the economy and the polity, to allow for more freedom of expression and political competition. A new constitution, introduced in 1989, removed the word *socialist* as the official designation of the country and guaranteed basic civil rights – such as freedom of association and freedom of expression. It did not even mention the FLN and accorded no special political status to the army, describing it only in the context of national defense. For a state whose legitimacy had been staked on the heroic achievements of the

---

[108] Ibid., *Algeria*, pp. 102–103.   [109] Roberts, *Battlefield Algeria*, p. 107.
[110] Evans and Phillips, *Algeria*, p. 142.   [111] Roberts, *Battlefield Algeria*, p. 20.

armed revolutionaries of the FLN, these were momentous changes. For one half of the population another change was perhaps even more significant – and ominous: the guarantee of equal rights for women, incorporated into the previous constitution of 1976, was removed from the 1989 version, as a concession to the Islamists and reflecting the *fait accompli* of the Family Code.[112]

The new constitution opened up new space for political competition. Algerian "newspapers became the liveliest and freest in the Arab world, while political parties of nearly every stripe vied for members and a voice."[113] Although religious political parties remained banned, in February 1989 a broad political movement called the Front Islamique du Salut (Islamic Salvation Front) or FIS was founded. It was allowed to compete electorally and handily beat the FLN in local and provincial elections in June 1990, partly because the secular parties boycotted them. Many Algerians blame the FLN for creating the conditions that gave rise to the FIS. They recognize that, however different their political programs, the FLN contributed to the rise of the FIS by opening itself up to charges of corruption and by closing off other avenues for peaceful political change. They illustrate the point with a play on words with the two organizations' initials, drawing on the fact that in French FIS rhymes with *fils*, the word for "son." The play on words focuses on the contrasting implications for women (represented by the common female name, Fatima) of their competing political and social programs. So FLN, they say, stands for *Fatima libre la nuit*, Fatima (is) free (to go out) at night. FIS means *Fatima interdite sortir*, Fatima (is) forbidden to go out. Yet, despite these different approaches to Fatima, they conclude, *FIS est fils du FLN*, FIS is the son of the FLN.

In the face of the major electoral challenge from the FIS, the Algerian government responded by imposing an electoral law that blatantly favored the FLN. In response, the FIS called a general strike and sent its supporters into the streets. President Chadli Bendjedid declared martial law on June 5, 1991, but allowed elections to go forward in December. FIS candidates won absolute majorities in 188 of 430 electoral districts, while the FLN took only 15. Some members of Bendjedid's cabinet, fearing a complete FIS takeover, forced the president to dissolve parliament and to resign on January 11, 1992. They declared the elections void and formed a High Council of State to rule the country under army dominance. In February 1992, violent demonstrations broke out throughout the country, and the government declared a state of emergency, banned

---

[112] Toth, section on Chadli Bendjedid and Afterward in Metz, *Algeria*.
[113] Ibid.

the FIS, and imprisoned its leaders.[114] What followed during the rest of the decade was a horrendous orgy of violence, perpetrated mainly by Islamist gangs, both in the countryside and in urban areas. There was also evidence that figures in the Algerian military and secret services instigated some of the massacres, to distract attention from their corruption, maintain a state of fear, and attract foreign support for their campaign against Islamist terror.[115]

If Islamist leaders on the one side, and corrupt military officers on the other, were the instigators of the violence, its foot soldiers were primarily unemployed youth. Women became their main targets. "By joining extremists," the BBC reported, "the men get the chance to seize hold of power, something lacking in their daily lives."[116] That the men wanted to use that power to destroy women can be explained in part by perceptions of competition for jobs and status and in part by the pervasive anti-women attitudes that they had been hearing from the Islamists all their lives. Young men came to resent the perceived advances in women's progress at a time when they saw their own prospects declining. The fact that a key manifestation of their dim prospects was their inability, for lack of economic means, to attract a bride and raise a family, goes some way towards explaining why women and children became a focus of their violent attacks.[117]

Objectively one might not expect that women posed such a threat to male employment or professional advancement. In the mid-1950s, before the revolution, only about 7,000 women were registered as wage earners. Fifteen years after independence that number had grown nearly twenty-fold to 138,234 women engaged in full-time employment outside the home, but that figure represented only 6 percent of the labor force. By the mid-1980s the number had grown to about 250,000, and by 1989 to 316,626, but again representing only 7 percent of the total workforce. Compensating in some respect for the low proportion, one might argue, was the high visibility of women in certain sectors of the workforce. Many "were employed in the state sector as teachers, nurses, physicians, and

---

[114] Ibid.
[115] Stathis N. Kalyvas, "Wanton and Senseless?: The Logic of Massacres in Algeria," *Rationality and Society*, 11, 3 (1999); John Sweeney and Leonard Doyle, "Algeria Regime 'Was Behind Paris Bombs,'" *Manchester Guardian Weekly*, November 16, 1997; John Sweeney, "Police Role in Algerian Killings Exposed," *The Observer*, January 11, 1998; Robert Fisk, "Algeria Terror Touches the World," *The Independent*, January 7, 1998; Evans and Phillips, *Algeria*, esp. pp. 223–225, 268–270.
[116] British Broadcasting Corporation, "'The Lost Generation,'" February 16, 1998, http://news.bbc.co.uk/2/hi/middle_east/57133.stm.
[117] Omar Carlier, "Civil War, Private Violence, and Cultural Socialization: Political Violence in Algeria (1954–1988)," ch. 4 in Anne-Emmanuelle Berger, ed., *Algeria in Others' Languages* (Ithaca, NY: Cornell University Press, 2002).

technicians," for example.[118] These figures did not include women working as unpaid family members in the rural labor force.

Females were also increasingly visible in education, and on a trend that portended eventual parity. In 1957 there had been only 116,340 Algerian girls in elementary school and 1,558 in high school, from a female population of more than 4 million, half of whom were under twenty years old. The proportion of female students in the 1980s at secondary schools and technical colleges ranged from 38 to 44 percent. By the academic year 1990–1991, females made up nearly 47 percent of a secondary school cohort of 752,264 students.[119]

Promoters of "traditional values," especially if that meant keeping women in their place, found a welcome audience among unemployed and underemployed men. In the early 1990s, Algeria's labor force was growing rapidly and included some 5.5 million unskilled agricultural laborers and semiskilled workers. More than 50 percent of the labor force was between fifteen and thirty-four years old. Almost 40 percent of the labor force either had no formal education or had not finished primary school.[120] Even among the better educated, resentment builds when opportunities diminish. As Ali Kouaouci argues, the age group of fifteen to twenty-four years old "is particularly vulnerable and potentially explosive. These individuals are generally well-educated but not all are successful in entering the labour market or integrating into ordinary patterns of social life through marriage. In most countries facing population crises, these young people challenge in several ways a social order that cannot offer them a position that corresponds to their expectations."[121]

Kouaouci carried out a comparative study to indicate that indeed the situation in Algeria was graver than in neighboring countries. "Between 1950 and 1990," he found, in Algeria "the number of 15–24-year-olds increased from 1.63 to 5.13 million, multiplying 3.14 times while the overall population multiplied 2.85 times" – a higher ratio "than Morocco and Tunisia, which had relative increases of 2.91/2.68 and 2.61/2.31, respectively ... Out of 1.26 million unemployed Algerians in 1991, 826,957, or 65 per cent, were less than 25 years old. The cohort made

---

[118] Deeb, section on Men and Women in Metz, *Algeria*.

[119] Lazreg, *Torture*, p. 168; Deeb, section on Education in Metz, *Algeria*; and the table, provided by the US Library of Congress, at http://lcweb2.loc.gov/frd/cs/algeria/dz_appen.html#table2. For more recent figures on education and literacy, see Kamel Kateb, *La fin du marriage traditionnel en Algérie? (1876–1998): une exigence d'égalité des sexes* (Saint-Denis: Éditions Bouchène, 2001), pp. 78–79.

[120] Boulos A. Malik, section on Labor and Employment, John P. Entelis with Lisa Arone, section on Role of the FIS, and Mary-Jane Deeb, section on Toward a Modern Society, all in Metz, *Algeria*.

[121] Kouaouci, "Population Transitions," p. 35.

up as much as 40 per cent of the workforce in 1987. ... this means that for every Algerian eligible for retirement in 2000, more than five young people were available, hypothetically, to fill his or her position."[122] No wonder that there would be a sense of competition and resentment against women, who by tradition (and by law, with the 1984 Family Code) should not be working outside the house at all.

A further culturally based, gender-related source of male resentment is the fact that Algerian women typically marry younger than men, and during many periods there are far fewer women of the appropriate age than men. The legal age for women to marry is eighteen years old, whereas for men it is twenty-one. As Kouaouci explains, "when cohorts of young people produced by the 'baby boom' reach adulthood, a shortage of marriageable women develops owing to the fact that men generally marry younger women." In 2005, for example, there were 200,000 more men in the 20–24 age range than women in the 15–19 age range.[123]

This factor seems to have been at work in the period of unrest that preceded the outbreak of Algeria's civil war. "Between 1986 and 1992, the proportion of 25–29-year-old men who were both employed and married decreased by almost half, while those who were neither employed nor married doubled. Among 20–24-year-olds, the proportion of employed married men fell by two-thirds, while men who were both unemployed and unmarried were the only group of 20–24-year-olds to increase in size."[124]

In 1991, only 22 percent of the age cohort of 15–29 years was employed. Were the rest in school? Unfortunately not. The Algerian educational system, like much of the rest of the country, was in crisis. In 1991, as Kouaouci describes,

approximately 400,000 youth were excluded from the system – 16,000 left prior to completion of the elementary (*fondamental*) cycle of nine classes, 159,000 left prior to completion of the secondary cycle (including 105,000 who failed the *baccalauréat* exam), and the system "oriented" 197,000 toward the employment market. The vocational training sector announced its objective of absorbing 100,000 of these youth by 1992. What was to become of the remaining 300,000? It is in 1992 that armed violence broke out and became generalised, with young males being the main participants.[125]

For young Algerian men the combination of no job, no education, and no marriage prospects came at a time when the Algerian state was ill-suited

---

[122] Ibid., pp. 34–35.
[123] Ibid., p. 35; Deeb, section on Men and Women in Metz, *Algeria*.
[124] Kouaouci, "Population Transitions," p. 37; for further details on marriage patterns, see Kateb, *La fin du marriage*.
[125] Kouaouci, "Population Transitions," p. 40.

to provide any relief. As in many countries during the period of the late 1980s, structural adjustment policies and the drop in oil prices led to heavy foreign borrowing by an Algerian government desperate to maintain a basic standard of living for its population. The country's "debt service-to-export ratio increased from approximately 30–35 to 60–70 per cent, leaving it no choice but to accept further indebtedness to cover the costs of food imports, pharmaceutical goods and maintaining a function-ing economic apparatus." By 1988, Algeria's debt service had reached 87 per cent of export revenues. Under the circumstances, the country's level of imports dramatically declined as the cost of living continued to rise.[126]

The Black October riots of 1988 were a consequence of the economic crisis, popular disdain for the weak Benjedid and his corrupt army cro-nies, and the humiliating challenge to the masculinity of young Algerian men. The riots also became one the causes of the government's further liberalization. Pressed by the World Bank and International Monetary Fund as a condition of further loans, the Algerian government freed prices on staple goods, rendering 14 million Algerians, nearly half of the population, dependent on social welfare to survive. At that point, "4 mil-lion Algerians had no income at all."[127]

The economic crisis was compounded by a housing shortage. Again Kouaouci provides valuable comparative statistics. In 1992, the year the civil war broke out, an average of 3.18 persons shared a bedroom in Algeria, compared with 2.93 in Tunisia and 2.0 in Morocco. In Algeria the situation was made worse by the youth bulge. In 1992, sons and daughters represented approximately 27 percent of household members in Morocco, for example, compared with 64 percent in Algeria.[128] A sur-vey at the time indicated the level of desperation experienced by young people. In answer to the question "In case of a problem, with whom do you primarily confide?" 33.5 per cent of respondents answered "nobody." Mothers were the most frequently cited confidant (20.5 percent), fol-lowed by friends (18.8 percent), but a full 20 percent of respondents declared that they had no friends at all, with 54 percent reporting only a few. When asked where they would most prefer their place of employ-ment if they could have a job, young women answered near to home. Young men wanted to be at least 100 kilometers away.[129]

The situation was ripe for Islamists to step in with social-aid programs and a critique of the failures of the incumbent government that resonated with much of the population. Male youths were particularly susceptible to such an appeal, especially to the extent that it made scapegoats of

---

[126] Ibid.   [127] Ibid., pp. 36–37.   [128] Ibid., p. 37.   [129] Ibid., p. 41.

the young women who were unavailable to them for demographic and economic reasons. Kouaouci writes that they suffered a "triple frustration ... They exhibit affective and sexual frustration due to non-marriage in a conservative society that condemns extra-marital relations, material and financial frustration due to unemployment and their dependence on parents, and political frustration due to their exclusion from the process of decision-making that affects them."[130]

The linguistic divide came into play too, as Arabic-speaking men of limited education enjoyed fewer job prospects than educated francophone women – many of them the daughters of the FLN elite. During the 1980s these unemployed young men became known as *hittistes*, from the Arab word *heta* or wall – because they congregated around and leaned on the walls of their neighborhoods all day, with nothing better to do. They referred to the foreign-educated, francophone children of privilege as *chi-chis*, whose lives "revolved around shopping at the new mall at Riadh el-Feth, sunning themselves at specially reserved beaches in skimpy costumes and dancing to Michael Jackson at open-air discos."[131] As Evans and Phillips point out,

The *hittistes*' view of the world was marked by a strong strain of misogyny; they knew that in sexual and emotional terms *chi-chi* women were beyond their reach and this sense of rejection made them angry and resentful. Favourite *hittiste* pastimes included baiting the *chi-chis* by picking their pockets, stealing their cars or, in the case of women, harassing them with lewd gestures and remarks.[132]

The *hittistes*' turn to religion only reinforced their misogynistic tendencies. They were particularly drawn to the young cleric Ali Belhadj, who demanded that women not be allowed to attend secondary school or university and that they wear head-to-toe hijabs. In his sermons he claimed that "women who imitate Marilyn Monroe or Brigitte Bardot will only produce abortions" and "effeminate offspring" and would destroy Islam's traditional family values – not least the dominance of men over women. As Evans and Phillips suggest, "for young men, unsure of their position in society, such an assertion of traditional gender roles, reaffirming their status as guardians and protectors, was empowering. Many male converts transformed their guilt at their previous 'sinful' lifestyles into anger and violence against women."[133]

With the passing of the Family Code and the 1989 Constitution, "the state had given men the license to treat women as minors whose actions

[130] Ibid., pp. 37–38.   [131] Evans and Phillips, *Algeria*, p. 110.
[132] Ibid., p. 111.   [133] Ibid., pp. 132–134.

were now subjected to constant surveillance."[134] Not only urban, professional, or secular women were at risk. The radical clerics targeted Sufi practices, widespread in rural areas, that combined Islam with superstitions about the "evil eye," local saints known as *marabouts*, miracles, and a general blurring of the line between religion and magic, the sacred and the profane. These practices, pagan in origin, were "long associated with the supposed dominance of women in the countryside, and had to be rooted out, condemned as the expression of an obscurantist Islam."[135] Not surprisingly, it fell to men to carry out the task.

If the notion of "guardians and protectors" seems cruelly at odds with the violence these young men inflicted on women, we should consider one further explanatory factor: some of the armed Islamist groups were led by "Afghans" – Algerian veterans of the war against Soviet occupation of Afghanistan.[136]

The returning veterans were to have a huge impact in 1989 as they appeared at the head of demonstrations in combat fatigues, beards and *pakols*, the round woollen hats donned by the *mujahidin*. These veterans, lithe and muscular, were God's own warriors; a stark contrast to the government where there were no more heroes, only grey, faceless bureaucrats devoid of any higher purpose. Unsurprisingly the Afghan look took off amongst sections of Algerian youth, becoming a statement about their rejection of the Chadli regime.[137]

That the behavior of the armed Algerian Islamists should resemble the violent repression of women characteristic of the Taliban is no coincidence.

The worst violence came in the late 1990s, as the Algerian government reacted to the Islamist violence by creating an antiterrorist force of fifteen thousand men. Wearing black balaclavas to hide their identity and avoid reprisals, they were known as the "ninjas" because of their resemblance to the Ninja turtle cartoon characters. They "became infamous for a whole host of torture techniques including electric shocks, sexual abuse with bottles, beatings with sticks, especially on the genitals," as well as a variant on waterboarding known as *chiffon* – named after the cloth soaked in filthy water and put over the victim's face to simulate drowning.[138] Under pressure from the army and rejected by the Islamist politicians of the FIS, the armed groups in the *maquis* became desperate. As Evans and Phillips suggest, "as male societies based upon the cult of the strong," the groups "were under constant pressure to assert themselves as fighting men." Afraid to appear weak, yet with no chance

[134] Ibid., p. 127.   [135] Ibid.
[136] Ibid., pp. 134–137, 185–186; Roberts, *Battlefield Algeria*, p. 154.
[137] Evans and Phillips, *Algeria*, p. 137.   [138] Ibid., p. 188.

of overthrowing the regime, the group members sought "other ways of expressing their masculinity." They chose kidnapping, forced "temporary" marriages (known as *zaouedj el moutaa*), and rape of women and girls as "a way of playing out their pent-up frustrations and asserting their power and sexual domination."[139] Sometimes the sexual violence was harnessed to "strategic" purposes, as armed marauders carried out campaigns of mass rape and murder, targeting particular villages or neighborhoods for elimination.[140]

Whatever the motives, the effect on women was devastating. As one human rights activist put it, "All the young women who have been abducted and then flee away or are thrown away by the armed groups after they have been raped for weeks or months, they are the living dead. They are destroyed psychologically – totally destroyed."[141]

Legacies of violence

Throughout the world the volatile combination of youth unemployment, overcrowding, and sexual frustration has been a sure recipe for violence.[142] In the Algerian case, the situation was exacerbated by what some have termed a "culture of violence" dating back to the devastation of the war of independence.[143] In June 1957, as the French were celebrating their brutal victory in the Battle of Algiers, a schoolteacher in the Casbah asked her pupils, aged ten to fourteen years, to write a composition in French on the topic, "What would you do if you were invisible?" Here are some of the typical responses:

> "I would kill all French soldiers."
> "I'll free prisoners."
> "I will place a bomb at the Milk Bar" (as Zohra Drif did the year before).
> "I'll go all the way to Guy Mollet [French prime minister] and Robert Lacoste [French governor general of Algeria] and I'll kill them."
> "I'll free my three brothers held prisoner by the soldiers; I'll massacre all the French people, young and old, on the way."

---

[139] Ibid., p. 219.
[140] Kalyvas, "Wanton and Senseless?"
[141] Caroline Brac, quoted in British Broadcasting Corporation, "Abortion Plea for Algerian Rape Victims," March 5, 1998, http://news.bbc.co.uk/1/hi/world/middle_east/62514.stm.
[142] See, for example, United Nations Office for the Coordination of Humanitarian Affairs, *Youth in Crisis: Coming of Age in the 21st Century* (February 2007); N. G. Egbue, "Socio-Cultural Factors in Nigerian Male Youth Violence: Relationship with Education and Employment," *Journal of Social Sciences*, 12, 1 (2006), pp. 1–10.
[143] "'The Lost Generation.'"

"I'll steal French women's jewelry as Massu's men do [to Algerian women]; they take pictures of women to give to the men. They cannot take Algiers. It belongs to Arabs."

"I'd take a cord and strangle the last of the paras on patrol in the tunnel in my neighborhood ... And if they dared do what they usually do, I'd torture them and some, before I kill them. And I'll have a job like my teacher; I'll buy a villa ... and be a Sultan of the whole world but not France."

Marnia Lazreg, who lists these responses in her book *Torture and the Twilight of Empire*, observes that despite the widespread use of sexual violence in the Algerian war, these children focus on a different kind of sexual violation: "The sexual component of paratroopers' actions was retained not so much in the form of rape, but as something that was morally offensive: taking pictures of women and passing them to men."[144] This reaction is similar to the one the French soldier-photographer Garanger experienced when taking photos of Algerian women for identification cards.

There is no doubt that these children were traumatized by the events they witnessed and endured through the eight years of brutal violence that resulted in Algeria's liberation. In their early twenties in the late 1960s, they would be the parents of the baby-boom generation that caused the "youth bulge" in the late 1980s. It is perhaps not so surprising that people so psychologically damaged as children would raise their own children, who – when facing problems – confide in nobody; have few or no friends; and participate in a reenactment of the worst violence of their parents' childhood, violence even beyond Gillo Pontecorvo's cinematic imagination in *The Battle of Algiers*.

[144] Lazreg, *Torture*, pp. 187–188.

3   Yugoslavia: archetype or anomaly?

> Both politicians and private citizens search for scapegoats and ways to differentiate in the distribution of scarce resources, such as jobs, among citizens with equal rights. The most likely result of this scapegoating in Yugoslavia is always a rise in nationalist antagonisms ... nationalist incidents, religious revival, and antifeminist backlash.
>
> Susan Woodward, 1986[1]

> If women fail to participate in bringing political decisions and in defending their rights, I am afraid that democracy in Eastern Europe will be of masculine gender. And, what is worse, it will wear boots.
>
> Slavenka Drakulić, 1991[2]

The wars that attended the breakup of the Socialist Federal Republic of Yugoslavia in the early 1990s brought issues of gender and violence to the front page of newspapers and on to television screens. Nationalist rhetoric justified policies of violent "ethnic cleansing" that included organized campaigns of mass rape and other sexual atrocities as a core part of the strategy. The association of nationalism with violence against women seemed to fit very well Virginia Woolf's contention that nationalism was a mainly male sentiment, fostered by a system of discrimination against women. One study of female survivors of the war in Bosnia and Herzegovina reflected Woolf's basic argument in its very title: *This Was Not Our War*.[3] Even more to the point was the title of Cynthia Enloe's insightful essay on the making of a Serbian rapist: "All the Men are in the

---

[1] Susan L. Woodward, "Orthodoxy and Solidarity: Competing Claims and International Adjustment in Yugoslavia," *International Organization*, 40, 2 (Spring 1986), pp. 505–545.

[2] Slavenka Drakulić, quoted in Jasmina Lukić, "Media Representations of Men and Women in Times of War and Crisis: The Case of Serbia," ch. 14 in Susan Gal and Gail Kligman, *Reproducing Gender: Politics, Publics, and Everyday Life after Socialism* (Princeton University Press, 2000), p. 403.

[3] Swanee Hunt, *This Was Not Our War: Bosnian Women Reclaiming the Peace* (Durham, NC: Duke University Press, 2004).

Militias, All the Women are Victims."[4] By putting it so starkly, Enloe deliberately raises questions about the merits of such broad generalizations. Do the wars of former Yugoslavia really constitute an archetype of male nationalist violence confronting female peace-loving cosmopolitanism?

The wars in former Yugoslavia, according to an important study of their origins by V. P. Gagnon, Jr., "are often held up as *the* paradigmatic examples of ethnic conflict," of "extremist nationalism leading to violence."[5] One common version attributes the conflict to "ancient hatreds" among groups that had been forced to live together under the Austro-Hungarian and Ottoman empires and then communist Yugoslavia. A somewhat more sophisticated version suggests that unscrupulous elites manipulated public opinion to generate fears and mobilize the population to fight against rival national groups. Gagnon's careful examination of attitudes among the main groups – Serbs, Croats, and Bosnian Muslims – in the years preceding the outbreak of war, finds little support for either explanation. Instead, he argues that the fighting in Bosnia was provoked by political leaders in Belgrade (the capital of Serbia and of federal Yugoslavia) and Zagreb (the capital of Croatia) and carried out primarily by forces from outside the localities. The magnitude of the violence reflected not the depth of hatred between members of the local population, but rather the difficulty that the external forces faced in trying to tear apart communities that had lived peacefully together for decades.[6] They had to resort to extreme violence and atrocities to do so. To paraphrase the writer Miroslav Karaulac, Bosnians had acquired the "fatal habit of living together," which the armies fighting against them were attempting "to correct" by means of a bloodbath.[7]

Srđan Dragojević's 1996 film *Pretty Village, Pretty Flame* (*Lepa sela, lepo gore*) portrays all three competing explanations for the war in Bosnia-Herzegovina: ancient hatreds, elite mobilization of nationalist sentiment, and external destruction of a local multiethnic community. Its treatment of gender issues conveys a sense of the prevailing relationship between men and women and attitudes about gender before and during the war. The film appeared at a time when the regime of Slobodan Milošević was

---

[4] Reprinted as "The Politics of Masculinity and Femininity in Nationalist Wars," ch. 7 in Cynthia Enloe, *The Curious Feminist* (Berkeley, CA: University of California Press, 2004).

[5] V. P. Gagnon, Jr., *The Myth of Ethnic War: Serbia and Croatia in the 1990s* (Ithaca, NY: Cornell University Press, 2004), p. xix.

[6] A compatible account, drawing on different materials, is found in Eric D. Gordy, *The Culture of Power in Serbia: Nationalism and the Destruction of Alternatives* (University Park, PA: Pennsylvania State University Press, 1999).

[7] Quoted in William Pfaff, "Invitation to War," *Foreign Affairs*, 72, 3 (Summer 1993), p. 104, with no reference.

coming under increasing popular pressure for the disastrous wars it had launched to distract attention from its criminal mismanagement of the economy. As Pavle Levi describes, *Pretty Village, Pretty Flame* "was one of the most popular films of the decade in Serbia, its aesthetically accomplished portrayal of ethnic animosity attracting almost as many people to the movie theaters as the antigovernment demonstrations would attract to the streets sometime later."[8] It is a fitting vehicle for exploring the relationship between gender and nationalist violence.

This chapter begins with a brief history of Yugoslavia, followed by a discussion of ethnic differences and interethnic relations in Bosnia-Herzegovina and Croatia – the sites of the worst violence of the Yugoslav wars. It then turns to competing explanations for the origins of those wars, and summarizes the most promising accounts. It next discusses the relationship between gender and violence in Yugoslavia, with particular attention to the wartime campaigns of mass rape in Bosnia. Finally it turns to the film to explore the way it portrays the relationship between gender attitudes, misogynistic language, and violent nationalism.

Yugoslavia's history: conflict and coexistence

Modern Yugoslavia was the product of two world wars. World War I saw the demise of the three continental European empires – the Ottoman, Habsburg (Austro-Hungarian), and Russian – with the last eventually reconstituted as the Soviet Union. The Kingdom of Serbs, Croats, and Slovenes was founded at the end of 1918, and renamed the Kingdom of Yugoslavia (land of the South Slavs) just over ten years later. Despite advocacy by Croatian nationalists for greater autonomy and external pressure from fascist Italy and Nazi Germany, Yugoslavia remained intact until World War II. Invasion in April 1941 by the armed forces of Germany, Italy, Hungary, and Bulgaria brought Yugoslavia to an end and led to the emergence of Croatia as a Nazi puppet state. Armed resistance forces opposed the German occupation of Yugoslavia. The two main groups were the Chetniks (*Četnici*), mainly Serbs who supported restoration of the monarchy, and the communist-dominated partisans, led by Josip Broz "Tito" and organized into multiethnic guerrilla units. The partisans' main base of support was mountainous Bosnia. The Chetniks were incapacitated by the Nazi policies of collective punishment, by which the Wehrmacht executed a hundred Serb civilians for every German soldier killed. A Croatian nationalist militia, known as the

---

[8] Pavle Levi, *Disintegration in Frames: Aesthetics and Ideology in the Yugoslav and Post-Yugoslav Cinema* (Stanford University Press, 2007), p. 140.

Ustashe (*Ustaše*, the plural of *Ustaša*), rounded up Serbs, Jews, Roma, and others, interned them in concentration camps, and carried out numerous massacres, sometimes with the support of local Muslims. In addition to fighting against the Nazis, both the Chetniks and the communists battled the Ustashe – and fought each other. Chetniks conducted massacres of Croat and Muslim civilians in retaliation for the Ustasha atrocities. The victorious partisans, in turn, carried out reprisals against supporters of both the Ustashe and the Chetniks, and summarily executed their fighters when they fell into partisan hands.

In all, more than a million Yugoslavs perished during the carnage of World War II, but the country managed to liberate itself from Nazi occupation largely by its own efforts. The communists led the way to victory, according to Catherine Samary, because they promoted "a Yugoslav federalist project." They rejected both the "idea of resurrecting a 'unitary' Yugoslavia or its social and national policies" and the "idea of building 'ethnically pure' nation-states imposed by fascist means." Thus, "the Partisans made a multiethnic antifascist resistance possible because they stood *both* for recognition of differences *and* for unity. This is why they won."[9]

The country that emerged – the "second Yugoslavia" – was a federation of socialist republics, reflecting both the popularity of the communist partisans and the ideal of a multiethnic state. Its main components were the republics of Bosnia and Herzegovina, Croatia, Macedonia, Montenegro, Serbia, and Slovenia. Two provinces of Serbia – Kosovo and Vojvodina – enjoyed autonomous status within the republic, based on their substantial populations of Albanians and Hungarians, respectively. With the exception of Slovenia, whose population was rather homogenous, the other republics were ethnically mixed, with no single *narod*, or national group, holding a majority in Bosnia and Herzegovina.

The violence that engulfed Yugoslavia in the early 1990s was part of a strategy by communist elites fearful of losing power as their counterparts in eastern Europe did a couple of years earlier. Inspired by the rise of the Solidarity trade union movement in Poland in the early 1980s, the advent of a reformist leadership in the Soviet Union at mid-decade, the fall of the Berlin Wall in November 1989, and the subsequent peaceful transformations of communist dictatorships, many Yugoslavs began demanding comparable economic and political reforms in their own country. The economic crisis of the previous decade had discredited the communists' ideology, the prospect of democratic elections left them with

---

[9] Catherine Samary, *Yugoslavia Dismembered*, trans. by Peter Drucker (New York: Monthly Review Press, 1995), p. 49.

no source of appeal. As Zoran Pajić put it, "nationalism was a life-boat for them ... a tool to homogenize people and create the constituency that, in the reality of the one-party system, they had never had."[10] Thus, the Yugoslav leaders turned to violence to provoke fears of ethnic conflict. As Gagnon explains, the point was not, as many observers have suggested, to *mobilize* the population under the banner of nationalism. Leaders such as Slobodan Milošević in Serbia and Franjo Tuđman in Croatia were mainly interested in retaining control, preferably over a passive populace. Their goal was "to silence, marginalize, and demobilize challengers and their supporters in order to create political homogeneity at home." This, in turn, served their political and economic interests: "to maintain control of existing structures of power, as well as to reposition themselves by converting state-owned property into privately held wealth, the basis of power in a new system of a liberal economy."[11]

Slobodan Milošević made a name for himself and consolidated his power in Yugoslavia in the late 1980s by provoking fears of "genocide" against the Serbian people. Milošević was an unlikely candidate for nationalist rabble rouser. With a background in economics, he came to head a major Belgrade bank in the late 1970s, traveled extensively to the United States and western Europe, and spoke English. He entered politics under the patronage of Serbian communist leader Ivan Stambolić who promoted his election as leader of the League of Serbian Communists in 1986. Milošević's apparently favorable attitude towards foreign trade and liberalization of the Yugoslav economy endeared him to western leaders, who thereafter found it difficult to recognize him as the war criminal he became. Milošević rose to prominence by focusing on the situation in Kosovo, an autonomous province of Serbia with a predominantly Albanian Muslim population. Because of the importance of Kosovo to Serbian history, Milošević decried the decline in Serbian birth rates and concomitant loss of influence of Serbs in the province. As Kosovar Albanians agitated for greater autonomy in the province where they represented 90 percent of the population, some Serbs organized protests of increasing violence. On a trip there in 1987 Milošević posed as the defender of Serb rights in Kosovo – a role that he found served his political interests well.[12] His fear-mongering about the status of Serbs in Kosovo, in the Krajina in Croatia, and in Bosnia-Herzegovina began to alarm the leaders of the other Yugoslav republics who feared

---

[10] Zoran Pajić, "'New Democracy' and the Challenge of Ethnic Politics," *Balkan War Report*, 21 (August/September 1993), p. 18.

[11] Gagnon, *The Myth of Ethnic War*, p. xv.

[12] An excellent account of the rise of Milošević is found in Laura Silber and Allan Little, *Yugoslavia: Death of a Nation*, revised edn (New York: Penguin, 1997).

a resurgent Serbian nationalism. Milošević replaced leaders in Kosovo, Vojvodina, and Montenegro with his own loyalists in what he called an "anti-bureaucratic revolution" and he revoked the autonomous status of Vojvodina and Kosovo, ruling the latter with an increasingly repressive hand. He was now in a position to impose his views on the collective presidency that governed Yugoslavia.

Some members of the communist elite, such as the leaders of Slovenia and Croatia, concerned about the dominant role that Milošević's Serbia was coming to play, opted for their republics' secession – a risk inherent in the structure of "subversive institutions" that comprised the Yugoslav federation.[13] The two republics declared their independence in June 1991. Milošević appears at first to have wanted to preserve the federation, but then to have decided that his interests would be best served by claiming to seek, through the use of violence, to create a "Greater Serbia," a project particularly associated with more extreme nationalists, such as Vojislav Šešelj. He ordered the Yugoslav National Army (*Jugoslovenska narodna armija* or JNA), whose units were still deployed on Croatian and Slovenian territory, to use force to prevent the republics' secession. The JNA campaign against Slovenia was a half-hearted effort, a "phoney war," as the authors of an outstanding day-to-day chronicle of the demise of Yugoslavia put it.[14] Milošević was not interested in defending the small minority of Serbs in Slovenia, some 37,000 of whom became refugees in Serbia. He was more interested in Croatia, with its large Serb population in the Krajina, and he encouraged the region's violent secession from the newly independent Croatian state.

With the departure of Croatia and Slovenia, Milošević's Serbia was in a position to dominate rump Yugoslavia. The leaders (and citizens) of Bosnia-Herzegovina would have most preferred that Yugoslavia remain intact. But without the counterweight to Serbian power posed by Croatia and Slovenia, Bosnia's second-best choice was independence. When the Bosnian government declared independence in April 1992, it expected that the transformation of its border with Serbia into an international boundary would somehow provide protection. Instead, the international community stood by as Milošević sent the army ostensibly to defend Bosnia's Serb population. But, as in Croatia during the summer of 1991, the real goal was to expel non-Serbs from the territory that Milošević claimed for Greater Serbia, by whatever brutal means necessary. The model was the destruction in August 1991 of the town of Kijevo, a

---

[13] Valerie Bunce, *Subversive Institutions: The Design and the Collapse of Socialism and the State* (Cambridge University Press, 1999).
[14] Silber and Little, *Yugoslavia*, ch. 12.

Croatian village surrounded by Serb-held territory in the Krajina. A twelve-hour bombardment by heavy artillery of the Yugoslav army was followed by a sacking and burning of the town by local Serb paramilitaries and JNA conscripts. The JNA commander was Lieutenant Colonel Ratko Mladić, a Serb from southeastern Bosnia who would go on to lead the renegade Bosnian Serb army there in a campaign of mass atrocities that resulted in his indictment at The Hague for war crimes.[15]

Although Milošević posed as the champion of Serb minority communities in Croatia, Kosovo, and Bosnia, his wars brought untold devastation to his own *narod* and provoked a massive flow of a half million Serb refugees into Serbia proper. In fact, the refugee crisis and the suffering of ordinary Serbs played right into the hands of Milošević and his allies. As Gagnon explains, "by using the image and discourse of injustices being perpetrated against innocent civilians by evil others defined in ethnic terms," Milošević and the other "conservative elites managed successfully to divert attention away from the demands for change toward the question of these injustices. The violence thus served to silence and marginalize the proponents of fundamental change."[16]

What constitutes difference? Bosnia's ephemeral ethnicity

The war in Bosnia from 1992 to 1995 witnessed the deaths of some 100,000 people, mostly civilians, and the expulsion of some 3 million people from their homes.[17] The war became the symbol of ethnic conflict and the rise of nationalism in the wake of the end of the Cold War. Bosnia was an unlikely choice to demonstrate the power of national or ethnic difference, however. The three main "ethnic" groups are usually designated as Serbs, Croats, and Muslims, but what was the source of their differences? Ethnicity is typically associated with cultural features, such as language, cuisine, customs, religion. In the case of the Bosnians, however, all three groups shared a common Slavic language, once known as Serbo-Croatian, and they spoke the same local dialect. A Serb from Sarajevo and a Serb from Belgrade could sound quite a lot different from each other, whereas Serbs, Croats, and Muslims of a given locale of Bosnia

---

[15] Ibid., pp. 170–172.

[16] Gagnon, *The Myth of Ethnic War*, p. 181.

[17] The number of people killed is in dispute, with early figures of 200,000–250,000 now appearing to be too high. See Lara J. Nettlefield, "Research and Repercussions of Death Tolls: The Case of the Bosnian Book of the Dead," ch. 7 in Peter Andreas and Kelly M. Greenhill, eds., *Sex, Drugs, and Body Counts: The Politics of Numbers in Global Crime and Conflict* (Ithaca, NY: Cornell University Press, 2010).

and Herzegovina would sound the same. Regarding cuisine, all Bosnians enjoyed similar food, including "Turkish" coffee and *rakija* (fruit brandy) or *šljivovica* (plum brandy) – sometimes called the "Muslim national drink," an indication of the extent to which that group ignored Islam's ban on alcohol. Bosnia's Muslims did tend to avoid pork, although that prohibition broke down in Yugoslavia's last decades, and many Muslims, although not preparing pork at home, might eat it if served in a restaurant or someone else's home. Bosnian Muslims practice other customs that one might associate with Islam, such as taking off their shoes before entering the house, as before entering the mosque – but so do Bosnia's Croats and Serbs.[18] Although many Muslims have recognizable variants on Arabic first names, many others received neutral-sounding names from their parents. Surnames are often shared between all three groups in Bosnia. For example, the surname of Radovan Karadžić, the indicted war criminal and political leader of the Bosnian Serb forces, is a common Muslim name, with Turkish roots.

The journalist Peter Maass noticed the similarities between the Bosnian groups even in the midst of his coverage of the war. "It was one of the ironic aspects of wartime Bosnia," he wrote, "that a Serb warlord would interrupt an anti-Muslim tirade to take a sip of his beloved Turkish coffee." Maass suggests that "too many Serbs forgot when they began waging war on their neighbors" that "a Serb in Bosnia has quite a bit in common with a Muslim in Bosnia. Banja Luka's Serbs and Muslims adored the same Oriental-sounding music, shared the same regional accents, and their jargon was the same too."[19]

Religion remained the primary ethnic marker for those who wanted to assert the differences between Bosnia's three main communities. But even here, the assertion was problematic. A survey of ethnic composition and religious affiliation, undertaken in 1990, is particularly revealing. At that time, Muslims made up 43.7 percent of the population; Serbs, 31 percent; and Croats, 17.3 percent. When asked their religious belief, the proportions reporting the expected answers – Islam, Orthodox Christianity, Roman Catholicism – were only 16.5, 20, and 15 percent respectively. Fully 46 percent of the population claimed *no* religion. Many Bosnians of Muslim heritage indeed sought to avoid calling themselves Muslim, a term which did not achieve the status of a "nationality" equivalent to Serb, Croat, or Slovene until 1971, when it appeared as an option on the census. Some Bosnian Muslims preferred the name *Bošnjaci* or

---

[18] Omer Hadziselimovic, "Unwilling Warriors: Bosnian Muslims," *The Iranian*, November 19, 2003, www.iranian.com/History/2003/November/Bosnia/index.html.
[19] Peter Maass, *Love Thy Neighbor: A Story of War* (New York: Vintage Books, 1997), p. 84.

Bosniaks, the historical term they gave themselves during the Ottoman period, and one distinct from the regional name *Bosanci* (inhabitants of Bosnia).[20] Ironically, as the Bosnian Muslims sought to avoid the religious designations, some Bosnian Serbs and Croats rejected the national ones – arguing that their ancestors had lived for generations in Bosnia, not in Serbia or Croatia. If forced to pick a source of difference with their neighbors, they would choose religion – calling themselves Bosnian Catholics or Bosnian Orthodox. The point is that most Bosnians did not want to choose. They were comfortable with their identities as residents, for example, of Sarajevo, of Bosnia-Herzegovina, of Yugoslavia, and with whatever other attributes of identity suited them in any particular situation: student, worker, athlete, musician, woman, man.

Some observers, seeking to explain the violence that engulfed a Bosnian community whose members shared so much in common, have embraced Freud's concept of the "narcissism of minor differences."[21] This seems a bit of a stretch. Evidence summarized by Gagnon of professional surveys conducted by Yugoslav social scientists demonstrates a high level of support for ethnic pluralism and tolerance. A 1989 survey of Bosnian youth found, for example, that 77 percent rejected the statement that "one always needs to be cautious" towards people of a different nationality. The following year, a survey reported that 33 percent of young people preferred to identify themselves as Yugoslav, with equal proportions of each main national group responding that way. The same survey reported that 81.6 percent of young people agreed with the statement, "I am a Yugoslav and cannot give priority to feeling of some other belonging." A broader survey of the population in 1989 found that 80 percent of the respondents considered interethnic relations in the places where they lived to be positive and 66 percent thought Bosnia-Herzegovina had the most stable interethnic relations in all of Yugoslavia. When asked whether ethnicity should be taken into account when choosing marriage partners, large majorities answered no: 66 percent of Croats, 77 percent of Muslims, 80 percent of Serbs, and 93.4 percent of those who identified themselves as Yugoslavs – many probably the product of, or participant in, a mixed marriage themselves. Indeed, one survey from 1981 showed that 16.8 percent of all marriages in Bosnia were interethnic and that 15.8 percent of Bosnian children were products of mixed marriages. The proportion in cosmopolitan Sarajevo was much higher. As one demographer explained, given the average family size in the republic, "at least

---

[20] Hadziselimovic, "Unwilling Warriors."
[21] Michael Ignatieff, *The Warrior's Honor: Ethnic War and the Modern Conscience* (New York: Metropolitan Books, 1998).

one half of the population of Bosnia-Herzegovina has interethnic family relations."[22]

As Gagnon suggests, "the experience of living with others led Serbs in Bosnia to have a very different and more positive view of ethnic pluralism than Serbs in homogeneous Serbia."[23] That positive view posed difficulties for the Serb nationalists' plan for creating a homogeneous political and territorial space. Thus, "it was no coincidence that the worst violence in the Yugoslav wars occurred in the most ethnically mixed and tolerant regions of the country, places where such notions had a strength and reality that came from a shared sense of community. Exactly because of the strength of those bonds, horrible levels of violence and atrocities were the only way to construct and impose new 'clear' borders of ethnicity."[24] A law professor from Sarajevo University, writing during the war, drew similar conclusions. In Bosnia-Herzegovina, he wrote, "it has not been easy to persuade the ordinary man to see that his friend, neighbour, or even spouse belongs on the other side of the barricade."[25] Interviews conducted among refugees who had fallen victim to "ethnic cleansing" both in Bosnia-Herzegovina and in the mixed Serb–Croat regions of Croatia indicated that "the majority of those questioned do not mention any particular conflicts among neighbors before the war, much less explain the war in this way."[26]

Explanations that focus either on "ancient hatreds" or on elite-driven nationalist mobilization appear ignorant of the high degree of tolerance among groups in Yugoslavia. Instead, they attribute the four and a half decades of peace following the end of World War II to the dictatorial rule of Marshal Tito. Even though Tito died in 1980, and the war broke out eleven years later, proponents of these explanations suggest that it was only a matter of time before the putatively artificial communist internationalism that Tito enforced would give way to interethnic strife. This account is similar to what Ronald Suny has dubbed the "Sleeping Beauty" theory of nationalism, because it depicts "eruptions of long-repressed primordial national consciousnesses" as "expressions of denied desires liberated by the kiss of freedom."[27] Others employ the metaphor

---

[22] Srđan Bogosavljević, quoted in Gagnon, *The Myth of Ethnic War*, pp. 41–42, where the survey data are also presented.

[23] Gagnon, *The Myth of Ethnic War*, p. 40.

[24] Ibid., p. 28.

[25] Zoran Pajić, "The Structure of Apartheid: The New Europe of Ethnic Division," *Balkan War Report*, 21 (August/September 1993), p. 3.

[26] Samary, *Yugoslavia Dismembered*, p. 91.

[27] Ronald Grigor Suny, *The Revenge of the Past: Nationalism, Revolution, and the Collapse of the Soviet Union* (Stanford University Press, 1993), p. 3.

of a pressure-cooker, with nationalist passions ready to burst out, once the lid of repression is lifted. This conception of nationalist animosity finds no support in the surveys of public opinion before the war cited by Gagnon.

Grievance and greed: economic sources of conflict

Some analysts have resisted such monocausal explanations and have sought to provide more context for the outbreak of conflict. Particularly compelling are arguments that point to the economic situation that faced Yugoslavia in the early 1980s, as it suffered from the worldwide recession that followed the oil price shocks of the previous decade and then approached the challenge of liberalization and privatization. Unlike the countries of the Soviet bloc, nonaligned Yugoslavia had always been open to the international economy and western investment; its economic system of self-management, whatever its faults, was far less centralized than the Soviet-type economies. That openness allowed for an influx of loans from the World Bank, International Monetary Fund, and private commercial banks flush with "petrodollars" from the dramatic rise in oil prices. The decentralized nature of the economy, with most decisions made at the republic level or even more locally, led to a rash of ill-considered borrowing, because firms and republics could count on the federal government as the guarantor of repayment. The loans were intended to finance export-led growth, but the recession of the early 1980s dried up an already limited market for Yugoslav products and left the country heavily in debt. In fact, Yugoslavia never managed to match the influx of foreign money with an outflow of export goods. Instead, it exported workers to northern Europe in a mainly unsuccessful attempt to have their remittances of foreign currency balance the current account.[28]

In facing the economic crisis, the Yugoslav government accepted the advice of experts from the international financial institutions and sought to implement an "austerity" plan of the sort that characterized the so-called Washington consensus. The policies led to the liquidation of many insolvent firms, with resulting mass unemployment. The country ended up with a combination of high unemployment (15 percent by 1985) and continued inflation (more than 50 percent a year from 1980 until the

---

[28] Woodward, "Orthodoxy and Solidarity." For a fuller treatment, see her *Socialist Unemployment: The Political Economy of Yugoslavia, 1945–1990* (Princeton University Press, 1995). For the general argument about petrodollars and foreign loans, see Laura D'Andrea Tyson, "The Debt Crisis and Adjustment Responses in Eastern Europe: A Comparative Perspective," *International Organization*, 40, 2 (Spring 1986), pp. 239–285.

hyperinflation of the war years). By 1984, average household income had fallen to 70 percent of what was considered the official minimum amount for a family of four to sustain itself.[29] Moreover the attempts to recentralize in the interest of economic austerity provoked resistance from the republics and simultaneously discredited the communist ideology, which was no longer seen to serve the interests of the workers.[30]

The economic argument accounts rather well for Slovenia's decision to secede from the federation in 1991. It was the most prosperous, most Europe-oriented republic, and it had the best prospects for success as an independent state – particularly given the considerable encouragement it received from Germany and Italy, which were eager to welcome it as a trading partner and market for their investments. There is also some merit to the general argument that "at a time when economic stagnation precluded the growth to which regions had gotten accustomed, perceptions of economic injustice developed along regional lines" and exacerbated interethnic tensions.[31] The vast disparity in economic performance also contributed to tensions, with unemployment in the mid-1980s at only 1.5 percent in Slovenia, but 50 percent in Kosovo, for example.[32] In Belgrade in 1991 the unemployment rate reached 50 percent for young men in their twenties – the prime age for recruitment to paramilitary gangs.[33]

High unemployment could also be related to demands for women to stay out of the workforce and have babies instead – an early warning sign of impending militarized nationalism. It might also be responsible for the phenomenon, mentioned in the previous chapters, that Chris Dolan has called the "proliferation of small men." He found, based on his study of northern Uganda, that when a large number of young men are unable to fulfill society's expectations of what it means to be a "full man" (for example, to have a job capable of attracting a wife and supporting a family), they disproportionately fall victim to alcoholism, engage in violence, commit suicide – or join an armed militia.[34]

---

[29] Woodward, "Orthodoxy and Solidarity," p. 544.

[30] Susan Woodward, *Balkan Tragedy: Chaos and Dissolution after the Cold War* (Washington, DC: Brookings Institution, 1995); Milica Zarković Bookman, *Economic Decline and Nationalism in the Balkans* (New York: St. Martin's Press, 1994).

[31] Bookman, *Economic Decline*, p. 86.

[32] Woodward, *Balkan Tragedy*, p. 51; Woodward, *Socialist Unemployment*.

[33] "By 1985 59.6 percent of the total registered unemployed were under the age of twenty-five (and 38.7 percent of people under twenty-five were unemployed)." Woodward, *Balkan Tragedy*, p. 57.

[34] Chris Dolan, "Collapsing Masculinities and Weak States – A Case Study of Northern Uganda," in Frances Cleaver, ed., *Masculinities Matter!* (London: Zed Books, 2003), pp. 57–83. One can recognize some of the "small man" phenomenon in discussions of how

The main link between economic distress and ethnic conflict is presumed to be the process of finding others to blame. Consider the observations of one specialist, writing about the Yugoslav economic crisis in the mid-1980s, before the situation became drastically worse in the second half of that decade. She argued that "both politicians and private citizens search for scapegoats and ways to differentiate in the distribution of scarce resources, such as jobs, among citizens with equal rights. The most likely result of this scapegoating in Yugoslavia is always a rise in nationalist antagonisms." She pointed particularly to tensions in Kosovo and adduced evidence of "nationalist incidents, religious revival, and antifeminist backlash" as early as 1981–1984.[35]

In most accounts of the origins of the wars in Yugoslavia, Serbian nationalism comes in for most of the blame. Some observers also point to the actions of Croatian nationalists in reviving symbols of the Nazi-backed Ustasha regime which made Serb residents of the Krajina region, in particular, feel insecure.[36] All the more striking, then, are Gagnon's findings that show the Serb minorities in both Croatia and Bosnia "were among the strongest proponents of peaceful coexistence." Survey data from the late 1980s showed "very high levels of positive coexistence, little evidence of resentments or suppressed violence, and the growing attractiveness, especially among young people in Bosnia, of a Yugoslav identity."[37] People were certainly concerned about the deteriorating economy and growing inequality, and the surveys indicate a high priority given to economic and political reform. But the surveys also demonstrate that the inequalities that bothered most respondents were not those between national groups. A 1990 poll in Croatia revealed that two-thirds of Croats and three-fifths of Serbs believed that both groups were treated equally (or disadvantaged equally). Another poll put the figure at 80 percent of Croats and Serbs who denied that the other group was privileged in any way. These results are all the more surprising for having come in the midst of an electoral campaign during which Serbian and Croatian nationalist politicians sought to foster perceptions of injustice and inequality as sources of grievance against the other community. Polls taken in May and June 1990 did show some sensitivity to these issues, as

women in eastern Europe deal with the difficulties that faced their men during the communist era and the postcommunist transition. See especially Slavenka Drakulić, "The Language of Soup," ch. 11 in her *How We Survived Communism and Even Laughed* (New York: Harper, 1992), pp. 104–112.

[35] Woodward, "Orthodoxy and Solidarity," p. 543.

[36] On the role of symbols, in particular, see Bette Denich, "Dismembering Yugoslavia: Nationalist Ideologies and the Symbolic Revival of Genocide," *American Ethnologist*, 21, 2 (1994), pp. 367–390.

[37] Gagnon, *The Myth of Ethnic War*, p. 34.

16 percent of respondents in Croatia claimed to perceive inequality "in relations between nationalities." But this was roughly the same amount that perceived inequality between the republics, and rather less than the proportion who were sensitive to inequality "between those with political power and regular citizens" (21 percent) or "between rich and poor" (19 percent).[38]

As the economic situation in Serbia deteriorated, Slobodan Milošević, the communist-leader-turned-nationalist, sought to distract attention by complaining of the mistreatment of Serbs (to the point of "genocide"), especially in Kosovo and Croatia's Krajina. Through his manipulation of the mass media, he appears to have convinced many residents of Yugoslavia that interethnic relations had worsened. By late 1989, Croats, for example, had come to believe that relations between nationalities in Yugoslavia were either very bad or mostly bad (77.6 percent). Remarkably, however, neither Croats nor Serbs in Croatia itself believed that relations were bad within their own communities. Among Croats 66 percent characterized them as mainly good or very good, 25.5 percent as average, and only 8.7 percent as mainly or very bad. Serbs, a minority in Croatia, were even more positive, with figures of 72.1, 23.4, and 3.5, respectively. Asked about threats to the national rights of their groups, 82.7 percent of Croats and 87.3 percent of Serbs denied them. Comparably high numbers from both groups rejected the notion that interethnic marriages were more unstable than others, at a time when 29 percent of Serbs living in Croatia took Croatian spouses. Gagnon quotes the summary of one of the main survey researchers: "At the end of 1989 signs of tensions between nationalities in Croatia were hardly discernible…Croats, Serbs, and Yugoslavs were convinced of the possibility of a life together unburdened by considerations of national similarities or differences."[39]

Although ordinary Yugoslavs became increasingly preoccupied with economic conditions, it was the elites who viewed the problem through the prism of nationalism. As Gagnon demonstrates, the top leaders used ethnically inspired fears and violence to prevent challenges to their control of political and economic resources. But even before they resorted to such extreme measures, the elites were sensitive to the distributional implications of ethnic identity. The structure of the Yugoslav economic and political system depended in part on a balancing of privileges and benefits among the national groups within and between the republics. For example, the "balance of political forces" in Bosnia and Herzegovina, as Gagnon explains, "in part took the form of an institutionalized 'ethnic

---

[38] Ibid., pp. 37–38.   [39] Nikola Dugandžija, quoted in ibid., p. 36.

key,' whereby all positions from the top down were carefully allocated across ethnicities. In effect, this ethnic key created an incentive structure whereby elites and prospective elites were ensured positions in the bureaucracy." The ethnic categories were self-identification as Muslim, Serb, Croat, or "other" (including Yugoslavs, as well as minority groups such as Roma or Slovaks). One reason for the Bosnian elite's commitment to preservation of the Yugoslav federation was a selfish one: "Any change in the status of the republics would threaten to disrupt this balance within the elite, though there would be minimal impact on the wider population."[40]

For Gagnon these incentives provide an explanation for an otherwise surprising discrepancy in the public opinion polls. Members of the League of Communists of Bosnia-Herzegovina were far more likely to express nationalist sentiments than was the population at large: 29 percent versus 8 percent. "It also helps explain why, despite the fact that ethnic ties were not a major fault line among the wider population itself, they remained important for elites and aspiring elites" who also were troubled by the growing identification of Bosnia's young people with the label Yugoslav. So, even though the Bosnian communists shared the conservative orientation of their Serbian counterparts regarding market reforms and political liberalization, they came into conflict with the Serbian conservatives' proposals for centralizing institutional reforms that would disrupt the pattern of ethnically distributed benefits that the Bosnian elites enjoyed.[41] Their tolerance for Serbia's centralizing project vanished altogether once Croatia and Slovenia had opted out of the federation, leaving no counterweight to Belgrade's power.

The republic held a referendum in March 1992, boycotted by the Bosnian Serbs, who had preemptively declared their own Serbian Republic of Bosnia-Herzegovina, later called the Republika Srpska, in January. With the referendum approved, the Muslim and Croat members of the collective Bosnian presidency voted for independence, while the Serbs voted against. Although in the minority, the Serbs held one key advantage: the Yugoslav National Army. Anticipating Bosnia's bid for independence, Milošević had ordered the replacement of all JNA officers stationed there by Bosnian Serbs who had been living outside the republic. Thus, when war broke out, the JNA followed orders from Belgrade and cooperated with the Bosnian Serb paramilitaries who sought to carve out an "ethnically cleansed" territory linked to Serbia. Preparations had been made long before. The 1991 plan, code-named Ram, anticipated

---

[40] Ibid., pp. 72–74.   [41] Ibid.

"stage-managed interethnic incidents and the occupation of strategic points by the federal army," relying primarily on militias recruited by the Serb nationalist party, SDS, from the Serb population of Bosnia.[42]

Once the war broke out, another sort of "economic factor" came into play, as violence was combined with widespread looting of the property of those expelled from the territory – a common feature of pogroms and ethnic conflict everywhere.[43]

Media manipulation: "Television was more important than history"

Although many people in Yugoslavia opposed the wars against Slovenia, Croatia, and then Bosnia, Milošević attempted to persuade them that violence was necessary, first, to preserve the Yugoslav federation, and, failing that, to protect Serb populations from attack. The main resource at his disposal was mass media and particularly television. As Peter Maass explains, "Milošević controlled television absolutely, refusing to let independent stations have any national frequencies. State television maintained a monopoly, and Milošević, a well-trained communist who understood the power and importance of propaganda, met or talked on a daily basis with the director of Radio-Television Serbia, whom he appointed and replaced, as necessary." Newspapers and magazines maintained a degree of independence, but with the hyperinflation that accompanied the war and imposition of economic sanctions by the United States and the European Community, "few people could afford to buy them anymore."[44]

For Maass, "the most amazing thing about the role of television was that it not only had the power to form people's opinions, it could change those opinions overnight."[45] He provides two examples. In April 1993, when Milošević opposed the Vance–Owen Plan for ending the conflict in Bosnia and state television described it as unfair, only a third of the population of Serbia supported it. When Milošević came to fear US intervention in the war, he reversed his position, and so did all the television stations. By May, nearly two-thirds of Serbs polled supported the plan. His second example is the 1993 election campaign, when Milošević's

---

[42] Xavier Bougarel, "Etat et communautarisme en Bosnie-Herzégovine," *Cultures et Conflits*, 13 (December 1994), quoted in Samary, *Yugoslavia Dismembered*, pp. 94–95.

[43] The relationship between crime and warfare in the context of the Yugoslav wars is explored in Peter Andreas, *Blue Helmets and Black Markets: The Business of Survival in the Siege of Sarajevo* (Ithaca, NY: Cornell University Press, 2008).

[44] Maass, *Love Thy Neighbor*, p. 227.

[45] Ibid., pp. 226–227.

Socialist Party gained twenty-two seats in the parliament, despite coming under attack from extreme-right nationalists and at a time when the inflation rate was outpacing Weimar Germany in the days of Hitler's rise to power. Maass attributes Milošević's success to the TV monopoly and he quotes the analogy offered by an independent Serb journalist: "You must imagine a United States with every little TV station everywhere taking exactly the same editorial line – a line dictated by David Duke," the notorious white supremacist and Ku Klux Klan leader. "You too would have war in five years."[46] And, he might have added, using Maass' example, the subsequent acceptance of an externally dictated peace settlement, if that is what the television advocated. For, as Gagnon has argued, Milošević did not always take the extreme nationalist position. He took the position that served his personal political interests, even if it meant abandoning his fellow Serbs in Bosnia, the Krajina, or Kosovo.

In the years preceding the outbreak of war, Milošević in Serbia and Franjo Tuđman in Croatia used television to rekindle memories of the massacres of World War II, often using graphic documentary footage of atrocities. As Ian Traynor put it, television itself became "more important than history."[47] Television took "history" very seriously in its own way, using it at every manipulative turn to link current events to various historical parallels from World War II and the Balkan wars earlier in the century – especially ones that involved sexual violence.[48]

Once the wars began, the state-dominated media continued to manipulate the populations under their control. Tanja Ljujić-Mijatović, a Serb from Sarajevo, offers an example of the Serbian media's portrayal of the Bosnian war: "Today I meet people from Serbia who really didn't know Sarajevo was destroyed, and they're amazed at what they see. They actually thought we Sarajevans were shooting at ourselves."[49] Media manipulation became a weapon in the war itself. Rada Sesar, a Bosnian Serb journalist originally from a village outside Pale, had studied at Sarajevo University, married a Bosnian Croat, and had two children. She described in an interview how the "Serbs used the media in the most terrible way, isolating their coverage area," after bringing it under military control. "They 'cleansed' the region so they could do whatever they wanted; radio and TV signals were provided from Serbia for their territory in Bosnia, and all other relays were destroyed so other media couldn't reach them."[50]

---

[46] Ibid.   [47] Traynor, quoted in ibid., p. 227.
[48] I owe this formulation to Holly Case, who provided many valuable comments on this chapter.
[49] Hunt, *This Was Not Our War*, p. 93.   [50] Ibid., p. 92.

Did the Serb monopolization of the media make any difference? Sesar gives an example of the seemingly incredible effect of the propaganda on her own mother: "Take my mother, who – with all due respect – even after the time we spent in Sarajevo, still can't believe that someone was shooting at the city from the outside. During the war, she was in her mid-seventies, listening to the broadcasts from Serbia about how 'those Muslims' were destroying the capital … For her, it was 'the Muslims' who were shelling Sarajevo."[51]

Throughout the war, Serbian state-controlled media enflamed tension by heightening ethnic stereotypes and playing on people's sexual fears. In Bosnia Maass interviewed a Serb woman whose village had been "cleansed" of Muslims in the opening days of the war. He asked whether the fighting had been heavy.

"Why, no, there was no fighting between Muslims and Serbs in the village," she said.

"Then why were the Muslims arrested?"

"Because they were planning to take over the village. They had already drawn up lists. The names of the Serb women had been split into harems for the Muslim men."

"Harems?"

"Yes, harems. Their Bible says men can have harems, and that's what they were planning to do once they had killed our men. Thank God they were arrested first."

She wiped her brow.

"How do you know they were planning to kill the Serb men and create harems for themselves?"

"It was on the radio. Our military had uncovered their plans. It was announced on the radio."

Maass challenged her, asking how she knew the radio was telling the truth.

"Why," she demanded to know, "would the radio lie?"

"Did any of the Muslims in your village harm you?" Maass inquired.

"No."

"Did any Muslim *ever* do anything bad to you?"

She seemed offended.

"My relations with Muslims in the village were always very good. They were very nice people."[52]

Such stories support Gagnon's contention that the local populations in mixed Muslim–Croat–Serb areas of Bosnia were not seething with resentment and eager to attack their neighbors. The atrocities often required

---

[51] Ibid., p. 92.　　[52] Maass, *Love Thy Neighbor*, pp. 113–114.

outside organization and agitation, bolstered by a constant barrage of media disinformation and invocation of historical and pseudo-historical memories.

Women and nationalism in Yugoslavia

If ordinary people were unmoved by the elites' attachment to ethnically based privilege, and unreceptive to calls to war, ordinary women were even less so. That is the expectation one draws from Virginia Woolf's anti-nationalist hypothesis about women wanting no country. It is also the view conveyed by many feminist observers in Yugoslavia and abroad. Cynthia Cockburn, for example, views the history of women in Yugoslavia as characterized largely by violence and economic discrimination. Expressing a view familiar from Woolf's *Three Guineas*, Cockburn suggests that "if you see home as a 'golden cage' you may suspect that homeland too has its contradictions." Seeing "violence as a continuum – from domestic violence (in and near the home) to military violence (patrolling the external boundaries against enemies) and state violence (policing against traitors within)" tends to make "women question the pursuit of political movements by violent means."[53]

Yet, as Cockburn points out, a principled commitment to non-violence does not fully characterize Yugoslav women's experience. Many women in Yugoslavia had embraced violent resistance to Nazi occupation during the 1940s. Two million women joined the Anti-Fascist Front of Women and some hundred thousand fought in regular partisan military units. Twenty-five thousand were killed in action and forty thousand wounded.[54] Women expected the new socialist society that emerged from the war to improve their situation, but, as Cockburn explains, "'emancipation' was always the brothers' policy for the sisters, not something the sisters achieved in their own design." Even by its own Marxist standards, where equality would be achieved by "women's equal participation with men in the paid labour force," Yugoslavia failed. As late as 1981, two-thirds of women remained outside the formal economy. Yugoslavia boasted one of the world's highest rates of university-educated women, yet they were little represented in the top administrative and management positions – another reason for their lack of interest in the elite distribution of privilege by nationality.

[53] Cynthia Cockburn, *The Space between Us: Negotiating Gender and National Identities in Conflict* (London: Zed Books, 1998), pp. 44–45.

[54] Ibid., pp. 156–157, citing Andjelka Milić, "Women and Nationalism in Former Yugoslavia," in Nanette Funk and Magda Mueller, eds., *Gender, Politics and Post-Communism* (London: Routledge, 1993).

While urban women were successfully pursuing higher education, their rural sisters were losing ground. An astounding 17 percent of women (mainly in the countryside) remained illiterate in 1981 – four times the rate for men.[55]

The atmosphere in Yugoslavia for a critique of the status of women was not very encouraging. Interest in feminism emerged in the late 1970s mainly as an urban phenomenon, associated with educated professional women with knowledge of the West. In Zagreb in 1979, a discussion group was formed under the rubric "Women and Society," with similar ones founded in subsequent years in Belgrade, Ljubljana, Sarajevo, and Novi Sad. As they began explicitly identifying themselves as feminist, the women came in for strong criticism. The official state women's organization condemned them as "enemies of the people" and pro-capitalist.[56] For female veterans of the partisan war, in particular, "feminism was synonymous with disloyalty," according to the novelist and journalist Slavenka Drakulić.[57] It was even more threatening to the men in power. As Cockburn describes, they "saw nothing to gain from questioning the 'naturalness' of male leadership and female domesticity. All else under socialism might be seen as amenable to social reconstruction – not gender."[58]

As the socialist model itself became discredited, pressure for democracy mounted. Women were active in the movement and many of them sought to provide alternatives to the nationalist program promoted by Milošević. In 1986, prominent members of the Serbian Academy of Sciences and Arts had issued a "memorandum" deploring the state of the 40 percent of Serbs who lived in other Yugoslav republics. It "clearly announced that Serbs would 'take back Serb sovereignty over Serbia'" (by revoking the autonomous status of Vojvodina and Kosovo), as a "first step in the creation of Greater Serbia. The document defended 'Serbs' right to be brought together in a single state' and to protect the Serb diaspora from 'new dangers of genocide.'"[59] Svetlana Slapsak, a Serb academic who rejected the nationalist call, aptly termed the document a program for "preventive vengeance."[60] The memorandum was widely

[55] Cockburn, *The Space between Us*, pp. 157–158.
[56] Drakulić, *How We Survived Communism and Even Laughed*; Cockburn, *The Space Between Us*, pp. 159–160; Zorica Mršević, "Belgrade's SOS Hotline for Women and Children Victims of Violence: A Report," ch. 13 in Gal and Kligman, *Reproducing Gender*; Zorica Mršević and Donna M. Hughes, "Violence against Women in Belgrade, Serbia: SOS Hotline 1990–1993," *Violence against Women*, 3, 2 (1997), pp. 370–392.
[57] Quoted in Cockburn, *The Space between Us*, p. 160.
[58] Ibid., p. 159.   [59] Samary, *Yugoslavia Dismembered*, p. 75.
[60] Svetlana Slapsak, "Les alternatives serbes: y en a-t-il après la Bosnie?" *Migrations Littéraires*, 21 (Summer 1992), pp. 3–17, quoted in Samary, *Yugoslavia Dismembered*, p. 75.

condemned by the communist-controlled press, particularly in Serbia itself, but Milošević, the Party chief, refused to denounce it.[61]

Women were particularly alarmed at the way gender figured directly in the nationalists' fear-mongering about the fate of Serbs in Kosovo. As Cockburn explains, "it was a moral panic in the late 1980s concerning alleged rapes by Albanian men of Serbian women in Kosovo that intensified the Serb nationalist revival there." In Cockburn's view, women in Serbia were expected to draw the conclusion: "rape by alien men is the ultimate defilement" and only "domestic confinement of women safeguards their purity."[62]

The alarm over rapes in Kosovo was a classic example of Serbian media manipulation. Researchers later discovered that "in Kosovo there were two-and-a-half times fewer rapes than in 'inner' Serbia, and two times fewer than in Yugoslavia" as a whole. Of the 323 rapes reported between 1982 and 1989, fewer than 10 percent of the cases involved Albanian perpetrators attacking Serbian or Montenegrin victims – the great fear promoted by Milošević's media machine. There were no such rapes reported at all for 1987–1989, a period of peak nationalist hysteria in Serbia.[63]

In 1990, in anticipation of the first multiparty elections in Yugoslavia, feminists formed the Women's Lobby to resist nationalist pressures ("to have more babies for greater Serbia"), to campaign against the nationalist parties, and to promote interethnic tolerance and demilitarization. The efforts proved inadequate. The election "resulted in a Serbian Parliament with only 1.6 percent women (the lowest percentage in Europe), so women formed the Women's Parliament on 8 March 1991 to monitor new laws that pertained to women."[64]

Not surprisingly, many of the laws sought to restrict women's autonomy over decisions about reproduction. Abortion had been legal and readily available in Yugoslavia since 1951. Article 191 of the Constitution of 1974 guaranteed access to abortion in the context of "the human right to decide about the birth of one's own children." In April 1992, a new constitution eliminated Article 191. Nationalists (presumably women as well as men) called women who had abortions traitors to the Serb nation, comparing the number of abortions to the number of soldiers killed in the war.[65] Pressures on women to produce more babies, and consequent

---

[61] Silber and Little, *Yugoslavia*, ch. 1.
[62] Cockburn, *The Space between Us*, p. 162.
[63] Gagnon, *The Myth of Ethnic War*, p. 67.
[64] Lepa Mladjenović and Donna M. Hughes, "Feminist Resistance to War and Violence in Serbia," ch. 20 in M. Waller, ed., *Frontline Feminisms* (New York: Routledge, 2001).
[65] Ibid.

limitations on women's reproductive rights, were a significant component of the nationalist propaganda in Croatia as well. The goals were generally to increase the population of one's ethnic group vis-à-vis the others, and in the most militarized versions, to provide future soldiers for ethnic conflict.[66] The warning issued by Slavenka Drakulić in 1991 proved prescient: "If women fail to participate in bringing political decisions and in defending their rights, I am afraid that democracy in Eastern Europe will be of masculine gender. And, what is worse, it will wear boots."[67]

The demise of the socialist welfare state, the economic decline, and the rise of nationalism all combined to create a particularly difficult situation for women.[68] Consider the example of Slavica Stojanović, who did not consider herself a feminist "before the war." She was, however, inspired by her grandmother's experience to reject the type of nationalism fostered by her country's leaders:

My grandmother lived under the Austro-Hungarian rule and out of the experience of her youth she despised inter-ethnic conflicts which were provoked by rulers who had vested interests in creating animosity. My grandmother remembered the enthusiasm of the time when Yugoslavia was founded as a multi-ethnic country after World War I. She lived near the Italian border in the early years of fascism and openly opposed it. At the beginning of World War II she lived in Zagreb and was forced to leave because she was Serb. She came to live in Belgrade and her house was bombed in 1941 by the Germans and again in 1944 by the Americans. Until her death, a few years ago, at age 90, she called herself "Yugoslav." It was her political choice. I was raised with these ideas. When this war started I had to make a distinction between the values I wanted to retain from "Yugoslavia" and the material/territorial idea of Yugoslavia.

For consolation, Slavica turned to translating Virginia Woolf into Serbo-Croatian. She began teaching courses on women's literature, founded a feminist publishing house, and co-founded a center against sexual violence. Echoing Woolf, she declared: "The whole world is my country. I want to work for values that are more open than nationalism." But the

---

[66] Sonja Licht and Slavenka Drakulić, "When the Word for Peacenik was Woman: War and Gender in the Former Yugoslavia," in B. Wejnert, M. Spencer, and S. Drakulić, eds., *Women in Post-Communism, Research on Russia and Eastern Europe*, vol. II (Greenwich, CT: JAI Press, 1996), pp. 111–140; Patricia Albanese, "Leaders and Breeders: The Archaization of Gender Relations in Croatia," in Wejnert *et al.*, *Women in Post-Communism*, pp. 185–200; Rada Iveković, "Femmes, nationalisme et guerre ('Faites l'amour, pas la guerre')," *Peuples Méditerranéens*, no. 61 (1992), pp. 205–215.

[67] Slavenka Drakulić, quoted in Lukić, "Media Representations of Men and Women," p. 403.

[68] For an excellent overview, see Joyce P. Kaufman and Kristen P. Williams, *Women, the State, and War: A Comparative Perspective on Citizenship and Nationalism* (Lexington, MA: Lexington Books, 2007), esp. pp. 82–87.

independence movements that arose partly in reaction to fears of Serb domination posed a dilemma:

When Slovenia and Croatia wanted independence, I supported unity, but that meant I supported the war. I wanted to support unity, but I needed to respect their choice for independence and I couldn't support crimes. I had political doubts about the motivations of some people who wanted separate states. Because populations in the republics are so mixed I knew that separating Yugoslavia would be very difficult and risky. I am not happy with the nationalistic states with their patterns of domination.[69]

Once the actual fighting started, and war reports began appearing on television, the situation for women deteriorated markedly, although it is not certain whether actual incidences of domestic violence increased.[70] In any event, reports from a domestic-violence hotline founded in Belgrade are revealing about the relationship between media portrayals of the war and male violence at home:

In the autumn of 1991 the SOS Hotline started receiving calls from women who were battered after men watched the TV news (or special broadcasts) in which picture[s] of dead bodies were shown. The narratives were filled with hatred for "the enemy." Women reported that men became enraged after watching the nationalist propaganda and they beat women as a way to avenge their wounded national pride. Some women reported that they were beaten for the first time in their lives after the men watched one of the nationalist reports on Serbian victims of war...Women told SOS Hotline staff that their husbands cursed the Croats and Muslims in Croatia and Bosnia-Herzegovina while beating them. In some of these incidents the women were beaten so badly that an ambulance was called to take them for emergency treatment. In most of these cases the nationality of the woman was the same as her partner. The men displaced their hatred and anger onto a convenient target – the woman.[71]

Ironically, and tragically for women, the nationalist campaign for violent defense of innocent women and children in the Serbian diaspora contributed to violence against them at home. For women who endured direct violence in the conflict zones, even escape from the war offered no escape from male violence. Misogyny and generally discriminatory and patriarchal attitudes towards women continued beyond the war, worsening the lives of refugees who had already lost everything.[72] In one case,

[69] Mladjenović and Hughes, "Feminist Resistance to War and Violence in Serbia," p. 254.
[70] Mršević, in "Belgrade's SOS Hotline," p. 389, calls into question the claim that domestic violence by men against women "has increased dramatically since the war began."
[71] Mršević and Hughes, "Violence against Women in Belgrade," p. 126.
[72] For a review of several films that treat issues of masculinity and sexual violence in postwar Serbian film – including one by Srđan Dragojević – see Ivana Kronja, "The

encountered by volunteers at the SOS Hotline in Belgrade, a woman who had escaped with her children from the war in Bosnia sought refuge at her godfather's house. He raped her within the first week of her stay.[73] In another case, a woman in Serbia who hosted relatives of her husband – refugees from the war in Bosnia – found herself the victim of their patriarchal attitudes and potential violence:

> They are all men and none of them work. They wait for her to prepare their food, wash their clothes (even though there is no washing machine or running water in the house), iron their clothes and clean the house. She has a little garden to grow vegetables, but the men will not help with that either – gardening is not men's work. The men give her no money. So besides all the work in her home she cleans neighbors' houses for money.

In a cruel Catch 22, she has to keep her extra work outside the house secret, for fear that the men will take the money she earns "or beat her for causing them shame by showing that they are not capable of providing for the family."[74]

The attitude of some (male) police officers towards violence against women manifests an unmistakable misogyny: "It is a Serbian custom for a husband to beat his wife." These were the remarks of an officer on duty at a Belgrade police station in 1994, "made to a woman who had been brutally beaten by her husband throughout an entire night in front of their 2½-year-old child."[75]

Gender and the wars

The worst violence, of course, was suffered by those engulfed by the wars themselves. A popular gendered reading of war – and of the Bosnian war, in particular – sees all men as warriors and potential rapists and all women as victims. When Cynthia Enloe made the point in the title of a powerful essay exploring the motivations behind the actions of a Serb militia fighter who had confessed to multiple rapes, she did so to question such simple, "essentialist" understandings. "Accepting a priori the assumption that women are best thought of as victims in any nationalist mobilization that has turned violent dulls the analytical curiosity," she writes. "Ultimately, this dulled curiosity produces explanations that are naïve in their descriptions of power and camouflage men as ungendered

Aesthetics of Violence in Recent Serbian Cinema: Masculinity in Crisis," *Film Criticism*, 30, 3 (Spring 2006), pp. 17–37.
[73] Mršević and Hughes, "Violence against Women in Belgrade."
[74] Ibid.   [75] Mršević, "Belgrade's SOS Hotline," pp. 381–382.

actors."[76] Others have read the war that way without question. As Swanee Hunt wrote in her valuable collection of interviews with women survivors of the Bosnian war: "Bands of males may assert their manhood as warriors, but war affords women no corresponding empowering role; instead they become victims, not only displaced and damaged, mourning the loss of family members, but also prey for men on the enemy side."[77]

The first victim of the Bosnian war was a woman. In April 1992 Suada Dilberović, a young student from Dubrovnik, Croatia, who was studying medicine in Sarajevo, joined a peace march across the Vrbanja Bridge to Grbavica to protest the attacks on the city by Serb paramilitaries. As the multiethnic crowd crossed the bridge, the blond-haired, blue-eyed Muslim woman was shot in the chest and arrived dead at the hospital.[78] Many more women and girls would suffer and die in the course of the war and hundreds of thousands would be left homeless in its wake. The war in Bosnia was not, as the foreign governments and media sought to portray it, a civil war pitting the armed forces of one side against those of the other, with civilians caught in between. As Silber and Little explain, "the columns of refugees that spilled into Croatia in April and May 1992 were not fleeing the war zones. They had been driven from their homes on the grounds of their nationality. They were not the tragic by-product of a civil war; their expulsion was the whole point of the war."[79] The deliberate attacks against civilians and the campaign of mass rapes carried out by the Serb forces as part of the strategy of "ethnic cleansing" made the Bosnian war look very much like a war waged against women, even if in reality far more men perished.[80]

Women are typically considered the keepers of ethnicity – the ones who pass on language, custom, and cuisine to the next generations. In that respect, women in Bosnia were the ones who "reproduced cultural difference." But they also were a key element in the preservation of interethnic comity. As Cockburn points out, Bosnian women "took care of those little courtesies that kept Muslim, Serb and Croat families in touch with each other. It was precisely those threads of connection

---

[76] Enloe, "All the Men are in the Militias," p. 53.
[77] Hunt, *This Was Not Our War*, p. 179.
[78] Silber and Little, *Yugoslavia*, pp. 226–228.   [79] Ibid., p. 244.
[80] Alexandra Stiglmayer, ed., *Mass Rape: The War against Women in Bosnia-Herzegovina*, trans. by Marion Faber (Lincoln, NE: University of Nebraska Press, 1994); Beverly Allen, *Rape Warfare: The Hidden Genocide in Bosnia-Herzegovina and Croatia* (Minneapolis, MN: University of Minnesota Press, 1996); Teresa Iacobelli, "The 'Sum of Such Actions': Investigating Mass Rape in Bosnia-Herzegovina through a Case Study of Foca," ch. 10 in Dagmar Herzog, ed., *Brutality and Desire: War and Sexuality in Europe's Twentieth Century* (New York: Palgrave Macmillan, 2009).

spun by women that the ethnic aggression was directed towards tearing asunder. Aggression that was, *de facto*, by men."[81]

But it is not true that women were only victims in the war, that it afforded none of them an "empowering role," as Hunt put it. Much as every generalization about the peaceful nature of women in politics must acknowledge exceptions such as Indira Gandhi and Margaret Thatcher, so must we remember the roles of Mirjana Marković and Biljana Plavšić, among others, in the Yugoslav wars. Marković, a sociologist and daughter of prominent partisans, contributed to the atmosphere of fear and tension in the late 1980s with her warnings about threats to the "national dignity of Serbia." In the 1990s she used her independent political influence as leader of the Yugoslav United Left political party to support the ambitions and criminal policies of her husband, Slobodan Milošević. When he fell from power and went on trial at The Hague, she fled to exile in Moscow, where the Russian government rejected requests for her extradition.

Plavšić, known like Thatcher as the "Iron Lady," became the Serb representative in the collective presidency of Bosnia that still nominally governed the republic as the war broke out in April 1992. Sent with her Muslim counterpart to investigate atrocities perpetrated by Serb irregulars in the town of Bijeljina, she arrived in the deserted, destroyed town and warmly greeted the leader of this textbook example of "ethnic cleansing." Zeljko Raznatović, known as Arkan, was a notorious Serb warlord, later indicted by the International Criminal Tribunal for the former Yugoslavia and wanted by Interpol for crimes ranging from bank robbery to genocide.[82] He moved to Belgrade after the war, was elected to parliament, and enjoyed a high-profile life until he was gunned down, gangland-style, in a hotel in January 2000. In 1996 Plavšić said of Arkan, "when I saw what he'd done in Bijeljina, I at once imagined all his actions being like that. I said 'Here we have a Serb hero. He's a real Serb, that's the kind of men we need.'"[83] Plavšić later worked as deputy to another indicted war criminal, Radovan Karadžić, and publicly supported his plan to partition Sarajevo, one that crowded the Muslim residents into a limited area of the old town, while making broad swaths of the outskirts available only to Serbs. Karadžić had little understanding or sympathy for Sarajevo's cosmopolitan character and tradition of

[81] Cockburn, *The Space between Us*, p. 206.
[82] Silber and Little, *Yugoslavia*, pp. 224–225.
[83] *On* (Belgrade), November 12, 1996, quoted in Slobodan Inić, "Biljana Plavšić: Geneticist in the Service of a Great Crime," translated from *Helsinska povelja* [Helsinki Charter], Belgrade, November 1996, and available at www.barnsdle.demon.co.uk/bosnia/plavsic.html.

tolerance and coexistence. He himself was an outsider, "an urbanized peasant from Montenegro," who had come to Bosnia's capital to study medicine – the first in his family for generations to receive higher education – and, if anything, he resented the unfamiliar ways and the snobbish attitude some Sarajevans had shown towards him.[84] Plavšić, originally from Tuzla, a Muslim-majority town, justified Karadžić's discriminatory plan by explaining that "it is the habit of the Muslims to live this way. They like to live on top of one another. It's their culture. We Serbs need space."[85] A virologist by training, former professor and Dean of the Faculty of Natural Sciences and Mathematics at Sarajevo University, and a 1971 Fulbright visitor at the Boyce-Thompson Institute in Yonkers, New York, Plavšić also brought her biological expertise to bear in analyzing the state of Muslim–Serb relations.[86] Bosnian Muslims, she argued, were "genetically deformed Serbs." Thus, she claimed, "we are disturbed by the fact that the number of marriages between Serbs and Muslims has increased." Such mixed marriages, she explained, "lead to an exchange of genes between ethnic groups, and thus to a degeneration of Serb nationhood."[87]

In 1996, Plavšić broke with her fellow Bosnian Serb nationalists to endorse the US-sponsored Dayton Plan to end the war in Bosnia by creating loosely affiliated, ethnically defined mini-states. Then Secretary of State Madeleine Albright praised Plavšić, and the US government funneled millions of dollars in aid to her region "to shore up political support" for her candidacy, as US officials put it.[88] She lost the election anyway to a candidate who opposed Dayton and favored union with Serbia. In January 2001 Plavšić flew to The Hague and surrendered to officials at the war crimes tribunal, where she had been under secret indictment. She began serving a jail term for crimes against humanity.

Contrary to traditional gender norms, some women did serve in the armed forces during the Yugoslav wars. A certain number of Muslim women joined the Bosnian army after having been raped. As one

---

[84] Silber and Little, *Yugoslavia*, p. 226.   [85] Ibid., pp. 232–233.

[86] Povjerljivo i podneseno zapečaćeno Tužilca protiv Momčila Krajišnika, Biljane Plavšic, document IT-00–39&40-PT of the International Criminal Tribunal for the Former Yugoslavia, September 30, 2002, www.un.org/icty/bhs/cases/plavsic/documents/factual-basis.htm.

[87] Quoted in Sarajevo's *Oslobodjenje*, May 1994, as reported in Patrick FitzPatrick, "It Isn't Easy Being Biljana," *Central European Review*, 2, 22 (June 5, 2000), www.ce-review.org/00/22/fitzpatrick22.html.

[88] Cable News Network, "US Plans Loan Package to Bolster Plavsic," August 27, 1997, www.cnn.com/WORLD/9708/27/bosnia.aid/. R. Jeffrey Smith, "Albright Warns Bosnia that Radical Victory Could Damage Economic Aid," *Washington Post*, August 31, 1998.

explained, "the main reason I put on a uniform is to get revenge."[89] Men on all sides of the conflict tried to mobilize women to aid the war effort. As one woman, a Bosnian Serb interviewed by Swanee Hunt, described: "I was a journalist for what some considered a Muslim magazine. The Serbs came to my father and tried, at gunpoint, to mobilize me for civil defense, to make me prove my loyalty. My father managed to get me transferred to the medical corps."[90] Women served as medics on the Bosnian government side as well, perhaps more willingly, as they felt a stake in the defense of their multiethnic community.[91] Such behavior would confound Woolf's generalizations, because women would be acting in support of military activity, and for the purpose of defense, but, in essence, for an antinationalist cause – the preservation of a multiethnic Bosnia and Herzegovina.

Another aspect of the Yugoslav wars that challenges the male warrior–female victim dichotomy is the huge number of draft resisters. Gagnon describes the situation that arose as the JNA sought to keep Croatia from seceding and the Milošević regime sounded the alarm about impending genocide against the Krajina Serbs: "At a time when the Serbian media was filled with images of genocidal *ustaše* massacring innocent Serb women and children, the attempts to mobilize young men and reserve forces in Serbia to fight in Croatia were stunningly unsuccessful." Antiwar activists claim that in Belgrade only 5 percent responded to the call-up, whereas in rural areas the rate was about 20 percent. Other estimates suggest 15 percent response in Belgrade and 50 percent overall. Some 200,000 men reportedly went abroad to avoid the draft. Gagnon concludes that "between 50 and 85 percent of Serb men called up to fight in Croatia either went in to hiding or left the country."[92] An estimated 50,000 reservists who did join the army subsequently deserted.[93]

Particularly revealing of gender dynamics during the wars was the behavior of Serb volunteers. As Aleksandra Sasha Milićević points out in a fascinating study, men in Serbia fell into four categories in respect to military service, depending on whether they received call-up orders to report either as reservists or conscripts and whether they did report or tried to evade service. She focused her study on the men who did not receive a call-up letter, but who nevertheless chose to join the war. Although her face-to-face interviews were conducted necessarily with a relatively small sample, she turned up quite interesting findings. The

---

[89] Alexandra Stiglmayer, "The Rapes in Bosnia-Herzegovina," in Stiglmayer, *Mass Rape*, p. 99.
[90] Hunt, *This Was Not Our War*, p. 18.   [91] Ibid., pp. 20, 68–69.
[92] Gagnon, *The Myth of Ethnic War*, pp. 108–109.   [93] Ibid.

typical volunteer did not, for example, always fit Dolan's profile of the "small man" – young, unemployed, and unable to attract a wife. On the contrary, many of Milićević's interlocutors were married men, who, she points out, often abandoned their own families (without sometimes even informing their wives or children) in order to defend an abstract "family" – the Serbian nation. Moreover, they often lost their families, when their wives filed for divorce at higher rates than for those who did not volunteer.[94] The volunteers' insistence on fighting despite the wishes of their wives and children recalls the Quaker wife in *High Noon*, discussed in chapter 1. Her principled opposition to violence enabled her husband, the retired marshal, to take up his weapon again. If women by nature are peaceful, then it is the man's responsibility to defend the family and community with violence – and it is the sign of true masculinity to be willing to do so in the face of female opposition. It was this insight that led Virginia Woolf to suggest that her society of female "outsiders" react to men's interest in fighting by pledging not "to incite their brothers to fight, or to dissuade them, but to maintain an attitude of complete indifference."[95]

If antinationalist women in Belgrade faced difficult decisions about whether to support the deployment of the army in the interest of Yugoslav unity, men's decisions were a matter of life or death. In one case, a "reservist could not decide whether to join a group of deserters or remain with his unit, so he shot himself. Another took a tank from the front and drove it all the way to the Federal Parliament."[96] Maass asked an eighteen-year-old Serb named Boris, with a pony tail and John Lennon glasses, what he thought of the war and what he would do if he was drafted.

He shrugged his shoulders, as though I had asked a question that anybody with a double-digit IQ knew the answer to.

"The Serb people are being seduced. They don't know what is happening. They see what they want to see, or what others want them to see. I think it's pretty sick."

"What will you do when the army calls?" I asked.

[94] Aleksandra Sasha Milićević, "Joining the War: Masculinity, Nationalism and War Participation in the Balkans War of Secession, 1991–1995," *Nationalities Papers*, 34, 3 (July 2006), pp. 265–287.

[95] Virginia Woolf, *Three Guineas* (New York: Harcourt, Brace, 1966 [1938]), pp. 106–107. In Slavenka Drakulić, *The Balkan Express: Fragments from the Other Side of War* (New York: Norton, 1993), the author imagines if her daughter were a son, and how difficult it would be to persuade him not to fight. Much as Woolf posits, the more she argues against the war, the more the son is determined that he must fulfill his manly duty and seek revenge.

[96] Silber and Little, *Yugoslavia*, p. 177. For a similar account, see Zillah Eisenstein, *Hatreds: Racialized and Sexualized Conflicts in the 21st Century* (New York: Routledge, 1996), p. 56.

He shrugged his shoulders again. Another dumb question.
"I will go to the army. It's better than jail."[97]

Maass later visited some of the soldiers responsible for laying siege to Sarajevo and occasionally shelling it. Some of them were conscripts. "The soldiers were bored," he writes. "Only two exciting things ever happened in their besieging lives – they got an order to fire, or they got new porno magazines."[98] Maass sympathizes. "It was a horrible choice: Dodge the draft and get thrown in jail or join the army and fire mortars at your cousins."[99]

Many who chose to fire mortars at their cousins also chose to rape their neighbors. The extensive discussions about rapes during the Bosnian war have focused to a considerable degree on explaining their motivations.[100] Were the rapes manifestations of "war as usual," expected to happen in any war, but for some reason better documented in this one than in others? Were the soldiers who raped acting spontaneously or opportunistically or were the actions part of a premeditated strategy, directed from above? Did the rapes reflect the particular gender dynamics of Yugoslav society or a more widely shared "culturally related contempt for women that is lived out in times of crisis?" For analysts such as Catherine MacKinnon or Ruth Seifert, who coined that expression, pornography plays a key role as a source or reflection of men's contempt for women.[101]

The evidence compiled by journalists and human rights workers on mass rape in Bosnia reveals a wide range of motivations (or imputed motivations, because they are based on the impressions of the victims). Some men knew their victims and wanted to express their newfound power over them; some knew their victims and seem to have been forced by outsiders to participate in the rapes; some raped to punish women and girls who refused to tell them where money or gold was hidden; some raped as a means of torture before killing their victims; some raped with intent to impregnate their victims. There was considerable variation in venue as well, from outdoors, to individual apartments, to brothels, to large public facilities established as rape "camps."[102] Men as well as

---

[97] Maass, *Love Thy Neighbor*, pp. 108–109.
[98] Ibid., pp. 109–110. [99] Ibid., pp. 106–107.
[100] For more detailed consideration, see Ruth Seifert, "War and Rape: A Preliminary Analysis," in Stiglmayer, ed., *Mass Rape*, pp. 54–72; and Elisabeth Wood, "Variation in Sexual Violence during War," *Politics and Society*, 34, 3 (September 2006), pp. 307–341.
[101] Seifert, "War and Rape;" Catherine A. MacKinnon, "Rape, Genocide, and Women's Human Rights," in Stiglmayer, *Mass Rape*, pp. 183–196.
[102] Stiglmayer, "The Rapes in Bosnia-Herzegovina."

women were victims of rape and sexual mutilation of the most sadistic sort, suggesting that domination and terror were key elements.[103] Yet, according to Zillah Eisenstein, "less has been reported about the sexual abuse and torture of men because it destabilizes the very notion of gender that is central to nation building."[104]

There is little doubt that some considerable portion of the rapes of women, as well as violence against men, constituted part of a deliberate plan to terrorize Muslims into leaving particular territories forever. The Italian journalist Giuseppe Zaccaria obtained minutes from discussion of the Yugoslav army's so-called Ram Plan of late 1991, in which strategies for ethnic cleansing were developed, with evident allusions to rape:

> Our analysis of the behavior of the Muslim communities demonstrates that the morale, will, and bellicose nature of their groups can be undermined only if we aim our action at the point where the religious and social structure is most fragile. We refer to the women, especially adolescents, and to the children. Decisive intervention on these social figures would spread confusion among the communities, thus causing first of all fear and then panic, leading to a probable retreat from the territories involved.[105]

Evidence of intention to impregnate rape victims and keep them captive until it was too late to terminate the pregnancies comes from extensive testimony of the victims themselves and from photocopies of documents. One letter, from Milan Dedić, commander of the third battalion of the Serb army, to Mihajl Kertes, head of the Federal Customs Administration in Belgrade, reads in part:

> Sixteen hundred and eighty Muslim women of ages ranging from twelve to sixty years are now gathered in the centers for displaced persons within our territory. A large number of these are pregnant, especially those ranging from fifteen to thirty years. In the estimation of Boško Kelević and Smiljan Gerić, the psychological effect is strong and therefore we must continue.

The Serb military authorities were also involved in the trafficking of captives for prostitution. A document signed by Kertes reads: "In accordance with the Ministries of Health and Security, and upon the request

---

[103] John Borneman, "Toward a Theory of Ethnic Cleansing: Territorial Sovereignty, Heterosexuality, and Europe," in his *Subversions of International Order* (Albany, NY: State University of New York Press, 1998), pp. 273–317; Dubravka Žarkov, "The Body of the Other Man: Sexual Violence and the Construction of Masculinity, Sexuality and Ethnicity in the Croatian Media," ch. 5 in Caroline O. N. Moser and Fiona C. Clark, eds., *Victims, Perpetrators or Actors? Gender, Armed Conflict and Political Violence* (London: Zed Books, 2001).

[104] Eisenstein, *Hatreds*, p. 60.

[105] Giuseppe Zaccaria, *Noi, criminali di guerra: storie vere dalla ex-Jugoslavia* (Milan: Baldini & Castoldi, 1994), quoted and translated in Allen, *Rape Warfare*, p. 57.

of Dr. Vida Mandić and Colonel Loginov, it is established that a certain number of young women, the numbers to be agreed upon, will be transferred to Slavonia and Baranja for the needs of the Serb forces and also for the UNPROFOR officers." Zaccaria has also found a note signed by Loginov: "I suggest we send eighty or a hundred or so girls to satisfy the officers' needs."[106] The mention of UNPROFOR refers to the United Nations Protection Force, international "peacekeepers" stationed in Bosnia since March 1992. Within Bosnia they became as notorious for their involvement in prostitution and various black market activities as for their failure to protect anyone.[107]

One of the most bizarre and disturbing aspects of the Bosnian rapes is the claim of the rapists that they are seeking to impregnate their victims in order to force them to give birth to "little Chetniks" or future "Serb soldier-heroes." The idea that a child who is the product of a Serb and a Muslim will necessarily be a Serb (and a male) contains, as Beverly Allen points out, a "logical glitch." It is as bizarre as the theories of genetics à la Professor Plavšić, albeit with different expectations. As Allen suggests, such ideas are "based on the uninformed, hallucinatory fantasy of ultranationalists whose most salient characteristic, after their violence, is their ignorance."[108] Besides their ignorance about basic genetics, they also seem ignorant of the fact that a child's identity as a Serb or Bošnjak is not determined by biology at all, but dependent on culture and upbringing. Yet the ignorance itself is revealing of a more fundamental attitude towards women. The policy of genocidal rape, to the extent it depends on forced impregnation rather than simply territorial expulsion, "is possible only because the policy's authors erase all identity characteristics of the mother other than that as a sexual container."[109]

Aleksandra Milićević has described the cultural origins of the effacement of women's role in reproduction. "Traditional Serbian society," she explains, "was patrilocal and patrilineal (that is, property and power belong exclusively to men). Relationships among male kinsmen created formal social structures, and women were seen merely as links between fathers and sons." Even though socialist Yugoslavia attempted to recast gender relations to reflect egalitarian norms, many of the traditional attitudes persisted. The crises and wars of the 1990s brought them to the fore:

Men were seen as born into a family group and their loyalty was certain, especially because their own interests (as heirs and property holders) corresponded

---

[106] Allen, *Rape Warfare*, pp. 60–61.
[107] Dženita Mehić, "We are Dying of Your Protection," *Bulletin of the Atomic Scientists*, 51, 2 (March/April 1995), pp. 41–44.
[108] Allen, *Rape Warfare*, pp. 96–97.   [109] Ibid., p. 87.

to the group's interests. Their main duty was protecting the group against both physical and symbolic attacks. In contrast, women were seen as outsiders, "people who are in the group but not of it," and their loyalties were always in doubt. Women, in general, had to be controlled, since their sexual behavior (if inappropriate) revealed men's vulnerability to external challenges. Only by giving birth to a son (and preferably more than one) could they improve their position and legitimate their status within their husbands' kinship group.[110]

Thus there appeared a strong cultural predisposition for men to treat women as, at best, "empty vessels," and, at worst, potential traitors. Serb ignorance of genetics was hardly a prerequisite for forced impregnation of Bosnian Muslim women.

Moreover, not all of the rapists were ignorant of basic genetics. Some victims report their tormentors' telling them "how much they'd like to see us raise their kids," and singing "a mother raises a baby, he's half a Muslim, half a Serb." When they found out that the women were pregnant they were pleased. Alluding to Alija Izetbegović, the Bosnian Muslim leader, they would say such things as "very good, now Alija will have to provide for a Chetnik." The paradoxical result of such taunts was to make the women reject the genetic reality of their situation. As one of them later explained to Alexandra Stiglmayer, "I knew it wasn't my kid. I knew what I went through. It wasn't a child born of love or from a respectable marriage. If anyone had tried to show it to me after it was born, I'd have strangled them and the baby too … If I'd ever had any chance to kill the kid inside me, I'd have done it." As it turned out, the baby was taken from the mother immediately after the birth, as the doctors considered her suicidal. A British journalist smuggled the baby out of Sarajevo to England. "This kid has nothing to do with me," said the mother. "He can do whatever he wants to with it, it makes no difference to me."[111]

Thanks to the efforts of individuals such as *Newsday* reporter Roy Gutman, who first revealed the widespread evidence of rape in Bosnia, and Stiglmayer, who followed up with extensive interviews, as well as organizations such as Human Rights Watch, the Serb rape campaign was widely publicized as it happened. The publicity led to a curious backlash of sorts. Far from seeing the Bosnian war as a "war against women," some argued that *men* were its primary victims. Adam Jones was perhaps the most outspoken advocate of this view. He adopted the term "gendercide," coined by Mary Ann Warren in a 1985 book, to describe the situation in Bosnia, and he founded the organization Gendercide Watch

---

[110] Milićević, "Joining the War," p. 269.
[111] Stiglmayer, "The Rapes in Bosnia-Herzegovina," pp. 132–133.

in 2000 to "to confront acts of gender-selective mass killing around the world" by "working to raise awareness, conduct research, and produce educational resources on gendercide."[112] Jones summarizes the Bosnian war as follows:

Atrocities were committed by all sides and against all sectors of the population in Bosnia-Herzegovina between 1992 and 1995. But the Serb strategy of gender-selective mass executions of non-combatant men was the most severe and systematic atrocity inflicted throughout. The war in Bosnia can thus be considered both a genocide against Bosnia's Muslim population and a gendercide against Muslim men in particular.[113]

The largest massacre of the war – indeed the largest massacre in Europe since World War II – took place at Srebrenica, when United Nations and Red Cross relief officials allowed Serb militias to separate men from women and children.[114] Dutch "peacekeepers" with UNPROFOR stood by as the Serb soldiers murdered more than seven thousand men. One study cites prevailing "gender norms" as the main reason international relief workers ignored their own principles – that "humanitarian assistance should be provided without distinction" to "all individuals and groups who are suffering, without regard to nationality, political or ideological beliefs, race, religion, sex, or ethnicity" – and instead defined "civilians" to include women and children, but not unarmed men and teenage boys.[115]

Thus, one can agree with Cynthia Cockburn that in Bosnia, the "so-called ethnic war was totally gendered," without inferring that it was a war conducted mainly against women.[116] The Bosnian case reinforces our understanding that gender in warfare is not simply a matter of peaceful women and misogynistic, violent men – although misogyny clearly played a major role in the campaigns of mass rape. Cockburn's analysis also points to the complicated workings of gender (and nationalism) within peace activism as well as war. In the summer of 1991, for example, peace activists protested against the Yugoslav army's intervention in Croatia. Women and mothers of soldiers played a prominent part. As Cockburn points out, to the extent they objected to the launching of a

---

[112] Mary Ann Warren, *Gendercide: The Implications of Sex Selection* (Lanham, MD: Rowman & Littlefield, 1985). The Gendercide Watch website is www.gendercide.org.
[113] "Case Study: Bosnia-Herzegovina," www.gendercide.org/case_bosnia.html.
[114] "Case Study: The Srebrenica Massacre, July 1995," www.gendercide.org/case_srebrenica.html.
[115] R. Charli Carpenter, "'Women and Children First': Gender, Norms, and Humanitarian Evacuation in the Balkans 1991–95," *International Organization*, 57, 4 (October 2003), pp. 661–694.
[116] Cockburn, *The Space between Us*, p. 206.

civil war against fellow Yugoslavs, the protestors constituted a coherent peace movement. But if their main object was to keep their Croatian sons from serving in an army intent on crushing Croatia's independence or their Serb sons from dying on someone else's (Croatian) land, their nationalist sentiments got the better of their pacifism. Once that happened, the gender symbolism of mothers protecting their sons became counterproductive, at least as far as maintaining peace was concerned:

Certainly the presence of mothers against the military seemed usefully to undercut the claims of the leaders to be fighting to defend women and children. But the moral authority of the mothers derived precisely from the nationalists' system of values. It was yet one more denial of selfhood to women. The jingoistic and war-mongering media chose to ignore the presence of some men/ fathers in the demonstrations and hyped up the symbolism of mothers. The women's protests were ideal material for nationalist propaganda justifying the creation of separate republican armies.[117]

Pretty Village, Pretty Flame

At first glance, perhaps literally on first or even second viewing, Srđan Dragojević's *Pretty Village, Pretty Flame* may not seem well suited for an analysis of the gendered dimensions of the Yugoslav wars. First, there are few female characters, and only one – an American journalist – plays any significant part. Even she is a type, not fully developed. The biggest issue implicating gender in the wars – the mass rape campaigns – receives the barest of allusions.

Second is the matter of the film's "magic realism" style – perhaps the most common idiom for great Yugoslav films dating back to the classics of Dušan Makavejev. Indeed the opening frames offer a dedication "to the film industry of a country that no longer exists."[118] The movie's style – incorporating documentary footage, multiple narratives, flash-forwards and flash-backs, and hallucinatory memories and visions – has troubled

---

[117] Ibid., pp. 166–167. Another interesting element of gender and the peace movement concerns the role of gays and lesbians. In December 1990, Belgrade activists founded the group Arkadia, devoted to promoting the rights of lesbians and gay men, but soon came into conflict over nationalism. "When the decision was made to be non-nationalist," the men dropped out and "the group became predominantly lesbian." Donna M. Hughes and Lepa Mladjenović, "Feminist Organizing in Belgrade, Serbia: 1990–1994," *Canadian Women's Studies/Les Cahiers de la Femme*, 16, 1 (1995), pp. 95–97.

[118] Igor Krstić, "Showtime Brothers!" in Andrew James Horton, ed., *The Celluloid Tinderbox: Yugoslav Screen Reflections of a Turbulent Decade* (Telford: Central European Review, 2000), pp. 43–61. For Makavejev's comments on his techniques and Yugoslav film, see Ray Privett, "The Country of Movies: An Interview with Dušan Makavejev," *Senses of Cinema* (December 2000), www.sensesofcinema.com/contents/00/11/makavejev. html.

some critics. It seems to present Yugoslavia "as some great arena of madness." In Andrew James Horton's summary, "the whole idea of 'Balkan madness' has been criticized as presenting an image of Balkan violence as irrational and, therefore, unstoppable and uncontainable by the forces of reason. This depiction, the argument goes, is pro-Milošević in that it advocates violence as an inevitable outcome of the Yugoslav predicament."[119]

Third, and related, *Pretty Village, Pretty Flame* was made by a Belgrade-based director and tells the story of the wars from the perspective of Serbs from Belgrade and from Bosnia. Its point of departure is the life-long friendship of the Serb Milan and the Muslim Halil, both from a small Bosnian village on the River Drina bordering Serbia, and how they end up on opposite sides of the conflict. But we see only Milan's version of the story, and Halil barely makes an appearance after the war begins. The story of a Serb unit trapped in a tunnel is based on an incident that actually happened near Višegrad in autumn 1992. Vanja Bulić wrote an article about it in the magazine *Duga*, and later a book. He is credited as co-scriptwriter. The film uses actual footage of burning villages from the war as its backdrop.[120] A more literal rendering of the title would be "pretty villages burn prettily," a quotation from one of the characters, who adds that ugly villages remain ugly even as they burn.

By the year 2000, already more than 250 feature films and documentaries had been made related to the violent breakup of Yugoslavia.[121] Why choose this one for analysis, especially given the criticisms? In fact, all three of these aspects of the film – the "male dominance," the magic realism, and the Serb perspective – make the film especially appropriate for treating issues of gender, nationalism, and violence in the Bosnian war.

On the first point, we encountered a similar situation in chapter 2 with *The Battle of Algiers*. As Danièle Djamila Amrane-Minne pointed out, there women appeared in less than an eighth of the screen time, usually silent. The director portrayed the torture of male Algerian suspects,

[119] The first quotation is from his "Critical Mush," in Horton, *Celluloid Tinderbox*, p. 38; the second is from his "Vignettes of Violence," in the same collection, p. 112. The criticism has been made of Emir Kusturica's *Underground* as well – a more historically wide-ranging film. See Dina Iordanova, *Cinema of Flames: Balkan Film, Culture and the Media* (Berkeley, CA: University of California Press, 2001), and her *Emir Kusturica* (London: British Film Institute, 2002). See also the discussion in Levi, *Disintegration in Frames*, pp. 101–105.

[120] Mauro Ravarino, "Schermi di guerra: Le guerre jugoslave tra cinema, storia, e società," undergraduate thesis (*tesi di laurea*), University of Turin, Italy, 2005, pp. 83–91. I thank Michele Chiaruzzi for sending me a copy.

[121] Dina Iordanova, "Introduction," in Horton, *Celluloid Tinderbox*, p. 6; For an impressive overview of many of these works, see Ravarino, "Schermi di guerra."

but not the well-documented sexual violence and torture of women.[122] Yet the film still yielded powerful insights into gender and nationalist conflict. A film that does not directly address women or gender is more likely to reveal the taken-for-granted nature of gender relations in a particular society than one that deliberately takes a feminist perspective or addresses issues of concern to women.

Dina Iordanova appears to have had this point in mind when she remarked that "the cinematic world of former Yugoslavia today seems to be almost entirely dominated by men." For her, this confirms "the allegations of the profoundly macho character of Yugoslav culture made by political scientist Sabrina Ramet or feminist Beverly Allen."[123] Presumably that profoundly macho character has something to do with the extent of sexualized violence that prevailed during the war. Indeed, the macho nature of Yugoslav culture is apparent as soon as the characters in Dragojević's film open their mouths – although, for better or worse, much less apparent from the subtitles. The standard English swears are considerably more limited in their possibilities for conveying the vulgarity, and especially the sexism and misogyny, of the Serbo-Croatian variants. The phenomenon has attracted linguists who attended a conference in Novi Sad, Vojvodina in 1998 to discuss it. The conference was held to mark (and mock) the jubilee of the prediction made by the Hungarian-born Vojvodinian feminist and philologist Olga (Borsy) Penavin in 1973 that "the development of Socialism would lead to a society free of conflict, where there would be no reason for swearing."[124]

One thing apparent from surveying the list of common Serbian swears is that a remarkably high number of them express violence against women, particularly mothers.[125] It shares this feature with the Russian language, where the word mother (*mat'*) itself is used as a synonym for swearing. Characters in *Pretty Village, Pretty Flame* are constantly using expressions such as *pička ti materina* and *pizda ti materina*, variants on "(fuck) your mother's cunt" – even in the presence of their own mothers.

---

[122] Danièle Djamila Amrane-Minne, "Women at War: The Representation of Women in *The Battle of Algiers*," trans. by Alistair Clarke, *Interventions*, 9, 3 (2007), p. 342.

[123] Iordanova, "Introduction," in Horton, ed., *Celluloid Tinderbox*, p. 13. An exception would be the 2006 film *Grbavica* by Jasmila Žbanić, a work that directly addresses the issue of wartime rape and its postwar consequences.

[124] Bernard Nežmah, "Fuck this Article: The Yugoslav Lexicon of Swear Words," *Central Europe Review*, 2, 41 (November 27, 2000), translated from *Mladina* (Slovenia), www.ce-review.org/00/41/nezmah41.html.

[125] The "Insultmonger" website, accessed on August 8, 2006, listed 142 swears on its site for Serbian, www.insultmonger.com/swearing/serbian.htm, and 199 on its site for Bosnian, www.insultmonger.com/swearing/bosnian.htm. (Beware, the sites also include pornographic advertisements.)

The subtitles usually render these as "fuck you" or very often skip them altogether. Of course, subtitles in most films miss nuances of the original language, and swears are particularly difficult to convey and are often peculiar to a given culture. But, as we see in the chapter on Québec, what is missing in the translations of Québécois swears into ordinary English ones is a preoccupation with the Catholic liturgy and items in the ritual of the mass. Not every culture's swears evoke misogynistic, sexualized violence. If native English speakers were able to view literal translations of the dialogue in *Pretty Village, Pretty Flame*, they would gain an impression of a male-dominated culture preoccupied with sexual violence and incest. In other words they would recognize Yugoslavia as seen through the eyes of the clients of Belgrade's SOS Hotline or the inmates of the rape camps of Doboj or Foča.

Concerning the second point, about the film's style, European critics, in particular, have denounced the magic realism and surrealism of this and other Yugoslav films about the wars as "fascist." As Halligan explains, "the tempered and informed dissection of the origins and effects of nationalism" that the critics evidently desired "was continually frustrated by the use of an anarchic aesthetic of chaos."[126] Yet there is nothing about magic realism per se that leads to nihilism or moral relativism when it comes to political judgments about such issues as responsibility for the wars. The fantastic element of the film does not negate, but rather heightens the antiwar message. As Igor Krstić points out, "Dragojević seems to consider the Bosnian war from the Serb perspective as a re-enactment of war fantasies, drawn from the rich metaphorical vocabulary of Partisan and Vietnam films."[127] In this respect, the Bosnian war resembles the Russian wars in Chechnya, with Chechen fighters acting out fantasies of "Che Guevaras in turbans," as Georgi Derluguian put it, and Sylvester Stallone's *Rambo* inspiring soldiers on both sides.[128] A director who wanted to support one side's justification for launching a war would hardly choose to portray its soldiers as acting out movie fantasies. Horton, who called attention to the criticisms of Dragojević's style, ultimately rejects them, finding the movie "a blackly humorous and ironic depiction of war which ultimately shows the futility and idiocy of inter-ethnic hatred" – the factor promoted by Milošević as *casus belli*.[129]

Concerning the third point, the exclusive focus on the Serb perspective, in fact it makes more sense to speak of multiple Serb *perspectives*.

[126] Benjamin Halligan, "An Aesthetic of Chaos," in Horton, *Celluloid Tinderbox*, p. 86.
[127] Krstić, "Showtime Brothers!" p. 60.
[128] Georgi Derluguian, "Che Guevaras in Turbans," *New Left Review*, 237 (September– October 1999).
[129] Horton, "Vignettes of Violence," p. 106.

The movie tells the story of seven surviving members of a Serb military unit, trapped by Muslim fighters in a tunnel. The intensity of the conflicts that develop among them, combined with the flash-backs depicting their strongly divergent backgrounds and values, undermines the key premise of Milošević's wars: that they were fought to defend a common Serb identity and heritage. The film instead shows a war fought by supposed representatives of the Serbian *narod* who actually had less in common among themselves than did the members of the multiethnic community of Serbs, Croats, and Muslims they were trying to destroy. According to Mauro Ravarino, who has surveyed most of the films on the violent breakup of Yugoslavia, *Pretty Village, Pretty Flame* is anything but fascist or one-sidedly pro-Serb. Instead, it is "one of the key films for understanding the Yugoslav wars: a troubling and complex work that goes beyond the stereotypical readings of the conflict and doesn't accept compromises of any sort."[130]

The film begins wth a faux-documentary newsreel from 1971 on the dedication of the Tunnel of Brotherhood and Unity (*Tunel Bratsvo i Jedinstvo*), intended for a future highway connecting Belgrade and Zagreb. "Who says that the forces of nature can't be made to work for man?" intones the announcer. A crowd has been assembled, with workers and local residents, visiting dignitaries, a troupe of dancers in traditional costumes, a lively band, and groups of children in their Young Pioneer outfits. The film fades from black and white into color as the camera follows a young girl with a red scarf and a cushion on which rest the scissors intended to cut the red ribbon stretched across the mouth of the tunnel. As the color comes in, so does the intensity of the sound, with exaggerated noises heard on the soundtrack over the background music and murmurs of the crowd: a welcoming slap on the back of the girl's neck from the VIP poised to cut the ribbon, the steel swish of the blades as he tries them out right in front of her nose. Then a surreal and ominous mishap: the VIP, as he cuts the ribbon, slices into his own thumb. Blood spurts everywhere, including on to the little girl's face. The local official hosting the event covers the VIP's thumb with a handkerchief and frantically gestures for the band to continue playing. They strike up a frenetic tune and everyone dances wildly, including the VIP, who seems to have forgotten his injury completey.

From there the film jumps forward nine years to introduce Milan and Halil as boys about ten years old: blond, short-haired, and hardly distinguishable by their physical features – as Bosnians do not differ from each other physiologically by ethnic group, whether they are Serbs, Croats, or

---

[130] Ravarino, "Schermi di guerra," p. 17.

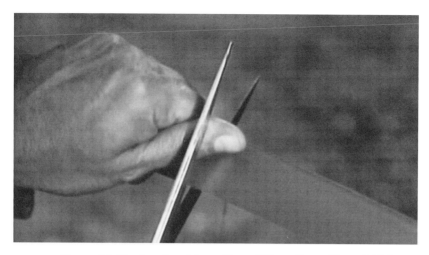

Figure 3.1 Cutting the ribbon. *Pretty Village, Pretty Flame* (1996)

Muslims. They stand in front of the tunnel, now deserted, the highway never having been completed. Local legend has it that an ogre inhabits the tunnel. If disturbed, Halil says, the ogre who lives in it will eat up the village and set all the houses on fire. For Dragan Bjelogrlić, who plays the adult Milan and also co-produced the film, "the ogre stands for the fear of difference, which the people of Bosnia never have been able to accept ... The ideologies of Communism, Brotherhood and Unity have tried to hide this ogre and lock him into a cave."[131] Another plausible reading, for those who know Suny's characterization of the literature on nationalism, is that the ogre represents the "long-repressed primordial national consciousnesses" ready to erupt if awakened. Better to let "Sleeping Beauty" stay asleep.[132]

Whether the ogre is the fear of difference, as Bjelogrlić suggests, or the fear that waking Sleeping Beauty will produce something very ugly, Milan and Halil propose to confront that fear with violence. One says he'll go and get his grandmother's knife. The other says he'll get his grandmother's gun. "We'll come back when we're better armed." Why do the weapons belong to their grandmothers rather than their grandfathers?

Noise from the tunnel, perhaps old equipment rattling in the wind, turns into the sound of rotor blades, as the credits role, and then the scene flashes forward to 1994. Wounded soldiers are being unloaded from a helicopter into a military hospital. Then the scene jumps back two

---

[131] Quoted in Krstić, "Showtime Brothers!" p. 59.
[132] Suny, *Revenge of the Past*, p. 3.

years to the spring of 1992, on the eve of war. Milan and Halil are playing basketball on a makeshift court next to a roadside tavern. Again, as with most of the cuts, the sound (in this case the ball hitting the backboard) precedes the visual, creating a sense of expectation and uneasiness in the viewer. The action on the court depicts a relationship characterized by affection, competition, friendly insults, physicality, and sometimes sudden bursts of anger. Throughout the movie multiple flash-backs to various incidents during their childhood and adulthood all portray these elements. When Milan and Halil get into arguments or physical conflicts, neither one is willing to back down.

This scene introduces another important character who is not one of the soldiers, but who plays a key role in the coming conflict. He is Sloba, the barkeeper – not coincidentally the nickname of Slobodan Milošević. As the two friends share a bottle of *rakija*, Sloba sits reading a Belgrade newspaper, and comments on the reports of interethnic violence. The headline reads "Barricades in Sarajevo." Halil asks. "Why don't you read our paper?" according to the subtitles. In fact he mentions specifically *Oslobodenje* (*Liberation*), the Sarajevo newspaper that managed to maintain its independence throughout the war. Sloba complains that it's too big, "like a sheet." Halil says he can spread it on the ground, kneel, and read. His expression just hints at a certain ill-feeling towards the barkeeper. "Right, it's good for Muslim prayers," cracks Sloba. This first utterance of a mild ethnic slur will turn into a torrent of far harsher ones as the movie progresses.

As Milan and Halil sit getting drunk and wondering aloud whether there will be a war, their Muslim neighbor Nazim drives up with his tiny car loaded with household goods, and a portrait of Tito strapped to its roof. He and his wife are taking the stuff to his brother-in-law in Tuzla. He insists that they are not moving, that they will be back soon, but he asks Sloba if he'll look after their house while they are gone and tries to give him the keys. "I feel uncomfortable," replies Sloba. "Something might happen." Nazim insists on handing him the keys and then moves to give him a farewell embrace. Sloba backs away. Milan, getting increasingly drunk and frustrated, slams his hand on the table, drawing blood. A quick cut forward to 1994 shows a seriously wounded Milan in a hospital bed in Belgrade, with his legs in casts, clutching a self-dispensing container of morphine. A crazy young male patient hobbles around on crutches and sings patriotic songs about past Serbian battles ("in 1913, the Bulgars attacked, the Serbs beat them back"). A male orderly, talking on the phone to his girlfriend, tries to get him to shut up. In the background we hear him telling her, "I'm gonna ram it to you, break you in two."

Figure 3.2 "Will there be a war?" *Pretty Village, Pretty Flame* (1996)

Now several of the key elements of the story are in place. The friends retain their close relationship but feel the strain of the tensions emanating from Belgrade and the viewer soon learns how things will turn out – at least for Milan. Sloba, the recipient and propagator of the nationalist fear-mongering, is also the first to introduce elements of ethnic conflict within the local community. His unwillingness to promise to look after Nazim's house foreshadows his future role as a prime organizer of the looting of local Muslim property, a role that he expands into a major career through contacts in the Serbian capital. During a later scene of burning houses and wild looting, we hear his voice saying, "I need a warehouse in Belgrade."

The next scene, flashing forward a short time, finds the village in flames. Milan is armed and in uniform, with the members of his military unit. They are inside the ransacked apartment of someone named Ćamil (as we learn when a woman calls on the telephone frantically looking for him). We see most of the soldiers who end up later following Milan into the tunnel to escape an attack. At this point, they wander around the apartment aimlessly, seeming not to understand the purpose of their mission there. Throughout the rest of the film we learn more about each soldier – his background, his political views, how he came to join the war – through fragmented flash-backs in parallel narratives, often getting to learn key elements of the story just after the character has died.

About Milan himself we learn that he is a mechanic and that he set up a car repair shop with his friend Halil. A flash-back shows us Halil's (Muslim) mother serving the young men brandy (*rakija*) to inaugurate their new garage. They drive into town to celebrate, the car radio blaring "All Yugoslavia Dances to Rock 'n' Roll" (*Igra rokenrol cela Jugoslavija*) by the Belgrade band Električni orgazam (one member of which, Zoran "Švaba" Radomirović, makes a cameo appearance in the film as a friend of Speedy who visits him in the hospital). Rock music was one of the most cosmopolitan, "internationalist" elements of Yugoslav culture and many musicians opposed the rise of nationalism and the wars. The Milošević regime tried to destroy the rock music scene and promote the genre known as "turbo-folk" as an alternative. One of the regime's favored singers, Svetlana Ražnatović (née Veličković), known as Ceca, became the bride of the notorious killer Arkan.[133] The soundtrack here seems to convey a sense of nostalgia for the old Yugoslavia, as the two friends drive off singing, to celebrate the opening of their new garage. Ominously, the camera tracks the car looking out from the tunnel. The car swerves off the road, becomes bogged down in mud, and the friendly excursion turns into a fight. Flashing forward to the war, the anthemic song continues to provide the soundtrack as a wild bunch of Serb fighters set Halil's house and the friends' garage on fire as they rove through the village on tractors and in trucks, looting all the Muslim homes and businesses.

In one of many clever montages, we see Milan and Halil posing in front of their new garage. Sloba notices that the sign hangs crookedly, as Nazim focuses the camera. Halil says, "Fuck the art, just pull the trigger." Cut forward to the looters at the same place. Milan, armed with a machine gun, starts firing at them, wounding several. He spots Sloba there, points the gun at him, and tells him to scram. "Where?" Sloba asks. "This is all mine and yours now." Then he asks suspiciously, "Did that bum Halil send you to guard his house?"

Milan had visited his mother earlier, apparently already having joined the militia, to tell her to go to Sloba if she needs anything. "No! I won't," she replies, suspecting Sloba's motives long before Milan does. As they talk, a motley group of Serb fighters drive up on a tractor and ask Milan's mother whether it is true that there is "a dangerous Muslim stronghold around here." She adamantly denies the ridiculous idea. They are drunk and singing. Milan stares at them, as the tractor drives across the field. He later comes back to his mother's house and finds it empty. He goes to Sloba's tavern, bustling with activity, and asked what happened. Sloba tells him that a group of Muslims had attacked the night before. "The bastards swam across the river, went through the village like wild fire." Two of them were caught, he claims. "They said they were from Halil's

---

[133] On the role and fate of rock music in former Yugoslavia, see Gordy, *Culture of Power*, ch. 4.

Figure 3.3 "Fuck the art, just pull the trigger." *Pretty Village, Pretty Flame* (1996)

detachment ... while they could still talk." Sloba implies that Halil was responsible for killing Milan's mother. "So you just think about guarding his house again," he warns. Milan takes his gun and starts smashing things in Sloba's store. "I should have killed you back then," he says. Part of him clearly doesn't trust Sloba's story, but he nevertheless imagines the worst. He goes to the cemetery with a shovel to search for his mother's grave, but freezes before he begins to dig – his hallucinogenic vision of a bloody knife and his terrified mother comes on the screen, highly stylized, as in a horror movie, in a way to make the viewer doubt that it had happened that way. The screen cuts to the battlefield, where Milan and his fellow soldiers come under fire, and, at his suggestion, seek shelter in the tunnel of the ogre. It is the first time he has ever dared enter it.

Each member of Milan's unit represents a certain type in Serbian society – but eventually we learn something about each of them that challenges our expectations. Milan himself is probably the archetypal Bosnian Serb from a peaceful mixed community, the sort of person who would respond to the surveys Gagnon cites by favoring high levels of peaceful coexistence and attachment to a Yugoslav identity. Gvozden Maksimović, the unit's commander, is a captain in the Yugoslav army. His name means "steely" or "ferrous," the same as *Stalin* in Russian. The actor who plays him, Velimir Bata Živojinović, is immediately recognizable by Yugoslav audiences for his portrayals of partisans in some

hundred films.[134] Gvozden is clearly still attached to the Yugoslav internationalist ideal and seems to think he is fighting to restore it, rather
than destroy it. He becomes sentimental when he hears the old partisan
songs or the hymns that children sang to Brotherhood and Unity. He
reminisces fondly of marching 350 kilometers on foot to Tito's funeral,
an event captured in ersatz newsreel footage and shown in flash-back.

Different from both of these characters in his attitude towards Yugoslav
identity or really any ideal is Velja. He has spent a fair amount of time
in Germany, leading a life of crime, from pick-pocketing to auto theft to
smuggling. As we learn later, he only recently returned to Belgrade from
abroad and he evinces little understanding of or appreciation for the
traditional ethnic tolerance of Bosnia-Herzegovina. He is also particularly violent in his language and behavior, including towards women –
suggesting that such traits are hardly limited to those who grow up their
whole lives in Yugoslavia. Velja represents an external force of the sort
that Gagnon describes when he writes of the outside elements that provoked conflict in Bosnia. Indeed, the International Criminal Tribunal
for the former Yugoslavia has indicted people like him who returned to
Yugoslavia only in 1992 to help tear the country apart.[135]

Two members of the unit are portrayed as stereotypes of ignorant
Chetniks, Serbian nationalists from the countryside. Their story unfolds
in flash-backs. In one scene the camera zooms in from behind the backs
of a group of villagers seated around a television set out in a field. The
TV is broadcasting the standard nationalist propaganda that accompanied the onset of the war: "Raging hordes of evil have risen up against
the entire Serbian people – Croatian communists, foreign mercenaries,
fanatics of Allah's *Jihad*. Just as they did 50 years ago, they are attacking the poorly armed Serbian defenders who are heroically holding their
own in this unfair battle." A middle-aged man named Laza spits in dis-
gust, stands up, kisses his young, blond wife on the cheek, and strides off
across the field towards the road, where a truck stops to pick him up. He
has decided to join the valiant Serb defenders.

His younger brother-in-law feeds his little daughter as she sits in her
high chair. He interrupts the feeding, lifting up her baby fork, and looks

---

[134] Krstić, "Showtime Brothers!" p. 47.
[135] Consider, for example, Milan Lukić, born fifteen kilometers north of Višegrad in 1967,
returned there in 1992 after having lived in Germany, Switzerland, and Obrenovac,
Serbia. On his return he organized a local paramilitary group sometimes called the
"White Eagles," with ties to the Višegrad police and Serb military units. He was
indicted, along with his brother and cousin, for war crimes and crimes against humanity, including the murder of many Muslims. See International Criminal Tribunal for the
Former Yugoslavia, case against Milan Lukić, Sredoje Lukić, Mitar Vasiljević, Case No.
IT-98–32-PT, www.un.org/icty/indictment/english/vas-ai010712e.htm.

up at Laza in amazement. As the TV announcer warns of the dangers facing Serbian children from the "new world order," he absent-mindedly puts the fork in his own mouth. This is Viljuška, "the Fork." He earns his nickname when he joins Laza on the front, keeping the little fork with him as a talisman. At one point later, Liza Linell, an American television reporter trapped with the Serb soldiers in the tunnel, videotapes him. He launches a diatribe on the glories of the Serb nation: "I recently saw on TV...the Serbs are the oldest nation. When the Krauts, English, and Americans 600 years ago were eating pork with their hands, we had this." He whips out his baby daughter's fork. "At the Serbian court, we ate with forks!" Overcome with emotion, he looks confused, then throws the fork on to the floor of the cave. Another member of the unit, the bespectacled "Professor," picks it up and says, "It's this fork that drove us into here, into this cave."

Petar, the "Professor," is from Banja Luka, the de facto capital of the self-styled Republika Srpska and, according to the 1991 census, a (bare) majority Serb-populated municipality. He is fond of reading poetry and prose about burning villages. For Srđan Dragojević and his audience, the Professor could be a stand-in for the members of the Serbian Academy of Sciences and Arts who put grandiose ideas about forks and genocide into gullible Chetnik heads.

The character Fork himself seems a caricature of a Chetnik – huge build, long hair, beard. His name comes from his insistence on Serbian cultural superiority, yet he himself appears an uncultured oaf. But he is less a caricature than a real-life type. Claims that Serbs invented the fork were apparently so widespread during the Yugoslav wars that journalist Peter Maass was relieved when he interviewed a Serb paramilitary leader named Dragan *not* to hear them: "He did not give me history lessons, which is what most Serbs do when they talk about their country. Dragan did not try to convince me of the historical glories of Serbia, that Serbs were eating with forks and knives before the British, or that a Serb invented the spoon, or that Serbs are defending Christian civilization from the infidel Turks."[136]

As Fork watches his brother-in-law leave, the camera moves to focus on Laza sitting in the truck that picked him up, observed from the perspective of the still unseen driver. Laza is agitated and explains his decision to join the army. "I said 'no more!' They commit genocide on the whole Serbian people and I sit by calmly. No more, buddy! Not another Kraut or Turk soldier will set foot here. No more!" The camera cuts to the driver, seen from Laza's perspective. He is olive-skinned and

[136] Maass, *Love Thy Neighbor*, p. 225.

bearded, and has a medallion representing the star and crescent of the Turkish flag hanging in his cab window. "*Ja, ja,*" he replies gamely in broken German, smiling. Laza becomes dimly aware that the driver is foreign. "How is it up there in Sweden? Cold, eh? But what a standard of living!" The sound of Middle Eastern music becomes increasingly audible and then blares as if from the radio as they drive along the highway.

Perhaps the most sympathetic character among the Serb soldiers is the English-speaking drug addict nicknamed *Brzi* or "Speedy." He arrives on the scene suddenly, when his comrades-in-arms are caught in the tunnel, by driving an old truck straight through the bombs and machine-gun fire to join them. He has brought a female doctor, but has remembered her too late. She was sitting on the passenger side of the truck, got shot during the drive into the cave, and was dead by the time he checked her. He also had another female passenger – a stowaway, the American reporter, Liza. Unlike the male characters, we learn nothing of her background or character. She remains two-dimensional, starting off as hostile, angry, and suspicious, but later becoming affectionate, caring, and even seductive. When she is discovered, Liza immediately becomes the focus of the men's rage and the pretext for a contest of sexual one-upmanship among them.

They discover that she is traveling on a visa issued by the Bosnian (Muslim-majority) government and launch into a series of threats and intimidating remarks.

GVOZDEN: "Milk her for information."
LAZA: "She's skinny. I say we slaughter her. She'll say we did it anyway."
     Velja, the thief, takes her camera bag.
LIZA: "Hey, give that back to me!"
     He knocks her to the ground.
MILAN: "What are you doing?" demands Milan.
VELJA: "Beating her. She's resisting a routine inspection." Fork nods in agreement.
MILAN: "Is that how you treat women?"
VELJA: "Only foreigners. Have you ever screwed anyone outside your village?"
MILAN: "Fuck you."
VELJA: "How they love spanking!"
     Liza gets up to leave, apparently not realizing that the tunnel is surrounded by Muslim forces.
VELJA: "Let the whore go. Anyway, if she stays with us, boys ... " He asks Laza to remind him of the expression. " ... we'll fill her with tadpoles."
     Velja crosses himself. Fork makes kissing noises. Sudden shooting and explosions come from the opening of the cave.
SPEEDY to Liza, in English: "Get down, you'll get shot."
LIZA: "Oh, yes, I'm fully aware of the Serbian concern for women in this war."

She dashes towards the tunnel entrance, provoking a firefight between the Serbs inside and the Muslims outside. Velja runs up to rescue her and throws her over his shoulder, but she assumes he is attacking her and resists, slapping him in the face. He knocks her down and the others lift her and tie her up.

Fork and Laza seem fascinated by her freckles and unfazed by the violent scene that just unfolded.

FORK asks Laza: "Do you think she has freckles all over her body?"
VELJA: "What are you staring at? She's not for you. She's cultured."
LAZA: "It's nicer with culture."
MILAN: "How about some respect?"

They find a plastic liter Coke bottle with some water in it and pass it around. Milan helps Liza sip some. Velja angrily grabs the bottle from them and in the confusion doesn't notice that someone has thrown a grenade into the cave. He is wounded and Liza offers to help. She has a first-aid kit in her bag.

VELJA: "If she comes near me, I'll strangle her."
SPEEDY: "If she goes for your cock, should I let her?"
LAZA: "Slaughter the bitch."

Then someone remarks, "Journalists are to blame for this mess" – a view that many survivors of the Yugoslav wars would endorse, but probably not with US reporters in mind.

Later the Coke bottle provides the opportunity for a bizarre bonding moment, as the lack of water makes the cave-mates increasingly desperate. Milan urinates into the bottle and passes it around to his thirsty companions, who try it with varying degrees of reluctance. Velja offers it to Liza, who initially resists and then finally tries it. Velja, the brute who grabbed the bottle rudely away from her when it contained water, now reassures her, in German, that it's sugar-free (*ohne Zucker*), then catches himself and does the best he can in English: "Excuse me...diet Coke." She laughs, holds her nose, and takes a sip. Everyone laughs. "She loves it, let's export it!" Velja raises his hand for a "high five" sign, and tells her "Now you're one of us." For him, that seems to mean: you hate the people we hate. He immediately hands her his gun, urging her to shoot, "boom-boom," and pointing towards the cave entrance, because a Muslim might be out there somewhere. He uses the epithet, *Balija*.

The Muslims outside wonder what the commotion is about inside. They provide an opportunity for the viewer to see the prevalence of misogynistic language that both sides share in their common male culture. Even the most educated (Petar, the Professor) or gentle (Speedy) partake.

"Where'd you get the water?" someone outside asks. The Professor shouts back that it came from a "mobile fountain...what I used to refresh your old lady with." The others congratulate him on this sophisticated version of the standard crude insult. "Well, Chetniks, you'll soon be eating shit," replies one of the Muslims.

Then Speedy pipes up. "We didn't come here to insult each other," he yells. The Muslims laugh uproariously. Speedy then tells a joke: "A Muslim girl is taking a monkey for a walk in Sarajevo. People asked her where she got it. 'From a member of UNPROFOR,' she answers. 'Well, why didn't you get an abortion?' they ask." Thus Speedy manages simultaneously to insult Muslim women (as whores who would have sex with foreign soldiers), UNPROFOR as an organization, and the African soldiers who served in it (some of whom appeared in an earlier scene). All the men laugh, inside and outside, and so does the American woman, who doesn't understand a word.

Speedy says, "Thank you, you're a wonderful audience," at which point Muslim fighters appear in the tunnel entrance and open fire. The Serbs return fire, hitting some of them. Speedy complains, "You killed my audience."

Relations between the two sides inside the cave – Serb men and American woman – gradually improve. Liza wants to film the autobiographies of the cave captives. Finally, we learn Speedy's story from flashbacks but also from his own telling.

The first flash-back is to an amusement park, 1992. A man appears, dressed in a children's-style cowboy suit, with a double holster and six-guns. He seems drunk or on drugs. Speedy is asking him for a fix, and promises to pay him tomorrow.

"All good kids are in bed asleep," the cowboy says, as the camera shows two young women, from the waist down only, stepping away from one of the rides and passing between the two men. The camera shows a mini-skirt with bare legs and a pair of cut-off shorts with bare legs. "I'm going to tuck these two in," vows the cowboy.

When Speedy pleads for his fix, the cowboy responds, echoing the call of the army recruiters: "Be a man!"

Cut to the hospital room in Belgrade, two years later, where Speedy seems unconscious, as he gives himself an overdose of morphine with the self-dispensing apparatus. Milan and the Professor look on in horror and shout for the nurse. She takes her time coming out of the nurse's station, fixing her hair, and walking in the opposite direction.

We learn later than Speedy became addicted to heroin while serving in the army in 1989, the year of *la dolce vita*, he says. Back in the tunnel, Liza proposes to film their story. Several, including Milan, say no. Velja says, "Let her. Anyway, they shit on us like we came from Hitler's testicles." Captain Gvozden worries that after filming "they put words in your mouth. What's it called?" He remembers: "Editing [*montaža*]. They can make us look real bad, sully us to hell."

Here director Dragojević inserts a double commentary: the Serbian TV approach to generating support for the wars in Croatia and Bosnia entailed doctoring films of Serb-perpetrated atrocities to make them look as if they were done by the other side. So footage of Bosnian Muslims and Croats being raped and abused by Serbian forces was dubbed and edited to appear that Serbs were the victims and the Muslims and Croats the perpetrators.[137] The second commentary is, of course, the self-referential joke: montage is one of the most effective techniques employed by the director in this movie. How could his character even temporarily forget the word?

Speedy ignores Gvozden's objections to Liza's filming, which she couldn't understand anyhow, and tells her in English, "Go ahead, you can do it. *Just do it*." He grins at his quotation of the Nike slogan. He volunteers to start and asks Liza what he should do, as she focuses the camera on him. Introduce yourself, she says. He begins, in English: "Please allow me to introduce myself. I'm a man of wealth and fame." Petar, the Professor, recognizing the Rolling Stones song, smiles and contributes a "whoo, whoo." Liza, behind the camera, smiles as well and joins in with her own "whoo, whoo." This is the first moment in their desperate situation of captivity when these people have managed to share a light moment and a smile – thanks to the song called "Sympathy for the Devil."

When Speedy continues his actual autobiography, he provokes a round of conflict among the Serb soldiers. He describes himself, sardonically, as "an unreformed drug addict, currently getting anti-drug war group therapy." He mentions that his father was a colonel in the Yugoslav army – Gvozden's ears prick up – and "a lush."

A verbal free-for-all erupts, as the differences between these men, who are all supposed to represent the Serbian nation, burst into the open. The captain accuses Velja of stealing from old ladies in Germany, taking advantage of people who earned their money honestly. Velja accuses him

---

[137] This practice has made it difficult for the Serbian side to gain credibility when it makes charges of atrocities committed by Muslims and Croats, especially when the purported evidence is broadcast on television before it is presented to courts. Consider, for example, the charges against Muslim and Croat commanders during Operation Storm, which expelled thousands of Serbs from their homes in the Krajina in July 1995: "Bosnian Serb Leader Files Charges against Muslim Commander," *Radio Free Europe/Radio Liberty Daily Report*, 10, 147, part 2 (August 11, 2006).

in turn of waging wars for the sake of rank, a criticism that Virginia Woolf would have endorsed. He then launches a torrent of sexualized abuse:

Do you think that one single house we burned – or ours that they burned – was honestly earned? If they were honestly earned, they wouldn't be so easy to burn. As long as Tito stuffed American dollars up your ass you did pretty well blathering about "Brotherhood and Unity." And then the time came to settle the bill! You jerked off for fifty years, drove fancy cars, screwed the best girls, and now you can't get it up … Well, I shit on that honor of yours and your whole honorable generation!

Gvozden, who is still holding the walkie-talkie, replies (according to the subtitles), "I'll shove this down your throat." What he actually says is "I'll fuck your mother." It probably makes a difference.

Gvozden is frustrated that he hasn't managed to contact his comrades to arrange a rescue. When he thinks he is getting through to them, he reaches the Muslims outside instead. At one point he has Ćamil on the line, a man of the same name as the one whose apartment the Serb unit looted. "We're in the neighborhood," Ćamil announces. Then, mocking the traditional Bosnian hospitality, he asks, "How about some coffee?" His real feelings of revenge come out in a threat: "We'll impregnate your mothers."

Finally the voice of Šumadinac comes over the walkie-talkie. Liza asks Speedy what's going on. He explains, "It's our *boys*. I mean, *our* boys." His English is good enough that he seems to have realized that the initial stress might have implied that it was "our boys" rather than "our girls." He corrects himself. It is *our* boys, rather than *their* boys. This war is strictly a boys' affair.

Šumadinac tells Gvozden that he can't send anyone to rescue them at this point. Gvozden replies, according to the subtitles, "What a unique slime you are." But his actual words in Serbian convey a threat of sexual violation of Šumadinac's mother. Again, the difference seems relevant.

The tunnel scenes represent not only the disintegration of Serb unity under pressure and the sexualized violence that remains so close to the surface. They also provide an opportunity for commentary on Muslim–Serb relations, where the same themes emerge. The Muslim soldiers in this film are even more stereotyped than the Serbs. We never see them. They are disembodied voices outside the tunnel or shadow figures moving past the entrance, guns ablaze. They are portrayed as sadists, engaging in activities that most observers have associated more with the Serbian side in the war, and secondarily with the Croats.

To some degree, the decision not to portray the Muslims was probably more an artistic choice than a political one. Krstić points out the extent to which *Pretty Village, Pretty Flame* draws on key Hollywood Westerns and films of the Vietnam war. This film resembles Stanley Kubrick's *Full Metal Jacket* (1987) and Francis Ford Coppola's *Apocalypse Now* as they keep the enemy "out there" in the jungle: most of the conflict takes place between characters on the same side. There are quite a number of direct references to those films as well. The Serbs burn villages to the sound of rock music, as in *Apocalypse Now*. The Muslims' wake-up call to the Serbs inside the cave – "Good morning, Chetniks!" – mimics Robin Williams playing Adrian Cronauer in Barry Levinson's *Good Morning, Vietnam!* (1987). Both the Bosnian Muslim characters and the director pay homage to the film, which came out five years before the outbreak of the Yugoslav wars. The gradual realization that there are former friends and relatives – not just Milan's friend Halil – among the besieging Muslim forces recalls Sam Peckinpah's *The Wild Bunch* (1969), where the gang pursuing the outlaws contains some of their former accomplices.[138] Finally, the gunplay that characterized the Serbs' use of weapons copies the idiom of American Westerns quite self-consciously.

At one point early on, the Muslims use their radio connection to broadcast the screams of Marko, "formerly yours, now ours," being tortured. "Bakir's a slow-hand circumciser," they announce. The reaction in the cave is immediate. Milan turns his anger on Liza: "Go over to their side now. Go!" He seems to want to punish her for his own impotence in the situation. She should pay for his humiliated masculinity. It is probably the same sentiment that motivated the Belgrade wife-beaters, reported on the SOS Hotline, as the wars in Croatia and Bosnia began. Laza, by contrast, directs his anger towards their enemies – "I'm going to fuck the living daylights out of them" – and makes a suicidal charge towards the cave entrance. Now it's Liza's turn to express her anger and frustration, and she does the best she can with the limited repertoire of English swears. Milan insists that she film the dying Laza. "It's not my fault you're killing each other. I'm just doing my goddamned job." She gets ready to film. "Fuck it, fuck it, fuck it! It's just a goddamned bad dream."

The film cuts to a peace demonstration outside the Belgrade hospital in 1994. We learn that the director intends to spare no one in this film. The demonstrators look rather well-to-do, mostly middle-aged, and many dressed in furs. They appear faintly ridiculous. The female nurses are watching from inside the room where Milan and Petar are staying. "They're cute," one remarks to another, pointing to "the chubby one in the fur coat." "Love and tolerance," he intones, through a bull horn,

---

[138] Krstić, "Showtime Brothers!"

as another protestor grabs it from his hand. Then they begin to sing, in English, "All we are saying, is give peace a chance." Inside the hospital the crazy patient continues his song about historic Serb battles. He is now up to 1941 and sings the words to the tune of John Lennon's song.

As with much else in the film, the hospital scenes serve to destabilize the image of Serbian nationalism – and masculinity. Milan and the Professor are both gravely wounded, but Milan – now a convinced anti-Muslim – seems determined to continue the fight when a Muslim prisoner of war is brought into the ward. The Professor seeks to dissuade him: "Let's retreat, Milan ... like men." The doctor in charge of the ward tries to explain why his Bosnian Serb patients are causing so much trouble: "It's a matter of cultural difference. You're both in a foreign country." Thus, Dragojević undermines two key premises of the war – the allegedly irreconcilable nature of ethnic differences within Bosnia and the Serbian nationalist sentiment that is supposed to justify the army's intervention to protect brother Serbs. The female Belgrade nurses also offer little support for the nationalist cause, nor do they fit the image of the true Serbian woman – producing sons to defend the nation. In one scene, a nurse announces with relief that she has finally had her period – she is not pregnant after all. They sing the popular song "Jugoslovenka," with its chorus embracing a Yugoslav, rather than a Serb identity.

Back in the tunnel (two years earlier), Dragojević provides the viewers another reminder of the contrast between the recent multi-ethnic past and the divided future. From outside the tunnel the Serb unit receives an offer of protection in return for surrender, as a voice announces, "I, Captain Muslimović, guarantee your lives." Gvozden seems to know Muslimović and calls back, reminding him that "we were in the barracks together." This is "Sergeant Maksimović, now captain...remember?" Muslimović taunts him, echoing precisely Velja's criticism: "How many burned villages will get you another stripe?" "You deserter cunt!" shouts Gvozden. Muslimović stands in the opening of the tunnel, firing his machine gun in Gvozden's direction. "You betrayed me!" he shouts. "Who is that?" Milan asks Gvozden. "My brother-in-law," he replies.

The Serbian word for brother-in-law is *kum*. That is the relationship between Fork and Laza. Fork is married to Laza's sister. *Kum* also can mean godfather, best man, or witness at a wedding. Its origins date back to the time when Christians in Serbia were persecuted, and written baptismal records could not be kept. Ethnologist Ivan Kovačević explains the significance of the institution of godfather: "It was an important and lasting channel of social links, sometimes stronger than family relations [which] could not be imperiled by quarrels over inheritance, land and other transactions. It is an institutionalized form of friendship, help and security."[139] There was a sexual taboo around godparents, who were not allowed to marry or have sexual relations with their godchildren. Thus, according to Serb tradition, the rape reported to SOS Hotline of a refugee woman by her godfather was a double violation. Many observers believe that a breakdown in respect for the institution of *kum* has coincided with the overall decline in Serbia in the 1990s.

By far the highest-profile betrayal of the *kum* tradition was carried out by none other than Slobodan Milošević himself, and it would not be surprising if Dragojević intended his film's various betrayals to echo that nationally consequential one. The case involved Ivan Stambolić, Milošević's patron and *kum*, the person most responsible for his rise to power. But in December 1987 Milošević turned against him, and in the best Stalinist fashion, engineered his dismissal from the post of president of Serbia. As described by Ljubinka Trgovčević, a historian and Central Committee member at the time, Stambolić was completely taken by surprise. "He comes from a patriarchal environment, where you don't hit your best friend and where you never betray your Party."[140] Milošević went well beyond betrayal. In August 2000, when Stambolić was working for the opposition and contemplating challenging Milošević in the upcoming election, he was assassinated, reportedly on Milošević's orders.[141] Thus the institution of *kum* explains the close relations between Chetniks Laza and Fork – keepers of the Serb tradition – and the sense of mutual betrayal experienced by the two estranged Yugoslav army captains, divided by Milošević's war.

One of the most disturbing scenes of the film comes when the Muslim forces send a brutalized woman staggering into the cave. The episode seems to epitomize the connection between misogyny and violence that many feminists find essential to understanding the war. Yet Dragojević does not allow for easy conclusions. He subverts many of the viewer's expectations. The scene follows a bizarre series of events in the interaction between the Serbs inside and the Muslims outside the cave. The Muslims play music for their captives, sentimental songs that remind the Serbs of first loves, patriotic songs that remind them of "brotherhood and unity," of all that they have lost. The Serbs make wisecracks and tell jokes, including the one at the expense of UNPROFOR, to the point where sometimes both sides are laughing uproariously together. Each

---

[139] Quoted in Milos Vasić, "The Role of 'Kum' in Serbian Politics," Vreme News Digest Agency No. 140, May 30, 1994, www.scc.rutgers.edu/serbian_digest/140/t140–7.htm.
[140] Silber and Little, *Yugoslavia*, pp. 45–47.
[141] Gagnon, *The Myth of Ethnic War*, p. 127.

such event is punctuated by a Muslim attack from outside or an individual Serb's suicidal lunge for the entrance.

Finally the Muslims announce, "Here comes a sex bomb, Chetniks," and they send the woman in "for your entertainment." It is a cruel trick. The Serbs assume the worst. "She can barely walk, she must be full of explosives." Then, without subtitles, "and we'll all go to our mother's cunt" (i.e., that will be the end of us). They must kill her before she gets too far. If it turns out that they are wrong, however, they will have killed another innocent victim. The tension mounts, as each solider is reluctant to fire, most of all Milan, who recognizes the woman as his grade school teacher, Mirjana.

"What's wrong with that woman?" Velja explains to Liza in broken German that her stomach must be loaded with bombs that will explode. As the other men fire their weapons to scare her back and beg her not to come further, he beckons her forward, perversely. "Come to me, baby, explode on me."

Then we see a strange identity transformation. Another innocent victim, the captive female American journalist, begins to sound like a macho Chetnik. "Somebody shoot her!" screams Liza. "Just fucking kill the bitch!" With the blackest humor, Dragojević has her unintentionally mimic Speedy mimicking a TV commerical: "Just do it, do it, do it!"

Speedy pleads with Milan to shoot Mirjana. Milan crosses himself, his eyes moist and his face distorted with remorse, as he aims his rifle. At that the screen flashes back to Milan's school days, as his classmates gather for a photo, and we see them from the perspective of the photographer "aiming" the camera. Teacher Mirjana scolds one of the Muslim students. "Samir, I'll scalp you like a Sitting Bull." The photographer issues military orders: "Tighten up your ranks, they can't fit in." Teacher Mirjana reports, "I have two 'missing-in-action.'" She finds Halil and Milan, sitting behind a building facing each other, each holding an egg, and playing a traditional game (that we saw Fork play earlier), hitting the eggs against each other to see which one breaks first. "What's this?" she demands. "We're banging each other," they answer. "First I'll do it to him, then he'll do it to me." The teacher seems angry, until one of the boys accuses her of being "against brotherhood and unity." She quickly puts on a cheerful smile and calls them to the photo, as the camera flashes forward to the tunnel.

Milan still has not managed to pull the trigger. But Fork does, through the broken window of the truck cab, shooting several times as the teacher falls to the ground. She does not explode and everyone realizes with a sinking feeling that it was a hoax. For someone who fits the stereotype of the Chetnik, Fork is obviously shaken by the unnecessary killing. Milan tries to reassure him: "You were the bravest." Here bravery is defined as the willingness to risk killing someone who might actually pose no harm, rather than to accept the risk of danger to oneself in order to spare a possible innocent.[142] Facing that choice, the others could not bring themselves to shoot. But Fork is not reassured. He declares he has had enough, that he is going home, and he walks out of the tunnel to his death.

Velja puts a gun to his own temple and contemplates suicide himself. He hesitates and then asks Liza, in English, "One kiss for a dead man?" She indicates to Speedy to film them and the viewer watches through the video camera, a series of long, sensual kisses. "Real Hollywood slobbering," says Velja. "This is worth waiting for … at least a while longer." Then he puts the gun in his mouth and pulls the trigger.

As Speedy and Liza stare in shock, the screen takes us back. Now that Velja is dead, we learn through a flash-back an important part of his story: how he ended up in the army. The scene takes place at his mother's home, where he has arrived unannouced from Germany with an apparently stolen car and a bag full of presents, evidently also illegally obtained. He greets his brother, Miloš, a second-year student in archaeology. As they are talking, two military officers come to the door. They ask for Miloš, who has ignored two call-up notices already. Their language is vulgar and "mother-oriented," like Velja's of a few minutes before. Like him, they also issue quick pro forma apologies to his mother in mid-sentence. Velja instantly pretends to be his brother, making the excuse that he has just returned from abroad, and goes off to join the army and die.

Outside the cave, events come to a head, as the Muslims begin dropping flaming canisters outside the entrance, to smoke their captives out. A voice greets them, "Good evening, Serbs" (not "Chetniks," which would be an insult coming from a Muslim). Milan recognizes it as Halil's. As Gvozden drives the truck (repaired by mechanic Milan) out the front of the cave to create a diversion, Milan and the others make ready to escape out the back. When Liza goes back for her camera, she is hit by gunfire and dies instantly. Milan picks up her camera, then throws it to the ground, and we watch him run out of the cave through the crooked viewfinder. Milan meets up with Halil, standing above the cave. "So, you

---

[142] In her essay "All the Men are in the Militias," Enloe calls attention to Christopher Browning's insight from his study of the "ordinary men" who carried out genocide on the Eastern Front during World War II: according to "the 'macho' values of the majority," it was considered "a positive quality to be 'tough' enough to kill unarmed, noncombatant men, women and children." The quotation is from Christopher Browning, *Ordinary Men: Reserve Police Battalion 101 and the Final Solution in Poland* (New York: HarperCollins, 1992), p. 185.

went into the tunnel?" he asks, as if in accusation: So, you Serbs woke the sleeping ogre of nationalism. They exchange further accusatons – Why did you burn down our garage? Why did you slaughter my mother? – and denials. So, who did it, then? asks Halil. The ogre? They make no move to hurt each other.

What are we to make of these developments? The conflict between Milan and Halil is revealed as the result of misunderstandings, misperceptions, and false accusations, fostered by others – most prominently the character known as Sloba – for their own gain. Things are not as they seem for other figures either. Velja, the most dishonest, violent, and misogynistic character, turns out to have sacrificed his life for his brother, when he could have avoided the war by returning to Germany. Liza, the independent American woman, initially critical of the Serbs' violent and sexualized nationalism, undergoes an apparent change of heart, embraces Velja, the misogynist-turned-sentimental suicide. And what of teacher Mirjana? Are we supposed to see her death as revenge for her offhand threats of violence to her Muslim pupils? As a consequence of the militarization of everyday life, as reflected in language even at a school? As a result of her inadequate commitment to Brotherhood and Unity? Or as punishment for an excess of Brotherhood and Unity? In a flash-back we had seen, through the eyes of the schoolmates Halil and Milan, their teacher having sex with Nazim, the Muslim postman, during recess. The date is May 4, 1980. The radio announcement of the death of Tito immediately cools the lovers' ardor and they both break out in sobs. Tellingly, however, the young schoolboys fail to summon even a tear, although they challenge each other to do so.

At a minimum, the scene of Mirjana's violent death seems to represent the limits of Dragojević's ability to address the Bosnian war honestly. As with the earlier sexual violence against Marko, the treatment of Mirjana represents much more the Serb paramilitaries' side in the Bosnian war than the Bosnian government's side. She was the one apparently abused to the point of not being able to walk properly and then treated, to use Beverly Allen's expression, as a "sexual container" – or, rather, her womb was used as a container for imagined explosives.

Here, perhaps, Dragojević does approach a certain truth, and a difficult one for the Serbs: the hoax that the Muslim forces carried out with Mirjana in the tunnel was cruel and sadistic in the extreme. Yet it depended on prior expectations by the Serbian men, that they could imagine a women with her identity eliminated, as a vessel or container, and homicidally dangerous. Such attitudes were not unknown in their own prewar culture and in their own wartime behavior. Indeed if it is difficult to watch some scenes in this film, and to listen to the violent misogyny of the men's language, it is far more difficult to read the actual accounts – of words and deeds – of the sexual atrocities that took place during the war.

The film closes with another ersatz newsreel. This one is projected into what was then the future: the fourth of July, 1999, American Independence Day. A new Tunnel of Peace is being dedicated, to be constructed "according to European and world standards." "Who says the Bosnian War destruction cannot be repaired in record time?" asks the announcer, echoing the predictions issued at the opening of the original tunnel three decades earlier. Then the scissors cut the red ribbon – and the thumb – and the blood gushes forth again. It is a pessimistic vision of the future of some of the successor states of postwar Yugoslavia, but one that is hard to gainsay.

Do the wars that broke up Yugoslavia represent an archetype of gender relations during nationalist conflict or an anomalous case of extremes and idiosyncracies? Consider what Cynthia Enloe suggested in her insightful essay "All the Men are in the Militias, All the Women are Victims": not all of the men joined militia forces. Many deserted from the army and many escaped abroad. Perhaps some of them felt diminished as men, for failing to stand up to the ideal of militarized masculinity. Others may have come to agree with one of Tim O'Brien's characters in "On the Rainy River," who comes close to escaping to Canada rather than fight in Vietnam, but loses his nerve: "I was a coward. I went to the war."[143]

What about the women? They were not all victims. Some, such as Biljana Plavšić, were perpetrators. Moreover, women did not suffer disproportionately compared with men, if by that we mean how many were killed.[144] Nevertheless, a distinctive feature of the wars of Yugoslav secession was the systematic campaign of mass rape perpetrated mainly by Serb forces as a tool of "ethnic cleansing." It is not typical of nationalist conflict, as there are many cases – such as the one discussed in the next chapter – where organized sexual violence was not a key element of the war.

How to explain why one case involves widespread sexual atrocity and another does not is beyond the scope of this work. The best systematic work on the topic has tended to focus on issues of discipline and training.[145] In the Yugoslav case, many of the perpetrators were undisciplined, poorly trained gangsters, yet many were also part of a chain of command

---

[143] Tim O'Brien, "On the Rainy River," in *The Things They Carried* (Boston: Houghton Mifflin, 1990), p. 63.

[144] Nettlefield, "Research and Repercussions of Death Tolls," p. 177.

[145] For an excellent example, see Wood, "Variation in Sexual Violence during War."

where the top leadership directed the mass rape campaign with specific political and territorial objectives.

The close analysis of *Pretty Village, Pretty Flame* suggested that the violence these leaders directed against women tapped into a reservoir of woman-hating sentiment among a certain spectrum of Serb men, reflected in the violent misogynistic language they use as part of their everyday speech. Scholars inclined towards a cultural explanation of sexual violence in the Balkans would find ample evidence in past wars, in practices of domestic violence and wife-beating, and even in sources such as Alex Comfort's *Joy of Sex*, where in his section on different forms of "national" sex, he depicts the Serbian form – *srpski jeb* – as a mock rape of a woman by a man.

Yet few elements of the Yugoslav wars are unique to that case, so one hesitates to rely on such a cultural argument. In fact, one particular element of the case stands out as almost archetypical, and we see it across several of the cases in this book. It is what Chris Dolan called the "proliferation of small men," the relationship between declining economic prospects and threatened masculine identities that piqued Enloe's curiosity in her examination of the case of an individual rapist in former Yugoslavia. The role of economic conditions in fostering nationalist violence reappears as a theme in the next chapter, and the implications for gender are taken up again in the book's conclusion.

4   Chechnya: virgins, mothers, and terrorists

> The war has changed the relationship between man and woman, mostly because we, the weaker sex, are more worried about our stronger partners than they are about us.
>
> Kalimat, a café owner in Grozny, 2000[1]

> During a war women can often do more with their voices and their desperation than men with trench mortars.
>
> Tamara, a Chechen refugee in Stráž pod Ralskem, Czech Republic, 2000[2]

Conflict between the central government of Russia and the secessionist republic of Chechnya erupted into open warfare within a few years of the violent disintegration of the Yugoslav federation. Indeed the causes of the breakup of the Soviet Union – nominally a federation of fifteen union republics – resemble those that contributed to Yugoslavia's demise.[3] A key difference is that little violence accompanied the initial Soviet disintegration, whereas the peoples of the Yugoslav successor states endured years of brutal warfare, barbaric "ethnic cleansing," and civil strife. Only with Moscow's armed attempt to put down the Chechen bid for sovereignty in 1994 did Russia witness a comparable level of violence.

With the formal dissolution of the Soviet Union at the end of 1991, Russia emerged as its largest and most populous successor state. Stretching across eleven time-zones, from Kaliningrad (the former Königsberg) in the west to Vladivostok in the east, the Russian Federation, as it is formally known, contained some hundred different ethnic groups or "nationalities," as they were called in Soviet parlance, speaking as many languages. Administratively Russia was divided into eighty-nine

---

[1] Quoted in Petra Procházková, *The Aluminum Queen: The Russian–Chechen War through the Eyes of Women*, trans. by Gerald Turner (originally: *Aluminiová královna: rusko-čečenská válka očima žen*) (Prague: Lidové noviny, 2002). Downloaded from www.berkat.cz/Dokumenty/Doc_2003/AluQueen/, and archived with the author, p. 46.

[2] Procházková, *Aluminum Queen*, p. 145.

[3] Valerie Bunce, *Subversive Institutions: The Design and Destruction of Socialism and the State* (Cambridge University Press, 1999); Veljko Vujačić, "Historical Legacies, Nationalist Mobilization, and Political Outcomes in Russia and Serbia: A Weberian View," *Theory and Society*, 25, 6 (December 1996), pp. 763–801.

"subjects" (*sub"ekty*). These ranged in size from the two cities of Moscow and St. Petersburg to the enormous territory of the resource-rich republic of Sakha (Iakutia) – at 3,103,200 square kilometers, about the size of the entire continent of Europe west of Russia. Twenty-one of these political units, including Chechnya, were designated "national republics" because they are considered the homeland of a major nationality. During the late 1980s several of these republics, such as Tatarstan and Bashkortostan, as well as Chechnya, sought greater independence from Moscow. Both Chechnya and Tatarstan refused to sign the Federative Treaty that formed the basis for relations between the central government of post-Soviet Russia and the regions, and Bashkortostan did so only after appending a separate bilateral agreement.[4]

In all of the cases except Chechnya, the poorest of Russia's eighty-nine regions, the Moscow authorities pursued a compromise solution that kept the republics from seceding. In the Chechen case, Russian President Boris Yeltsin chose war, ostensibly for fear that Chechen independence would provoke a rash of other secessions. As he put it in one of several volumes of ghost-written memoirs, "We cannot stand idly by while a piece of Russia breaks off, because that would be the beginning of the collapse of the country."[5] Yet Chechnya did break off.

Chechnya's attempt to achieve autonomy did not in itself threaten the disintegration of Russia. Moscow's violent reaction, however, helped spread the conflict by sending refugees fleeing into bordering regions of the North Caucasus and by provoking acts of terrorist retaliation elsewhere in Russia – some of them carried out by women.

Against all odds, Russia lost its first attempt to subdue Chechnya, a mountainous region slightly larger than the US state of Connecticut. Chechen rebels ambushed and destroyed ill-prepared Russian conscripts, as a demoralized Russian public demanded an end to the conflict. Despite managing to kill the leader of the Chechen independence movement, General Dzhokhar Dudaev, the Russian armed forces lost the war. When they withdrew from Chechen territory in 1996, the republic achieved de facto independence and an agreement with the central government in Moscow to negotiate its formal status over the next several years. Aslan Maskhadov, Dudaev's successor, faced internal opposition, mainly from Islamist radicals, and never managed to consolidate

---

[4] Details on the Russo-Chechen conflict come from Matthew Evangelista, *The Chechen Wars: Will Russia Go the Way of the Soviet Union?* (Washington, DC: Brookings Institution Press, 2002), unless otherwise indicated.

[5] Boris Yeltsin, *Midnight Diaries*, trans. by Catherine A. Fitzpatrick (New York: PublicAffairs, 2000), pp. 58–59.

his authority, despite coming to power in an internationally monitored election whose results Moscow accepted.

In the late summer of 1999 Maskhadov's opponents carried out an attack from Chechen territory on the neighboring Russian republic of Dagestan, in a bid to create an Islamic caliphate in the North Caucasus as an alternative to the secular state Maskhadov sought to govern. The conflict coincided with a series of devastating apartment bombings in several Russian cities. The bombing campaign went unexplained at the time, but was officially blamed on Chechens, and it served as further justification to resume the war. This second Chechen war, as it became known, initially proved surprisingly popular and helped secure the election of then prime minister, Vladimir Putin, as Yeltsin's chosen successor. In one of his own quasi-autobiographies, Putin justified the new invasion and bombardment of Chechnya with the same argument that Yeltsin had used: "What's the situation in the Northern Caucasus and in Chechnya today? It's a continuation of the collapse of the USSR." He spoke of the "Yugoslavization" of Russia.[6]

In many respects the Chechen case resembles less Yugoslavia than Algeria. Chapter 2 already pointed out some of the similarities. Russian imperial control over the North Caucasus region shares much in common with French colonial domination of Algeria: their similar origins in the first half of the nineteenth century, the way they pit the Christian identity of the colonizer against the Muslim identity of the colonial subjects, the nature of the anticolonial struggles, and the state's military response. A key difference is that the French–Algerian war ended with Algerian independence, whereas the opposition of Chechens to Russian domination has continued into the twenty-first century.

Regarding gender, Chechnya has witnessed many examples of sexualized violence and atrocities, but nothing on the scale of the mass-rape campaigns in Bosnia or the sex slavery and misogynistic bloodletting of the Algerian civil war of the 1990s. Nevertheless, women have been prominent victims of the violence of the Chechen wars – both directly, as targets of bombing and murder, and indirectly as the remaining survivors of the widespread "disappearances" and killings of their male family members. Some Chechen women have also engaged directly in violence themselves – including suicide terrorism, something rare in the Chechen experience of resistance to Russian rule and absent from our other cases as well.

In the use of cinematic sources, this chapter differs from the others in the book by going beyond the focus on a single key film. In the

---

[6] Vladimir Putin, *First Person: An Astonishingly Frank Self-Portrait by Russia's President* (New York: PublicAffairs, 2000), p. 139.

decade and more during which Chechens have been battling Russians and Russian filmmakers have been making movies about those battles, the treatment of Chechens, Russians, gender, nationalism, and violence has been in flux. In the earliest major film on the war, Sergei Bodrov's *Prisoner of the Mountains* (*Kavkazskii plennik*, 1996), most Chechens were treated rather sympathetically as fully developed human beings – a change from the way traditional Russian literature had portrayed them. The Russians presented in the film covered a range of personalities with varying moral qualities. Gender roles for women tended to fit a certain stereotype – peacefully inclined women, one Chechen and one Russian, who are nevertheless strong in defense of their families – whereas the male roles were somewhat more complicated. Two later films – Aleksandr Rogozhkin's *Checkpoint* (*Blokpost*, 1998) and Aleksei Balabanov's *War* (*Voina*, 2002) – represented a change in the treatment of the Chechens, where very few were portrayed in a positive light and most were unidimensionally evil. *Checkpoint* challenged traditional gender norms by depicting, among other unconventional female characters, a female Chechen sniper. *War* employed gender as a device for creating binary oppositions between Chechens and Russians, and between westerners (Europeans) and Russians. Some lesser films, such as Fedor Popov's *Caucasian Roulette* (*Kavkazskaia ruletka*, 2002) and even more so Aleksandr Nevzorov's television movie *Purgatory* (*Chistilishche*, 1998), take the demonization of Chechens and the violent proclivities of women to an extreme.

In some respect, the evolution of depictions of Chechens and of gender in Russian cinema since the start of the first war tracks the changes in government and popular attitudes towards the conflict and towards women. A creeping racism renders all Chechens potential terrorists. Chechen women become particularly suspect, and Russian women who had earlier received widespread admiration – journalists who risked their lives to report on the war, or mothers who traveled to Chechnya to rescue their sons – come under scrutiny, or worse, if they appear insufficiently loyal to the Russian government's cause.

Exceptions to this generalization of increasingly negative portrayals of Chechens and women include two very different films. Andrei Konchalovskii's *House of Fools* (*Dom durakov*, 2002) treats the Chechen conflict as an allegory. Its characters are mostly inmates of an insane asylum – ethnic Russians, Chechens, and other nationalities of the former Soviet Union – and come off as rather sympathetic and much saner than the people who launched the war. The film clearly draws inspiration from Milos Forman's *One Flew over the Cuckoo's Nest* (1975) and especially Philippe de Broca's *King of Hearts* (1966). Konchalovskii's film presents and challenges virtually all gender stereotypes as part of an effort to recover the basic humanity of people caught in a desperate situation. Aleksandr Sokurov's *Aleksandra* (2007) conveys a very different tone – primarily one of resignation. It offers some hope for reconciliation between Chechens and Russians in a form that would be familiar to Virginia Woolf – through the relationships of women who, in their personal interactions, behave as if they "have no country."

Two centuries of Russo-Chechen relations

Russia's first serious attempt to subdue Chechnya followed in the wake of the annexation of the Kingdom of Georgia under Tsar Aleksandr I in 1801 and the outbreak of war with Turkey in 1807. Russian authorities advanced strategic arguments to justify expansion – particularly the need to secure the route from Vladikavkaz to Tbilisi, Georgia's capital, through the Darial Pass. General Aleksei Ermolov led the effort to incorporate the mountain peoples of the region into the Russian Empire. The policies he pursued represent the worst of Russian approaches to the Chechens and they set the precedent for subsequent crimes of the Soviet and post-Soviet eras. Under Soviet rule, the Communist Party tended to portray Ermolov as the symbol of an enlightened civilizing mission. The Chechens, some of whom sought to blow up a statue of the general in Grozny in 1969, knew better.

Ermolov advocated a strategy of economic warfare against the recalcitrant mountaineers, destroying their crops and burning their villages. His forces perpetrated massacres against unarmed villagers and carried out the first mass deportation of Chechens, including sending captured prisoners into exile in Siberia. Mountain peoples who had moved to the fertile land between the Terek and Sunzha rivers were driven back up into the mountains, reversing a trend towards the more "progressive" economic and political practices that had followed the migration. As John Dunlop puts it, "by forcing the Chechens back up into the inhospitable mountains, Ermolov returned them to an economically and socially primitive state, thereby ensuring the existence of a fierce and dedicated opponent for the Russian Empire over the next half century (and beyond)."[7]

Paradoxically, Ermolov's military and economic policies "led gradually to a consolidation of Chechen society." The destruction of Chechen villages

---

[7] This summary of the history of Russian–Chechen conflict draws on John B. Dunlop, *Russia Confronts Chechnya: Roots of a Separatist Conflict* (Cambridge University Press, 1998). Some of the wording comes from my review, published in *Slavic Review*, 59, 1 (Spring 2000).

and other "harsh punitive actions drove many Chechens into the arms" of Islamic warlords. The Russian government during the Tsarist era carried out three major deportations, setting the precedent for Iosif Stalin's genocidal actions against the Chechen people in the 1940s. The deportations failed to break Chechen resistance, and instead contributed to an abiding attachment to the homeland and a smoldering sense of grievance.

Chechens, whose primary loyalty was typically local, formed their sense of a "national" identity initially in opposition to Russian military offensives – much as Algerians came to think of themselves as a nation in response to Ottoman and particularly French rule. The French army's conquest of Algeria in the early 1800s coincided temporally with the intensification of Tsarist Russia's military effort to control the North Caucasus. The experiences of the colonial military campaigns and the armed resistance from Muslim populations share much in common. A key difference is that Chechnya, geographically contiguous with the rest of Russia, only succeeded in gaining a temporary, de facto independence for two years (1997–1999). For the rest of its history it was subject to Tsarist Russian or Soviet communist rule. The Soviet system made full citizens of the peoples of the North Caucasus and the hundred or so other "nationalities" of the Soviet Union in a way that the most ardent French reformers never succeeded in doing for the vast Muslim majority of *Algérie Française.*

A major impact of the Soviet experience was economic development and modernization that brought in their train urbanization, education, secularization, and a high level of assimilation of Muslim groups. Soviet nationalities policy fostered teaching and codification of native languages and development of local culture as well as education in Russian.[8] Paradoxically, these Soviet policies helped contribute to the reemergence of nationalist and religious sentiment and a focus on "identity politics," as the old political and economic order broke down in the late 1980s.[9]

For the Chechens, and other groups in the North Caucasus, the benefits of modernization were often counteracted by measures of state repression against any signs of resistance to the Soviet order. Harsh repression was characteristic of Tsarist rule as well, but nothing compared to Stalin's

---

[8] Aleksei Malashenko, *Islamskoe vozrozhdenie v sovremennoi Rossii* [Islamic Revival in Contemporary Russia] (Moscow: Carnegie Center, 1998); Terry Martin, *The Affirmative Action Empire: Nations and Nationalism in the Soviet Union, 1923–1939* (Ithaca, NY: Cornell University Press, 2001).

[9] Martha Brill Olcott and Aleksei Malashenko, *Faktor etnokonfessional'noi samobytnosti v postsovetskom obshchestve* [Factors of Ethnoconfessional Identification in Post-Soviet Society] (Moscow: Carnegie Center, 1998).

mass deportation – the memory of which played a key role in mobilizing Chechen nationalism in the 1990s.

In the mid-1950s, following Stalin's death, Chechens and others began making their way back to their homelands in the North Caucasus. Finally in 1956 Stalin's successors, led by Nikita Khrushchev, officially permitted the deported groups to leave their places of exile, but discouraged them from claiming their former property and tried to prevent them from returning to the sites of their (destroyed) ancestral villages in the mountains. In 1957 the Soviet authorities reestablished a homeland for the Chechens and Ingush. The Checheno-Ingush Autonomous Soviet Socialist Republic (ASSR) was created by transferring back territory formerly assigned to the Dagestan ASSR and the North Ossetian ASSR as well as the area around the former capital of Grozny, which after the deportation had become a mainly Russian region (*oblast'*). Some of the territory of the Grozny *oblast'* which had formerly belonged to Checheno-Ingushetiia was transferred to Dagestan and the mainly Russian Stavropol' district (*krai*).[10] Intentionally or not, the new arrangement led to a dilution of the Chechen population within the autonomous republic – 41 percent, compared with 58.4 percent in 1939.[11] It also created conditions for competing territorial claims among the various other ethnic groups, leading to violence in some cases as the Soviet Union disintegrated. Some of the repercussions of such territorial machinations continued well into the twenty-first century and included a war between Russia and Georgia in 2008 over the disputed region of South Ossetiia.

Solidifying stereotypes in Chechnya

Although historical relations between Russia and Chechnya included long periods of peaceful development as well as war, it is the conflictual

---

[10] The following documents relate to the decision. They were found in the former archive of the Central Committee of the Communist Party of the Soviet Union (CPSU), later renamed the Russian State Archive for Contemporary History (Moscow): "O vosstanovlenii natsional'noi avtonomii kalmykskogo, karachaevskogo, balkarskogo, chechenskogo i ingushskogo narodov" [On the restoration of the national autonomies of the Kalmyk, Karachaev, Balkar, Chechen, and Ingush peoples], No. P60/24, from Protocol No. 60, of the session of the Presidium of the CPSU Central Committee, November 24, 1956; "O vosstanovelenii Chechno-Ingushskoi ASSR i uprazdnenii Groznenskoi oblasti" [On the restoration of the Chechen-Ingush ASSR and abolition of the Grozny region], decree of the Presidium of the Supreme Soviet of the Russian Soviet Federated Socialist Republic, n.d., F. 89, Op. 61, D. 8. Protocol No. 67, session of the Presidium of the CPSU Central Committee, January 5–6, 1957, item 32, "O territorii Checheno-Ingushskoi ASSR" [On the territory of the Checheno-Ingush ASSR], F. 89, Op. 61, D. 1.

[11] Dunlop, *Russia Confronts Chechnya*, pp. 78–79. A series of documents, from 1957 through 1964, have been declassified and published on the return of the Chechens and Ingush to the Caucasus. See the journal *Istochnik* [Source], 6 (1996), pp. 89–104.

aspect that came to dominate the discourse of the 1990s. One reason is that Chechens and the Russo-Chechen conflict had long been staples of Russian literature, dating back to the early nineteenth century poems and prose works of Aleksandr Pushkin and Mikhail Lermontov, continuing through Lev Tolstoi's writings later in the century, and into the post-Soviet era.[12] Many Russians entered that era with an image of Chechens that dates back nearly two centuries. It is a romantic image of a kind of noble savage: warm and hospitable to guests, fierce but fair with enemies, wild and cunning, with a strong martial tradition and an innate democratic form of social organization based on extended families and tribes.[13] That the image diverges considerably from reality is not so surprising, given that it is based largely on a highly romanticized portrait from the literary classics read by every Russian schoolchild.

Perhaps more surprising is that the self-identity of the Chechens, as revealed during the post-Soviet conflicts, stems from the same sources. One product of Soviet-era modernization is that the Chechens too read the Russian classics in school. Chechen fighters of the mid-1990s often modeled themselves on the legendary heroes of resistance to Russian rule, such as Kazi Mullah and Shamil', with an added dose of Che Guevara and Rambo, the 1980s Hollywood movie character.[14] Not even the top political-military leaders of the Chechen independence movement were immune from Russian literary influences – as, for example, when Dzhokhar Dudaev, the first president of separatist Chechnya, renamed his new state the Chechen Republic of Ichkeriia. As Harsha Ram explains, the toponym Ichkeriia, which applies only to the highland region of Chechnya, was familiar to the Chechen leader from the poems of Lermontov "whom Dudaev had often acknowledged to be his favorite poet," even if not the only source of the country's new name.[15] The Russian literary influence on the pro-Moscow Chechen regime of Ramzan Kadyrov, which took control in the wake of the second war, is presumably less. Kadyrov, who became Chechnya's president at age thirty,

[12] Ewa M. Thompson, *Imperial Knowledge: Russian Literature and Colonialism* (Westport, CT: Greenwood Press, 2000), esp. ch. 2; Harsha Ram, "Prisoners of the Caucasus: Literary Myths and Media Representations of the Chechen Conflict," Working Paper, Berkeley Program in Soviet and Post-Soviet Studies, University of California, Berkeley, 1999.

[13] On the problems with this image, which draws on flawed Soviet ethnographic and historical study as well as Russian literature, see Valery Tishkov, *Chechnya: Life in a War-Torn Society* (Berkeley, CA: University of California Press, 2003), esp. pp. 16–25.

[14] Zaidni Shakhbiev, *Sud'ba checheno-ingushskogo naroda* [The Fate of the Chechen-Ingush People] (Moscow: Rossiia molodaia, 1996); Dunlop, *Russia Confronts Chechnya*; Georgi M. Derluguian, "Che Guevaras in Turbans," *New Left Review*, 237 (September–October 1999), pp. 3–27.

[15] Ram, "Prisoners of the Caucasus," p. 1. Ichkeriia is not a traditional Chechen name, but rather of Turkish origin. In their own language the Chechens call themselves *Nokhchi*.

was poorly educated and spoke ungrammatical Russian, with a limited vocabulary. The Rambo influence, more than the Russian literary one, seemed to predominate among the members of his armed gangs – and as late as 2007 Kadyrov himself displayed a portrait of Che Guevara in his office in Grozny, next to the one of Vladimir Putin.[16]

Socio-economic change and the demise of the Soviet model

In the chapters on Algeria and Yugoslavia, we saw the role played by economic decline – and particularly widespread unemployment among young men – in contributing to the mobilization of violence. Unemployment was an endemic problem for Chechnya – a result, in part, of ethnic discrimination in employment. Returning to their homeland in 1957, Chechens found an economy in the throes of industrialization, based on extraction and refining of oil. They also found that in their absence many non-Chechens – Russians, Ukrainians, Jews, Armenians – had taken the new jobs in the petroleum sector. They lived in the capital city of Grozny, the center of the modern industrial economy, where Chechens remained a minority. As Georgi Derluguian explains,

When the Chechens and Ingushes returned from exile, there were twice as many of them as there were jobs available in the republic (even including the least desirable employment on collective and state farms). Structural unemployment continued and actually got worse towards the end of the Soviet period because the industrial growth had been slowing down. In the mid-1980s, according to official estimates, 40 percent of the rural labor force received wages below subsistence level, while close to 60 percent of adult women had no formal employment at all.[17]

Chechnya's main source of wealth – oil – saw a steady decline from peak production in 1971 of 21 million tons to a low of 4 million in 1991.[18] Even when the oil industry was thriving, it did not benefit local Chechens and Ingush. As Valerii Tishkov explains, "the paradox was that the industry and transport sectors badly needed more workers, particularly trained specialists, but because of ethnic discrimination,

---

[16] Åsne Seierstad, *The Angel of Grozny: Orphans of a Forgotten War*, trans. by Nadia Chijstensen (New York: Basic Books, 2008), p. 213.

[17] Georgi M. Derluguian, *Bourdieu's Secret Admirer in the Caucasus: A World-Systems Biography* (University of Chicago Press, 2005), p. 245.

[18] Taimaz Abubakarov, *Rezhim Dzhokhara Dudaeva: Pravda i vymysel* [The Regime of Dzhokhar Dudaev: Truth and Falsehoods] (Moscow: INSAN, 1998), p. 9. For comparable figures, see Michael McFaul and Nikolai Petrov, *Politicheskii al'manakh Rossii 1997* [Political Almanac of Russia, 1997], vol. II: *Sotsial'no-politicheskie portrety regionov* [Socio-political Portraits of the Regions], book 1 (Moscow: Carnegie Center, 1998), p. 291.

little was done to engage Chechen and Ingush youths in these fields." In the late 1980s, the largest petrochemical firms in Chechnya employed some 50,000 workers and engineers, of which only a few hundred were Chechen or Ingush.[19]

Emerging out of the disintegrating Soviet Union, Chechnya suffered an unemployment rate that reached, by some estimates, 40 percent. The breakup of the Soviet Union and Chechnya's later declaration of sovereignty only exacerbated the economic situation. Three-fourths of the goods produced in Chechnya, including oil products, were dependent on deliveries from Russia and other countries of the former Soviet Union. Although Dudaev had visions of making Chechnya into a second Kuwait, by provoking isolation of his republic from the Russian economy he did it great economic harm.[20]

Lack of work was a particularly serious problem for village dwellers.[21] During the Soviet era, Chechen men had compensated for the absence of local employment by engaging in seasonal work – in agriculture and construction – elsewhere in the Soviet Union. The combination of abundant agricultural products grown locally and income earned from outside the republic made Chechens feel relatively well off, even if according to official statistics their region was one of the poorest in the country. That all changed with the demise of the USSR and its integrated economy. The men who had worked as seasonal laborers no longer had jobs. According to Tishkov, "the labor surplus reached perhaps 100,000 to 200,000, or 20–30 percent of the able-bodied population. Later, these people became the main reserve for the armed struggle."[22] Derluguian elaborates: the labor migrations "had engendered a special sub-culture whose norms and rituals chiefly pertained to internal organization of migratory teams," led by a top male leader of "quasi-parental authority." Its members formed a "male peer group, essentially a fraternity, sometimes with internal ranks based on seniority or the recognition of individual merits." The teams "provided a modular and transposable pattern of micro-organization which in a changed situation could be put to quite different purposes, such as forming a chapter of a nationalist movement or a guerrilla band."[23] As the previous chapter suggested, a similar phenomenon characterized the war in Bosnia, when Serbian men working as *Gastarbeiter* in Germany returned home with their relatives and friends to form militias

---

[19] Tishkov, *Chechnya*, p. 41.
[20] Abubakarov, *Rezhim Dzhokhara Dudaeva*, p. 21.
[21] Ibid., p. 8.   [22] Tishkov, *Chechnya*, p. 41.
[23] Derluguian, *Bourdieu's Secret Admirer*, p. 246.

and engage in organized violence, as depicted in the character of Velja in the film *Pretty Village, Pretty Flame*.[24]

Chechnya's bid for independence

Economic conditions deteriorated sharply in the Soviet Union in the second half of the 1980s, in part as a result of Soviet leader Mikhail Gorbachev's unsuccessful attempts at reform. Economic discontent fueled political efforts on the part of activists in the union republics to exert greater sovereignty and control over their resources. The strongest movements for independence emerged in the Baltic republics of Estonia, Latvia, and Lithuania; their forcible incorporation into the Soviet Union during World War II was still widely resented by members of the population and never officially recognized by the United States and other countries. Estonia had declared its sovereignty in November 1988, to be followed by Lithuania in May 1989 and Latvia in July. There is a direct connection between the Baltic events and the war in Chechnya, namely in the person of Dzhokhar Dudaev, the leader of Chechnya's independence movement and its first president. Dudaev is a classic example of an assimilated and "Sovietized" Chechen: raised in exile in Kazakhstan, he attended Russian-language schools and Soviet military academies, married a Russian woman, and became a general – the first Chechen to hold that rank – in the Soviet air force. In his last official posting, Dudaev served in Estonia as commander of the strategic air base at Tartu. He is still widely admired in Estonia for his refusal to use his troops to suppress protests in favor of Estonian independence. The protest movements in turn inspired Dudaev to support similar independence efforts upon his return to Chechnya.

The big opportunity for Dudaev and other opponents of Moscow's rule came with the failed coup against Soviet President Gorbachev in August 1991. The local communist authorities in Grozny had failed to condemn the coup plotters, who sought to reverse Gorbachev's reforms, especially his proposal for a new Union Treaty to create a less centralized confederation of republics to replace the USSR. They thereby discredited themselves in the eyes of increasingly nationalist and anticommunist Chechens as well as among the supporters of Russian President Boris Yeltsin, whose symbolic role in defeating the coup had made him a hero. Yeltsin soon gave up on the possibility of reforming the Soviet Union and

---

[24] See International Criminal Tribunal for the Former Yugoslavia, case against Milan Lukić, Sredoje Lukić, Mitar Vasiljević, Case No. IT-98–32-PT, www.un.org/icty/indictment/english/vas-ai010712e.htm.

in concert with the leaders of Ukraine and Belarus withdrew the Russian Federation from the USSR, leading to its disintegration by the end of the year and depriving his rival Gorbachev of a job.

Yeltsin's circle also sought to undermine certain regional authorities who had supported the coup plotters. Mass demonstrations in Grozny gave them a pretext to withdraw support from the Soviet-era leadership of Chechnya, even though, as Tishkov reports, the demonstrations in Sheikh Mansur Square (formerly Lenin Square) did not have an obvious political objective: "These were not political actions, but rather a demonstration of solidarity, free spirit or libertarianism, and militancy, mobilized and directed by local leaders." Unemployed men "were the backbone of the demonstration and guaranteed its spirit by performing the traditional zikr" dance.[25]

Dudaev took advantage of the "social anarchy" that prevailed in Chechnya, as one of his erstwhile supporters described it.[26] His forces seized government buildings and the radio and television center. They disrupted a session of the local Supreme Soviet (parliament) and caused the death of Viktor Kutsenko, the elderly head of the Grozny city council and an ethnic Russian, who was either thrown out of a window or fell trying to escape.[27] Yeltsin declined to intervene in support of the local authorities – a decision he soon came to regret (and to reverse), as Dudaev increasingly moved to assert Chechen sovereignty and his own authority.

Dudaev outmaneuvered his opponents and staged elections in October 1991, becoming Chechnya's president and issuing a declaration of sovereignty the next month. As Aleksandr Cherkasov and others have pointed out, the Russian war against Chechnya could have broken out at any point after that. The Russian parliament rejected Chechnya's declaration and President Yeltsin decreed a state of emergency in the republic and dispatched 2,500 interior ministry troops.[28] He secretly armed and funded Chechen opponents of Dudaev. The Chechen president responded to Yeltsin's challenge by declaring martial law and mobilizing forces for the defense of Chechen sovereignty. Under threat of Russian

---

[25] Valery Tishkov, *Ethnicity, Nationalism, and Conflict in and after the Soviet Union: The Mind Aflame* (London: Sage, 1996), pp. 200–201.

[26] Abubakarov, *Rezhim Dzhokhara Dudaeva*, p. 50.

[27] Tishkov, *Ethnicity, Nationalism, and Conflict*, pp. 201–202; Timur Muzaev, *Etnicheskii separatism v Rossii* [Ethnic Separatism in Russia] (Moscow: Panorama, 1999), pp. 37–38; Carlotta Gall and Thomas de Waal, *Chechnya: Calamity in the Caucasus* (New York University Press, 1998), pp. 95–96. Although Kutsenko is a Ukrainian surname, most sources identify him as Russian.

[28] Aleksandr Cherkasov, "The Driving Force behind the Chechen Wars," in Tanya Lokshina, ed., *Chechnya Inside Out* (Moscow: Demos, 2007), p. 42.

invasion, most of Dudaev's erstwhile opponents rallied to his side – a phenomenon that was repeated under his successor, Aslan Maskhadov, when Russia invaded again in 1999.

War after war

There was nothing inevitable about the Chechen war, however. As we have seen, many other regions of the Russian Federation, including resource-rich Tatarstan and Bashkortostan, had sought greater autonomy from the central government and had issued declarations of sovereignty. Yeltsin had worked out agreements with the leaders of those regions – formalized as "treaties," to enhance the illusion of independence – to produce a system that became known as "asymmetric federalism." Dudaev's mercurial personality and provocative rhetoric would have made it more difficult for Yeltsin to strike a deal with him than with the leaders of the other regions. But Yeltsin did not bother to try and refused even to meet with Dudaev. He thought he could easily overthrow the upstart Chechen's regime in short order.

In some respects Russia could have won the first war in Chechnya. Its armed forces destroyed the capital and gained nominal control of all the other major population centers. Chechen troops were forced to retreat to the mountains and conduct a guerrilla campaign. If Moscow had used economic aid to win over the civilian population, it might have employed police methods to deal with the remaining rebel forces. Instead the Russian forces treated the residents of Chechnya – including thousands of ethnic Russians and Russian speakers of mixed ethnicity who lived in Grozny – indiscriminately as enemies. The occupying Russian army – with drunken and drugged soldiers robbing, harassing, and otherwise maltreating civilians – did little to try to win over hearts and minds.

The Chechen resistance forces turned the tide of the war and expelled the Russian troops by some of them becoming what Moscow had always branded them: terrorists. Among the more dramatic terrorist attacks of the first war was the June 1995 seizure of a hospital at Budennovsk, when Chechen fighters, led by Shamil' Basaev, took more than a thousand hostages. That action in turn was justified as a response to a well-documented massacre of civilians by Russian troops at the village of Samashki in April, and, for Basaev, a Russian attack on his home village less than two weeks earlier that had killed several members of his family.[29] The Budennovsk crisis was resolved when the then Russian prime minister, Viktor Chernomyrdin, negotiated a release of the hostages by

---

[29] Gall and de Waal, *Chechnya*, pp. 242–247.

telephone – shown live on television in fact – in return for safe passage of their kidnappers. The Chechen terrorists' main stated objective – ending the war with a withdrawal of Russian troops – was not achieved, as the war dragged on and inspired further terrorism from the Chechen side.

In January 1996 Chechen fighters, led by Salman Raduev, seized another hospital in Kizliar, over the border in Dagestan. Not satisfied with keeping the patients and medical staff captive, they went off and rounded up more people from their homes, until they had assembled between two and three thousand hostages. Russian forces quickly attacked the hospital but stopped when the Chechens began to execute their captives. Local Dagestani officials then negotiated safe passage for the terrorists, on the Budennovsk model, but Russian forces reneged on the deal and attacked the Chechen convoy just as it was about to cross a bridge into Chechnya. The Chechens retreated into the village of Pervomaiskoe with their hostages. The Russian forces attacked with *Grad* rockets, yielding a death toll of many scores of people, including hostages.[30]

Soon the Russian armed forces began engaging in similar terrorist actions, including seizing a hospital in August 1996, the regular taking of hostages, and use of civilians as human shields.[31]

With its army in shambles and its citizens thoroughly demoralized, the Russian government finally began to take seriously the need to end the war. Russian popular support for a military resolution of the conflict, already low to begin with, fell to such depths that Yeltsin felt his chances for reelection in serious jeopardy. Several additional factors contributed to the Russian decision to pursue peace. In April 1996, the Russian army assassinated Dudaev. The Chechen president was talking by satellite phone to a Russian member of parliament who was trying to arrange negotiations between Dudaev and Tatarstan's president, as a first step towards direct negotiations with Yeltsin or Chernomyrdin. Nearby Russian forces used the satellite signal to target Dudaev with a guided missile that killed the Chechen president and two of his aides.[32]

The assassination of Dudaev removed an unpredictable and unreliable negotiating partner. He was succeeded by his vice-president, Zelimkhan Iandarbiev, and by Aslan Maskhadov as commander of the armed forces. With competent Chechen leaders in place, there still remained an unpredictable and unreliable negotiating partner on the Russian side, namely,

[30] See the eye-witness account of Enver Kisriev, published in the *Bulletin* of the Conflict Management Group, "Ethnic Conflict Management in the Former Soviet Union" (March 1996), pp. 13–23.

[31] Aleksandr Cherkasov, "Terrorism and Counter-terrorism during the Chechen Wars," in Lokshina, *Chechnya Inside Out*, pp. 77–81.

[32] Gall and de Waal, *Chechnya*, pp. 318–321.

Yeltsin. But the Russian president was motivated to change – at least in appearances.

Popular opposition to the war was widespread, especially among women. An organization called the Committee of Soldiers' Mothers supported efforts of parents to travel to Chechnya and rescue their sons from the army or at least find out how they died and recover their bodies. The committee, with branches throughout the country, kept the war's human costs in the public eye.[33] The prominent role of mothers reinforced the gendered understanding of war as a mainly male activity which women would naturally oppose. Yet the cooperation of Chechen women in the release of Russian soldiers does not necessarily imply shared opposition to the war, Virginia Woolf-style antinationalism, or even gender solidarity. Why would Chechen women not support opponents of the Russian invasion? Helping pacifistic Russian women get their soldier sons out of Chechnya would not preclude endorsing the parallel efforts of male Chechen fighters to expel the Russians through violent means.

A turning point in the war came on August 6, 1996 when some 1,500 of those fighters, led by Maskhadov, stormed Grozny and pinned down the nearly 12,000 Russian troops supposedly defending it. The Russian command reacted with typical brutality and deceit. On August 20 General Konstantin Pulikovskii, commander of the Russian forces, issued an ultimatum: all Chechen fighters must leave Grozny or he would order an air and missile attack on their positions. The general gave the civilian population forty-eight hours to leave the city, but waited barely a day before launching a devastating attack. As for negotiations, Pulikovskii announced that "there was no longer anything to talk about" with Maskhadov. Pulikovskii's optimism was misplaced. The August assault cost the Russian army some 494 dead, 1,407 wounded, and 182 missing in action. Estimates of civilian deaths ranged around 2,000, and more than 220,000 refugees fled the carnage.[34]

Yeltsin finally faced reality and appointed General Aleksandr Lebed' to negotiate a Russian withdrawal. On August 31, 1996 Lebed', Maskhadov, and their associates signed an agreement on "principles for the determination of the basis of relations between the Russian Federation and the Chechen Republic." It became known as the Khasaviurt Accord, after the town in Dagestan where it was negotiated. The document formally

---

[33] Valerie Sperling, "The Last Refuge of a Scoundrel: Patriotism, Militarism, and the Russian National Idea," *Nations and Nationalism*, 9, 2 (2003), pp. 235–253; Brenda J. Vallance, "Russia's Mothers – Voices of Change," *Minerva: Quarterly Report on Women and the Military*, 18, 3–4 (2000), pp. 109–128.

[34] Gall and de Waal, *Chechnya*, ch. 15. For a first-hand account, see the interview with Elza Duguyevova in Procházková, *Aluminum Queen*, pp. 19–21.

left the status of Chechnya's relationship to Russia undecided until December 31, 2001, and, therefore, subject to further negotiations.[35]

The lesson learned by many Chechens – at least the ones with guns – was that Russia was vulnerable to terrorist acts, that the Russian people were easily demoralized, and that their leaders would heed their views and withdraw the army as the costs of war mounted. That Russian women would feel obliged to take the initiative to rescue their sons only reinforced the impression of an irresolute male leadership susceptible to violent pressure. These inferences, favorable to terrorism, proved incorrect during the second war, when terrorist acts served only to provoke further Russian brutality.

The second Chechen war broke out before the two sides could work out a modus vivendi. In August 1999, Islamist opponents of President Maskhadov staged a raid across the border into Dagestan led by Shamil' Basaev and "Emir Khattab," a Saudi immigrant to Chechnya married to a Dagestani woman. The attack coincided with a rash of bombings of apartment buildings in several Russian cities, and together these helped draw Russia back into war.

The resumption of war shocked and dismayed most Chechens. In an interview with a BBC reporter, Basaev acknowledged that in Chechnya "some women curse me" because his military activities in Dagestan had provoked a renewal of Russian bombing.[36] Indeed, few Chechens supported Basaev's continued military provocations, especially when they jeopardized Chechnya's hard-won independence and peace. Few were willing to support the holy war that he, his friend Khattab, and their "band of madmen" had promoted. Such a characterization was typical of the ordinary Chechens interviewed by reporter Anne Nivat. One woman referred to Basaev as "that criminal" who "should have been arrested a long time ago." A group of Chechen men who did not join the fight against the new Russian invasion insisted that "all of us here would willingly fight the Russians for our independence, but not as long as Shamil' is leading the troops."[37]

---

[35] "Printsipy opredeleniia osnov vzaimootnoshenii mezhdu Rossiiskoi Federatsiei i Chechenskoi Respublikoi," signed by A. Lebed', A. Maskhadov, S. Kharlamov, S. Abumuslimov, August 31, 1996, Khasaviurt, in the presence of T. Guldimann, head of the OSCE mission in Chechnya. Published in *Nezavisimaia Gazeta*, September 3, 1996.

[36] Transcript of BBC Russian Service's telephone interview with Basaev, posted by Tom de Waal to Johnson's Russia List, Center for Defense Information, Washington, DC, October 4, 1999 (originally online at www.bbc.co.uk/russian/2909_4.htm).

[37] Anne Nivat, *Chienne de Guerre: A Woman Reporter Behind the Lines of the War in Chechnya*, trans. by Susan Darnton (New York: Public Affairs, 2001), pp. 15–16, 250.

If the first Chechen war was Yeltsin's responsibility, the second quickly became associated with Vladimir Putin, Yeltsin's chosen successor. The Chechen forces led by Basaev and Khattab invaded Dagestan just two days after Yeltsin appointed Putin as prime minister. Unlike Yeltsin, who at the outbreak of the first war had disappeared for days to have an operation on his nose, Putin visibly and publicly took control. As Yeltsin rhapsodized, "within a matter of weeks, he had transformed the situation within our power ministries. Each day he would bring together the heads of each ministry or agency into his office. He forced them to gather all their resources into one united fist."[38] It may seem surprising that Yeltsin, whose career had nearly collapsed in the wake of the disastrous first war in Chechnya, decided that the best instrument for dealing with the North Caucasus three years later was a "united fist." Equally surprising, the Russian public seemed to agree. Three months into the war, pollsters found that 77 percent of respondents in St. Petersburg and Moscow approved of the invasion. Even in the provinces the approval rate averaged 64 percent, despite the fact that the regional media often portrayed the local impact of the war – deaths of hometown police and soldiers, for example – more truthfully than in the capitals. Along with support for the war itself Putin's personal approval rating soared, from 35 percent when Yeltsin appointed him in August to 65 percent in October, as he escalated the war. As one Russian journalist explained, "the secret of this popularity is in the single forceful expression which Putin used about Chechnya – 'We will wipe them out.'"[39]

Remarkably, Putin retained a high level of popularity over the course of many more years of war. Dramatic increases in the price of oil and gas helped a lot. These were key Russian exports whose revenues filled the federal coffers and allowed for continuing subsidies for the population. So did restrictions on the media that prevented Russians from getting a true picture of the war's costs.

Within a few years of the resumption of war, Russian forces had gained control of most of Chechen territory, except for the impenetrable mountain strongholds that would continue to shelter the tenacious guerrilla fighters. Even after most of Chechnya was bombed into rubble, and thousands of its citizens killed, driven away, or "disappeared" into internment camps and mass graves, the country remained a dangerously insecure place, with frequent guerrilla attacks, assassinations, and abductions.

---

[38] Yeltsin, *Midnight Diaries*, p. 336.
[39] Andrei Shukshin, "Putin Thrives on Russians' Pain – Pollster," Reuters report from Moscow, October 22, 1999, on JRL; Fedor Gavrilov, "Enemies are Learning from Each Other," *St. Petersburg Times*, October 22, 1999; Sarah Karush, "Chechen War Hits Home in Provinces," *Moscow Times*, December 7, 1999.

Moscow's attempts to "normalize" the situation in Chechnya proved difficult. Russian troops alienated the local population with their vicious tactics and gave rise to a wave of terrorist attacks increasingly perpetrated outside Chechnya. These included the siege of Moscow's Dubrovka Theater in October 2002, where more than eight hundred members of the audience were held captive; an attack at a rock festival outside Moscow in July 2003; several suicide truck bombings; a suicide attack against the Moscow metro system; and the brutal seizure of a school in Beslan in September 2004, where some 330 hostages died (including children, parents, and grandparents), when Russian forces and local vigilantes stormed the building as the terrorists set off explosives. As one chronology of these events put it, "three years after the start of the counterterrorism operation" – the name that Putin gave to the second Chechen war – "terrorism had returned to Russia."[40]

Putin blamed Aslan Maskhadov for all of these crimes, branded him an international terrorist, and refused to negotiate anything but the terms of his surrender. In March 2005, Russian forces succeeded in assassinating Maskhadov, eliminating the last hope for a negotiated peace with the separatists. In the meantime, Putin sought to reinstall pro-Moscow forces in control of Chechnya. Elections held in October 2003 were denounced internationally and by local representatives as fraudulent. They yielded victory for the Kremlin-backed candidate, Akhmat Kadyrov, but his assassination seven months later necessitated yet another round. He was eventually succeeded by his son Ramzan. As direct Russian control of the region gave way to "Chechenization," ordinary Chechens continued to suffer at the hands of the new president's armed gang of *Kadyrovtsy*.

Women, violence, and Islam

In Russian popular consciousness the high-profile terrorism of the first years of the new millennium bore a woman's face – an unprecedented development in Chechnya's long history of struggle with Russia. Eighteen of the fifty Chechens who seized the Dubrovka Theater were women, as were the drivers of several truck-bomb attacks, the suicide bombers of the Moscow subway and concert, and some of the terrorists at Beslan. Between June 2000 and June 2005, women carried out 47 of 110 bombing attacks and 22 out of 27 suicide attacks (81 percent).[41] They became

---

[40] Lokshina, *Chechnya Inside Out*, pp. 26–27.
[41] Anne Speckhard and Khapta Ahkmedova, "The Making of a Martyr: Chechen Suicide Terrorism," *Studies in Conflict and Terrorism*, 29, 5 (2006), pp. 429–492.

known as *shakhidki*, the Russian feminine version of the Arabic word for martyr.

The Chechens who seized the Dubrovka Theater demanded an immediate end to Russia's war in Chechnya and a withdrawal of the army. They threatened to blow up the building if their demands were not met. After a tense fifty-eight hours, Russian special forces piped in a debilitating gas and then stormed the theater. They killed the Chechens and freed the hostages, although more than a hundred of them later died from the effects of the gas. Some wondered why the Russian forces did not arrest the perpetrators when they had the chance. A possible answer – particularly regarding the women *shakhidki* – was provided to journalist Fred Weir by Zainap Gasheeva, the Chechen co-director of Ekho Voiny (echo of war), an antiwar coalition of Chechen and Russian women: "It makes no sense from a police point of view not to capture the culprits and interrogate them," she said. "But I believe our authorities did not want those women to ever tell their stories in a courtroom or anywhere else. They were killed to shut them up about the horrors that led them to commit such an act of despair."[42] As Weir reports, "surviving hostages confirm that their female captors spoke of ruined lives and personal agony." Alla Illyichenko, an accountant who was attending the theater performance and was taken hostage, reported that "the *shakhid* woman sitting next to me said her brother was killed last year and she lost her husband six months ago. She said: 'I have nothing to lose, I have nobody left. So I'll go all the way with this, even though I don't think it's the right thing to do.'"[43]

Journalists reported similar motives of the women who participated in the siege of the Beslan schoolhouse. As Peter Baker describes,

The Beslan attackers included two women dressed in black, with scarves covering their faces and explosive belts around their waists. As the attackers trained guns on more than 1,200 children, parents and teachers in the gymnasium, the school's director, Lydia Tsaliyeva, begged them to release the students, according to her deputy, Olga Sherbinina. "Let the kids go and the adults stay," Tsaliyeva said. "Feel mercy for the young." Sherbinina recalled one of the fighters answering: "Who felt mercy for my children? My house was bombed, and five of my children were killed."[44]

Whatever the motives of the *shakhidki*, the role they played in the violent seizure of the theater and other terrorist acts runs contrary to the

[42] Fred Weir, "Chechen Women Join Terror's Ranks," *Christian Science Monitor*, June 12, 2003.
[43] Ibid.
[44] Peter Baker, "'New Stage' of Fear for Chechen Women," *Washington Post*, October 19, 2004.

gendered expectations, articulated by Virginia Woolf and many others, of peaceful women. In the field known as postcolonial studies, a debate has emerged over whether feminists misunderstand women who support Islamist movements by improperly imputing to them liberal notions of individual agency.[45] In the Chechen case, it is still uncertain how much agency women possessed. Clearly many of them were motivated by feelings of despair and desire for revenge. Yet their actions were often controlled by men. In the Dubrovka Theater, for example, men made all the decisions. When members of the literally captive audience requested permission from their female captors to use the restroom, for example, they were told to ask the men. These women, clad in explosives, were effectively walking suicide bombs. They never detonated themselves, however, because – in one interpretation, at least – their male overseers became distracted by the Russian attack, and neglected to issue the order.[46]

Putin characterized the hostage takings at Moscow and Beslan as entirely about international Islamist terrorism and nothing else. He linked the Chechens to the al Qaeda terrorist network. The Dubrovka crisis provided a vivid image to reinforce Putin's framing of the Chechen conflict as an international terrorist conspiracy, one intimately connected to political Islam: bearded men in combat fatigues, toting machine guns, and wearing green headbands with Arabic slogans, and veiled female suicide bombers issuing communiqués to the al Jazeera TV network. Yet these images were not typical of Chechnya, but of a small minority of Islamist extremists, known as Wahhabis.

The Wahhabis sought to impose a form of religious and social practice quite alien to the traditions of Chechnya and were much resented by most of the populace. Not least, their insistence on limiting women's sphere of activity to the household and imposing the use of the veil contradicted decades of modernizing policies of the Soviet era and the everyday reality of wartime Chechnya – where women were obliged to play prominent roles in the absence of fathers, sons, husbands, and brothers. In areas where the Wahhabis took control, some women suffered terribly, with those accused of adultery, for example, subjected to torture and public

---

[45] See, e.g., Saba Mahmood, "Feminist Theory, Embodiment, and the Docile Agent: Some Reflections on the Eyptian Islamic Revival," *Cultural Anthropology*, 6, 2 (2001), pp. 202–236.

[46] Anne Speckhard, Nadejda Tarabrina, Valery Krasnov, and Khapta Akhmedova, "Research Note: Observations of Suicidal Terrorists in Action: The Chechen Terrorist Takeover of a Moscow Theater," *Terrorism and Political Violence*, 16, 2 (Summer 2004), pp. 305–327.

abuse.[47] Nevertheless, some members of Chechen society – including young people who had known nothing but the violence and degradation of war through their entire lives – were susceptible to the appeal of the Wahhabis. Apparently some of the female suicide bombers fit this profile. In that respect they resemble the young adherents to radical Islam in Algeria during the same period.

For the modern Russian public, the Wahhabi understanding of the proper role of women also seemed alien and tended to reinforce the tendency to see Chechens as Others. Ironically, the image of the ideal Wahhabi woman – passive, submissive to men, and with a sphere of activity limited to the home – seemed to conflict with other images of Chechen women that the Russian public routinely encountered: women as snipers attacking Russian troops, women taking Russian children hostage, women as suicide bombers destroying Russian civilians. Some of the most influential images came not from the television news programs or documentaries, which under antiterrorism laws became increasingly limited in what they could show, but through the medium of the popular film. Before turning to some of those films, we review the background of gender relations in Chechnya and Russia and the role that Islam and local traditions played.

Gender between tradition and modernity

The previous chapters attested to the visible impact the clash between modernity and tradition can have on women. As in Algeria, women in Chechnya faced competing demands from modernizing colonial (in this case Soviet) authorities to enter the urban workforce and abandon traditional dress and customs, and from family and clan members to maintain the patriarchal order of village life. As with Yugoslavia, the Soviet Union's communist ideology added the further dimension of official sex equality. Gender relations in Chechnya have received relatively little attention from scholars. Much of what passes for knowledge – especially on such "exotic" topics as abduction of brides and polygamy – contains an admixture of myth and fantasy distilled from the early colonial ethnographers, the Russian literary tradition, and even popular Soviet culture. The purpose of this section is to convey a sense of the basic character of gender relations and to what extent they represented male domination and female submission, before I turn to analysis of the films.

---

[47] C. J. Chivers, "In Chechen's Humiliation, Questions on Rule of Law," *New York Times*, August 30, 2006.

Fortunately, for our purposes of understanding the role of gender in Chechen culture before and during the post-Soviet wars, some collections of interviews with Chechen and Russian women and men offer valuable insights. Particularly useful are the interviews conducted by Petra Procházková in a collection titled *The Aluminum Queen*.[48] Procházková served as a war correspondent for the Czech daily *Lidové noviny*, reporting from Grozny under Russian bombardment, from the site of mass graves after the Samashki and other massacres, and at the scene of the Budennovsk hospital siege, where she and other journalists offered to exchange themselves for the hostages taken by Chechen terrorists. She temporarily left journalism to run a day-care center and work for a humanitarian-aid organization in Grozny until the Russian government declared her *persona non grata* in 2001 (after which she moved to Afghanistan).

In 2000 Procházková was asked to carry out interviews of the women she served in her humanitarian work – young, old, Russian, Chechen, with and without families. The transcripts provide useful and sometimes surprising information about traditional gender relations in Chechnya, and particularly how the wars transformed them. Another valuable source is the collection of stories gathered by Tanya Lokshina and members of the Russian human rights organization Memorial and published in 2007.[49] Other interview material comes from the work of the anthropologist Valerii Tishkov, and the journalists Anne Nivat, Anna Politkovskaia, and Åsne Seierstad. The evidence from these interviews suggests that there are certain core generalizations about gender relations in Chechnya, but much variability in practices.

One question is the extent to which Chechen practices reflect traditional Muslim customs and to what degree that entails subordination of women. Typically analysts point to a tension between local customary law, known as *adat*, the Islamic law of *Shari'ia*, and the legal code of the secular Soviet or Russian federal authorities. In many areas, Chechen practice reflected a mix of the three. Consider, for example, the case of polygamy. In Islamic law, a man can take up to four wives if he can treat them fairly and provide for them. According to Chapter 14 of the Russian Family Code, however, polygamy is illegal: a person will not be allowed to marry if he or she is officially married already. During the wars, guerrilla leaders frequently took more than one wife. As one of Tishkov's interlocutors reported, "It's the vogue now to compete with

[48] Procházková, *Aluminum Queen*.
[49] Tanya Lokshina, ed., *Chechnia: Zhizn' na voine* [Chechnya: Life in War] (Moscow: Demos, 2007); an abridged English translation appeared as *Chechnya Inside Out*.

each other for the greatest number of wives."⁵⁰ Ramzan Kadyrov, who became Moscow's chosen president of Chechnya, had advocated polygamy when he served as acting premier in 2006: "Statistically, women outnumber men in Chechnya because of the ongoing war. Polygamy could be an extremely important factor for the Chechen nation. Shariat laws allow that. That is why every man who can maintain such large families should have four wives. I can only welcome this idea." The Russian press reacted negatively, as did many Chechen women.⁵¹

As a matter of practice, polygamy existed in Chechnya even during the Soviet era. Chechen women commonly married as young as fifteen or sixteen years old, even though the minimum legal age in Russia was eighteen years. Among Petra Procházková's interlocutors were women from a range of backgrounds, many of whose husbands had more than one wife. Consider the example of Kalimat, the owner of a small café in Grozny, whose husband had taken a second wife. When asked about the practice of polygamy, she replied, "That's our tradition. A man can have up to four wives and the wife must sit at home and put up with it patiently. I suppose that's the way it should be."⁵² Polygamy was also practiced in mixed marriages between Chechen men and Russian women, as Zhenya, an elderly Russian woman interviewed by Procházková, reported of her granddaughter's situation: "Polygamy has never been anything unusual in Chechnya. We're accustomed to it. Anya's husband had another wife, a Chechen." The wife of a minister in the Chechen separatist government told Procházková of how her husband had fled the country in the wake of the Russian invasion in 1994, to promote the cause of Chechen independence abroad. He took a second wife while living in Turkey. "At that moment he actually had two wives," she reported. "However, that's not as objectionable here as it is in your country. He told me everything and explained it all to me. As our laws require there had to be a meeting of all our near relatives and the situation was sorted out. In the end we remained friends."⁵³

Zoya, another Russian woman interviewed by Procházková, described how she got married to a Chechen man in a village in Kazakhstan in 1957 after her mother had died: "I was simply in a hurry to get married. Dad didn't take much care of me anymore and it was very hard being a single girl in a wild country." It turned out that her husband, Said, already had a wife and two children, who lived with his mother. Moreover, "to tell you the truth, we didn't get married officially." Said

⁵⁰ Tishkov, *Chechnya*, p. 146.
⁵¹ "Chechen Women Furiously Reject Suggestion on Polygamous Family," Pravda.ru, January 16, 2006.
⁵² Procházková, *Aluminum Queen*, p. 68.   ⁵³ Ibid., pp. 105–106.

later returned to Chechnya when the republic was reconstituted and gave Zoya the option to follow or not. She moved to Chechnya, where Said set her up in a small house which came under bombardment during the wars of the 1990s. She ended up living in a bomb shelter nearby, where Said eventually joined her.[54]

My point in recounting these stories is to suggest the difficulty of making generalizations about gender relations in Chechnya. For a practice that was formally illegal, and rare as far as outsiders knew, polygamy turns out to have existed in a wide variety of forms, including some that seem rather surprising for the Soviet Union – a country often characterized as totalitarian in its social control.

Certain elements of gender relations reflected everyday practices and traditions that varied from place to place or even from family to family within the same place – again challenging our notions of the homogenization of society under Soviet rule. Liza Ibragimova, a Chechen woman interviewed by Procházková, described a tradition according to which mothers are never allowed to see their sons-in-law. It is not a Chechen tradition, but one common in neighboring Ingushetiia, and it affected Ibragimova because her daughter Luiza married an Ingush man named Ruslan who could never meet his wife's mother: "We must never meet in our lives. We can't even pass each other on the street … The Ingush family that Luiza married into is in fact very modern; you could even call it international; after all, Ruslan's mother is a Russian. They have lots of Lithuanian relatives. But they observe that law."[55] However "modern" Ibragimova considered her son-in-law's family, there are plenty of elements of her own family's traditions that would not seem to qualify. For example, there is a strict hierarchy of gender and age in the order by which family members are allowed to marry, and severe consequences for those who violate it. Ibragimova explained, for example, that her younger daughter "hasn't the right to marry until her elder brother has got married. He could even kill her if she did."[56]

Procházková collects considerable information from her interlocutors on the apparent subordination of women in Chechen society. But some of them deny it. In her interview with Kalimat, for example, Procházková ventures the impression that a Chechen woman "doesn't have much freedom" compared with Europeans or Americans, that because of the husband's dominant role "you sometimes seem downtrodden." Kalimat responds: "That's total nonsense. There was nothing like that in our home and those traditional attitudes no longer apply in

[54] Ibid., p. 177.   [55] Ibid., pp. 115–116 (Liza Ibragimova).   [56] Ibid., p. 121.

Chechen households."[57] This is the same person who said that a woman whose husband has four wives is expected to "sit at home and put up with it," and "that's the way it should be."[58] For every family that might find a given tradition archaic, another family will practice it, take it for granted, and find it natural.

Abduction of brides and forced marriages are practices that one might expect to be more common in legend and literature than in real life. Actually, many residents of the Soviet Union would have associated them with a movie – a popular comedy loosely based on the Caucasus captivity narrative called *Kavkazskaia plennitsa* (dir. Leonid Gaidai, 1966) – literally "female prisoner of the Caucasus" (known as *Kidnapping Caucasian Style* in its US release). Oksana Sarkisova refers to it as an "Eastern," because, like the American Westerns, it played a significant role in creating and sustaining legends.[59] The movie's enduring legacy, its "near-cult status," in Bruce Grant's words, is attested by its widespread availability on DVD in post-Soviet Russia and the establishment of an eponymous Moscow restaurant, with props, stills, and clips from the movie.[60] Yet, despite its comedic appeal, the practice of abducting brides was real and it has continued in the region into the twenty-first century. As in other Muslim regions of the former Soviet Union, bride kidnapping in Chechnya is sometimes a consensual practice, the result of either an inability of the couple to persuade their parents to agree to the marriage or a lack of funds to afford a wedding.[61] But it also occurs against the wishes of the woman. In 2008 in the town of Piatigorsk in the Russian North Caucasus I met a young woman of Chechen and Ingush descent who had escaped three attempted abductions while growing up in Ingushetiia. According to local custom, if she had been abducted and remained with her captor overnight, she would have been obliged to marry him and he would have had to negotiate a payment to her family.

The topic of abducting brides is close to two others linked to our theme of gender and violence: kidnapping and rape. Kidnapping for ransom, for exchange of prisoners, and as a demonstration of status is a long tradition in the Caucasus and a practice that Russian imperial armies adopted as soon as they came into contact with the region as

---

[57] Ibid., p. 54.   [58] Ibid., p. 68.
[59] Oksana Sarkisova, "Skazhi mne, kto tvoi vrag: Chechenskaia voina v rossiiskom kino" [Tell Me, Who is Your Enemy: The Chechen War in Russian Cinema], *Neprikosnovennyi Zapas*, no. 6 (2002), p. 26.
[60] Bruce Grant, "The Good Russian Prisoner: Naturalizing Violence in the Caucasus Mountains," *Cultural Anthropology*, 20, 1 (2005), p. 53.
[61] Derluguian, *Bourdieu's Secret Admirer*, p. 45; Cynthia Werner, "Women, Marriage, and the Nation-State: The Rise of Consensual Bride Kidnapping in Post-Soviet Kazakhstan,"

aspiring conquerors. Present-day descendants on all sides of the conflict have continued the practice. In response to the September 2004 terrorist seizure of the Beslan schoolhouse, for example, Russian authorities in Chechnya rounded up "the entire extended families of Maskhadov, the former Chechen president, and of Chechen warlords Shamil' Basaev and Doku Umarov. Maskhadov's brother was in the tent where the men were kept, and his elderly sister was in a nearby building with the women and children," including a five-month-old baby.[62]

Kidnapping was rife during the brief period of Chechen independence, 1997–1999, as opponents of Maskhadov sought to undermine the authority of his rule and his attempts to improve relations with Russia. When the Russians reestablished control after launching the second war in September 1999, they engaged in widespread kidnapping and "disappearances" of suspected rebels and sympathizers – and of people with no connection to the resistance, whom they would then ransom or try to turn into informers, if they allowed them to live at all. Their Chechen proxies, led by Ramzan Kadyrov, continued these practices. One prominent example is "Magamed Khanbiev, the former Ichkeria minister of defense, who sided with the pro-federal Chechen government after 40 members of his family, primarily women, were taken as hostages by Kadyrov's security service in early spring 2004."[63]

Rape is a taboo subject in Chechen society. It is a capital crime and one traditionally kept under control by the threat of vengeance – the "blood feud" (*krovnaia mest'*) which is part of the traditional *adat* system of justice.[64] In some respect, the custom of a man's forcible abduction of a woman to be his bride could be seen as a way of redefining what otherwise would be considered rape. In one of Procházková's interviews, Zhenya described how she and her two granddaughters were kidnapped from a bomb shelter by Chechen and Arab fighters. The kidnappers persuaded fifteen-year-old granddaughter Anya that they had killed her grandmother and that the only way to spare her little sister, also named Zhenya, was for Anya to become the bride of an Arab named Ahmed. The grandmother expressed her own ambivalence about how to understand what happened to Anya:

I really do think that nobody raped her in the actual meaning of the word. She told me about her wedding night. Imagine that he apparently said to her: "Anya,

in Pauline Jones Luong, ed., *The Transformation of Central Asia: States and Societies from Soviet Rule to Independence* (Ithaca, NY: Cornell University Press, 2004), pp. 59–89.

[62] Kim Murphy, "During School Siege, Russia Took Captives in Chechnya," *Los Angeles Times*, September 7, 2004.

[63] Tanya Lokshina, "'Chechenization' of the Conflict, or the 'Political Process' in the Chechen Republic," in Lokshina, *Chechnya Inside Out*, p. 93.

[64] Amjad Jaimoukha, *The Chechens: A Handbook* (London: Routledge, 2005).

you're a virgin and I don't want to cause you any pain. I won't do anything you don't want me to do" … So she doesn't have any dreadful sexual experiences. I won't ever let anyone say she was raped. She was properly married … She told me he treated her in an exemplary fashion. He never insulted her and was always tender and considerate. Perhaps he really was in love with her.[65]

Yet later in the interview, when Zhenya begins to generalize about gender relations in Chechnya, she adds a more critical element:

They claim that they respect their womenfolk, but it's as easy to respect your dog. Here in the Caucasus, the man is always something more than the woman. If a man takes a fancy to a girl and he decides to have her, it doesn't matter very much whether she wants to or not. If she doesn't take him freely, he abducts her and then the whole family has to agree. Otherwise the girl is disgraced and no one will marry her afterward. So the Chechens don't think that what happened to Anya was much of a crime. They didn't rape her, but instead that Arab took her for his wife properly.[66]

As we saw in the case of Algeria in the 1990s, such "instant marriages" often served to give a veil of Islamic propriety to outright rape.

Sexual violence and the limits of peacemaking

Chechens' motivation for defending their territory against Russian attack entailed the conventional gendered notion of war as male defense against threats to the women and children, or what Tishkov calls "defense of the procreative sphere." One forty-year-old man he interviewed provided this explanation: "When the troops approached our village, we already knew about the massacres in Grozny and Samashki. Everyone [male?] who could handle arms swore on the Qur'an to die before permitting the disgrace of our women."[67]

Terms such as the "disgrace of our women" refer evidently to male concerns that "their" women will be raped by Russian soldiers – a fate considered worse for the women than death. Rape has played a role in the historical relations between Russia and Chechnya since the beginning, as Russian soldiers and officers committed sexual violence in the course of militarily subjugating the peoples of the North Caucasus. Historians have written, for example, of how the campaigns led by General Ermolov in the early 1800s entailed rape and enslavement of Chechen women to serve as concubines for his officers.[68] Yet even these practices have been romanticized in the Russian literary canon. In Mikhail Lermontov's prose work, *A Hero of Our Time*, for example,

[65] Procházková, *Aluminum Queen*, pp. 90–91.   [66] Ibid.
[67] Tishkov, *Chechnya*, pp. 141, 99.   [68] Jaimoukha, *The Chechens*, p. 42.

Pechorin kidnaps a young Circassian beauty named Bela against her will and keeps her captive in his room. He eventually wins her affection by buying her gifts.

Post-Soviet Russia's wars in Chechnya have not produced evidence of systematic campaigns of rape, as we saw in the case of Yugoslavia and Algeria in the 1990s. The Russian army has apparently not attempted to use rape as a means of "ethnic cleansing," to destroy Chechen communities in order to make room for Russian settlers, for example. Moscow evidently harbored no intention of repopulating Chechnya with ethnic Russians, or creating ethnically "pure" land bridges to Russian territory, as Serb forces did in Bosnia. Nevertheless, there is plenty of evidence of individual cases of rape and torture of Chechen women and men by Russian soldiers and police officials.[69]

"That's something we don't talk about here" is the response Petra Procházková typically received when she broached the subject of wartime rape. "Only a handful of cases received publicity, the rest were hushed up," explained Elza Duguyevova. "A lot of our young women are in prisons all over Russia. If they come home, they'd be better off shooting themselves. If anyone laid a hand on them they'd be written off for good here in Chechnya. It's a kind of law. A sullied daughter is worse than a dead one to her father. It's a terrible disgrace."[70]

Not that the victim or her father always had a choice: some daughters ended up both sullied and dead. One of the few cases where a Russian officer was brought to trial for his crimes involved the abduction, rape, and murder of a young Chechen woman, Elza Kungaeva. A year and a half into the second war, Colonel Iurii Budanov was the only Russian military official put on trial for war crimes. The incident began on March 26, 2000, when Budanov and his troops went on a drinking binge in double celebration of Vladimir Putin's electoral victory and the birthday of Budanov's daughter. At one point Budanov's drunken assistant ordered Lieutenant Roman Bagreev to fire an artillery barrage at a neighboring village ostensibly to test the military preparedness of his soldiers. When the lieutenant refused to commit such an illegal act, Budanov ordered

---

[69] Anna Politkovskaya, *A Small Corner of Hell: Dispatches from Chechnya* (University of Chicago Press, 2003), pp. 51–53, 86–87; Medical Foundation for the Care of Victims of Torture, "First Reliable Evidence of Widespread Rape in Chechen Conflict," www.torturecare.org.uk/news/latest_news/64, citing a report of April 2004. For a thorough report, including many additional sources, see Diana Tsutieva, "Rape and Other Forms of Sexual Violence in Chechnya," memorandum prepared for Chechen Advocacy Network, December 1, 2004 (archived with the author).

[70] Procházková, *Aluminum Queen*, p. 27.

him beaten and thrown into a pit for the rest of the night. He became the main witness against Budanov.[71]

According to several witnesses, Budanov then drove into the village and barged into the Kungaev home in the middle of the night. He initially tried to abduct a sixteen-year-old girl, but when she screamed and resisted, he grabbed her eighteen-year-old sister Elza instead. He then brought her back to his lodgings, where he allegedly beat and raped her, and strangled her to death. Military authorities arrested Budanov, but friends in high places managed to protect him from suffering the full consequences of his crimes. For example, although a military autopsy of Kungaeva's body found evidence of vaginal and anal damage consistent with rape, the prosecutor dropped that charge early on in the proceedings. Budanov argued that Kungaeva was a suspected sniper and he had accidentally killed her when he flew into a rage as he was interrogating her.

According to Anna Politkovskaia, Budanov's tank regiment had been involved in fierce battles during the previous month in which some of the colonel's close friends had been killed, perhaps by snipers.[72] This history may account for why Budanov thought he could exculpate himself from the charge of murder by accusing Kungaeva, and why the public responded sympathetically. There is, however, no evidence to back up his charge, and much to call it into question. For one thing, the fighting the previous month took place some eighty kilometers from Kungaeva's village, and all of the other elements of his story – that someone gave him a photo of Kungaeva as a leading suspect, for example – proved false. Budanov ultimately ended up in prison with a ten-year sentence, but multiple efforts by his military superiors to secure a diagnosis of "temporary insanity," to arrange pardons, or to reduce his jail time for good behavior undermined any sense that the Russian government was committed to eradicate crimes of sexual violence against Chechen women. The newspaper *Moscow Times* titled one of its articles about Budanov, "Insane 'Heroes of Our Time,'" a reference to the colonel's literary predecessor, Pechorin.[73]

Although Budanov was arrested and ultimately received a prison sentence, the reaction from Russian leaders and the general public did not augur well for further prosecution of war crimes – or justice for crimes of sexual violence. A sizable proportion of Russian public opinion sympathized with Budanov. Forty-two percent of those questioned about the

[71] Agathe Duparc, "L'impossible procès d'un 'héros russe,'" *Le Monde*, April 13, 2001.
[72] Politkovskaya, *Small Corner of Hell*, pp. 39–40.
[73] "Insane 'Heroes of Our Time," *Moscow Times*, June 25, 2002.

colonel's murder of the young Chechen woman claimed that he "was justified in doing so and should not be punished. Thirty-two percent said the trial was arranged to smear the military, with only 11 percent saying that they believe the colonel is guilty and should be punished."[74] Defense Minister Sergei Ivanov "voiced his support and sympathy" for Budanov when he was put on trial, calling him "a victim of circumstances."[75] Ivanov, like Vladimir Putin a former St. Petersburg resident and KGB agent, was known as Putin's "eye and arm," and his views were probably not far from the president's on the matter.[76] Indeed, Putin is on record as considering rape a joking matter. The incident in question took place in October 2006 and concerned then Israeli President Moshe Katsav, who was under investigation for rape and sexual harassment of several women. At the end of a press conference in Moscow with visiting Israeli Prime Minister Ehud Olmert – and thinking the microphones were off – Putin said, "Say hi to your president. He turned out to be quite a powerful guy. Raped 10 women! We're all surprised. We all envy him!"[77]

Despite the subordinate position of women in traditional Chechen society and the violence they face during military conflict and occupation, many observers accord a particular role to women when it comes to matters of war and peace. Derluguian suggests, for example, that Chechen mothers exert a certain influence in deciding whether or not their sons will fight with the anti-Russian resistance. If she has only one son, a mother is less likely to send him off to battle than if she has several.[78] Procházková's interviews suggest that the practice is much more variable. Kalimat, a Chechen mother of two sons, aged eighteen and twenty, told her, for example, that she had to beg them "literally on my knees" to get them to flee Grozny to their grandmother's village rather than stay and join the "home-guard units that sprang up all over the city." As Kalimat described, "it really is hard for a man to sit at home and just watch the city being turned into a heap of rubble and an enormous graveyard. My boys simply wanted to go and do something because doing nothing and feeling helpless can even drive a man mad." Young Chechen men, like males throughout the world, were

---

[74] RFE/RL Newsline, 5, 107, Part I, June 6, 2001, quoting *Izvestiia*, June 5, 2001.

[75] Ian Traynor, "Russia Prepares to Draw More Blood in Chechnya," *The Guardian*, June 8, 2001; "Defense Minister Says Budanov 'A Victim Of Circumstances,'" RFE/RL Newsline, vol. 5, no. 94, part I, May 17, 2001.

[76] Carlo Bonini and Giuseppe D'Avanzo, "Tutti gli uomini del presidente: Così Putin impone l'ordine in Russia" [All the President's Men: How Putin Imposes Order in Russia], *La Repubblica*, July 16, 2001.

[77] Tom Parfitt, "Putin Praises Sexual Prowess of Israeli President," *The Guardian*, October 20, 2006.

[78] Derluguian, *Bourdieu's Secret Admirer*, p. 32.

brought up to associate willingness to fight with masculinity. Meeting the cultural expectations for men implied consequences for the rest of the family as well – an insight that Kalimat's eldest son expressed when he asked, "Mummy, wouldn't it be better for you too if I died somewhere in combat instead of before your eyes here at home, like an old woman?"[79]

Another tradition, mentioned by several twenty-first-century Chechens, reflects a belief that women enjoy a particular influence in preventing or resolving conflicts. Chechen women are supposed to have the power to stop a fight by dropping a kerchief between the combatants "or by sending one of her children holding a mirror to face the fighters."[80] As Tamara Abuzaidova told Procházková, "when two men fight or when a blood feud is declared between two families, only a woman can stop it. In some places it's an old woman, in others a young girl who has to throw her headscarf between lads who are raring for a fight."[81] Such traditions were no match for the Russian army, nor were they adequate to prevent bloodshed between rival Chechen criminal gangs or the depredations of the *Kadyrovtsy*.

Whatever role one thinks Chechen women played according to tradition – making peace or deciding whether to send their sons to fight – the years of violence that followed the Russian invasion of 1994 eventually turned some of them into fighters themselves. "Something has come unglued at the very heart of Chechen society," argued Irina Zvigeskaia, of Moscow's Institute of Oriental Studies. "It is almost unheard of for Chechen women to fight. They are traditionally the heads of the household and the peacemakers in Chechen society. Many things must have changed irrevocably for Chechen men to accept this terrible new role for women in battle."[82] Russian cinema of the 1990s and beyond portrayed many of the factors that led to a transformation of gender norms in Chechnya and a new violent role for women.

Chechnya on screen

The outbreak of war between the Russian authorities and the Chechen separatist movement in December 1994 brought Chechnya to the movies – or, more precisely, back to the movies. During the Soviet era, the film industry had represented Chechnya and the North Caucasus in

[79] Procházková, *Aluminum Queen*, p. 46.   [80] Jaimoukha, *The Chechens*, p. 91.
[81] Procházková, *Aluminum Queen*, p. 131.
[82] Fred Weir, "Chechen Women Join Terror's Ranks," *Christian Science Monitor*, June 12, 2003.

various ways. Sarkisova identified several categories of representation, each based on a particular notion of us–them (*svoi–chuzhie*) and corresponding to the ideological notions in vogue at a given time. In the era of the 1920s, filmmakers presented Chechnya and other regions as captives of the Tsarist "prison house of nations" and made movies (e.g., *Zelimkhan*, 1929) depicting the national groups' efforts to achieve independence according to the "class principle." Peasant and working-class representatives of the national minorities fought against both the Tsarist regime and their own nationalist bourgeoisie. In the 1930s, "in the service of the theory of Soviet (inter)nationalism," when the regime sought to consolidate its control over the national republics, "Chechnya gradually disappears from the screens as an independent theme." In the darkening years preceding World War II, films began to represent the region again with a theme of borders that pitted "us" and "ours" against threatening foreign Others, as in the 1939 film, *Patriot*.[83] Following the cultural thaw initiated by Nikita Khrushchev, filmmakers enjoyed more leeway to explore their own themes, but even in comedies such as *Kidnapping Caucasian Style* (1966) many of the stereotyped representations and tropes of the earlier eras reappeared.

The highly acclaimed *Prisoner of the Mountains* (1996) by Sergei Bodrov was inspired by the contemporaneous war, but also heavily influenced by the romantic tradition of Russian literary treatments of the Caucasus, in which gender had always come into play. The film shares its title – literally, "Prisoner (or Captive) of the Caucasus" – with an 1822 narrative poem by Pushkin, an 1872 short story by Tolstoi (based on his military service in the region in the 1850s), and another short story by a contemporary Russian writer, Vladimir Makanin. Its antiwar tone is reminiscent of Tolstoi's later, posthumously published *Hadji Murat*.[84] It reflects several themes of Lermontov's *A Hero of Our Time*. According to Gary Shteyngart, Lermontov's novel provides an even more direct connection to the film, and to cinema in general. "In many ways, Lermontov's narrative style anticipates the world of cinema; its influence, direct or not, can be found not only in the work of early Soviet filmmakers such as Sergei Eisenstein but also in more recent postmodern films." For such an early

---

[83] Sarkisova, "Skazhi mne, kto tvoi vrag."

[84] Tolstoi's story is available in a translation by Hugh Aplin, *Hadji Murat* (London: Hesperus Press, 2003); Makanin's story is included in the collection *The Loss: A Novella and Two Short Stories*, trans. by Byron Lindsey (Evanston, IL: Northwestern University Press, 1998). Makanin's story is actually entitled "Kavkazskii plennyi," or "Captive [literally, "Captured"] of the Caucasus." A film version, called *The Captive* (*Plennyi*) was made by Aleksei Uchitel in 2008.

exemplar of the Russian novel, Lermontov deploys a fragmented narrative style, where events take place early on that are not understood until later "flashbacks" fill in the relevant background.[85]

In cinema, as in literature, gender comes into Russia's relations with Chechnya in a way familiar to many colonial situations.[86] According to Paula Michaels, "Russian literary tradition envisioned the Caucasus as feminine, sensual, and weak, a perception that supported its military conquest and political domination." She quotes Katya Hokanson's description of the region as "a province of wild freedom in the Russian imagination" and explains that "the Caucasus became a place to be tamed by the Russians, and the literature of that time reflects this imperialist drive."[87] Other analysts have suggested that Russia's legitimacy as a state vis-à-vis its colonial territories was premised in part on a binary relationship between "notions of hegemonic masculinity (e.g. the soldier, men of the dominant ethnic/racial group or institutionalized hegemonic masculinity embodied by the state or the military)" and "notions of subordinate masculinity (e.g. the enemy, the deserter, the refugee, the homosexual or the national minority)."[88] In Michaels' view, the film *Prisoner of the Mountains* challenged the prevailing characterization of Russia's relations with the Caucasus in its sympathetic portrayal of the Chechens. She saw in the film a hopeful sign of changed cultural values that would reject the traditional Russian imperial approach.

Bodrov's film is apparently set in the midst of the war that Russia launched against Chechnya in 1994 to put down the armed separatist movement. There is, however, little to identify the political context and no mention of Chechnya per se, giving the film a certain timeless quality that further reinforces its link to nineteenth-century literary predecessors, despite the presence of late twentieth-century weaponry. The movie is beautiful, filmed in the mountains of Dagestan, an autonomous republic of the Russian Federation bordering Chechnya. Residents of Dagestani villages were themselves later drawn into the war when it resumed in

---

[85] Gary Shteyngart, Introduction to Mikhail Lermontov, *A Hero of Our Time*, trans. by Marian Schwartz (New York: Random House, 2004), p. ix.

[86] Richard C. Trexler. *Sex and Conquest: Gendered Violence, Political Order and the European Conquest of the Americas* (Ithaca, NY: Cornell University Press, 1995). Thanks to Charles Niven for calling this book to my attention.

[87] Paula A. Michaels, "Prisoners of the Caucasus: From Colonial to Postcolonial Narrative," *Russian Studies in Literature*, 40, 2 (Spring 2004), p. 55, quoting Katya Hokanson, "Literary Imperialism, *Narodnost'*, and Pushkin's Invention of the Caucasus," *Russian Review*, 53 (1994), pp. 336–352.

[88] Maya Eichler, "Russia's Post-Communist Transformation: A Gendered Analysis of the Chechen Wars," *International Feminist Journal of Politics*, 8, 4 (December 2006), p. 487.

autumn 1999, following the attack by Islamist militants from Chechen territory. The musical score incorporates indigenous instruments and melodies, much as *The Battle of Algiers* does. It also conveys a certain documentary style and includes depictions of everyday life, including a wedding and a funeral, agricultural work, and children's play.

The element of gender appears in the movie's opening scene, as Russian army conscripts parade naked before an indifferent female medical staff, as their commanding officer refuses to tell them where they will be deployed. The storyline is a variant of a traditional captivity narrative, and, although the location is never specified, the audience assumes it takes place in Chechnya. From the medical examination, the film cuts to an extraordinary panoramic view of the Caucasus Mountains and then zooms in to track Russian soldiers on an armored personnel carrier traveling through a mountain pass. A group of men in local dress are pulling a cart full of hay. As if to highlight their Otherness, a Russian officer calls out, "Hey, non-Russians! Stop!" The Chechens block the road with the cart, as shots ring out from the surrounding hills. The Russians have been ambushed.

Only two of the Russians survive and are taken prisoner. One of the prisoners, named Ivan "Vanya" Zhilin (played by Sergei Bodrov, Jr., the son of the director), falls in love with the young Chechen girl, Dina, whose family is holding him and his Russian compatriot, Sasha, hostage. Dina's father hopes to trade the Russians for his son, Dina's brother, a school teacher imprisoned at a local Russian military base. The young Chechen was apparently caught up in a *zachistka*, an indiscriminate sweep operation of the sort that the French carried out in Algeria and the Americans conducted in Iraq. Meanwhile the Russian soldier's mother, also a school teacher, travels to Chechnya to try to arrange the exchange, as many Russian women, members of the Committee of Soldiers' Mothers, sought to do in the mid-1990s.[89]

Taking prisoners in this fashion has a long heritage in Chechen tradition, which is part of the reason the captivity narrative plays such a central role in the Russian literary canon. Among Chechens, certain norms govern the practice and give the holder of the prisoner particular rights. Capturing and holding hostages to trade for those one's enemy has captured has long been common in the region and elsewhere; in fact, it is the basis for the reciprocal relationship that has evolved into the Geneva Conventions' provisions for treating prisoners of war and repatriating them after the end of conflict. In the Caucasus prisoners were also taken for the sake of ransom. One of the humanizing elements of Bodrov's

---

[89] Amy B. Caiazza, *Mothers and Soldiers: Gender, Citizenship, and Civil Society in Contemporary Russia* (New York: Routledge, 2002).

Prisoner of the Mountains, as opposed to some of its literary forebears (such as Tolstoi's story), is that the Chechen who holds the Russian prisoners is interested not in ransom, but in the return of his son.[90]

One of the great achievements of Bodrov and his actors is to portray the story's characters as fully human, at the same time as they represent recognizable types drawn from the Russian literary heritage: Abdul-Murat, the stern patriarch; Dina, his innocent virgin daughter; Vanya, the equally innocent and green soldier; Sasha, the cynical veteran, who models himself on Sylvester ("Sly") Stallone, the actor who portrays Rambo; Maslov, the callous base commander; and a half-crazed Chechen rebel warlord who apparently has fought both with and against the Russians – another Rambo figure transported from Hollywood to the North Caucasus. In one scene, the Chechen Rambo temporarily kidnaps Sasha and Vanya from their kidnapper, Abdul. He makes them perform the potentially suicidal mission of walking through a minefield laid by the Russian forces, in order to identify the location of the mines. Sasha appears to recognize the Chechen commander, perhaps from Abkhazia, a region of the post-Soviet republic of Georgia, where a couple of years earlier Chechens and Russians had fought with the Abkhaz separatists against the Georgian government forces.[91]

Like Pontecorvo, Bodrov has relied on nonprofessionals for some of the roles – particularly that of twelve-year-old Dina, played with affecting self-assurance by Susanna Mekhralieva. In contrast to Tolstoi's "Prisoner of the Caucasus," where the author attributes an "anonymity, exoticism, and childlike barbarism" to the local people to accentuate their differences from the superior Russians, "Bodrov's lens uses costume, dance, music, and other cultural elements to humanize his Others." He portrays not "Caucasian otherness, but sameness," according to Michaels. "Their clothes, music and facial features differ from those of the Russians, but they are average men, women, and children, who sing and dance, laugh and live like the Russian characters in the film and the Russian audience itself."

Bodrov's use of nonprofessional actors creates a sense of "realism and authenticity [that] strengthens the audience's perception of the film as an accurate representation of the enemy and calls into question the images seen nightly on TV news broadcasts."[92] Sarkisova sees the director's ethnographic approach as intending to convey, "for the time being" at least,

---

[90] Sarkisova, "Skazhi mne, kto tvoi vrag." For a summary of Chechen traditions regarding prisoners see Alexander Mnatsakanyan, "'Heroes' and 'Villains' of the Chechen Wars," in Lokshina, *Chechnya Inside Out*, p. 55.
[91] Cherkasov's discussion in Lokshina, *Chechnya Inside Out*, p. 77.
[92] Michaels, "Prisoners of the Caucasus," pp. 56, 71.

Figure 4.1 Dina guards her prisoners. *Prisoner of the Mountains* (1996)

a "dotted boundary between 'ours' and 'others' inhabiting the archaic world of the past."[93] Whatever the extent of Bodrov's interest in highlighting a common humanity between the two communities, the portrayal of Chechens is unusually sympathetic.

Prisoner of the Mountains conveys the complexity and ambiguity of gender and nationality in contemporary Russia's identity landscape. Sasha, the experienced combat veteran, hired as a *kontraktnik* to fight in Chechnya, at first appears the epitome of a macho soldier of fortune; yet he gradually and grudgingly develops an affection for Vanya, to whom he is chained in a dirt cellar. The night of their planned escape they listen to a transistor radio and begin dancing together to Louis Armstrong's "Let My People Go," whirling joyfully around the cell until they collapse together on the floor.

Much of the history of Russo-Chechen relations, both its cooperative and conflictual elements, is embodied in the character of Hasan, Dina's brother-in-law, who helps guard the prisoners. Hasan was sent to Siberia, not with the 1944 deportation, but in the post-Stalin years, as punishment for a crime. He had killed his wife, Dina's sister, after she had run off with a Russian geologist. Dina – who seems to have accepted her sister's fate with equanimity and gets along well with Hasan – explains to the Russian prisoners that he used to love to sing, particularly Russian songs, but he could no longer do so: "the Russians" had cut out his

---

[93] Sarkisova, "Skazhi mne, kto tvoi vrag."

tongue as punishment for talking back to the prison guards – an allusion to the Chechens' legendary refusal, described by Aleksandr Solzhenitsyn and others, to bow down to Russian authority even in the prison camps of the Gulag. Sasha responds, "Of course, who else but the Russians?" He seems to recognize, at least from the Russian perspective, the harmful habit of stereotyping the Other and the misunderstanding and hostility that it engenders. Sasha then asks Hasan to sing a tune, promising to help him out. As Hasan hums, Sasha jokes: "It sounds familiar. Remind me of the words would you?" Hasan smiles. These two killers, who have ample reason to hate each other, managed nevertheless to find a common bond.

Prisoner of the Mountains appears at first to offer a traditional portrayal of gender roles in violent nationalist conflict. In fact, the feminist literature, as we saw in chapter 1, suggests that there are at least *two* traditional – and mutually inconsistent – roles.[94] The first is for women to support their men as they defend the nation (and *their* women) with violence. Dina plays this role, as she cooks and tends house for her father (apparently a widower), and helps guard the prisoners he has ambushed and captured. The second is for women to oppose war because it offends their maternal instinct and their purpose of fostering life. Vanya's mother plays this role, as she travels to Chechnya to rescue her son. Here, too, however, Bodrov complicates the picture. The mother is portrayed as sincere and conciliatory in a conversation with Abdul, as she seeks to arrange the exchange of her son for his. But when Maslov, the Russian commander who holds Abdul's son captive, explains to her that the Chechens cannot be trusted, that even children attack Russian soldiers, she cannot contain her emotions and begins hitting him. She turns her anger on "her own" rather than on the Others. Dina, too, is shown as more complicated than one might expect. When Abdul first returns with the prisoners, he hands Dina his guns, which she takes with a familiar confidence. The camera frames her in the doorway of the underground cellar, as the viewer looks out from the captives' perspective.

Later, when her brother is killed in an attempted escape from the Russian base – thereby eliminating the basis for the prisoner exchange – Dina at first accepts the consequence that Vanya must now die too rather than go free. By this time, Sasha has already been killed, following an escape attempt in which he committed two murders. By Chechen

---

[94] For a discussion, see Cynthia Enloe, *The Morning After: Sexual Politics at the End of the Cold War* (Berkeley: University of California Press, 1993); and Joane Nagel, "Masculinity and Nationalism: Gender and Sexuality in the Making of Nations," *Ethnic and Racial Studies*, 21, 2 (March 1998), pp. 242–269.

Figure 4.2 Dina takes the guns. *Prisoner of the Mountains* (1996)

Figure 4.3 Abdul returns. *Prisoner of the Mountains* (1996)

tradition it would be appropriate for Vanya to suffer the consequences of his fellow soldier's transgressions. He has already been moved from the underground cellar to an open pit. Yet Dina eventually wavers, as Vanya persuades her to let him go (much as the Circassian maiden sets the hero free in Pushkin's "Prisoner of the Caucasus"). Abdul returns, however, before Vanya can make good his escape – leaving the audience temporarily in suspense about the Russian's fate. Viewers soon learn that Abdul will violate the Chechen tradition of blood vengeance by allowing Vanya to flee, but the Russian army carries out its own bloody revenge anyhow, not realizing it is unnecessary, by destroying the village.

According to Michaels, Bodrov portrays the range of Chechen and Russian characters, men and women, in a more nuanced and multidimensional way than would have been expected by a Russian audience steeped in the literature of Pushkin, Lermontov, and Tolstoi. A likely exception, in my view, is Tolstoi's *Hadji Murat*, published in 1912, which offers comparably multidimensional portraits of many of its characters (not to mention a strong anti-imperialist message). Michaels explains:

> Bodrov did not merely update the setting to make an antiwar political point but metamorphosed his characters and their motivations based on the reality of more than a century of historical transformations. His pacifist, humanist Zhilin…is the product not only of the late twentieth-century concept of cultural relativism but of a culture grappling with how to reshape its identity in the face of imperial collapse. Bodrov's violent, cool, macho "Sly," the bitter child of Soviet military culture and its unfortunate adventurism, conveys Russia's weariness from its centuries-long struggle to keep its empire intact. Together, Zhilin and Sasha articulate a transformation in Russia's attitude toward its place in the world and its empire.[95]

The outcome is a sympathetic picture of the Chechens' plight and of the senselessness of the Russian war – views consistent with Russian popular opinion of the time. Yet the transformation Michaels identified was short lived. Russian attitudes shifted, as the situation in Chechnya worsened and the conflict reignited. The new perspective implied a different approach to gender as well.

From romantic realism to crude caricature

Aleksandr Rogozhkin's *Checkpoint* (1998), released two years after Bodrov's film, eschews a portrayal of women as essentially peaceful, innocent, and conciliatory. His female characters include a Chechen prostitute, a Chechen sniper, a Russian army officer, and a western human rights investigator. The straightforward setting of the captivity narrative gives way to an environment of uncertainty and confusion (evoking in some respects *Apocalypse Now*), as a Russian military unit is deployed to a remote region of Chechnya, ostensibly to deal with the threat of a sniper. The soldiers set up camp and become the sniper's targets. They have many interactions with the local Chechen community, reflecting a further elaboration of the themes of revenge killing and mistaken identity that *Prisoner of the Mountains* introduced.

---

[95] Michaels, "Prisoners of the Caucasus," pp. 73–74.

Figure 4.4 Violating "the unwritten rule not to search women and children." *Checkpoint* (1998)

We see again the perennial mix of cooperation and conflict – sometimes in the same action, as when Chechen women trade sex for bullets. A young Chechen woman who calls herself Masha brings her older mute sister to the Russian post to offer her for sex with the soldiers. One soldier takes the sister off to the woods as Masha talks to his buddy and asks whether he wants to be next. "No, I don't enjoy that," he replies. He inquires whether Masha also sells herself. She says no, that she is married. He asks whether her sister is married and she replies that she used to be. What about her husband? "Was he killed?" Referring obliquely to her sister's rape, she answers, "No, when your guys ruined her, he left her. Now she's of no use to anyone." We recognize the same sentiments about the shame associated with rape in Chechen society as we saw in the interviews Petra Procházková and others conducted with female victims of the second Chechen war.

In both Bodrov's *Prisoner of the Mountains* and Rogozhkin's *Checkpoint* the possibility arises of mutual understanding and even romantic love between Chechens and Russians – in each case a Chechen female and a Russian male. Yet tragedy intervenes to destroy the possibility of the personal relationship, symbolically signaling the hopelessness of the broader Russo-Chechen political relationship. In *Checkpoint*, Masha gradually becomes fond of the Russian soldier she first meets when she escorts her

Figure 4.5 Madam investigator arrives. *Checkpoint* (1998)

sister the prostitute. "You are kind and handsome," she tells him, setting the scene for the film's tragic surprise ending.

The ending comes as the culmination of a series of episodes of senseless violence that result from accidents and misunderstandings and are often shrouded in ambiguity. In an early scene, Russian soldiers raid a house and find a crippled young Chechen boy hammering on an unexploded mine. As the soldiers flee, the mine blows up, killing the boy and destroying his home. Was he a suicide bomber or an innocent victim? As the horrified villagers and dismayed Russian solders return to the scene, one Chechen woman grabs a soldier's gun and begins firing. She accidentally kills a Chechen police officer, and the Russians, in turn, fire at her.

The film posits a gendered division of labor when it comes to the Russians' committing potential war crimes and investigating them. Alisa, a stout, middle-aged lieutenant, interviews the Russian soldiers one by one in a small office, almost as naughty school boys are called to the principal. A Canadian woman leads a delegation to investigate the incident on behalf of the Organization for Security and Cooperation in Europe (OSCE). Her portrayal by Rogozhkin and her treatment by the other characters reflect the growing Russian suspicion of western interference in the Chechen conflict that ultimately resulted in expulsion of the OSCE mission from Chechnya. As we saw in the previous chapter,

Figure 4.6 Naked welcome. *Checkpoint* (1998)

such suspicions of international organizations are widely portrayed in Yugoslav films on the violent breakup of that country as well – and the representatives of the United Nations or the international press are commonly played by women.

That women represent the West and the OSCE in *Checkpoint* is hardly coincidental, as the film presents a clear sexualization of the relationship between East and West. The Canadian investigator interviews the Russians in a makeshift office with a large pin-up of a bare-breasted woman on the wall. The Russian officer dealing with her delegation proposes that "it's definitely time to roll up this OSCE," but he deliberately mispronounces the Russian acronym, OBSE, to reproduce a variant of the most common Russian profanity, suggesting essentially, "Fuck them." As the investigator departs, she tells the officer, somewhat seductively, but rather unrealistically, "If you're ever in Canada, give me a call." He kisses her hand and bids her "Bon voyage."

Oksana Sarkisova, in her insightful overview of the Chechen wars as portrayed in Russian cinema, refers "without a shadow of condescension or sarcasm" to Bodrov's *Prisoner of the Mountains* as an example of "cinema of the intelligentsia" (*intelligentskoe kino*). Filled with "politically correct decorations," it tried to portray "war with a human face."[96]

---

[96] Sarkisova, "Skazhi mne, kto tvoi vrag."

Checkpoint already represented a small step away from that ideal-type, although both films share what Sarkisova calls a "slowed-down, 'anti-adventure' tempo." Subsequent Russian films treating the Chechen theme took several leaps away from the ideal-type intelligentsia film in both form and content. Their crude stereotypes and vivid depiction of wanton violence reflected – and shaped – the popular understanding of the ever-worsening situation in Chechnya.[97]

When the Russian troops withdrew from Chechnya in 1996, they left behind a chaotic and increasingly lawless territory, the de facto independent Chechen Republic of Ichkeriia. Aslan Maskhadov, the military commander of Chechnya's secessionist war, was elected president in January 1997, but he faced opposition from warlords – particularly Shamil' Basaev and Salman Raduev – former allies who came to challenge his authority in the postwar interval. Chechnya saw a rash of kidnappings for ransom and a veritable slave-trade, much of the activity conducted with political motives (to undermine Maskhadov), but much also for reasons of greed and revenge. When the conflict spread beyond Chechnya's borders in autumn 1999, as Islamist radicals sought to carry out *jihad* and forge a North Caucasus Islamic state, the Russian armed forces again intervened and resumed a brutally destructive war.

Such is the political context for Aleksei Balabanov's 2002 film, *War*. It uses as its main narrative device the reminiscences of Ivan Ermakov, a former Russian soldier who was held captive in Chechnya. The film tells the story of an English couple, two actors performing Shakespeare's *Hamlet* in neighboring Georgia, who were kidnapped by a Chechen warlord along with the soldier and a Russian captain (Sergei Bodrov, Jr., who played Vanya in *Prisoner of the Mountains*). The film evokes Grigorii Chukhrai's *Ballad of a Soldier* (*Ballada o soldate*, 1959), the classic war film of Khrushchev's thaw era. In Galina Zvereva's words "resemanticized citations" from Chukhrai's film – particularly as Ivan travels back from the "front" to visit his hometown – fulfill an important function in *War*.[98]

The kidnapping of the English couple recalls a real event that transpired during the summer of 1997, part of complicated story of intrigue worthy of a movie script in itself. Russian troops had left Chechen territory

---

[97] For evidence of popular indifference to the human rights abuses perpetrated by Russian troops in Chechnya – and racist, even exterminist views about Chechens expressed in some focus groups – see Sarah Mendelson and Theodore Gerber, "Casualty Sensitivity in a Post-Soviet Context: Russian Views of the Second Chechen War, 2001–2004," *Political Science Quarterly*, 123, 1 (Spring 2008), pp. 39–68.

[98] Galina Zvereva, "'Rabota dlia muzhchin?' Chechenskaia voina v massovom kino Rossii" ["Work For Men"? The Chechen war in Popular Russian Cinema], *Neprikosnovennyi Zapas*, 6 (2002).

in accordance with the Khasaviurt Accord that ended the first war in August 1996. Chechnya's status was supposed to be negotiated between the conflicting parties by December 2001. In the event, the second war, launched in September 1999, led Moscow to renege on its commitment. In the intervening period, however, Aslan Maskhadov, whose election as president was recognized by the Russian government and international electoral monitors, tried to work out a *modus vivendi* with Moscow. His bargaining leverage was limited to what was left of Chechnya's prewar role in the Soviet-era system of oil transshipment and refining. Some officials in Moscow were ready to deal, whereas others remained suspicious of Chechen intentions and preferred to see the experiment in independence fail. The proponents of cooperation succeeded in negotiating a series of agreements on general economic cooperation. One of its advocates was Boris Berezovskii, a media and oil magnate then serving as deputy secretary of Yeltsin's Security Council. Berezovskii sought to bolster the prospects for the Russo-Chechen agreements by promoting them to Russian television audiences on his NTV channel a week before they were actually signed on May 12, 1997.

As an incentive to further economic cooperation, Ivan Rybkin, the Security Council secretary, suggested "offering Grozny a share of tariffs from oil exports via Chechnya" – a proposal that Maskhadov's predecessor, Dzhokhar Dudaev, had floated to an unresponsive Yeltsin administration in 1992.[99] The May agreements seemed to bear fruit, at least as far as the oil factor was concerned, on July 3, 1997, when Geidar Aliev, the president of Azerbaijan, signed an agreement in Moscow endorsing the shipment of Caspian oil through Chechnya. Western support for the proposal came in the form of partnership with British Petroleum.

The day after the oil agreement was signed, Jon James and Camilla Carr, two British volunteers at a home for troubled children, were kidnapped at gunpoint in Grozny.[100] A number of observers have suggested that the kidnapping of British citizens was intended to wreck the BP–Azerbaijan deal and thwart Chechnya's integration into the international oil market. In response to the kidnapping President Maskhadov

---

[99] "Berezovskii Details Russian–Chechen Agreements," RFE/RL Newsline, vol. 1, no. 25, part I, May 6, 1997. The main document is *Soglashenie mezhdu Pravitel'stvom Rossiiskoi Federatsiei i Pravitel'stvom Chechenskoi Respublikoi Ichkeriia* [Agreement between the Government of the Russian Federation and the Government of the Chechen Republic Ichkeriia] signed by V. Chernomyrdin and A. Maskhadov, May 12, 1997. Thanks to Vakha Khasanov, former Chechen "ambassador" to Moscow, for giving me a copy in November 1998.

[100] Information from online BBC reports: http://news.bbc.co.uk/hi/english/uk/newsid_125000/125327.stm; http://news.bbc.co.uk/hi/english/uk/newsid_175000/175919.stm.

ordered an antiterrorist brigade to storm the headquarters of warlord Arbi Baraev in Urus-Martan, where he suspected the captives were being held. The operation failed, owing to unanticipated resistance from forces loyal to Salman Raduev.[101] On August 18, 1997 three NTV journalists abducted in Chechnya in mid-May were freed through the efforts of Berezovskii. He and NTV director Igor' Malashenko acknowledged that the captives were ransomed for "a seven-figure dollar sum."[102]

Maskhadov's opponents continued to try to wreck Chechen–Russian relations. On May 1, 1998 they kidnapped Valentin Vlasov, Yeltsin's envoy to Grozny. Vlasov met and was held in the same location as the two British captives, Carr and James – evidence that the kidnappings were part of a coordinated plan.[103] The British couple were released on September 20, 1998, after fourteen months in captivity, thanks to a deal worked out between Berezovskii and Raduev. Berezovskii reported that he had secured their release by donating computers and medical aid to Raduev, but most observers consider these a euphemism for a substantial ransom. Leaders of republics neighboring Chechnya criticized Berezovskii, suggesting that Raduev now had "more computers than some Russian intelligence services possess." Taped telephone intercepts of conversations between Berezovskii and Movladi Udugov, a former deputy prime minister and Maskhadov rival, suggest that Berezovskii was indeed involved in sending money to ransom some victims of Chechen kidnappings.[104]

In this case, Berezovskii flew Jon James and Camilla Carr back to London in his private jet. But his efforts were not an act of individual altruism. In addition to his business affairs, Berezovskii was at that time also serving as a government official in the Commonwealth of Independent States (CIS), the organization that brought together most of the countries that had made up the Soviet Union. In fact, in an interview with Russian media, Raduev made clear that "Berezovskii was dealing with us not as a politician-businessman, but as the executive secretary of the CIS." As such, one of Berezovskii's goals was to further

[101] Shamsutdin Mamaev and Nikolai Babichev, "Prestupnye promysly" [The Criminal Fields], *Kommersant"Vlast'*, November 3, 1998, pp. 18–20. In Russian, *promysel* means both "trade" or "business" and "field," as in oil field.
[102] "NTV Journalists Released in Chechnya," RFE/RL Newsline vol. 1, no. 98, part I, August 19, 1997; "Berezovskii, Malashenko on Russian Journalists' Release," RFE/RL Newsline, vol. 1, no. 99, part I, August 20, 1997.
[103] Mamaev and Babichev, "Prestupnye promysly," p. 19; "Forgiven but Not Forgotten," *The Guardian*, February 17, 2000.
[104] "Chechen, Ingush Presidents Criticize Berezovskii," RFE/RL Newsline, vol. 2, no. 212, part I, November 3, 1998.

economic cooperation in the Caucasus region, including the shipment of Azerbaijani oil across Chechnya to Novorosiisk.[105]

Neither Moscow nor western governments were, however, satisfied that the situation in Chechnya was adequately secure to proceed. Two weeks after the release of James and Carr, for example, four engineers (three British citizens and one New Zealander), employed by a British telecommunications company, were kidnapped in Grozny. President Yeltsin's personal envoy, Vlasov, was still held captive. He was released on November 13, 1998, presumably with Berezovskii's intervention. On the same day kidnappers captured Herbert Gregg, an American teacher at an orphanage in Dagestan's capital of Makhachkala.[106] He was eventually released, but the four engineers were not so lucky. They fell victim to a botched rescue operation by Maskhadov's government.[107] Their captors executed them and left their severed heads by the roadside; the bodies were found a week later. In early December a senior official of the Grozneft oil company was kidnapped in Grozny and the chief of the Chechen antikidnapping unit was assassinated.[108] With such grisly determination Maskhadov's opponents made it clear that they were not giving up their attempts to thwart his plans to use the oil pipeline as a means of improving relations with Russia.

In Pontecorvo's *Battle of Algiers*, as chapter 2 pointed out, the disturbingly vivid depictions of torture failed to convey the full horror of the practice during the real Battle of Algiers – not least because the film showed no women undergoing torture. Something similar can be said about the difference between Balabanov's *War* and the actual war in Chechnya. However gruesome and gratuitous the violence and however Byzantine the intrigue in Balabanov's movie, Chechen reality in the decade following the Russian invasion of 1994 was far worse.

War is an apparent allegory for the state of relations between Chechnya, Russia, and the West at the time. The Chechens are all portrayed as subhuman terrorists – a view that many Russians were coming to hold, according to evidence from focus groups.[109] The warlord who holds the

---

[105] Paul Klebnikov, *Godfather of the Kremlin: Boris Berezovsky and the Looting of Russia* (New York: Harcourt, 2000), pp. 261–264; Mamaev and Babichev, "Prestupnye promysly," p. 19.

[106] Evgeniia Borisova, "US Teacher Kidnapped in Dagestan," *Moscow Times*, November 13, 1998.

[107] "Four Foreign Hostages Slain in Chechnya," RFE/RL Newsline, vol. 2, no. 236, part I, December 9, 1998; "Chechen President Sheds Light on Hostages' Murder," RFE/RL Newsline, vol. 2, no. 237, part I, December 10, 1998.

[108] "Chechen President Calls for Coordination in Combating Crime," RFE/RL Newsline, vol. 2, no. 231, part I, December 2, 1998.

[109] Mendelson and Gerber, "Casualty Sensitivity." Seierstad, *Angel of Grozny*, heard similar views in her travels in Russia.

prisoners is named Aslan, probably to support Vladimir Putin's characterization of the rebel Chechen president as a terrorist, even though the
real Aslan (Maskhadov) represented the moderate wing of the armed
separatist movement. The British actors, John and Margaret, are naive,
emotional, and incompetent. The Russian captain, Medvedev, and soldier, Ermakov, are, by contrast, strong, stoic, sensible, and skilled. For
some reason Margaret, supposedly a British Shakespearean professional,
is played by an actress (Ingeborga Dapkunaite) who speaks halting,
accented English and has very few lines anyhow – perhaps a further sign
of the director's disdain for his potential foreign audience and expectation that his domestic audience will not notice or care. Margaret is
completely undeveloped as a character and serves merely as a symbol of
feminine vulnerability and an object of masculine desire or misogynistic
violence.

The core of the story revolves around the warlord Aslan's attempt
to obtain a ransom for his captives. He releases John with a demand
to raise two million pounds in ten days or Margaret will be gang-raped
and beheaded. He also frees Ivan, who knows some English, to acknowledge his help in communicating with the British captives and the outside world, and to let him try to get Captain Medvedev ransomed or
exchanged. Although John fails to raise the full amount, he returns to
Russia (with no knowledge of the country or the language) to seek
out Ivan for help in rescuing Margaret. Some of John's ransom money
comes from a British source who would like John to film his exploits
for a documentary, so he carries around a video camera and dictates an
ongoing narrative into the microphone, looking alternatively silly and
reckless.

Balabanov relies on standard gender stereotypes to convey his views
of the West and Russia. As Sarkisova points out, the director portrays
Ivan as John's alter-ego ("Ivan" is "John" in Russian) with juxtaposition
of binary characteristics that are supposed to represent the difference
between Russia and the West – "strength and weakness, experience and
naiveté, practicality and idealism, masculinity and femininity."[110] The
point here is "to demonstrate Europe's interest in what is going on" in
Chechnya, but also its "inability to direct events, and, consequently, its
dependence on the 'rule of the fist' adopted by Russia for the salvation
of European civilization" in the face of terrorists – that same "united
fist" that Yeltsin praised at the outset of the second Chechen war.[111]
As Sergei Lavrentiev, a Russian film critic, exalted, "this is perhaps
the first film that shows that the world has changed; that obeying the

---

[110] Sarkisova, "Skazhi mne, kto tvoi vrag."   [111] Ibid.

laws of ... political correctness will result in the destruction of Western civilization." In his view the Russo-Chechen conflict "fits perfectly" on to "the thematic diagram of a classical western," including the moral affirmation it is supposed to provoke in its viewers: "Carrying out his orders, Ivan behaves with the Chechens in the same way as the heroes of well-known American cowboy's [sic] films behaved towards the native Indians."[112]

The director conveys the view that Russia has the right approach to terrorism, as the effeminate British John comes to adopt what superficially appears to be the behavior of the masculine Russian Ivan. At first, for example, sensitive John is shocked by Ivan's use of violence against Chechen civilians; the film portrays it as unintentional but necessary for the success of the rescue mission. Later, when John realizes that Margaret, although still alive, has indeed been raped, he goes off on a killing spree of his own, shooting Aslan and wrecking the basis for the deal to rescue Margaret and Medvedev. The message seems clear: when Russians use violence, they maintain control (a masculine attribute), even if they must sometimes sacrifice innocent civilians. When westerners overcome their feminine reluctance to use adequate violence, they become emotional, lose control, and overreact (feminine attributes).

Despite John's botching of the rescue, Margaret and Captain Medvedev manage nevertheless to flee with John and Ivan. They barely escape by crossing the mountains to Georgia on foot. On his return to England John makes a lot of money from his documentary, even though the traumatized Margaret leaves him. The video footage ends up providing evidence for war-crimes allegations against Ivan, as he calmly reports to a journalist in the course of narrating the film. This film-within-a-film technique (or film as a film, in this case) we also saw in *Pretty Village, Pretty Flame*, as the American journalist's video camera captures her own death in the tunnel. In this case, the technique conveys a political message as well, and one rather unsettling. As Zvereva suggests, the situation of the "hero" Ermakov, on trial for war crimes, "clearly reflects the reality of the 'affair' of Colonel Budanov."[113] He was the officer accused of raping and murdering Elza Kungaeva, yet lauded and protected by many high-level political and military officials. In Balabanov's film only Chechens commit rape, while Russians face accusations – backed by western evidence – of war crimes that were necessary to defeat terrorists. Only "political correctness" of the sort practiced in the West could prevent viewers from recognizing the injustice inherent in this situation. As the

[112] Sergei Lavrentiev's review of *Voina* from 2002 is available at www.kinokultura.com/reviews/Rwar.html.
[113] Zvereva, "'Rabota dlia muzhchin?'"

film critic Lavrentiev comments, "the Englishman, true to the traditions of the protection of any 'oppressed minority', naturally and logically acts in such a way that leaves the saviour of his bride ... behind bars."[114]

The real-life fate of Camilla Carr and Jon James diverged from that of Balabanov's couple. Carr was indeed raped by one of her captors, but rather than seek revenge, both she and James came to terms with their ordeal and even became representatives of an initiative called the Forgiveness Project.[115]

In six years' time, from *Prisoner of the Mountains* in 1996 to *War* in 2002, Russian cinematic portrayal of the Chechen war had changed dramatically. Sergei Bodrov had offered archetypal, but nonetheless human, characters recognizable from the Russian romantic literary treatments of the Caucasus. Their portrayal acknowledged Chechens' grievances as a proud, but colonized people and presented Russians as ranging from good-hearted but misguided to malign and domineering. Gender roles were generally consistent with what we would consider the traditional understandings of the role of men and women in nationalist conflicts. Rogozhkin's *Checkpoint* complicated and broadened the gender landscape, by portraying Chechen women as whores and murderers, and Russian women as military officers, and by introducing European and North American women to represent the West's intervention in the Chechen conflict as monitors of human rights. Finally, Balabanov brought his audience nearly up to date by reflecting the official Russian understanding of the Chechen situation as a Manichean conflict pitting the forces of Chechen barbarity against the civilizing mission of Great Russia. Here the West plays an unwelcome role as an inept and hypocritical meddler, gendered as female or effeminate. Judging by the observations of a Spanish journalist reporting from a Moscow cinema, *War* struck a chord with the Russian public. In the final rescue scene, Russian army helicopters swoop down as the Chechens nearly catch the fleeing Margaret and the two Johns and whisk them off to safety. The audience enthusiastically applauded.[116]

From "White Stockings" to "Black Widows"

During the course of the Chechen wars, Russian film portrayals of women have come a long way from what we saw in *Prisoner of the Mountains*: gentle

---

[114] Lavrentiev, review of *Voina*.
[115] "How We Met: Jon James and Camilla Carr," interviews by Peter Stanford, *Independent on Sunday*, January 11, 2004.
[116] Pilar Bonet, "Iván, el nuevo héroe de Rusia," *Edición Impresa Internacional*, April 18, 2002, review of *Voina*.

Dina is supportive of her father (taking the rifles from him), yet sympathetic to his Russian prisoner, Vanya. Vanya's school teacher mom is a "soldier's mother" in the early post-Soviet sense – strong and determined to rescue her son, even by defying a corrupt government that has embarked on a wrongheaded war.[117] Women in subsequent movies are snipers: they take the rifles and kill people with them. Russian mothers still want to find their sons in Chechnya, but they loyally support their government's wars.

In Chechnya, the Russian rumor mill probably always exaggerated the presence of female snipers of the sort depicted in *Checkpoint*. Female guerrillas were not nearly as numerous as in the Algerian *maquis*, for example. Both Russian and foreign journalists have, however, documented individual cases of female fighters. A Reuters reporter, for example, described how "Shakhidat Baymuradova, a rifle slung on her back, fought alongside her husband in the ranks of Chechen rebels until he was killed by Russian troops in 1999." Four years later, "she strapped explosives to her waist and blew herself up at a Muslim festival where pro-Moscow officials had gathered. At least 16 people were killed."[118] A Russian journalist reported on the case of Fatima, a 23-year-old Chechen woman who served as a sniper in the militia commanded by Ruslan Gelaev and acknowledged killing two Russian soldiers. The report described her as the eighth female sniper captured up to that point, just a few months into the second war. She had first become a fighter when she followed her husband, a Wahhabi from Dagestan, and joined the forces commanded by Khattab. When her husband abandoned her, she joined Gelaev's group.[119] One of Tishkov's interlocutors mentions a "women's battalion" that his sister joined after she fell under the influence of foreign Wahhabi Arabs.[120]

All of the cases of which I am aware involved Chechen women or women from the region. There does not seem to be any factual basis for the stories of "White Stockings," women from the Baltic republics of Latvia, Lithuania, and Estonia. Indeed, it may be that the main source of such legends is the 1998 television film written and directed by journalist Aleksandr Nevzorov called *Purgatory* (*Chistilishche*). It opens with a scene of two women in fatigues, one blond, the other dark-haired,

---

[117] For an insightful discussion of the Committee of Soldiers' Mothers attempt to fashion an alternative form of patriotism that does not depend on blind obedience to the state, see Sperling, "Last Refuge of a Scoundrel."

[118] Clara Ferreira-Marques, "Chechnya's Suicide Widows are New Threat for Russia," Reuters, May 27, 2003.

[119] "V Komsomolskom sdalas' v plen zhenshchina-snaiper" (A Female Sniper Taken Prisoner in Komsomolskoe), Lenta.ru, March 24, 2000, www.lenta.ru/vojna/2000/03/24/komsomolskoe/.

[120] Tishkov, *Chechnya*, pp. 173–174.

speaking accented Russian, and firing snipers' rifles at wounded Russian soldiers and the medical team trying to evacuate them. Nevzorov's film is an unrelenting orgy of violence, essentially an extended battle between Chechen fighters and their foreign supporters, on one side, and Russian soldiers on the other. The director misses no opportunity to portray racist stereotypes in all their gory detail: an Arab warlord cutting off the head of a Russian soldier, a group of Chechens nailing another Russian soldier, whose legs have already been blown off, to a cross. In an interview, Nevzorov claimed that in his film he "could not permit any falsehood. I demanded and created the world of war as it is."[121] Some of his images are undoubtedly based on the reality of a war that witnessed brutal atrocities on all sides. Yet some – such as a group of African-American soldiers fighting with the Chechens – are pure fantasy. The "White Stockings" seem to be something in between. There were some female fighters, but apparently not from the Baltic republics.

Baltic women appear threatening to the psyche and self-esteem of a particular type of Russian male – the one that favors the binary racist opposition between Russian/white and Chechen/black – for the Baltic "White Stockings" are whiter than he is, yet support the Chechen side. He is primed to see citizens of the Baltic states as traitors for their resistance to incorporation in the Soviet Union, their role in destroying it, and their sympathy for the beleaguered Chechens.[122]

A later film, Fedor Popov's *Caucasian Roulette* (*Kavkazskaia ruletka*, 2002), portrays a female *Russian* sniper named Anna – the ultimate traitor. She had married a Chechen warlord named (again) Aslan and began killing her fellow Russians – the soldiers fighting in Chechnya – for money. After giving birth to a son, Anna has second thoughts about her career – and the one that likely awaits him. She spirits him away from his father for safe-keeping, and tries to escape on a freight train. There she meets another mother, an older woman named Maria, who is heading to Chechnya to try to rescue her own son – a conscript in the Russian army who has been taken prisoner by … Anna the sniper's Chechen husband! The film treats the themes of gender and war by portraying the maternal instinct, but in the service of a superficial political message: Maria supports her son's service in defense of his country, despite her personal stake; whereas it is only Anna's personal connection to her son that makes her recognize herself as a traitor. Maria carries a photograph of

<hr>

[121] "Aleksandr Nevzorov pokazal 'Chisilishche,' kotoroe strashnee ada" [Aleksandr Nevzorov showed "Purgatory," which is Scarier than Hell], *Komsomol'skaia Pravda*, October 22, 1997, quoted in Zvereva, "'Rabota dlia muzhchin?'"

[122] Legends of rifle-bearing women appear in histories of earlier wars outside Russia. The proto-Nazi German *Freikorps*, for instance, included examples of *Flintenweiber*

Anna posing with her sniper's rifle and has clearly been following her in hopes of discovering the whereabouts of the baby. The viewer suspects that she might be somehow working for Russian intelligence. How else would she be able to track Anna's moves and know so much about her? Maria's plan is to offer to trade Anna's baby to Aslan – who has also been pursuing Anna to get his son back – in return for her own son.

The story of *Caucasian Roulette* represents a peculiar variant on the role of the Committees of Soldiers' Mothers, whose members traveled to Chechnya to try to arrange such exchanges with their Chechen counterparts. In fact, when she first meets Maria and learns only that she is seeking to rescue her son, Anna inquires whether she is a member of the Soldiers' Mothers organization. Maria replies that she is working on her own. As Daniel Wild points out in a thoughtful review, one could understand the film as seeking to render the Chechen conflict "entirely as a matter of gender." It

manages to marginalize the role of men to such an extent that they are solely represented by one, perhaps already archetypal figure of contemporary Russia, the train conductor, whose work environment consists of porn movies, Penthouse posters, and old Brezhnev pictures. His jovial and loquacious simplemindedness, as he wheels and deals his way around any obstacles with only his own immediate benefits and gratification in mind, stands in stark contrast to the solemn battle of the two mothers and emphasizes how meaningless his contributions are within a larger context.[123]

This reading is consistent with the traditional relationship between gender and nation in Russia. As Helen Goscilo puts it, "from time immemorial, the dominant Russian iconography has projected nationhood as female, its ethos and moral identity metaphorized as maternity ... As the personification of stoic patience and all-forgiving self-abnegation, Mother Russia embraced her native or prodigal sons."[124] In another respect, however, the film violates expectations – consistent also with Virginia Woolf's hypothesis – of female solidarity in the face of masculine militarism. In the standard story, the success of the Soldiers' Mothers in rescuing their sons depended on the sympathy and support of Chechen mothers and their mutual antipathy to Moscow's war. In *Caucasian Roulette*, two *Russian* mothers represent contrasting extremes – one supportive of

(rifle-women) in its memoir literature and fiction. See Klaus Theweleit, *Male Fantasies, volume I: Women, Floods, Bodies, History* (Minneapolis, MN: University of Minnesota Press, 1987), pp. 70–79.

[123] Daniel Wild, review of Fedor Popov's *Caucasian Roulette* (2002), www.kinokultura.com/reviews/R7–05kavkazruletka.html, posted in 2005.

[124] Helen Goscilo, "The Gendered Trinity of Russian Cultural Rhetoric Today – or the Glyph of the H[i]eroine," ch. 4 in Nancy Condee, ed., *Soviet Hieroglyphics: Visual Culture in Late Twentieth-Century Russia* (Bloomington, IN: Indiana University Press, 1995), p. 69.

the Russian war, the other opposing it with violence. Their relationship represents what Anna describes as the Caucasian variant of Russian roulette: instead of a revolver with a single bullet in one chamber, the gun is nearly full of bullets, with just one empty chamber. Far from cooperating in a common pacifist-inspired endeavor to rescue their sons, Anna and Maria are locked in a zero-sum confrontation that only one of them will survive.

Although its title is clearly intended to evoke the Russian roulette scenes of Michael Cimino's 1978 film *The Deer Hunter, Caucasian Roulette* is not in the same league as that film or any of the major films discussed so far. Popov's plot is contrived and convoluted. His cinematography depends on standard clichés of the thriller genre. He creates a claustrophobic atmosphere, as most of the action takes place in a train, and introduces suspense only when Russian troops board it in search of the sniper. A climactic scene of armed confrontation between Anna and the conductor, who had spent most of the journey trying to seduce her, is rendered particularly implausible when he grabs Maria as a hostage to try to get Anna to drop her weapon. The viewer wonders why he thinks this cold-blooded killer would be moved at the prospect of another dead Russian, especially one with whom she has dealt so antagonistically through most of the film. That the women seem to find a common bond, as they escape in the wake of Anna's shooting of the conductor, seems no more plausible.

For a phenomenon that has little real-world veracity – "White Stocking" female snipers working for the Chechen resistance – Russian cinema has depicted it in a remarkably wide variety of ways. The Baltic snipers in *Purgatory* are soulless automatons; the Chechen sniper in *Checkpoint* expresses human, even romantic feelings for one Russian, while killing others; the Russian sniper in *Caucasian Roulette* exudes evil, kills for money, yet loves her baby and feels the early stirrings of remorse.

Even as Russian directors were exploiting the violent potential of women by portraying them as vicious snipers, a new and more terrifying role for women came to displace the cinematic one: suicide bombers.[125] To complement the sobriquet White Stockings, the media invented Black Widows. The expression conveyed the impression that these were Chechen women who had suffered the loss of husbands, brothers, and fathers at the hands of the Russian armed forces, and were intent on revenge.

As in Algeria, once some women became engaged in armed struggle no woman was even nominally immune from searches, arrests, and torture. In Chechnya the occupying forces felt compelled to violate what one of

---

[125] John Reuter, *Chechnya's Suicide Bombers: Desperate, Devout, or Deceived?* (Washington, DC: American Committee for Peace in Chechnya, 2004).

the soldiers in *Checkpoint* calls "the unwritten rule not to search women and children." Their plight resembles that of the French soldiers in *The Battle of Algiers*. In the reality of the Chechen war, as in the Algerian one, soldiers increasingly came to employ violence against women. Indeed, with the advent of the Black Widows, the desperate women who killed themselves to avenge family members "disappeared" by the Russian *zachistki*, women became a target of choice for the Russian soldiers and their pro-Moscow Chechen allies. One Chechen policeman named Ali told the French journalist Anne Nivat about Operation Fatima, which sought to find out which women had particularly suffered during the war, how many relatives they had lost, and so forth. "We then retain those individuals before they have even committed the least crime! We check all the women with a sad demeanor, who are both young and all dressed in black."[126] Similarly, another police official told a Reuters reporter in May 2003 that "some days ago we got a message telling us to pay special attention to women in mourning or in Muslim clothes." He then ventured his own opinion on the matter: "'women should not die this way,' he added, shaking his head. 'War is a man's affair. It is our fault these things happen.'"[127]

When *The Battle of Algiers* first appeared in 1966, its depiction of women wielding revolutionary violence alongside men seemed to many audiences hopeful and liberating. After many more decades of terrorist violence carried out throughout the world by nonstate actors as well as agencies of the state, one wonders whether most people hold such a romantic view of terrorism. The dramatic deterioration of the situation in Chechnya, as depicted in films produced over the course of just six years, should sound a warning of where spirals of state repression and terrorist resistance can lead. Unfortunately, the gender-egalitarian nature of terrorist violence, as portrayed in contemporary cinema, has made women fair game for abuses carried out by armies and police forces inspired by the example of the French in Algeria or the Russians in Chechnya. Judging by the testimony of human rights activists and journalists, women themselves did not feel particularly empowered by the prospect of engaging in violent resistance to Russian occupation or the arbitrary methods of the Kadyrov regime.

Gender role reversal and the promise of redemption

As we saw in the discussion of the Battle of Algiers – the film and the reality – as the French system of surveillance limited male mobility, female

---

[126] Anne Nivat, *La guerre qui n'aura pas eu lieu* [The War that Should Not Have Taken Place] (Paris: Fayard, 2004), pp. 128–129.
[127] Ferreira-Marques, "Chechnya's Suicide Widows."

Algerian militants came to displace men as the active participants in the resistance. Chapter 2 suggested that young men's resentment of women's roles in the resistance and in postwar Algeria may have contributed to the misogynistic character of the civil war that erupted in the 1990s. The aftermath of two brutal wars in Chechnya has also contributed to a strange reversal of gender roles – one that bodes ill for the republic's future.

The Chechen wars have witnessed the failure of Chechens to prevent Russian domination of their society. The legendary special powers of Chechen women to prevent conflict clearly fell short. The armed resistance of Chechen men enjoyed temporary success in driving out the Russian forces in 1996, but the second war crushed that resistance and any supporting elements in Chechen society in the most brutal and indiscriminate way. Resort to terrorist violence by desperate Chechen women only served to focus Russian repression on them.

When Chechens suffer violence against their family or community, tradition requires the surviving members to exact vengeance. This obligation typically falls on the male members of the family, and, like the willingness to fight, it serves to define masculinity. In discussion with the ethnographer Valerii Tishkov, one Chechen man described the role that concern for masculinity played in his decision to take up arms: "I began fighting at sixteen. My father had been shot dead from a helicopter, my oldest brother had been blown up by a land mine. It was my duty to take revenge or I would lose my honor before my neighbors. If not, how could I look them in the eyes?"[128] Some Chechens have described the impulse to avenge a death as a personal one, aside from the societal expectation. When Petra Procházková asked one woman how a mother's experience of the death of a child during wartime differs from a father's, she heard that the response may vary according to gender. The mother, she was told, "goes on living but she is constantly haunted by the thought that she should have died in place of her children. A father feels anger at his powerlessness, which in the case of our menfolk gradually turns into a desire to take revenge."[129]

Liza Ibragimova described to Procházková the Chechen obligation in this way: "According to tradition, every man who lost someone in the war should become an avenger and go on seeking the culprit of his relative's death and kill him. Vengeance is also inherited by his children. In this way vengeance becomes an unending process." She herself harbored doubts about the process, particularly in the context of the war with Russia. "Of course if one of your relatives dies in an air raid it is hard to

[128] Tishkov, *Chechnya*, pp. 141, 99.
[129] Procházková, *Aluminum Queen*, p. 62 (Kalimat).

discover which pilot dropped the bomb. And to take vengeance on the entire air force is a nonsense. So you spend your life repressing the hatred within you."[130]

Procházková's other informants described similar consequences for Chechen men if the circumstances make revenge impossible.

What is a husband to do if Russian soldiers start to insult his wife at a check-point, or if, on the contrary, they start paying her improper attention? He could, of course, leap on them as tradition demands, but it would be tantamount to suicide. So he swallows his pride and holds his tongue. The woman, on the contrary, has much more scope in a situation like that. She can laugh and get the soldiers to leave her fellow alone, to let him go and not beat or shoot him. Or she can start screaming hysterically, tear her hair and hope that it'll do the trick. She must gauge the situation accurately and act accordingly. The man is far more helpless and in fact has no choice. All he can do is behave meekly. And that is the greatest humiliation for our menfolk.[131]

In the discussion in chapter 2 of Algeria we considered whether the relative freedom of action women initially enjoyed during the war of independence and their educational advances in the postcolonial period may have spurred resentment by young, unemployed men who subsequently took out their anger and humiliation by engaging in misogynistic violence. Could such a pattern emerge in Chechnya as well? A number of women described a role reversal whereby they came to see themselves as responsible for protecting their weaker husbands – and it seemed to make them uneasy. "Most of the husbands sit at home," explained Elza Duguyevova. She described her own situation. "I'm also frightened to let mine out into the street on his own. When he has no choice but to go, I prefer to accompany him. I protect him, not him me. My husband is tall and well-built, which is the type that has most to fear from the Russians. They could pick him up at any moment without any reason and we wouldn't see him again, or he'd come back crippled. It's better for him to stay home," although he "finds it terribly degrading." In Duguyevova's view, "there is no greater humiliation" than "what a Chechen [man] feels like having a woman feed him … In the past if you couldn't feed your family you weren't considered a man."[132]

Kalimat, the café owner, confirmed that "the war has changed the relationship between man and woman, mostly because we, the weaker sex, are more worried about our stronger partners than they are about us."[133] Liza Ibragimova related Chechen men's humiliation to their fears for their masculinity and sexuality. "One shouldn't talk about such things,

---

[130] Ibid., p. 111.   [131] Ibid., p. 46 (Kalimat).
[132] Ibid., pp. 25–26.   [133] Ibid., p. 46.

but the war even destroyed people's love lives. I know from conversations with my women friends that their husbands also stopped being proper husbands, if you know what I mean. They simply disappeared from our bedrooms. As if that stress affected them more than us women."[134]

Chechens were not the only men damaged by the war. Police and soldiers who served in the Russian armed forces suffered the consequences of their time in Chechnya, including the post-traumatic stress that can result from the violence one inflicts on others (particularly in the case of torture), as well as from the fear and experience of violence against oneself.[135] Employers back in their hometowns were often unwilling to hire veterans of the Chechen wars, knowing the psychological problems they exhibited. Unemployment contributed to alcohol and drug abuse in a vicious circle.[136] *Chechentsy*, as the veterans were called, joined gangs or private security firms and fostered an atmosphere of violent lawlessness throughout Russia, a phenomenon captured in other films by Aleksei Balabanov, the director of *War*, such as *Brother* (*Brat'*, 1997) and *Brother II* (2000), and in *Alive* (*Zhivoi*, 2006) by Aleksandr Veledinskii.[137]

The effect on Chechen women of more than a decade of war and devastation, Elza Duguyevova told Petra Procházková, is that "we're a lot harder than we used to be. And our menfolk, on the contrary, are much softer. Quite simply an entire male generation has collapsed psychologically before our very eyes."[138] Yet there seemed to be a positive side, at least for the women, as they came to appreciate their own strength. As Liza Ibragimova put it, "during a war a self-respecting man cannot sit at home with his wife. So they all went off somewhere, some to the partisans, some to drum up public support, while some simply got lost and some hid so that they wouldn't be laughed at for doing nothing. And their wives stayed at home with the children. We discovered that we could manage without men."[139]

In Chechnya and elsewhere in the Russian Federation women had to compensate for men's weaknesses and dysfunctional behaviors. Not surprisingly, several of the later films addressing the Chechen wars feature strong women. Where men figure in these movies, they typically appear

---

[134] Ibid., p. 107.
[135] (Lt. Col.) Dave Grossman, *On Killing: The Psychological Cost of Learning to Kill in War and Society* (Boston, MA: Little, Brown, 1995).
[136] Rebecca Kay, *Men in Contemporary Russia: The Fallen Heroes of Post-Soviet Change?* (London: Ashgate, 2006), pp. 49–51.
[137] For a review of *Alive*, see Elena Monastireva-Ansdell, "Staying Alive in the Age of Blockbusters: War, Youth, Popular Culture, and Moral Survival in *Alive*" (2007). www.kinokultura.com/2007/15r-alive.shtml.
[138] Procházková, *Aluminum Queen*, p. 27. [139] Ibid., p. 107.

as indecisive or passive. Women form bonds with each other – even across ethnic or class lines – to cope with difficult situations.

March of the Slav Woman (*Marsh slavianki*, 2003), written and directed by Natal'ia Piankova, takes place literally on the periphery of the Chechen conflict, in a resort town in the Caucasus Mountains of southern Russia. A famous Moscow actress named Svetlana journeys by train to try to rescue her son Sasha who was serving in the army in Chechnya before she lost contact with him. She meets up with a group of crazed drug dealers, criminals, and Afghan war veterans who eventually lead her to her son. Sasha has escaped from prison after deserting the army and is now living with an older woman, Ol'ia, evidently from a lower social class and provincial background, who has a son his own age. The Chechen war is not represented directly in the film, nor are Chechens, although some of the characters by their accents appear to be members of other North Caucasus nationalities.

The Russo-Chechen conflict forms an important subtext, however. The emphasis on maternal love and female solidarity, for example, evokes the efforts of the Committee of Soldiers' Mothers to end the war and bring back their sons. In this case, the son himself is ambivalent about the war that he has fled. When the women propose a toast to peace, Sasha offers an alternative, "to victory!" As his mother and his lover become increasingly close emotionally, Sasha becomes more distant. He soon turns himself in to the local military garrison. Tormented by guilt for abandoning his comrades, he asks to rejoin them in Chechnya. The film ends on an ambiguous note. As Svetlana boards the train to return to Moscow, Ol'ia announces that she is pregnant. Svetlana is overjoyed, but the viewer may wonder whether the baby is destined for the same fate as the parents – to suffer the consequences of their government's misguided military adventures in the future.

House of Fools (2002), by the veteran Soviet-era director Andrei Konchalovskii, shares with *March of the Slav Woman* a focus on people affected by altered states of mind – in this case because some of them are living in an insane asylum and the rest are engaged in a senseless war. The film intersperses depictions of the crazed reality of the mental institution with fantasies from the imagination of the lead female character, Zhanna. She believes that the popular singer Bryan Adams (who plays himself in a cameo role) is her boyfriend, and dreams of him singing to her and courting her. As in *Pretty Village, Pretty Flame*, the film's characters represent a range of archetypes. But whereas Dragojević's types – nearly all Serbs, yet representing an extremely heterogeneous group – confound the assumption of a common national character, Konchalovskii delights in the kaleidoscope of Soviet *inter*nationalism. The hospital's inmates

Figure 4.7 Zhanna and Akhmed. *House of Fools* (2002)

include Slavs, North Caucasus Muslims, Armenians, and others. Their ethnic diversity is matched only by their diagnoses: pyromaniac, nymphomaniac, catatonic, transvestite. The Russian "prison house of nations" becomes the "mad house of nations."

The characters in *House of Fools* tolerate considerable deviation from the norms of traditional gender relations. The hospital inmates treat their cross-dressing fellow patient, for example, no worse than anyone else. The Chechen fighters too depart from their expected gender norms – the Rambo–Che Guevara model depicted in most of the other films. One Chechen in particular stands out. Akhmed appears in a bowler hat, clean-shaven, and tall. An actor by profession, he, like Zhanna, plays the accordion. He is self-conscious about his balding pate – thus the distinctly nonmilitary headgear. In a light moment, as the Chechens calm the patients after occupying the hospital, he offers to marry Zhanna – and she takes him seriously.

In this film the fantasies are not limited to the mental patients. Many viewers, especially in Russia, will find rather fantastic the director's image of Chechens who entertain hospital patients with music and dance, rather than hold them hostage and threaten them with execution. Skeptical viewers will, however, probably recognize the character of Vika as a caricature. A fierce antiauthoritarian, she rails against the dictatorial, militaristic Russian government, yelling "Down with fascism and Russian chauvinism." In a chaotic moment, as the Russian troops bombard the hospital, she grabs a gun and fires wildly, exclaiming what a joy it is to see the Chechens fighting for their freedom.

Figure 4.8 "Down with fascism and Russian chauvinism!" *House of Fools* (2002)

As Dragojević mocked the peace demonstrators outside the Belgrade military hospital in *Pretty Village, Pretty Flame*, so Konchalovskii appears to mock this embodiment of the "politically correct" liberal supporter of Chechen independence. Or does the director intend instead to mock the many Russians who would condemn any opponents of the war as traitors – by giving them such an obviously exaggerated target?

Other elements of Konchalovskii's film appear at first glance to fit the iconic symbols of the war as depicted in movies like Nevzorov's *Purgatory*. He even includes a Lithuanian female sniper – the classic White Stocking. Yet again the director includes that figure more to mock it than endorse it as a reflection of reality. As the Russian troops arrive and begin shelling the hospital (despite the large sign painted on the building, "There are sick people here"), the sniper enters Zhanna's room and starts firing out the window. Zhanna, sitting on the bed, fails to notice her. She has driven herself into an emotional turmoil, angry that Akhmed has apparently abandoned her after she has betrayed her beloved Bryan to accept the Chechen's marriage proposal. Bullets shatter the glass of the room's windows. Zhanna picks up some shards and begins stabbing them into the photo of Akhmed she holds in her hand. Another bullet hits the Lithuanian sniper, who falls bleeding to the floor. Only then does Zhanna notice the dead body; at the same time she realizes that her own hands are ragged and bloody. As the viewer grapples with the incongruity between this woman's fantasy world and the grim reality of her situation, Zhanna runs screaming from the room. The bloody

Figure 4.9 Zhanna and the "White Stocking" sniper. *House of Fools* (2002)

verisimilitude of Nevzorov's combat scenes is no match for the horror that Konchalovskii's surrealistic juxtapositions convey.

Konchalovskii's ending offers some hope, while defying gender stereotypes so dear to Chechen and Russian culture alike. As the Russians retake the hospital, their commanding officer experiences a panic attack and pleads for help with the head psychiatrist, who injects him with a sedative. From the Chechen side, as well, the director offers an example of a failure to uphold the expectations of militant masculinity. The camera pans across the hospital dining room and zooms in on Zhanna and the back of the head of a man standing in line in front of her. The viewer watches through her eyes as she recognizes Akhmed, who has apparently deserted his fellow guerrillas and donned a hospital gown. The patients, all of whom have revealed limitations in their grasp of reality throughout the film, immediately understand the situation and treat him as a fellow inmate, lest the Russian troops arrest him. Thus, Konchalovskii holds out some hope of love and redemption, but only within the house of fools, as the world outside remains even crazier.

Aleksandr Sokurov's 2007 film *Aleksandra* also offers some hope of redemption, but in a very different style, and by returning to familiar gender norms rather than challenging them. The film adapts a somber, realistic tone. In many respects it echoes Bodrov's *Prisoner of the Mountains*, the first feature film about the Chechen war, made more than a decade earlier. As with several of its predecessors, *Aleksandra* tells the story of a Russian woman who travels to Chechnya. In this case, the lead character, Aleksandra (played by the octogenarian opera soprano Galina Vishnevskaia), is an older woman, recently widowed, visiting her grandson, Denis, an army officer stationed on a military base near Grozny. Unlike *Prisoner of the Mountains, Caucasian Roulette*, or *March of the Slav Woman*, she is not seeking to rescue him from any captivity. Denis intends to remain on the base, where life is rather mundane. Although there is a sense of insecurity and tension, the movie depicts no violence whatsoever, no combat scenes. Indeed, *Aleksandra* marks a return to what Sarkisova termed the "slowed-down, anti-adventure tempo" that marked the first films of the Russo-Chechen conflict.

In some key features the film diverges quite a lot from Bodrov's *Prisoner of the Mountains*. Bodrov's film offers panoramic vistas of the Caucasus Mountains and Chechen countryside, conveying the promise of freedom. *Aleksandra*, by contrast, is set mainly on the outskirts of the destroyed capital city of Grozny, in the close, labyrinthine warren of the military base, amid the stalls of a dreary marketplace, and in the ruins of an apartment complex. Aside from the Russian soldiers, there are very few men in evidence – just a couple of young Chechens who eye the elderly Russian woman suspiciously as she ventures out to the market. This aspect is rather true to life for the period of "normalization" and "Chechenization" that followed the end of major combat and the near defeat of the separatist forces. As evidence from the interviews of Procházková and others suggested, many Chechen men had fled, been killed, or were staying at home for fear of being "disappeared."

In *Prisoner of the Mountains*, the main female Chechen figure is Dina, the young adolescent girl. She forms a bond with the captive soldier, Vanya Zhilin, while Zhilin's mother seeks common ground with Dina's father, Abdul, in order to arrange an exchange of their sons. In *Aleksandra*, the Chechen women are older; they are mainly widows who eke out their existence selling goods at an open market. One of them, named Malika, invites Aleksandra home to her apartment in a bombed-out building and they gradually become friends.

In *Prisoner of the Mountains*, Private Zhilin's mother tries to appeal to Abdul-Murat on the grounds that both she and his son are teachers. Abdul responds, "But we are enemies now." They study each other across the table in an outdoor café, as the camera alternates with close-ups of the two care-worn faces.

Although Abdul's answer reflects the reality of the Russian invasion and occupation of his country, it is not the answer that other Russian mothers received from the Chechen women who helped them rescue their sons during the early months of the first Chechen war. The Committee of

Figure 4.10 "But we are enemies now." *Prisoner of the Mountains*
(1996)

Figure 4.11 A soldier's mother. *Prisoner of the Mountains* (1996)

Soldiers' Mothers arranged to send some twenty groups of mothers to
Chechnya. More than a hundred captured soldiers were returned home
in January 1995 alone.[140]

Several Russian films about the Chechen wars convey a truism that
women find it easier to make common cause on the basis of their shared

[140] Sperling, "Last Refuge of a Scoundrel," p. 243.

motherhood than to achieve their goals in dealing with men. The women in *Caucasian Roulette*, although in direct competition to save the lives of their sons, find a way to cooperate. So do Svetlana and Ol'ia in *March of the Slav Woman*, even though they vie for the affection of Sasha – the son of one and the lover of the other. *Aleksandra* portrays two women who should not expect to find much ground for mutual sympathy. Aleksandra's grandson is an officer in the army that has destroyed Malika's country and decimated her menfolk. Yet they form a relationship of respect and find comfort in each other's company. The women go a long way towards blurring the we–they distinction evident in so many films about the Russo-Chechen conflict.[141]

One should not overinterpret the relationship between Chechen and Russian women as resembling Virginia Woolf's Society of Outsiders who claim "no country." It is not even apparent that the women necessarily reject violence. Remember in *Prisoner of the Mountains* the easy familiarity with which Dina takes her father's rifles, in support of his use of violence to capture the Russian prisoners. In *Aleksandra*, we see Denis invite his grandmother to climb into an armored vehicle. She complains only of the smell – of men and metal, as Denis explains. He then offers her a Kalashnikov rifle, which she accepts and handles without comment. The scene creates a certain tension, but one hesitates to read into it an explicit antiwar sentiment. In that respect the film offers a plausible reflection of popular Russian attitudes towards the Chechen conflict overall.

---

[141] Gender is not the only binary operating in *Aleksandra*. An alternative reading identifies generation as significant, an interpretation consistent with Sokurov's previous work in films titled *Mother and Son* (1997) and *Father and Son* (2003), and one that yields more pessimistic conclusions. As Nancy Condee points out, the old women may be friends, but the younger generation – the Russian officer Denis and the wary Chechen youth – may be destined to remain enemies: "Generational succession will eliminate the elderly women who have had much in common and it will raise to maturity the young men who, in their struggle to separate and (so far) to kill each other, also have much in common." Nancy Condee, "Sokurov's Chechnia: Aleksandr Sokurov's *Alexandra* (2007)," *Kinokultura*, updated October 2, 2007, www.kinokultura.com/2007/18r-alexandra.shtml. It does make sense to see *Aleksandra* as the third in a trilogy of generational films, much as Sukurov made his trilogy of films about the leaders Lenin, Hitler, and Hirohito around the theme of sovereignty, among others. See Susan Buck-Morss, "Visual Empire," *Diacritics*, 37, 2–3 (Summer–Fall 2007); and Nancy Condee, *The Imperial Trace: Recent Russian Cinema* (Oxford University Press, 2009), ch. 6.

5   Québec: *oui*, no, or *femme*

> I wish the women would hurry up and take over. It's going to happen, so let's get it over with. Then we can finally recognize that women really are the minds, and the force that holds everything together, and men really are gossips and artists. Then we could get about our childish work and they could keep the world going. I really am for the matriarchy.
>
> Leonard Cohen, 1968[1]

> Québec is a matriarchal society that has adjusted itself to the patriarchal international rules.
>
> Robert Lepage, 1998[2]

Bombings, kidnappings, and murder, mass arrests, and the deployment of soldiers and tanks on the streets. These are aspects of Québec nationalism little known outside of Canada. Nor is *Nô* – the 1998 film by director and playwright Robert Lepage that treats these episodes – as famous as some of the other films discussed in this book. Yet it is an insightful, funny, and award-winning exploration of the links between nationalism, gender, and violence, and one, unlike most of the films considered here, that offers a hopeful message. The separatist impulses that led to the violent events of October 1970 and the forceful response from the Canadian federal government did not portend a spiral of violence or a descent into civil war, as we have seen in so many other cases. Instead, for many years now the struggle over Québec's status within Canada has been waged by peaceful means: by negotiation and referenda. Lepage shares the views of Michel Tremblay, fellow playwright and pioneer of Québec national theater, that Québec society is essentially matriarchal. Does the status and role of women in Québec account for the notable absence of

---

[1] Quoted in William Kloman, "I've Been on the Outlaw Scene Since 15," *New York Times*, January 29, 1968. I am grateful to Michel Seymour for calling this remark to my attention, and for his thoughtful criticisms of an earlier draft of this chapter.

[2] Michel Coulombe, "Entretien avec Robert Lepage," in Robert Lepage and André Morency, *Nô: Scénario du film de Robert Lepage* (Québec: Les 400 Coups, 1998), p. 96.

violence in a nevertheless extremely contentious debate over the province's relationship to Canada?

Origins of French Canadian nationalism

Québec nationalism was born in the settlement of North America in the seventeenth century. The explorer Jacques Cartier had claimed Canada for France already in 1534. French immigration was limited mainly to those involved in the fur trade and did not amount to more than ten thousand people over the next century and a half. Nevertheless, King Louis XIV declared the colony of Nouvelle France and appointed a governor in 1609. Language and religion were important sources of coherence for the distinct society that emerged there. French became the common language of the settlers of Nouvelle France even before it came to dominate metropolitan France itself (whose population spoke various Celtic and Latin-derived languages). It was the language of ports and travel and was therefore understood by emigrants from France, even if it was not their first language. It remained the language of ports and travel as the French colonists created their settlements mainly along the St Lawrence and other rivers.

The influence of women on emerging Québec nationalism is evident already at this early stage because of how "women play a central role in the acquisition of language." The majority of women emigrating from France possessed a good knowledge of French and helped maintain the language within their families.[3] Roman Catholicism was the dominant religion of the immigrants from France, by contrast to the Protestantism of the English colonialists in North America.

The nature of the physical settlement of Nouvelle France and the meager resources that the king was willing to devote to the colony made for rather limited control and an inability to defend the region during conflicts with the native inhabitants of the area and with rival English settlers. In 1629, English forces took over Québec and controlled it for three years. In subsequent years France would cede increasing amounts of territory to England by treaty. Armed conflict in 1759–1760 culminated in the siege of the city of Québec and the Battle of the Plains of Abraham. In the Treaty of Paris of 1763, France gave up its North American territory to England, including Canada and the left bank of the Mississippi River. The English authorities proceeded to dismember Nouvelle France and create new administrative structures, establishing

---

[3] Françoise Épinette, *La question nationale au Québec* (Paris: Presses Universitaires de France, 1998), pp. 10–11.

the Province of Quebec and appointing a governor. Consequences for the population of French colonists, now numbering about seventy thousand, were immediate and severe. English common law replaced French civil law, Catholics were banned from holding high administrative offices, and English became the official language of government.[4]

Contemporary supporters of an independent Québec state are right to highlight the "destructive effects on the Québec nation of the English Conquest and the British and Canadian constitutional regimes that were its direct consequence."[5] But, as we know from the cases of the Russians in Chechnya and the French in Algeria, starting roughly during this same era, imperial repression can contribute to solidifying a national identity. So did English suppression of French culture, language, and religion stimulate a counterreaction that reinforced the Québec people's sense of its uniqueness. Resistance to English discrimination against the French language and Catholic religion led the British Parliament to pass the Quebec Act in 1774. It expanded the territory of Québec, restored French civil law (while maintaining British criminal law), and offered official recognition to the Catholic Church and freedom of religion to its adherents – something that did not happen in Britain itself for another half-century.[6]

The British were not only reacting to resistance from budding Québec nationalists but also hoping to prevent French Canadians from joining the rebellion of the American colonists south of the border. Indeed the American revolutionaries, convening in congress at Philadelphia, deliberately sought to incite the inhabitants of Québec, despite the efforts of the British Parliament. To that end, just four months after the passing of the Quebec Act, delegates to the first Continental Congress sent a letter under the signature of its president, Henry Middleton. The letter began by providing a basic primer on self-government, the benefits of basic rights such as a free press, trial by jury, and *habeas corpus*, and quoted at some length "your countryman, the immortal Montesquieu." These are the rights, the letter argued, that the French in Canada should enjoy, after having been "conquered into liberty" by the British forces and made part of what the Americans considered in principle a superior form of government. Yet the government of King George denied them such rights, as it did the American colonists. The letter sought to denigrate the concessions provided for in the Quebec Act. ("And what is offered to you by the

---

[4] Ibid., pp. 11, 14.
[5] Introduction to Andrée Ferretti and Gaston Miron, eds., *Les grands texts indépendantistes: écrits, discours et manifestes québécois, 1774–1992* (Montréal: Editions de l'Hexagone, 1992), p. 15.
[6] Claude Bélanger, "Quebec Act," Québec History website, Marianopolis College, www2.marianopolis.edu/quebechistory/readings/1774act.htm.

late Act of Parliament ... Liberty of conscience in your religion? No. God gave it to you.") Although the Americans insisted that "we do not ask you, by this address, to commence acts of hostility against the government of our common Sovereign," they did invite the residents of Québec to elect delegates to send to the next Continental Congress in May 1775 and to make common cause with the American revolutionaries ("to add yourselves to us, to put your fate whenever you suffer injuries which you are determined to oppose not on the small influence of your single province but on the consolidated powers of North-America").[7] This appeal constituted what might today be called an attempt at exporting American democracy, launched even before the founding of the United States as an independent country.

The French Canadians failed to heed the call to join the American revolt. Instead, English loyalists opposed to the revolution headed north, increasing the English-speaking population of Canada from 4 to 9 percent during the years 1778 to 1784. In 1791, the British passed the Constitutional Act dividing the colony into Upper and Lower Canada. During the next decades, the French inhabitants came increasingly to resent British rule and to organize themselves in opposition. They were joined by Irish and other immigrants who sought to establish an American-style republic. In the first decades of the nineteenth century, they formed the Parti Patriote and sponsored a boycott of English goods and the establishment of a "people's bank" as an alternative to the English-owned Bank of Montreal. They agitated for increased local powers, including an elected assembly, and in 1834 issued a set of 92 Resolutions to London. The British government took three years to respond with an outright rejection of the colonists' demands and repressive measures to keep the French population under control. In the autumn of 1837 resistance turned into armed rebellion, with the declaration of an independent Republic of Lower Canada the following year. British troops suppressed the revolt without much difficulty in a campaign of considerable brutality which included the burning and pillaging of rebellious settlements.[8]

In the wake of the failed rebellion, British authorities decided that assimilation to a dominant English culture was the best means for preserving the peace.[9] The Act of Union of 1840 brought Upper and Lower

---

[7] An Appeal to the Inhabitants of Quebec, Continental Congress, Philadelphia, October 26, 1774, www.historicaldocuments.com/AppealtotheInhabitantsofQuebec.htm.
[8] Mitch Abidor, "The Patriotes Rebellion," www.marxists.org/history/canada/quebec/patriotes-rebellion/introduction.htm.
[9] Épinette, *La question nationale*, p. 17. Particularly influential was the *Report of Lord Durham on the Affairs of British North America* (1839), Quebec History website, Marianopolis College, http://faculty.marianopolis.edu/c.belanger/quebechistory/docs/durham/index.htm.

Canada together in an effort to dilute French influence. The discriminatory policies that followed led to a mass emigration of French Canadians. In the decade 1840–1850, 35,000 left Québec for the United States. The figure doubled in the next decade.[10] Between 1840 and 1930 some 900,000 French Canadians immigrated to the United States. Although the proportion of the English-speaking ("anglophone") population of Québec peaked at about 25 percent in the mid-nineteenth century, the continued out-migration of French speakers ("francophone") helped to facilitate the increasing English dominance of the province.[11]

For the majority of francophone Canadians who chose to remain in Canada, the failure of the rebellion of 1837–1838, according to one author, "provoked in less than a generation a complete transformation" in their way of thinking. Rather than independence, they sought to forge alliances with the reformist elements of English Canada against "the favoritism and abuses of power of British governors and the economic interests with which they were identified."[12] The evolution of representative, democratic institutions in Canada was a slow process, as was its emergence as an independent country. Indeed, as one scholar put it, "Canada's transition from a self-governing British colony into a fully independent state was an evolutionary process, which arose in such a gradual fashion that it is impossible to ascribe independence to a particular date."[13] Others have stressed the nonviolent nature of the transition: "Canada peacefully and gradually evolved as a nation, quite unlike the United States, which became a separate independent country by means of armed revolution."[14] In the British North America Act of 1867, the Province of Canada (divided into Québec and Ontario) joined the colonies of New Brunswick and Nova Scotia in a federation to be known as the Dominion of Canada. The country "was granted powers of self-government to deal with all internal matters, but Britain still retained overall legislative supremacy."[15]

---

[10] "Emigration to the United States from Canada and Quebec, 1840–1940," Quebec History website, Marianopolis College, www2.marianopolis.edu/quebechistory/stats/goto-us.htm.

[11] "Anglophone Population of Quebec [%], 1766–1996," Quebec History website, Marianopolis College, www2.marianopolis.edu/quebechistory/stats/anglos.htm; Claude Bélanger, "French Canadian Emigration to the United States, 1840–1930," www2.marianopolis.edu/quebechistory/readings/leaving.htm.

[12] Dominique Clift, *Le déclin du nationalisme au Québec* (Montréal: Éditions Libre Expression, 1981), p. 84.

[13] Andrew Heard, "Canadian Independence" (1990), www.sfu.ca/~aheard/324/Independence.html.

[14] Sidney Allinson, http://experts.about.com/q/Canadian-History-2762/canada-independence.htm.

[15] Heard, "Canadian Independence."

Self-government did not necessarily mean democracy. Pierre Elliott Trudeau claimed in 1958 that "historically French Canadians have not really believed in democracy for themselves, and English Canadians have not really wanted if for others." For the former he had in mind, particularly, the antidemocratic orientation of the Catholic Church, whose influence on Québec's political life remained strong as Trudeau was writing. For the latter, Catholic conservatism provided an opportunity: efforts at democratization among French Canadians were "crushed, mainly by agreement between the English-Canadian governing class and the French-Canadian higher clergy."[16] As Francis Dupuis-Déri has demonstrated, even the English-Canadian political elite were ambivalent about participatory democracy. The founders of modern Canada, authors of the 1867 Constitution (as the British North America Act became known), tended, for example, to associate democracy with anarchy. Like "the founders of modern electoral regimes of the United States and France," they "were openly antidemocratic." They understood democracy "as a tyranny of the poor," who were "incapable of taking rational decisions compatible with the common good and easy prey for demagogues."[17]

The English-speaking population of Canada seemed generally satisfied that the gradual move towards independence would satisfy their interests. French Canadians, by contrast, often found their way of life threatened by the country's evolution and sometimes they reacted with violence. In 1870, for example, Manitoba, a region settled in part by colonists from Québec, became part of the Canadian federation. The federal government's moves to make property laws conform to Canadian standards (land divided into square lots, for example) contradicted the local practices that derived from Québec's traditions. An armed uprising resulted in concessions on the part of the federal government: recognition of existing property rights, acceptance of official bilingualism, and a distinct education system. The leader of the rebellion was Louis Riel, a 21-year-old member of the people known as the *métis* (descendants of mixed marriages between native peoples and French, Irish, or Scottish colonists), sometimes called the "father of Manitoba." He was arrested and sent into exile, but remained popular at home and was actually

[16] Pierre Elliott Trudeau, "Some Obstacles to Democracy in Quebec," originally published in the *Canadian Journal of Economics and Political Science*, 24, 3 (August 1958), revised and republished in Trudeau, *Federalism and the French Canadians* (Toronto: Macmillan, 1968), quotations at pp. 103, 106.

[17] Francis Dupuis-Déri, "Histoire du mot 'démocratie' au Canada et au Québec. Analyse politique des stratégies rhétoriques," *Canadian Journal of Political Science/Revue canadienne de science politique*, 42, 2 (June 2009), p. 323. I am grateful to Olivier Barsalou for calling this article to my attention and for his many excellent comments on a draft of this chapter.

elected several times to the Canadian House of Commons, where he was not allowed to serve. In 1885, he returned to lead another unsuccessful insurrection. This time his arrest was followed by execution.[18]

By the beginning of the twentieth century the use of violence to achieve rights for the francophone population of Canada had met with mixed results: usually repression, followed by some concessions. The first half of that century saw mainly resistance to violence on the part of the Québécois – in particular an unwillingness to participate in the violence of the two world wars. Many Québécois, believing that "this participation in a European war under British command could not but reflect a colonial dependence, refused to join and to be considered British subjects." Anticonscription riots broke out and were severely put down by police and federal armed forces.[19] Opposition to Québec's involvement in World War II stemmed from similar concerns, augmented by a certain anti-Semitism (directed particularly against the large anglophone Jewish population of Montréal) and sympathy for fascism that characterized part of the Québec nationalist movement (and was widespread elsewhere) in those years.[20]

Women and the early nationalist movement

The rebellion of 1837–1838 for an independent republic in Lower Canada, had it been successful, would not necessarily have improved the lot of women. In many respects French female immigrants to North America enjoyed a higher status than women elsewhere, including in Europe. In 1663, Catholic nuns founded a school for girls in Montréal, at a time when there was no school for boys.[21] Under the Constitutional Act of 1791, certain owners and tenants were granted voting rights, without mention of sex. Many women took advantage of what may have been an oversight – the only women in the entire British Empire entitled to vote – until the right was revoked in 1849.[22] The (male) leaders of the movement for independence were mostly hostile to women's

---

[18] Épinette, *La question nationale*, p. 18.   [19] Ibid., pp. 17–18.
[20] Esther Delisle, *Myths, Memory and Lies: Quebec's Intelligentsia and the Fascist Temptation, 1939–1960*, trans. by Madeleine Hébert (Westmount, Québec: Robert Davies Multimedia, 1998). The original, published in French, came in for some criticism. See, e.g., Luc Chartrand, "Le mythe du Québec fasciste," *L'Actualité*, 22, 3 (1 March 1997), http://aix1.uottawa.ca/~fgingras/doc/quebec1930–45.html.
[21] Patrice LeClerc and Lois A. West, "Feminist Nationalist Movements in Quebec: Resolving Contradictions?" in Lois A. West, ed., *Feminist Nationalism* (New York: Routledge, 1997), pp. 220–246, at p. 222.
[22] "Right to Vote of Québec Women," website of the Directeur général des élections du Québec, www.electionsquebec.qc.ca/en/women_quest_equality.asp.

political rights. Louis-Joseph Papineau, leader of the Parti Patriote from 1826, had this to say on the topic eight years later: "It is revolting to see women dragged by their husbands and daughters, by their fathers, often against their will, to hustings. Public interest, decency, and the modesty of women demand that these scandals never reoccur."[23] Views hostile to women's political independence did not always coincide with a preference for violence as the means to French Canada's political independence. In the case of Papineau, for example, he favored continued efforts to persuade the British Parliament to allow Canadian self-rule and promoted economic boycotts as a means of pressure. When the attempt by British forces to arrest the leaders of the independence movement in 1837 led to armed rebellion, Papineau fled to the United States.

Had the armed rebellion succeeded it could well have made some Québec women worse off. Consider the Declaration of Independence of Lower Canada, drafted by Robert Nelson in 1838 from his exile in the United States. Point 8 calls for the immediate abolition and prohibition of the so-called *douaire coutumier*, an amount of money set aside as part of a marriage contract to provide for the material welfare of a surviving wife in the event that her husband died. In general, marriage contracts made according to the *Coutume de Paris*, adapted for the frontier life in Nouvelle France, were quite egalitarian and effectively protected the property rights of women.[24] But the male rebels saw them mainly as a legacy of the feudal system that had been implanted in Nouvelle France and were eager to abolish all remnants of that system, even ones that were favorable to the status and wellbeing of women.

Regardless of the fate of the independence movement, women's status continued to decline in Québec under English rule. The Québec Civil Code of 1866 in particular eroded women's legal rights. In marriage, in contrast to the more egalitarian status they had previously enjoyed, women would henceforth be considered under the authority of their husbands, and treated as minors or persons with mental disabilities.[25] Only in 1964 was a bill passed to end the legal incapacity of women, allowing them, for example, to file lawsuits on their own behalf. It was sponsored by Claire Kirkland-Casgrain, the first woman elected to be a member of Québec's National Assembly.[26]

---

[23] Quoted in *La Minerve*, February 3, 1834, cited in "Right to Vote of Québec Women."
[24] Suzanne Boivin Sommerville, "Marriage Contract in New France according to *La Coutume de Paris*/The Custom of Paris," *Michigan's Habitant Heritage* (journal of the French-Canadian Heritage Society of Michigan), 26, 3 (July 2005); Bettina Bradbury, "Debating Dower: Patriarchy, Capitalism and Widows' Rights in Lower Canada," copy generously provided by the author.
[25] LeClerc and West, "Feminist Nationalist Movements," p. 222.
[26] Ibid., p. 228.

In the rest of Canada, as in the United States and much of Europe, suffrage movements had earned women the right to vote, in part as acknowledgment of their roles during World War I. If women were willing to support their country's wars, the argument went, they should be allowed to elect its leaders. In fact, Dupuis-Déri dates Canada's rulers' interest in the language of electoral democracy – not only for women but generally – to World War I. Canadian leaders, who governed a constitutional *monarchy*, invoked defense of *democracy* then and during World War II because it appeared "effective for facilitating mass mobilization of the population in the war effort."[27]

Despite the new language of democracy, Québec's women found themselves lagging behind women elsewhere in Canada in basic civil and political rights. The Canadian federal government granted women the vote in 1918. In Québec, however, the conservatives rejected a role for women in the political sphere. Thus, as LeClerc and West point out, "by 1918 all Canadian women could vote in federal elections, although Québec women could still not vote in provincial elections."[28] Even though some of their ancestors were voting already a century earlier, Québec women did not achieve the right to vote again in their own province until April 1940. Even then the Catholic Church continued to oppose a woman's right to vote "because it goes against the unity and the hierarchy of the family."[29] Opponents of women's suffrage revived the pejorative meaning of democracy to criticize it. Among them was Henri Bourassa, a prominent politician from Québec, grandson of Louis-Joseph Papineau, and founder of the newspaper *Le Devoir*. In a series of essays written in 1918 to protest legislative efforts towards women's suffrage in Canada he argued that the reform contradicted the "good sense" of the Gospels, which favored the family as the basic social unit and the "hierarchy of authority" vested in the male head of the household. By contrast, the "feminist thesis" was "antisocial" and consistent with "the fundamental principle" of the "so-called democratic regime," which insisted on the vote as a guarantor of rights. Demonstrating an affinity for his grandfather's polemical tone, as well as antifeminist views, Bourassa titled the first article in the series "Désarroi des cerveaux – triomphe de la démocratie": disarray of the brains – triumph of democracy.[30]

As in the United States, World War II brought important changes to Canadian women. Despite widespread popular opposition to Québec's

[27] Dupuis-Déri, "Histoire du mot 'démocratie,'" p. 333.   [28] Ibid., p. 225.
[29] Communiqué by Cardinal Villeneuve, March 1, 1940, quoted in LeClerc and West, "Feminist Nationalist Movements," p. 225.
[30] Dupuis-Déri quotes this article and two succeeding ones from *Le Devoir*, March 28 and 30, and April 1, 1918, in "Histoire du mot 'démocratie,'" pp. 334–335.

involvement in the war, the government encouraged women to abandon their traditional roles in order to work in armaments plants as mechanics, welders, and electricians. The federal government provided funds for childcare centers in order to allow mothers to work, but French Canadian families availed themselves little of the service. With a population of 3.3 million, Québec received just six centers, whereas Ontario, with only a slightly larger population of 3.8 million, received twenty-eight. Moreover, only one of the six in Québec was used by francophone families, who mostly relied on relatives or private childcare facilities.[31]

The Quiet Revolution

The origins of contemporary Québec nationalism date to the so-called Quiet Revolution (*Révolution tranquille*) of the first half of the 1960s. This was the point at which traditional support for the rights of the francophone population of Canada as a whole gave way to a focus specifically on Québec and its transformation from a province to an aspiring quasi-sovereign state. The sources of this transformation were economic, cultural, and demographic.[32]

The nationalist movement's focus on Québec rather than French speakers in greater Canada was partly a reflection of the demographic reality. Whereas in 1941 one in nine children outside Québec was from a French-speaking family, by 1976 the figure was only one in twenty-one.[33] There were comparably significant changes within the province, in urbanization and population. At the dawn of the twentieth century, 75 percent of Québec's francophone population lived in rural areas. Industrialization, especially during and after World War II, began to change the situation. By 1951, 67 percent of the population lived in cities; by 1971, the number reached 78 percent.[34] As more women joined the workforce, Québec experienced a dramatic decline in the birth rate, from 29.7 per thousand in 1957 to 16.3 per thousand in 1968, although in general the province lagged behind the rest of the country in this demographic transition.[35]

---

[31] LeClerc and West, "Feminist Nationalist Movements," p. 225. On population statistics, see www2.marianopolis.edu/quebechistory/stats/pop-caqc.htm.

[32] Vincent Berdoulay, "Stateless National Identity and French Canadian Geographic Discourse," ch. 11 in David Hooson, ed., *Geography and National Identity* (Oxford: Blackwell, 1994), pp. 184–196.

[33] R. P. Beaujot, "The Decline of Official Language Minorities in Quebec and English Canada," *Canadian Journal of Sociology*, 7, 4 (Fall 1982), pp. 367–389.

[34] Jan Erk, "Is Nationalism Left or Right? Critical Junctures in Québécois Nationalism," *Nations and Nationalism*, 16, 3 (2010), p. 432.

[35] Épinette, *La question nationale*, p. 21; Clift, *Le déclin du nationalisme*, p. 67; Danielle Gauvreau and Diane Gervais, "Women, Priests, and Physicians: Family Limitation

The greater role accorded to governments worldwide in the wake of the Great Depression and subsequent war encouraged the provincial administration to take on more responsibilities in the sphere of health and education, previously dominated by the Catholic Church, and in control over the economy, influenced heavily by US capital. A number of groups promoted socialism as the answer to the dominance of Anglo-Canadian and US firms in the Québec economy, an ideology that also favored a growing role for the state. Some proponents of social democracy and language and cultural rights for Québec, such as Pierre Elliott Trudeau and Gérard Pelletier, founders of the journal *Cité Libre* in Montréal in 1950, believed that federalism could still serve Québec's interests. Others advocated sovereignty.[36]

For Québec's administration to play a modernizing role in fostering nationalism as a route to sovereignty and possible independent statehood required a change of government. From 1936 to 1960, with the exception of four years during the war, Québec's government was dominated by the conservative Union Nationale party, led by the prime minister, Maurice Duplessis, until his death in 1959. Duplessis' brand of nationalism favored maintenance of the traditional social order, with heavy reliance on the Catholic Church, although he did promote some initiatives of modernization, such as expansion of primary education.[37] Dissatisfaction with his conservative rule led to a period of government by the Liberal Party and to the rise of a number of political challenges from separatist forces. Although ideologically the Liberals opposed both statism and nationalism, they took initiatives that ultimately gave the Québec state the wherewithal to make a bid for greater sovereignty. In 1962, the nationalization of the energy sector, based mainly on hydroelectric power, gave a big impetus to industrialization and provided a nationalistic slogan under which the Liberals could seek reelection: *Maîtres chez nous*, Masters in Our Own House.[38]

The minister of national resources responsible for nationalizing the energy sector was a rising young politician, René Lévesque. Whereas some of his colleagues were encouraged by the success of the nationalization program to push for a more socialist or social-democratic orientation for the Liberal Party within federal Canada, Lévesque's own proclivities led in a more nationalist direction.[39] In 1967, he left the Liberal Party

in Quebec, 1940–1970," *Journal of Interdisciplinary History*, 34, 2 (Autumn 2003), pp. 293–314.
[36] Trudeau, *Federalism and the French Canadians*.
[37] Clift, *Le déclin du nationalisme*, ch. 1.   [38] Ibid., pp. 36–37.
[39] For reflections on Lévesque from one of his former Liberal Party colleagues, see Jean-Paul Lefebvre, *Qui profiterait de l'indépendance du Québec?* (Montréal: Les Éditions Varia, 1998), pp. 13–19.

when he failed to persuade fellow party members to support sovereignty for Québec "in association with" Canada. He founded the Mouvement Souveraineté-Association to pursue that goal, and then, in 1968, a new political party, the Parti Québécois.

The political program of the new party contained a number of goals that would have served the interest of women, including a minimum wage, wage parity between women and men, state-funded medical insurance and health care. It advocated a negotiated independence from Canada with flexible "association" – an economic necessity in the days before the North American Free Trade Agreement, when the specter of tariffs imposed by both the United States and the rest of Canada could have menaced Québec's economy.[40] A core goal of the Parti Québécois was to bolster the French language, by "affirming French as the sole official language of a sovereign Québec."[41]

Language and sovereignty

Language has played a central role in the evolution of modern Québec nationalism and it is central to Robert Lepage's film. *Nô* was based originally on a segment from Lepage's eight-hour play *Les sept branches de la rivière Ota* (*Seven Streams of the River Ota*) called "Les mots" (The Words), and it was performed by the actors from his theater troupe.[42]

As one scholar has written, "the weight of words" rests heavily in the "individual and collective memory of the Québécois," providing the vocabulary for the history of nationalist consciousness: "domination, alienation, collective, colonization, conquest, occupation, dispossession, neglect, defeat, survival, rupture ..."[43] Policies governing words and language – English, French, and the local Québécois dialects – have provoked the most contentious political debates.

One of the founding documents of the Quiet Revolution was a book, *Les insolences du Frère Untel*, published in 1960 anonymously by a young teaching friar at a rural Catholic school in Québec.[44] It was essentially a

---

[40] Most contemporary sovereigntists still consider close economic relations with Canada crucial to Québec's economic wellbeing, but criticize the neoliberal project associated with NAFTA. See, e.g., Michel Seymour, "L'état et la mondialisation" (n.d.), www.ipsoquebec.org.

[41] Épinette, *La question nationale*, pp. 56–57.

[42] Aleksandar Dundjerovic, *The Cinema of Robert Lepage: The Poetics of Memory* (London: Wallflower Press, 2003), p. 28.

[43] Épinette, *La question nationale*, p. 47.

[44] *Les insolences du Frère Untel* (Montréal: Les Éditions de l'Homme, 1960). The text is now available online: http://classiques.uqac.ca/contemporains/desbiens_jean_paul/insolences_frere_untel/insolences.html. The author was later revealed to be Jean-Paul

treatise on language and education and an attack on the Catholic Church for its retrograde effect on both. Frère Untel first became known when he wrote a letter to André Laurendeau, a journalist for the Montréal daily *Le Devoir*, that the newspaper published. Frère Untel was responding to a column Laurendeau had written complaining about the degradation of the French language, especially among young people, in Québec. The journalist had coined the term *joual* to describe the language – a distortion of the French *cheval* (horse). He thereby both suggested its rural origins and indicated the main problem of pronunciation: swallowing consonants and mispronouncing and slurring vowels. Or, as Frère Untel later wrote, to speak *joual* is "to talk as one might suppose horses would talk if they hadn't already opted for silence."[45] Frère Untel endorsed Laurendeau's critique and provided examples from his own students. In his book, he placed much of the blame on the church and the provincial government that followed its wishes. From the church's perspective, "the essential thing is Heaven, not French. One can be saved in *joual*." When the Department of Public Instruction was established in the last century, the objective of the authorities was "to avoid two perils": "Protestantization" and "Anglicization." "They didn't have a goal to reach; they had a precipice to avoid. They knew where not to go, but they hadn't clearly decided where to go."[46]

Frère Untel's book found a ready audience. As the editor of the English translation predicted, the "book will do much to destroy the myth of the isolation of French Canada from European movements." The well-read and erudite author would enrich his readers with "Continental currents of thought – intellectual, social, religious, literary," in the style of a Québécois Mark Twain: "Here is the opening to democracy and liberalization of institutions in Quebec that the rest of Canada has allegedly been waiting for. There will be no turning back. The fresh air is doing its work. Let's welcome it!"[47]

Frère Untel devoted a chapter to the role of women in education. His general concern was that teaching be treated as a serious profession and that teachers develop more of a sense of political maturity and responsibility. He noted that women made up nearly two-thirds of the teachers in Québec, but that their average term of service was about half that of male

---

Desbiens. I thank an anonymous (only because I neglected to ask her name) bookseller in Montréal for indicating to me the importance of this book and selling me a used copy of the English translation, *The Impertinences of Brother Anonymous (Frère Untel)*, trans. by Miriam Chapin (Montréal: Harvest House, 1962).

[45] *Les insolences* (downloaded as Microsoft Word text), p. 17. Translations are mine.

[46] Ibid., pp. 19, 26.

[47] Editor's Note, *The Impertinences of Brother Anonymous*, p. 12.

teachers, with many of them keeping their positions for only four or five years.[48] He urged a greater public role for women in what he claimed was already "our matriarchal North America." "We don't have to deplore the advent of women in History. She has been so silent up to this point. Until now History has been made by men, exclusively. Considering what the men have made of History, we don't see why women shouldn't concern themselves with it a bit."[49]

Despite his apparent good intentions, Frère Untel seems to have missed the main explanation for the fact that women did not remain teachers long enough to develop a professional consciousness. During the time he was writing, school boards required that any woman who became engaged to be married had to leave her teaching position (the requirement was also common in the United States at the time).[50] Nevertheless Frère Untel's advocacy of higher status for women working outside the home as teachers marks a sharp contrast to the views we encountered in chapter 3 of Serbian and Croatian nationalists demanding that women leave the workforce and return home to give birth to future soldiers.

In addition to his proposals for educational reform, Frère Untel advocated a role for the state in preserving the French language. "Language is a public good and it is up to the state to protect it as such." The state protects moose and trout and national parks, he pointed out. "The Québec state should require, by law, respect for the French language, as it requires, by law, respect for trout and moose."[51] The "little brother," as he referred to himself, proposed some specific measures, tongue in cheek:

(a) Absolute control of radio and TV. Writing or speaking *joual* is forbidden under pain of death;

(b) Destruction by the provincial police, in a single night … of all commercial signs in English or *joual*;

(c) Authorization for two years to shoot on sight any official, minister, professor, or priest who speaks *joual*.

---

[48] *Les insolences*, esp. pp. 73–74.

[49] Ibid., p. 74.

[50] Marie-Thérèse Bournival, "When Cracks Appear in the Varnish," in Louise Malette and Marie Chalouh, eds., *The Montreal Massacre*, trans. by Marlene Wildeman (Charlottetown, Prince Edward Island, Canada: Gynergy Books, 1991), p. 71.

[51] *Les insolences*, p. 20. Some linguists now argue that the accent of French spoken in North America is actually closer to what used to be spoken in Paris before the Revolution. See Jean-François Cliche, "L'accent québécois sous la loupe d'un phonéticien," *Le Soleil*, March 4, 2008, an interview with Jean-Denis Gendron, summarizing his book *D'où vient l'accent des Québécois? Et celui des Parisiens?* (Québec: Les Presses de l'Université Laval, 2007).

"To heal ourselves," he insisted, "we must take energetic measures. The axe! The axe! We must work with the axe ... This is not a time for nuance."[52]

Undoubtedly, Frère Untel's readers appreciated his references to Tolstoi, Sartre, Céline, and other "Continental currents of thought," as his translator suggested. But perhaps they appreciated more his calls to action, his proposals – similar to those above, but without the axes or death penalty – that the state forbid the use of English in advertising: "Name yourselves and advertise yourselves in French, or I [the government] don't recognize you." That way, there would no longer be businesses called "Chicoutimi Moving, Turcotte Tire Service, or Rita's Snack Bar."[53] Untel's French-speaking readers, at least, would recognize these business names as representative of a common practice in Québec: even if all members of a workforce were francophone, they would be obliged to speak English among themselves to suit their anglophone boss or owner. Perhaps these calls for direct government action, with an implication, however humorously presented, that they would be backed by the state's monopoly of force, accounted for a considerable degree of the book's popularity.

In any case, it sold more than a hundred thousand copies in a matter of weeks at a time when a press run a tenth that size in Québec would have made for a *best-seller* (an English expression that, decades after the Quiet Revolution, has still not found a preferred French translation).[54]

Many of Frère Untel's proposals struck a chord with the francophone population of Québec. A series of language laws, in particular, sought to bolster the position of the French language in the province. His criticisms of *joual*, however, fared less well. In fact, use of *joual* in the work of Michel Tremblay and other founders of the *nouveau théâtre Québécois* contributed to the development of a genuinely national culture, independent of both English Canada and France.[55] The language laws were intended to deal mainly with the threat of Anglicization. In 1969, Bill 63, the *Loi pour promouvoir la langue française au Québec*, required all children not born to native English-speaking families to attend schools where they would be taught in French. This law met resistance from some immigrant groups, including Italians, who preferred to have their children study in English. In 1974, the Liberal government of Robert Bourassa passed Bill 22, the

---

[52] *Les insolences*, p. 19.   [53] Ibid., p. 20.

[54] Jean-Paul Desbiens' book is referred to as a *best-seller* in numerous French-language websites from Québec, including one announcing his receipt of an honorary doctorate from the Université du Québec à Montréal in October 2004: www.uqam.ca/nouvelles/2004/04–180.htm.

[55] Dundjerovic, *The Cinema of Robert Lepage*, p. 14.

Loi sur la langue officielle. As Claude Bélanger summarizes it, the law seems to address well Frère Untel's concern about the encroachment of English, if not making any particular reference to *joual*:

The law proclaimed French the official language in Quebec, set up a *Régie de la langue française* to supervise the application of the bill, imposed on all public institutions the duty to address the public administration in French, made French the official language of contracts, forced corporations to give themselves a French name and to advertise primarily in French in Quebec as well as to seek a certificate of francization which could only be obtained when it was demonstrated that the business could function in French and address its employees in French.[56]

The law was actually something of a compromise (and thus was criticized from both sides) because it provided space for an English-language educational sector and allowed for some exceptions to the French-only economic rules (such that contracts could be written in English only, for example, if both parties desired it). When the Parti Québécois came into power in 1976 it passed a new "charter" of the French language (*Charte de la langue française*), Bill 101, eliminating some of the pro-English compromises of the previous legislation. According to Bélanger, the anglophone community's resentment of the bill has been "sharpened by sometimes plainly petty application of it by overzealous bureaucrats, called 'the language police'" – heirs of Frère Untel's "axe" method for saving the French language in Québec.

The true heirs of the violent methods proposed in jest by Frère Untel were the members of the Front de Libération du Québec (FLQ), or *felquistes*, as they were known. They provide the link between our themes of gender, nationalism, and violence in Québec, and their actions of October 1970 provide the background for Robert Lepage's movie.

The FLQ and the October Crisis

Lévesque and his Parti Québécois were committed to a nonviolent route to a sovereign Québec, but others were not. Inspired by the anticolonial movements and wars of "national liberation" in the Third World, a group of young students, teachers, and workers, mainly from the poorer neighborhoods on the east side of Montréal, formed the FLQ in 1963.[57] They began a campaign of bombings, using mainly

---

[56] Claude Bélanger, "The Language Laws of Quebec," August 23, 2000, www2. marianopolis.edu/quebechistory/readings/langlaws.htm. Most of my information on the language laws comes from this site.

[57] Mitch Abidor, "Le Front de Libération du Québec," Canada History Archive, www. marxists.org/history/canada/quebec/flq/introduction.htm.

dynamite and Molotov cocktails. Their first target, in March 1963, was a Canadian army base in Montréal. The next month the bombing of an army recruiting office in Sherbrooke killed the night watchman and led to the arrest of twenty-three FLQ militants, much of the group's original membership.

Pierre Trudeau, long a critic of Anglo-Canadian discrimination against Québec, had joined the Liberal Party in 1965 and become Canada's minister of justice and attorney general in 1967. He rejected the nationalist *tiers-mondisme* and violence of the FLQ. As a social democrat and former labor lawyer, he criticized the implied economic policies of the separatists, however revolutionary their rhetoric. Economic policy should not be based on the assumption "that workers would be ready to accept a drastic lowering of standards of living for the mere pleasure of seeing a national middle class replacing a foreign one at the helm of various enterprises." He decried "sentimental campaigns to promote the purchase of home-produced goods, or appeals to racial feeling" as "subterfuges hiding the desire of owners of business and industry to protect their profits against foreign competition."[58] Against the *felquistes*, Trudeau quoted their own favorite, Frantz Fanon, on Third World nationalists' tendency to displace foreigners to the economic benefit of the national *bourgeoisie*, to appeal to racial resentment, and to create a single-party "dictatorship of the national-socialist type." Without mincing words, Trudeau claimed that the separatism of the self-styled FLQ revolutionaries represented "a national-socialist counter-revolution."[59]

So much for Trudeau's image of the FLQ's ends. What of their violent means? In his 1958 essay on the obstacles to democracy in Québec, Trudeau had argued that French *Canadiens* had always treated political activity as a defense of ethnic, not democratic, rights. Whereas an 1837 rebellion of English settlers "in Upper Canada was a clear struggle for democratic self-government, most of Papineau's followers took up their pitchforks to fight for national self-determination." The *Canadiens*, he claimed, fought then "as they would eventually rally for electoral battles or parliamentary debates whenever their ethnic survival seemed to be imperiled, as men in an army whose sole purpose is to drive the *Anglais* back. And, as everyone knows," he added, "the army is a poor training corps for democracy, no matter how inspiring its cause."[60]

---

[58] Trudeau, *Federalism and the French Canadians*, p. 12.
[59] Trudeau quotes Fanon, *Les damnés de la terre*, in *Cité Libre*, May 1964, translated and reprinted in his *Federalism and the French Canadians*, pp. 211–212.
[60] Trudeau, "Some Obstacles," pp. 105–106.

The 1963 arrests of the FLQ bombers had failed to stop the movement. By 1966 a new group of about twenty activists, led by Pierre Vallières and Charles Gagnon, relaunched the bombing campaign. Targets included the site of a Liberal Party rally in June 1966 and the headquarters of the Lagrenade shoe company, whose workers were on strike. That bombing was carried out, "in solidarity" with the strikers, by *felquiste* Rhéal Mathieu and resulted in the death of the company's receptionist. In 1967 Mathieu was sentenced to nine years in prison for the woman's death. In the 1990s he resumed his violent activities, in support of the French language, by firebombing three coffee shops to protest their English name, Second Cup. He was tried and convicted by a jury in 2001, by which time he had in any case partially achieved his objective. The chain changed its name to Les Cafés Second Cup.[61]

On October 5, 1970 the FLQ kidnapped James Cross, the British trade representative, in an effort to publicize its cause and to force the government to release the jailed FLQ members, whom the organization considered political prisoners. Although the number of FLQ members actually engaged in violence was never very large, the Canadian federal government saw the organization as a grave threat. Pierre Trudeau, a native of Québec, had become Canada's prime minister in April 1968. According to declassified cabinet records of the October Crisis, Trudeau feared that broadcasting the FLQ's political manifesto – one of the key demands of the kidnappers – might spark a broader popular movement for Québec separatism. Indeed the group's critique of Anglo domination of Québec society and its demands for change met with widespread agreement among the francophone population of Québec and were treated sympathetically by the French-language press. In fact, one newspaper, *Québec-Presse*, had already published the FLQ manifesto back in June 1970.[62]

On October 8, 1970, the government authorized the Canadian Broadcasting Company to have an announcer read the FLQ manifesto over the air. Among other things the statement demanded: "the total independence of Quebeckers, united in a free society, purged forever of the clique of voracious sharks, the patronizing 'big bosses' and their henchmen who have made Quebec their hunting preserve for 'cheap labor' and unscrupulous exploitation." It maintained that francophone people of Québec "are terrorized by the closed circles of science and culture which are the universities and by their monkey directors," and

---

[61] Http://en.wikipedia.org/wiki/Rh%C3%A9al_Mathieu.

[62] Raphael Cohen-Almagor, "The Terrorists' Best Ally: The Quebec Media Coverage of the FLQ Crisis in October 1970," *Canadian Journal of Communication*, 25, 2 (2000), unpaginated online version; Épinette, *La question nationale*, pp. 58–59.

it called upon "production workers, miners, foresters, teachers, students and unemployed workers" to "take what belongs to you: your jobs, your determination and your liberty."[63]

On October 10, another FLQ cell kidnapped Pierre Laporte, Québec's deputy premier and minister for labor and immigration (whom the separatists dubbed "minister for unemployment and the assimilation of the Québécois").[64] The FLQ took full advantage of the media's preoccupation with the crisis by issuing multiple communications and playing two of Montréal's main radio stations off against one another for access to the group's latest demands. In the meantime, Trudeau's government in Ottawa had authorized negotiations with the kidnappers, but had also prepared for the deployment of hundreds of troops and sought, unsuccessfully, permission of the Québec government to send them to the province. With negotiations going nowhere, on October 14, a number of prominent public figures, including Claude Ryan, editor and publisher of the respected Montréal daily *Le Devoir*, and Parti Québécois leader René Lévesque, issued a statement urging the government to comply with the FLQ demands. Trudeau and his fellow Liberal Party members had long sought to associate their former colleague Lévesque and his new party with the terrorists and to blame the francophone press, especially Ryan, for instigating violence.

At a meeting of the Cabinet Committee on Security and Intelligence on the morning of October 14, Trudeau argued against making concessions for fear that they would increase support for Québec separatism. Instead, he advocated immediate action that "might have to include rigid control of the mass media and strong counter-propaganda action by the government."[65] The next day, after the government of Québec finally agreed to request the intervention of the Canadian armed forces – that "poor training corps for democracy" – Trudeau's Cabinet decided to declare a state of emergency, issue an ultimatum to the kidnappers, and begin arresting FLQ members. At 4 a.m. on October 16, the government invoked the War Measures Act, suspending civil liberties and banning the FLQ. It sent tanks into the streets and to the airport, and immediately launched a campaign of mass arrests, rounding up without warrants some 497 citizens over two days. After a short time, 435 of them were released without charges, and the remaining 62 were charged under the War Measures Act and the criminal code.

---

[63] Quoted in Cohen-Almagor, "Terrorists' Best Ally," unpaginated.
[64] Pierre Vallières, *The Assassination of Pierre Laporte: Behind the October '70 Scenario*, trans. by Ralph Wells (Toronto: James Lorimer, 1977), p. 63.
[65] Cohen-Almagor, "Terrorists' Best Ally," unpaginated.

Sixteen people were eventually sentenced for the kidnapping and murder of Laporte.[66] Sympathy for the FLQ remained high among the francophone population. Some three thousand students demonstrated in support of the group in Montréal on October 15. Only with the announcement on October 17 that the FLQ cell had executed Pierre Laporte did the tide of public opinion turn against the organization. At that point the francophone media began to side with the government. The English-language press, already hostile to Québec separatism, went to something of an extreme in its anti-FLQ stance. On October 17, the front-page headline of the *Vancouver Sun* blared "New FLQ Warning: 'Women and Children Next.'" In what turned out to be a hoax, it reported that FLQ terrorists had tortured a woman in Hull, Québec, to put pressure on the government to meet its demands. As Jean-Paul Desbiens, our erstwhile Frère Untel and by then an editorialist for *La Presse*, wrote on October 24, "there would be a lot to say about the lack of intellectual rigor on the part of the written and spoken press."[67]

Because of the crucial role that the killing of Laporte played in reversing public sentiment, some FLQ activists, most notably Pierre Vallières, have suggested that the federal government somehow orchestrated it. He accuses the Trudeau government of deliberately overreacting to the FLQ actions of October 1970. "The FLQ was not attempting to bring about a coup d'état," he claims, "but simply to win the release of the political prisoners while scoring a propaganda victory. In this context, the Cross kidnapping was intended as an act of 'armed propaganda' and not the beginning of a war of attrition against the existing system."[68] That claim seems at variance with the threats issued in the FLQ manifesto, broadcast, according to the kidnappers' demand, on Canadian radio. Referring to the Liberal Québec provincial government of premier Robert Bourassa, the manifesto predicts that "in the coming year Bourassa is going to get what's coming to him: 100,000 revolutionary workers, armed and organized!"[69] As if to back up the threat (and inadvertently echoing the government's rationale for deploying the army), Michel Chartrand, a labor union leader and FLQ sympathizer, declared, "we are going to win because there are more boys ready to shoot Members of Parliament than there are policemen."[70]

---

[66] Ibid.; Épinette, *La question nationale*, pp. 58–59. "The October Crisis," http://en.wikipedia. org/wiki/October_Crisis; Vallières, *Assassination of Pierre Laporte*, p. 191. The numbers differ somewhat in these various accounts.

[67] Both articles cited in Cohen-Almagor, "Terrorists' Best Ally," unpaginated.

[68] Vallières, *Assassination of Pierre Laporte*, p. 59.

[69] "The FLQ Manifesto," in Marcel Rioux, *Quebec in Question*, trans. by James Boake (1971), http://english.republiquelibre.org/manifesto-flq.html.

[70] John Gray, "How Trudeau Halted the Reign of Terror," *The Globe and Mail* (Toronto), September 30, 2000.

Chartrand's reference to "boys" seems appropriate. Virtually all of the prominent *felquistes* were young men.[71] One notable exception was Louise Lanctôt, who joined the FLQ with her then-husband, Jacques Cossette-Trudel, and participated with her brother, Jacques Lanctôt, and several others in the kidnapping of James Cross.[72] They were eventually allowed safe passage to Cuba as part of the agreement that led to the release of Cross. As we have seen, the *felquistes* drew inspiration from Third World revolutionaries. They also considered themselves Québec's equivalent of the Weathermen or Black Panthers – hardly role models for gender-egalitarian relations. As Anna Marie Smith has suggested, "the national-ists of all stripes looked south with envy, and somehow their americaphilia was not supposed to contradict their opposition to anglophone Canada."[73] Closer to home, the FLQ militants fancied themselves the heirs of the rebellion of 1837–1838. The prospects that their goals and methods would have advanced women's status and wellbeing are comparably dubious.

The War Measures Act remained in force until April 30, 1971. It led to the total defeat of the FLQ, membership of which was in any case never very large, and the popular rejection of a violent route to independence, even among the substantial numbers of Québécois who sympathized with that cause. But Pierre Trudeau was mistaken if he expected that taking extreme measures against the FLQ would discredit the long-term goal of Québec separatism and its political vehicle, the Parti Québécois. Instead, he found himself heading in the same direction as the French in Algeria, who, having won the Battle of Algiers, went on to lose the war for Algérie Française. At first, the Parti Québécois was indeed hurt by the October Crisis. Trudeau's Liberals sought to taint the party with terror-ism-by-association and the PQ's membership dropped to 30,000. Three years later, however, it bounced back to 60,000 members, as erstwhile sympathizers of the FLQ renounced violence and embraced the PQ as the only feasible instrument for achieving Québec's independence.[74] In the provincial elections of 1976, the PQ won the largest share of votes and formed a government, with René Lévesque as premier. The PQ had run on a platform of calling for a referendum on Québec's status, with the goal of sovereignty, and it held the vote on May 20, 1980.[75]

Nô: "The culture survives because of the mothers"

The dates October 15, 1970 and May 20, 1980 form the chronological endpoints of Robert Lepage's film, with most of the action taking place

[71] Http://en.wikipedia.org/wiki/Front_de_Lib%C3%A9ration_du_Qu%C3%A9bec.
[72] Http://en.wikipedia.org/wiki/Louise_Lanct%C3%B4t.
[73] Personal correspondence.   [74] Épinette, *La question nationale*, pp. 59–61.
[75] Http://fr.wikipedia.org/wiki/Parti_Qu%C3%A9b%C3%A9cois.

during the October Crisis. The film tells the story of Sophie, an actress performing with a Québécois troupe at the World's Fair, Expo '70, in Osaka, Japan, and her boyfriend, Michel, a writer and sympathizer with the FLQ back in Montréal. It is a movie about plays and about plays on words. The title, *Nô*, is the French transliteration of the traditional Japanese theater, usually spelled *Noh* or *Nō* in English. Its second meaning relates to the referendum of May 1980 on Québec sovereignty. In the director's words, "it's a play on words with the English word 'no,' which corresponds to the response of the Québécois to the referendum."[76]

The movie is made up of a series of parallels or binaries, starting with a basic gender divide, masculine–feminine, but with a particular Québécois slant. As Lepage describes, "in Québec still men are silent. It's the women who provoke change, who build society." Repeating Frère Untel's generalization, he asserts that "Québec is a matriarchal society," but one that "has adjusted itself to the patriarchal international rules." For example, "we inherited the American Indian tradition where the grandmother and the women's council have absolute power, a magic power."[77] "The men go and hunt and the women take care of the politics; they are the ones who decide."[78] After initially encouraging intermarriage between French settlers and the native population, the French colonial authorities sought to dilute the latter's influence, passing a law, for example, that made it illegal to dress like the native population, to wear similar make-up or earrings. The new approach rejected the native matriarchal tradition in favor of a reassertion of male authority. "With *Nô*," claimed Lepage, "I was interested in this heritage, as it appeared to me in 1970."[79] At a press conference following the opening of the film at the 1998 Montréal Film Festival, he explained that "there were two battles: the men fought for their language, their culture, with bombs, while the women were seeking to reappropriate their bodies."[80] Ultimately, he argues, "the culture survives because of the mothers, the women."[81]

Many of the film's parallels are visual: with events in Montréal filmed in black and white and those in Osaka in color; with the flash of a bulb in a photo booth or policeman's camera matched with the flash of a bomb

---

[76] Coulombe, "Entretien avec Robert Lepage," in *Nô: Scénario du film de Robert Lepage*, p. 100, hereafter referred to as "*Nô* script" for reference to the film dialogue. My translations sometimes differ from those in the movie's English subtitles.

[77] Coulombe, "Entretien avec Robert Lepage," p. 96.

[78] Interview with Lepage in Dundjerovic, *Cinema of Robert Lepage*, pp. 148–149.

[79] Coulombe, "Entretien avec Robert Lepage," p. 96.

[80] I found the quotations from the interview and downloaded them from a website called *Écran Noir*, www.ecrannoir.fr/films/filmsb.php?f=743. Lepage says something quite similar in the other interviews cited here.

[81] Interview with Lepage in Dundjerovic, *Cinema of Robert Lepage*, pp. 148–149.

exploding; with the nationalist violence of the writer Michel's friends (leftist revolutionaries) in Québec matched by the contemporaneous nationalist violence of the Japanese writer Yukio Mishima (mentioned in conversation only), who committed ritual suicide with his paramilitary unit after trying unsuccessfully to instigate a military coup to restore the emperor to full power. Both Michel and Sophie kept two clocks in their respective apartment in Montréal and hotel room in Osaka, set to the time in both cities, in a tragicomically unsuccessful attempt to keep track of what time it is for the other person.

The film opens in black and white, with a typewriter tapping out the setting, "Montréal, 15 October 1970." In the apartment of Michel and Sophie a television announcer reports the news of the FLQ kidnappings and the government's ultimatum. It then switches to news of Expo '70 in Osaka, with a reporter describing a *Noh* play about to be staged. The camera cuts to the Japanese stage, filmed in color, as the viewer hears the TV announcer summarize the play, and, in a sense, the movie we are about to see: "The Noh actor assumes the features of a young woman exile who, after having tried to drown her sorrows in a rushing stream, finds her way again thanks to the glow of a fire lit in burning letters by her warrior lover."[82]

Then we watch the play and watch Sophie and her Japanese colleague Hanako watching the play. In an interview, Lepage described the parallel he had in mind: "At the start of the film a *Noh* actor puts on the mask of a woman, straightens it and comes on stage. At the same moment, in Québec, a playwright in total identity crisis, far from the one he loves, puts on his revolutionary mask and enters the scene."[83]

Michel is rather forced into his revolutionary role, when two friends seek to hide in his apartment at 4 a.m. on October 17. The War Measures Act has gone into effect and hundreds of suspected militants and sympathizers are being hunted down. Michel hangs up on Sophie, who had called, mistakenly thinking it was four in the afternoon and knowing nothing about the crisis in Québec. She was preoccupied with her own personal crisis: an unexpected and possibly unwanted pregnancy. When she tells her fellow actresses about Michel's strange behavior, they immediately assume he has a mistress (an echo of the play they are performing). Thus Lepage links the personal and the political from the outset and shows how one can be mistaken for the other.

Abortion, along with the advertising and distribution of contraceptives, had been illegal in Canada since the nineteenth century. In 1967

---

[82] *Nô* script, p. 12.
[83] Coulombe, "Entretien avec Robert Lepage, " p. 100.

Figure 5.1 A male actor with a female mask. *Nô* (1998)

a bill introduced by the then justice minister, Pierre Trudeau, made an exception for cases of danger to the woman's health, as determined by a panel of three doctors. The same bill, which became law in 1969, made homosexuality and contraception legal because, as Trudeau explained, "the state has no business in the bedrooms of the nation."[84] Abortion, however, remained illegal, unless approved for health reasons, until 1988 when, after many court challenges, a ruling by the Supreme Court of Canada removed it from the Criminal Code.

In 1970, abortion was legal in Japan. In the film Sophie considers terminating her pregnancy there, with the help of her friend Hanako who offered to bring her to a clinic if she stayed an extra week in Japan. She feels some ambivalence about the decision – partly because she is not sure that Michel is the father. When she hears about the War Measures Act, she fears that Michel is in danger and decides to return straight home after the end of her production.[85] Michel is indeed in trouble. His friends have used his apartment to arrange a bombing and have borrowed one of his alarm clocks to use as the timer.

The scenes set in Montréal, and filmed in black and white, convey a certain documentary feel – with actual television footage from the period – and reflect the Québec film style known as *cinéma direct*. The placement of the camera gives the viewer the sense of being present on the scene. *Nô* exhibits a certain *film noir* quality as well. But it is the *film noir*

[84] Http://en.wikipedia.org/wiki/Abortion_in_Canada.
[85] In reality, Expo '70 had ended before the October Crisis, on September 13, 1970.

of the French New Wave of the late 1950s and early 1960s, rather than the original Hollywood version. Lepage's FLQ terrorists are "playing" terrorists the way François Truffaut's or Jean-Luc Godard's gangsters played at being Chicago (or Hollywood) gangsters, to great comic effect. When an interviewer described them as "operetta terrorists," Lepage felt obliged to explain why he portrayed them that way, when, according to him, contemporary Québec society tends to depict the *felquistes* as heroes. "I don't mock their motivations. These people were inspired, and something authentic was happening there. But, all the same, these were professors of philosophy going to plant bombs." One could justifiably poke fun at them, he suggests. But, as he explains, he himself was only twelve years old at the time of the October Crisis. The parents of some of his friends were militants or sympathizers. "I was a witness to their sincere militancy, just two steps away from ridiculous, and with blinders on."[86] There was a comic element to the state's response as well, at least in the eyes of a twelve-year-old, who remembers "the sight of a soldier in camouflage, with branches sticking out of his helmet, in an otherwise completely urban environment."[87]

Virtually all of the characters in the Montréal scenes are male – another reason for Lepage to have filmed them in black and white ("I associate feminine with color and masculine with black-and-white.").[88] He plays numerous sight gags, including some of a gender-bending sort. At one point an unlikely couple of police agents are staking out Michel and Sophie's apartment from an unoccupied apartment across the street. When a realtor unexpectedly arrives to show it to two clients, the cops stash their listening devices under the pull-out sofa bed and one of them hops on it, feigning a nonchalant pose. The clients, an evidently gay male couple, exchange a meaningful glance.

Lepage plays with gender in other ways. The Japanese *Noh* actors are all male, and put on masks to play female roles. Sophie, when we first see her in the audience, watching the play – and then in the ladies' room mirror feeling ill – also has a masculine air about her. Although dressed in a colorful blouse and miniskirt, she is very tall and her face is made up to emphasize her square chin, broad forehead, and high cheekbones.

Other gender identities are called into question. On stage with Sophie, when she performs in her own troupe's play, is François-Xavier. Both in "real life" and as the character Monsieur Petypon, he has a rather feminine quality, with a clean-shaven baby face and long, straight hair, typical

[86] Coulombe, "Entretien avec Robert Lepage," pp. 96–97.
[87] Dundjerovic, *The Cinema of Robert Lepage*, p. 100.
[88] Coulombe, "Entretien avec Robert Lepage," p. 100.

Figure 5.2 A female actor with a masculine face. *Nô* (1998)

of the era. He has fallen in love with Sophie, stimulated by an inadvertent act of violence during rehearsal as she tries unsuccessfully to execute a stage slap and keeps hitting him for real.

Several key scenes in the film involve confrontational conversations, with violent, emotional language. An early one addresses the question of language itself. As Michel's comrades are about to leave with their bomb, he asks for a look at the statement that will be sent to the press, with the group's list of demands – an apparent allusion to the FLQ manifesto. As a writer Michel is shocked at the poor quality of the writing. René, the statement's author, becomes increasingly defensive. Finally it is Michel who explodes:

Hey, isn't it you who said that our first battle is the language? Our first form of resistance is the language? The way we speak, the words we use … The words that aren't those of the oppressor? The will to transcend an alienated, miserable language, to become an adult, sovereign language! That's our battle too. Now that it's necessary to use it, the language, you deny the power of words.[89]

In Japan Sophie also experiences an outburst of nationalist sentiment – at an awkward dinner with Walter Lapointe, the cultural attaché from the Canadian embassy, and his wife, Patricia Hébert. They have come down from Tokyo to Osaka to congratulate the Québec theater troupe. The other actors have made excuses to skip the dinner, so Sophie is left

---

[89] *Nô* script, p. 49.

Figure 5.3 François-Xavier and Sophie. *Nô* (1998)

Figure 5.4 Michel. *Nô* (1998)

alone with them. Before politics intrudes on the scene, Sophie imbibes quite a bit of *sake* and tries to make conversation with Patricia. They venture into a discussion of the difficult choices facing women – choices about careers, children, family. Patricia represents a certain image of the modern woman. She is perhaps in her late thirties, somewhat older than Sophie, and she presents herself as a professional woman of sorts. She is married to Walter, but has not taken his surname. She was born in

Montréal, but moved to Paris with her family as teenager. She affects a more proper French than the typical Québec variant, but occasionally throws in a discordant, and therefore funny, colloquialism. Commenting on the esthetic beauty of *sushi* displayed on a plate, for example, she uses a slang word, common in France as well as Québec, for "very" (based on the word "cow") that the British might translate as "bloody." *Les couleurs et les formes des sushis, là ... Esthétiquement, c'est vachement réussi.* (The colors and the forms of the sushi there ... Esthetically, it bloody well works.)

Sophie asks whether Patricia and Walter have children. When Walter says "No, unfortunately," Patricia interrupts him. "You can't have your cake and eat it too," she explains. "When one wants a career, as in my case, well, one has to make a choice." The irony here is that Patricia does not appear to have an independent career.[90] She is a diplomat's wife and does not seem to enjoy that job very much. She had studied acting in Paris, but did not cater to the "exhibitionist aspect" and particularly disliked the "collective" approach. She believes that "creation is an essentially solitary act," and has dabbled in a style of Japanese painting called *sumie*. She studies Japanese language and literature. In short, her decision not to have children does not seem imposed by demands of a professional career.

Patricia's opinion serves as a stand-in for a larger point that Lepage wants to make about gender and Québec society. As Dundjerovic explains, "Lepage came to film from a background of collective creations in theatre" that developed in the 1960s. It was "a form of cultural resistance" to the patriarchal structures that Tremblay, Frère Untel, and others believed the English had imposed upon what had been a matriarchal Québec society: "By replacing individual ownership over creation, analogous to the capitalist-patriarchal model, with a collective-communal model, theatre groups sought to reform the production and organizational nature of artistic creation." Thus, in this single scene, one character's simple expression of distaste for theater collectives represents the tension between nationalist "Québec's theatrical collective creation and colonial-bourgeois French theatre" – and, of course, a kind of in-joke, since Lepage and the movie's actors all come from the world of collective theater.[91]

The discussion moves from the personal to the political rather suddenly. Sophie seems to want children. "I wonder if it's maybe possible for

---

[90] This irony may not be intentional, given that the character of Patricia in the original work on which the movie is based was pursuing a doctoral degree and worked on documentary films while living in Tokyo with her diplomat husband. See Robert Lepage and Ex Machina, *The Seven Streams of the River Ota* (London: Methuen, 1996).

[91] Dundjerovic, *The Cinema of Robert Lepage*, p. 15.

Figure 5.5 At the sushi restaurant. *Nô* (1998)

a woman to have a child, to have a career, even to raise her child herself. Because, nowadays, women, we're liberated. Come on!" "You think so?" replies Patricia. "Good luck!"[92] The conversation remains strained, in part because Patricia hated Sophie's play. The difficulty she has finding something nice to say about it is obvious. The play itself is a minor farce by Georges Feydeau, a Parisian playwright from the turn of the century, and no one seems to understand why a Québécois troupe was invited to perform it in the Canadian pavilion at the World's Fair.[93] Is this, then, what passes for Canadian culture – the best that either the anglophone or francophone communities can muster? Patricia finally comes up with some transparently insincere compliments ("interesting ... amusing ... refreshing!"). At that point Sophie bursts out with her own criticisms of the play, spiced with ample Québécois profanity, and then launches into a political tirade, with even more profanity. For better or worse, the swears, known as *sacre* (for "sacred") in Québécois French, are untranslatable, or, rather, meaningless in translation, because they mostly come from the Catholic mass and literally refer to seemingly innocuous parts of the ritual: tabernacle, chalice, host, ciborium. Here is her outburst, with the swears left in the original:

You, you're a diplomat, aren't you? Are you going to explain to me how it happened that a French director came to Montréal to teach us to speak with

---

[92] *Nô* script, pp. 52–53.
[93] That a troupe from Québec put on a turn-of-the-century French play, George Feydeau's *La Dame de Chez Maxim*, at Expo '70 is Lepage's invention.

a French accent in a bad French play, and that that's what represents Canada at the World's Fair at Osaka? Well, I'll tell you why. Because we're a colonized people! Colonized, *tabarnak*! Yes, *ta-bar-naque*! I said it, *tabarnak*! That really makes me want to swear (*sacrer*), *hostie de calice de tabarnak de saint-ciboire d'hostie de saint-ciboire de christ de sacrament*! Even General de Gaulle said it: "*Vive le Québec libre*," *tabarnak*![94]

And Walter responds, "Well, I don't think he said '*tabarnak*.'" Patricia tries to reassure Sophie that they are aware of the nationalist sentiment and the crisis back home. Then she tells Sophie about Yukio Mishima and the ultranationalist army he has formed.

The pacing of their exchange recalls the scene from Marguerite Duras' script for Alain Resnais' 1959 film, *Hiroshima Mon Amour*. The Japanese man insists that the French woman has seen nothing at Hiroshima ("tu n'as rien vu à Hiroshima"), and she repeats that she has, and he repeats that she has not.[95]

PATRICIA: Vous connaissez Mishima?
SOPHIE: Non.
PATRICIA: Vous connaissez pas Mishima!
SOPHIE: Beh non! Je le connais pas, Mishima.

Inevitably, Hiroshima figures in this film, set in Japan twenty-five years after the atomic bombings. Sophie's friend, Hanako, is a victim of the Hiroshima attack, a *hibakusha*, blinded by the explosion. She also happens to be the most stable and capable character in the film, always ready to help Sophie in her troubles. Hiroshima comes directly into the film in a quick montage that cuts from Hanako and her fellow interpreter and boyfriend Buchanan getting their picture taken in a photo booth. As the flash bulb explodes, Lepage cuts to the mushroom cloud – perhaps the only one of his many clever montages that seems a bit too forced.

Lepage's montages are inspired by Jean Cocteau – a fellow playwright-turned-filmmaker. In *Testament of Orpheus* (1960), Lepage explains, Cocteau "always challenges you, he always says, 'Well we're here in this room and now if we want to go into the world of death, or something, we have to go through the mirror'. But he can't go through the mirror the same way; every time he has to find a different way. If you look at the film there's seven different ways that he uses the idea of going through a mirror, there's not one single repeat." For Lepage, the transitions in *Nô* usually involve darkness or light, and often explosions – of a flash bulb or a

---

[94] *Nô* script, pp. 58–59. Charles de Gaulle issued this cry at Montréal City Hall in July 1967, on the occasion of his visit to Expo '67.
[95] Other similarities to *Hiroshima Mon Amour* are mentioned by Dundjerovic, *Cinema of Robert Lepage*, pp. 101–102.

bomb. One scene in the Montréal apartment of Michel and Sophie ends in darkness when Michel tosses his shirt over the camera lens – Lepage's tongue-in-cheek homage to *cinéma direct*.

Lepage's goal of combining and contrasting the personal and the political, the violent and the humorous, is reflected in the very structure of the film. Although his characters wonder why the Canadian government has decided to put on Feydeau's comedy alongside the more serious *Noh* production of the Japanese theater company, Lepage has his reasons. A common tradition in Japanese theater was to perform short comical pieces, known as *Kyōgen*, during intermissions in the main program of the *Noh* performance. These were very similar in spirit to Feydeau's farces, employing mistaken identities, multiple entrances and exits, and other techniques that Lepage adopts for his movie. Lepage has structured *Nô* to keep his audience laughing even while he engages such serious concerns as the limits of national and individual autonomy, and the relative merits of confrontation versus compromise in personal and political relations.

At first glance, Lepage seems to be contrasting the private, personal issues affecting Sophie in Osaka with the public, political issues confronting the FLQ and its sympathizers in Montréal. Yet, as one observer points out, "the Montréal sub-narrative has more to do with the boys playing roles than anything serious and life-determining." The Osaka sub-narrative, by comparison, "carries a life importance," representing "decisions that ordinary people make, which are significant in their lives."[96] In his temporal comparison Lepage brings the personal and the political together, linking Sophie's major personal choice in 1970 – whether or not to have an abortion – with a major political choice for the Québec nation ten years later – whether or not to secede from Canada and give birth to an independent Québec. As it turns out, Sophie's choice is moot. When she returns to find the ruins of her apartment, the police investigators from across the street treat her rather roughly and she miscarries. The film changes from black and white to color as the viewer, looking out from the window of the bombed-out apartment, spots the blood running down her leg.

Lepage "uses pregnancy and miscarriage as a metaphor for the political conditions in Québec," as Dundjerovic points out.[97] In Sophie's

---

[96] Dundjerovic, *Cinema of Robert Lepage*, p. 107.
[97] Ibid., p. 114. Salman Rushdie, in *Midnight's Children* (1981), used the birth – coinciding with India's independence from Britain – and life of his character Saleem Sinan to recount the subsequent political history of India and Pakistan. As with Rushdie's apparent model – Laurence Sterne's *The Life and Opinions of Tristram Shandy* (first volume published in 1759) – the birth of the main character takes place much of the way into the novel, giving the author ample opportunity to fill in additional background, including about both characters' preoccupation with noses.

Figure 5.6 Backstage. *Nô* (1998)

case, she faced violence in any event – if not the violence that caused her to miscarry, then the violence of going forward with an unwanted pregnancy. Carol Gilligan described the decision on abortion in those terms: "The occurrence of the dilemma itself precludes nonviolent resolution." Barbara Johnson elaborates: "The choice is not between violence and nonviolence, but between simple violence to a fetus and complex, less determinate violence to an involuntary mother and/or an unwanted child."[98] The FLQ's unsuccessful reliance on violence parallels the failed pregnancy. With the War Measures Act, Trudeau felt obliged to resort to the threat of violence to destroy the FLQ. But would a successful "revolution" by the hapless *felquistes* have yielded a better, more peaceful result?

The peaceful alternative of negotiation and referenda, despite setbacks, offers more promise for the future – as the concluding scene of *Nô* implies. It takes place on the evening of May 20, 1980 in Sophie and Michel's apartment – a more upscale place than their basement flat of ten years earlier. The movie ends on a hopeful note, despite the news that comes across the television screen: the referendum on Québec's sovereignty has failed by a large margin. More than 59 percent of the voters

---

[98] Barbara Johnson, *A World of Difference* (Baltimore, MD: Johns Hopkins University Press, 1987), p. 191. She quotes Carol Gilligan, *In a Different Voice* (Cambridge, MA: Harvard University Press, 1982), p. 94. I thank Diane Rubenstein for the point and the reference.

Figure 5.7 Sophie arrested. *Nô* (1998)

rejected what was, after all, a rather tentatively worded proposal. The question posed on the ballot was:

The Government of Quebec has made public its proposal to negotiate a new agreement with the rest of Canada, based on the equality of nations; this agreement would enable Quebec to acquire the exclusive power to make its laws, levy its taxes and establish relations abroad – in other words, sovereignty – and at the same time to maintain with Canada an economic association including a common currency; any change in political status resulting from these negotiations will be effected with approval by the people through another referendum; on these terms, do you give the Government of Quebec the mandate to negotiate the proposed agreement between Quebec and Canada?[99]

Sophie finds the results "really depressing." Michel, looking much more like a yuppie than the revolutionary intellectual of ten years earlier, waxes philosophical. "It confirms my theory … that the people who have a collective project are always a bit disadvantaged compared to those who don't have a project. In the sense that the people who don't have a project always have the force of inertia with them. The idea is that it takes more energy to change the political forms, the social forms, than … than to do nothing." He tries an analogy and seems to be hinting at something. It's like "a couple who are trying desperately to find a common reason or a common project, but it's sterile, you know? There's no common identity

[99] Http://en.wikipedia.org/wiki/1980_Quebec_referendum.

Figure 5.8 "They've become bourgeois." *Nô* (1998)

which is really...I don't know." Sophie seems to know what he's driving at, but she lets him flounder around with words like "sterile," "posterity," and "common project." She makes him admit what's on his mind: "You want to talk about a child, isn't that it? Isn't that what you're saying?"

Sophie wonders aloud what Michel would have said ten years ago if she had wanted to have a child. It was different then, he says. "We were busy changing the world." Now they both have careers, they have means. "Times have changed. What do you think about it?" She says, "Yeah." "Yeah," he repeats. "That's like a yes of 40.5 percent, right. Or a yes of 49?" "I don't know...A yes of 50 percent." Michel tries to talk her into at least a yes of 50.5 percent, "a simple majority." The closing notes of the script indicate that "the two lovers kiss with an ardor that presages a fertile future."

Lepage explains the optimistic ending to what, for the supporter of a sovereign Québec that he appears to be, should be a sad story. He suggests that the Québécois, like the Irish, don't mourn when someone dies, or when a project founders. "They make love, they make children, they dance. It's admirable." As for his characters, Michel and Sophie, at the end of the film "they've become bourgeois, but I don't love them any less."

Yvette and the 1980 referendum

Sophie and Michel have focused inward on a "common project" of domesticity and childrearing to deal with their disappointment about public life: the fact that the people of Québec remain "colonized" by Canada, as Sophie (and Lepage) puts it. So their situation was not entirely positive, despite the hope implied by the end of Lepage's film. Tension over issues related to women and the family was rife in Québec society in the run-up to the referendum of 1980 and may well account for its defeat. The "Yvette phenomenon" played a certain role as well.

As in any nationalist movement, feminist and national goals were often at odds in the campaign for Québec's sovereignty.[100] A common slogan in the women's movement in the late 1960s was *Pas de libération des femmes sans Québec libre, pas de Québec libre sans libération des femmes*, "No women's liberation without a free Québec, no free Québec without the liberation of women." In fact francophone women found a great deal of support for their concerns within the mainstream nationalist movement and the Parti Québécois. But pursuing sovereignty often meant forsaking alliances with anglophone women who did not share that goal. In 1970, for example, even a seemingly straightforward project of working together for abortion rights foundered on the francophone separatist women's refusal to join in a march on Ottawa because they did not recognize the authority of the Canadian federal government. Rejecting the coalition with the community of English-speaking women, many Québec feminists counted on the Parti Québécois to carry out their agenda – and hoped that the reforms would put Québec ahead of the rest of Canada on women's issues.

The advent of the Parti Québécois to provincial power in 1976 augured well for this strategy. The budget of the Conseil du Statut de la Femme, established in 1973 to advise the government on women's issues, was increased from several hundred thousand Canadian dollars to more than a million. "Between 1970 and 1979," as LeClerc and West describe, "the Parti Québécois platform had changed from peripheralizing women under 'family and childhood' to attempting to accommodate women in their dual roles as worker and housewife-mother." As represented in Lepage's character of Sophie, Québec women in the 1970s saw their status improve as they became involved in the new economy and entrepreneurship, gained access to the professions, and enjoyed increases in their income.[101]

Yet tensions remained between fostering women's independence in the public sphere and encouraging traditional nationalist focus on the home and family. They became apparent during the campaign on

---

[100] This paragraph draws mainly on LeClerc and West, "Feminist Nationalist Movements," pp. 229–231.
[101] Ibid., pp. 230–231.

sovereignty, brought to the surface by an off-hand remark from Lise
Payette, the Parti Québécois minister responsible for the status of
women. Her remark was directed against Madeleine Ryan, the wife
of Claude Ryan, former editor and publisher of *Le Devoir*. During
the October Crisis of 1970, Liberal Party leader and Canada's prime
minister, Pierre Trudeau, had accused Claude Ryan of siding with the
terrorists who were seeking Québec's independence. Now, ten years
later, the two politicians were on the same side of the barricades, with
Ryan, having become leader of the Québec branch of the Liberal Party
in 1978, campaigning against the sovereignty referendum in favor of
federalism. Lise Payette sought to criticize his position by targeting
his wife. She made reference to Yvette, a character in primary school
books, who helped her traditional mother at home while her brother
Guy pursued exciting adventures outside. Payette charged that Ryan's
wife, Madeleine, was an Yvette, afraid to challenge tradition by taking
Québec out of Canada.[102]

Payette's remark led to an astonishing backlash. On March 30, 1980, a
group of 1,700 women held a *brunch des Yvettes* at the Château Frontenac
in Québec City. A week later, at a rally that turned out to have been
organized by the Liberal Party, 14,000 women gathered at the Montréal
Forum to denounce Lise Payette and urge support for federalism and a
"No" vote on the referendum. Many analysts believe that the Yvette issue
contributed to the defeat of the sovereignty bid. Ironically, it was "the
nationalist image of women as mothers upholding the nation" that "led
to an antinationalist vote."[103] A further irony is that the Parti Québécois
itself eventually came to adopt pro-natalist policies typical of a nationalist movement (proposing, for example, in the 1981 electoral campaign,
financial rewards for having more children), which would have been
quite congenial to the Yvette stereotype.

The stinging defeat of the sovereignty referendum – sometimes
referred to as the *renérendum*, because PQ leader René Lévesque had
staked so much of his political reputation on it – ultimately resolved
nothing. Citizens of Québec remained dissatisfied with their province's
relationship to federal Canada. The next fifteen years saw what one ana-
lyst has called "a series of veritable constitutional psychodramas," and
another has dubbed "the traumatism of referenda."[104] Under the Liberal
government that came to power following the PQ's defeat in 1985,
Québec sought to negotiate an accord with the Canadian government

---

[102] Ibid., pp. 233–234; entries for Claude Ryan, http://en.wikipedia.org/wiki/Claude_Ryan,
and Lise Payette, http://en.wikipedia.org/wiki/Lise_Payette.
[103] LeClerc and West, "Feminist Nationalist Movements," pp. 233–234.
[104] Épinette, *La question nationale*, p. 82; Lefebvre, *Qui profiterait*, pp. 11–12.

to recognize the province as a "distinct society." The concern at the time was that Canada's emerging identity as a "multicultural" society (formalized in the Canadian Multiculturalism Act adopted in 1988) would come at the expense of Québec's claims to distinctiveness, that Québec's French heritage and culture would be considered just one among many – engulfed in what Pierre Trudeau once called "polyethnic pluralism."[105] Negotiations to satisfy Québec's concerns resulted in the Meech Lake Accord of 1987, which did recognize Québec society's distinct status and allowed for the transfer of various federal powers – over issues such as immigration, for example – to the provincial level. By this point, however, some of the other Canadian provinces – all of which were required to endorse the agreement for it to go into effect – had begun to resent what they saw as Québec's special pleading, and they rejected the accord.

Québec reacted to the rejection of the Meech Lake Accord by scheduling another referendum on sovereignty in 1995. It was defeated by the narrowest of margins, 50.58 percent "No" to 49.42 percent "Yes." A record 93 or 94 percent of the more than five million registered Québec citizens voted. They had evidently learned something about the practice of democracy, despite Trudeau's doubts of a couple of decades earlier. About 60 percent of francophone voters favored sovereignty. The heavily populated Montréal region voted "No", however, thanks to the substantial representation of "allophones" – people whose first language is neither French nor English. Regions with large aboriginal populations also tended to vote against sovereignty.[106] To some extent these votes represented a backlash against the remarks of Lucien Bouchard, a pro-sovereignty politician who was later elected premier of Québec. Campaigning for the referendum at a meeting of a women's group in Anjou, he asked, "Do you think it makes any sense that we have so few children in Québec? We're one of the white races that has the fewest children. It doesn't make sense!"

Bouchard managed simultaneously to offend two groups, while revealing his conservative tendencies.[107] First, he offended the "nonwhite" immigrants, who are arguably the real hope for the future economic prosperity of Québec, given the declining birth rates that Bouchard decries.[108] Second, Bouchard offended women who do not want to be

---

[105] Trudeau, "New Treason of the Intellectuals," originally published in *Cité Libre* (April 1962), reprinted and translated in *Federalism and the French Canadians*, quotation at p. 165.

[106] Http://en.wikipedia.org/wiki/1995_Quebec_referendum.

[107] In 1988 Bouchard became minister of the environment in the Progressive Conservative Party government of his friend Brian Mulroney. He left the conservatives and founded the Bloc Québécois only after the failure of the Meech Lake Agreement in 1990.

[108] On the importance of immigration, see Lefebvre, *Qui profiterait*, pp. 33–34; on the relationship between sovereignty and the multinational and immigrant character of

forced into the role of "mothers of the nation" by the pro-natalist policies that his comments imply.[109] As in the 1980 referendum, nationalist images of upholding the nation by emphasizing women's traditional
obligations as mothers led to an antinationalist outcome. But this time
a pro-sovereignty politician (Bouchard) was promoting women's traditional roles, whereas as the previous occasion a pro-sovereignty politician
(Payette) was mocking them.

For some critics, the suspicion that racist sentiments underpinned some
of the pro-sovereignty efforts was reinforced when PQ leader and Québec
premier Jacques Parizeau, on acknowledging defeat, blamed it on "money
and the ethnic vote."[110] According to this view, the PQ already expected
that immigrants would vote against sovereignty; the party sent out
activists to "monitor" polling places, intimidating foreign-looking voters
and throwing out "spoiled" ballots.[111] From the pro-sovereignty side came
charges, rendered plausible by the statistics, that Ottawa had "fast-tracked"
approval of citizenship for recent immigrants, so that they could vote
against the referendum.[112] Democracy at work, with all its flaws.

Relevant to this book's comparative examination of separatist movements, J. A. S. Evans has made a particularly strong claim of racism in
connection with the immigrant vote in the 1995 referendum: "There had
always been racist undertones to the separatist cause. Quebec independence was a dream which only a 'pure wool' Quebecker could fully understand. An immigrant from Haiti, Greece, or Lebanon, or even the United
Kingdom, might be not unsympathetic, but the Heavenly City of the

contemporary Québec society, see the essays in Michel Sarra-Bournet, ed., *Le pays
de tous les Québécois: Diversité culturelle et souveraineté* (Montréal: VLB éditeurs, 1998);
and Claude Bariteau, *Québec: 18 septembre 2001* (Montréal: Editions Québec Amérique,
1998).

[109] On policies such as the "bucks for babies" scheme to pay families 500 dollars for having a child, see "The Cradle's Costly Revenge," *The Economist*, January 8, 2009, www.
economist.com/world/americas/displaystory.cfm?story_id=12891035.

[110] Michael Seymour has suggested interpreting Parizeau's remark "as the expression of
frustration and resentment against immigrant groups for actions performed by them,
actions that he chose to interpret as the expression of not wanting to be part of the
Québec nation ... Parizeau does not realize that one could feel part of the Québec
nation and still be against secession. In any case, Parizeau interpreted the massive vote
of immigrant groups against secession as a self exclusion from the Québec nation," even
if Parizeau's own vision of the nation was more inclusive. Personal communication.

[111] J. A. S. Evans, "The Present State of Canada," *Virginia Quarterly Review*, 72, 2 (Spring
1996), www.vqronline.org/articles/1996/spring/evans-present-state-canada.

[112] "The statistics compiled by the analysts of Citizenship and Immigration Canada demonstrate that some 43,855 new *Québécois* obtained their Canadian citizenship in the
year of 1995. About one quarter of these (11,429) were given during the month of
October. It was the first time that Québec residents received more citizenship certificates than Ontario residents. It has not occurred again since. Looking into the data for
a longer period of time, we see that the increase in certificate attributions jumped by
87% between 1993 and 1995. The year of 1996 saw a drop of 39% in the attributions

Québécois de souche – the 'Old Stock' – relegated them to the sidelines."
Writing in the mid-1990s, in the wake of the brutal wars of Yugoslav
succession, he added a somewhat inflammatory comparison: "Quebec
separatism had more in common with the racial nationalisms of Serbia
or Croatia than with the ethnicities of a modern multicultural state."[113]
Most supporters of Québec sovereignty – and a peaceful route to achieve
it – would find such a charge offensive, even racist.

The intellectuals behind the sovereignty movement are far from the
equivalent of the members of the Serbian Academy of Sciences and Arts
described in chapter 3. In issuing their notorious 1986 memorandum
they offered what one Serbian scholar criticized as a program for "preventive vengeance."[114] Even a cursory look at the website of IPSO, Les
Intellectuels pour la Souveraineté, belies any such comparison.[115] Its 2007
Declaration of Principles, for example, stresses the group's commitment
to "political liberalism," "pluralism of points of view," and "diversity of
beliefs," and its expectation that sovereignty will "reinforce the feeling
of national belonging and the search for common values, such as the
French language, solidarity, citizens' taking charge of their present and
their future, peace, and respect for the dignity of persons."[116] Some of its
members have advocated a "socio-political" conception of the Québec
nation – multicultural and multiethnic.[117]

Québec separatists have not advocated the equivalent of "greater
Serbia" – nor would they have the means to pursue it, as Slobodan
Milošević had the Yugoslav National Army.[118] If armed violence resulted
from a declaration of Québec independence, it would more likely come

---

of citizenship certificates." Pierre O'Neill, "Le camp du NON a-t-il volé le référendum
de 1995?" *Le Devoir*, November 8, 1999, www.vigile.net/9911/vole.html.

[113] Evans, "The Present State," unpaginated.

[114] Svetlana Slapsak, "Les alternatives serbes: y en a-t-il après la Bosnie?" *Migrations
Littéraires*, 21 (Summer 1992). See the discussion in chapter 3.

[115] Www.ipsoquebec.org.

[116] "Déclaration des principes," adopted May 28, 2007, www.ipsoquebec.org.

[117] See, in particular, Michel Seymour's contributions to the www.ipsoquebec.org website,
such as "Letter to Canadians" and "On Redefining the Nation," which also appeared
in *Cahiers du département de sociologie*, Université de Montréal, 97–01 (1997). The views
of Seymour and others on the importance of tolerance for diversity and rejecting a
nationalism that denies cultural pluralism and the rights of minorities have come under
criticism by some for, of all things, the supposed intolerance of their "antidiscrimina-
tory ideology." See Mathieu Bock-Coté, "Le multiculturalisme d'état e l'idéologie anti-
discriminatoire," *Recherches sociographiques*, 50, 2 (2009), pp. 348–364.

[118] In 1962, in his "New Treason of the Intellectuals" (p. 159) Pierre Trudeau suggested
that the logic of Québec separatism would lead to territorial expansion: "If there is
any validity to their principles they should carry them to the point of claiming part of
Ontario, New Brunswick, Labrador, and New England; on the other hand, though, they
would have to relinquish certain border regions around Pontiac and Temiskaming and
turn Westmount into the Danzig of the New World."

from the Canadian government and its army or from opponents of the initiative.[119] Indeed, since the mid-1970s opponents of a sovereign Québec have raised the specter of partition, with pro-Canada regions seceding from the newly independent country, and presumably demanding armed defense – the recipe that led to the violent disintegration of Yugoslavia.[120]

Even if the comparison is not fully valid, one still wonders why Québec has thus far avoided the devastating violence of former Yugoslavia. Did October 1970 constitute a kind of inoculation? Or does the legacy of "matriarchy," whether imagined or real, make a difference? If so, will it endure?

Choosing not to choose: "So what's the problem?"

In the decades following the 1980 referendum that concludes Robert Lepage's film, Québec's status within Canada remained ambiguous. A number of changes during that time have, however, affected the relationship between gender, nationalism, and violence. First, women's opportunities have continued to grow and women have little by little broken down many traditional barriers to their advancement. Second, some men seem to feel threatened by women's progress. Although the potential for violence in the service of nationalism seems low in Québec, everyday "domestic" violence continues to threaten and preoccupy women, relegating sovereignty and independence to rather lower places on their list of priorities. Third, the increasing ethnic diversity of Québec has meant that the project of sovereignty based on the traditional values of the descendants of the original settlers – the *Québécois de souche* – is a lost cause. Here again is potential for resentment and violence of the "angry white male" sort against the newcomers.[121] A countervailing force is the emphasis on

---

[119] I am grateful to Michel Seymour for discussion of these points.

[120] William F. Shaw and Lionel Albert, *Partition: The Price of Quebec's Independence: A Realistic Look at the Possibility of Quebec Separating from Canada and Becoming an Independent State*, (Montréal: Thornhill, 1980); Scott Reid, *Canada Remapped: How the Partition of Quebec will Reshape the Nation* (Vancouver, BC: Pulp Press, 1992). For a legal assessment asserting Quebec's right to territorial integrity following secession, see Thomas M. Franck, Rosalyn Higgins, Alain Pellet, Malcolm N. Shaw, and Christian Tomuschat, *The Territorial Integrity of Quebec in the Event of the Attainment of Sovereignty*, Report prepared for Québec's Ministère des relations internationales, 1992; and Michel Seymour, "Le partenariat, une réponse à la tentation partitionniste," (n.d.), IPSO website, www.ipsoquebec.org.

[121] See, for example, some of the responses to the online discussion of the question, posed by Radio Canada in June 2006, "Are We Racist in Quebec? Sommes-nous racistes au Québec?" June 30, 2006, www.radiocanada.com/radio/maisonneuve/30062006/74964.shtml.

multiculturalism and gender equality embraced by many in Québec society, including segments of the sovereignty movement itself.

Women in Québec made considerable progress since the Quiet Revolution. Already in 1975 the province adopted a charter of rights and liberties, the *Charte Québécoise des droits et libertés*, that officially banned discrimination on the basis of sex. At the federal level it was not until 1987 that the Supreme Court of Canada declared systematic discrimination in the hiring of women to be unlawful.[122] On contraception and abortion rights the province went further and faster than the rest of Canada. Thus, many women continued to support the sovereignty agenda and the Parti Québécois, because both seemed to serve their interests as well or better than Ottawa was doing. Yet once the PQ came into office, women (and men) began to judge it on its performance, not only on its ideology.

In 1980, in the run-up to the referendum on sovereignty, a Québec women's organization, the Regroupement des Femmes Québécoises or RFQ, sought to bring together nationalists and socialists with the goal of putting feminist issues at the top of their common agenda. It established a referendum committee that proposed a campaign to encourage women to vote neither "*Oui*" nor "*Non*" on the ballot, but rather "*FEMME*" (woman). The majority of the RFQ rejected the proposal and the attendant disagreements ended up undermining the organization as a whole.[123] Two decades later, however, many Québécoises seemed to have adopted that position. According to opinion polls, their concern about issues related to health and education was consistently greater than that of men, and they supported sovereignty less. In surveys taken between 1998 and 1999, for example, the differences between men's and women's views were striking in the proportions agreeing to the following statements: (1) that the quality of health services should be a priority for discussion during the campaign (women 46.1 percent, men 28.9 percent); (2) that the predicted budget surpluses should be spent on health and education (women 47.4 percent, men 36.3 percent); (3) that tax breaks were less important than salary increases for state employees, many of whom are women (women 45.8 percent, men 34.3 percent); (4) that more investment should be made in the health sector (women 63 percent, men 48 percent).[124]

The pollster, whose findings were published in *La Presse*, a Montréal daily long associated with federalist positions, summarizes the results

---

[122] "Women's Rights," Canadian Human Rights Commission website, www.chrc-ccdp.ca/en/browseSubjects/womenRights.asp.

[123] LeClerc and West, "Feminist Nationalist Movements," p. 232.

[124] Guy Larocque, "Les femmes disent un NON pragmatique au PQ," *La Presse*, July 30, 2001.

as "an appreciable difference between the vote of Québec women and men in choice of government as well as on the national question," where women have tended to be more critical of the Parti Québécois. "The disaffection of women is perhaps less ideological than pragmatic," he suggests, given the crisis in health care and education. He then draws the implications for the sovereignty debate: the possible instability that would attend the accession of Québec to sovereignty is more likely to "chill the ardor of those [females] whose hands are full than of those [males] who dream of the glorious future."[125] So, in this view, although women seemed appreciative of the advances they had made under the banner of sovereignty and nationalism, they also sought to avoid backsliding and to pursue further improvements rather than risk their accomplishments in the uncertain future sovereignty.

In addition to the concern about backsliding, the years following the 1980 referendum also gave rise to fears of backlash. Some have suggested that the "Yvette phenomenon" of the referendum campaign was itself a harbinger of a backlash against feminism.[126] A much greater shock for the community of Québec feminists, and women in general, came on December 6, 1989. On that day, Marc Lépine, twenty-five years old, walked into the École Polytechnique of Montréal with a hunting rifle, ordered the men separated from the women, then proceeded to murder fourteen women and wound another thirteen – most of them engineering students – before killing himself. It took about twenty hours for the media to realize that this mass murder was directed specifically at women, even though Lépine carried a suicide note in which he vowed to kill "the feminists who have ruined my life" (he does not seem to have known his victims personally). Lépine appended a list of nineteen women whom he spared for "lack of time," including some well-known public figures and several female police officers. "Feminists have always enraged me," he wrote. "They want to keep the advantages of women (e.g., cheaper insurance, extended maternity leave preceded by a preventive leave etc.) while seizing for themselves those of men."[127]

Despite the killer's clearly expressed intention to punish women, the initial reporting of the massacre – "a mad gunman has opened fire on students at the Polytechnique in an unexplainable act" – remained the dominant framing.[128] Lépine was described as insane, even though he

[125] Ibid.
[126] LeClerc and West, "Feminist Nationalist Movements," pp. 233–234.
[127] The text of his suicide letter is appended to Malette and Chalouh, *The Montreal Massacre*.
[128] Sylvie Bérard, "Words and Deeds," in Malette and Chalouh, *The Montreal Massacre*, p. 75.

was coldly calculating in having cased out the school on many occasions in the past, having put down the reasons for his actions in writing, and having carried out his murders systematically. His actions were described as inexplicable, even though he explained them as directed against women because of their demands on men and their achievements. Even though the French language has two genders, the francophone press insisted on using only the masculine to describe the murder victims, thereby masking the killer's misogynistic motives. As one critic pointed out, "the French language, conservative though it may be, has access to the following: *étudiante*, *employée*, *amie* and, more recently, *professeure*" – all feminine forms.[129] Letters to the editors of the leading newspapers had to point out the obvious implications of the crime that the reporters had neglected to highlight: "The note he left shows that he deliberately chose women and, furthermore, that he didn't choose just any women students. He decided to slay young women destined for a profession still practiced mainly by men."[130] Adam Jones, founder of Gendercide Watch, includes the Montréal massacre and its aftermath as one of the case studies on his website and describes them as a personally "transforming experience. I had never seriously examined the gendering of violence in our society, and around the world, before those 14 women died."[131]

At the time, however, much of the media and the political authorities (the Liberal Party was then in power) played down the gendered dimension of the violence. They urged caution and a *silent* demonstration of respect for the victims – followed by continued silence. Talking about misogyny, they claimed, would only lead to more violence. Such a prediction reinforced the fears among women that some men actually shared Lépine's antifemale hostility. Indeed radio stations broadcast some male callers' comments to that effect, and many years later one could find such views on the internet, prompting some observers to suspect a campaign to rehabilitate the murderer as some kind of martyr for men's rights.[132] Women speculated that "the progress made by Quebec women during this past century – the access to education, better salaries, acquisition of political and legal rights, sharing of household tasks, assertion of control over their bodies and their pregnancies" – might

---

[129] Mireille Trudeau, "The Common Assassination of Women," in Malette and Chalouh, *The Montreal Massacre*, p. 73.

[130] Denise Veilleux, "Just for the Record," originally published as a letter to *Le Devoir*, December 9, 1989, reprinted in Malette and Chalouh, *The Montreal Massacre*, p. 40.

[131] "Case Study: The Montréal Massacre," www.gendercide.org/case_montreal.html.

[132] Micheline Carrier, "Des hommes veulent réhabiliter Marc Lépine," December 4, 2002, http://sisyphe.org/article.php3?id_article=226 -.

have resulted in a situation where "thousands of men are against these changes."[133] They wondered, "has Quebec feminism known such success that we must now speak of a 'suppressed' sexist misogyny?"[134] The appearance in 2009 of Denis Villeneuve's *Polytechnique* – a feature film, not a documentary – did little to resolve the debate over the murders of twenty years earlier.[135]

Some observers noted how threatening it might seem to men such as Lépine – an indifferent student, rejected for enlistment in the army – to see women make inroads into such institutions as the university, and even a male-dominated engineering school. If he could not bolster his masculinity as a soldier or a successful engineer, Lépine would do so as a mass murderer – a chilling prospect if other disgruntled males followed his lead. At the same time, however, the longer-term implications of a growing role for women in education and the professions, if the trend could be sustained, were promising. Some comments are reminiscent of Virginia Woolf, in her more hopeful moments, musing about the potentially transformative effect of women in higher education: "Opening the university to women does not simply mean that women will have access to professions previously reserved for men, but that an improved sharing between the sexes in their orientation toward the citizenry as a whole is expected to develop gradually ... The university is one of the bastions of resistance toward women. In this regard, the presence of women in universities implies real social transformation."[136]

Even more encouraging are the findings of the 2008 report of the Consultation Commission on Accommodation Practices Related to Cultural Difference, formed at the initiative of the Québec government. Its authors, the historian Gérard Bouchard (the brother of Lucien) and the philosopher Charles Taylor, sought to understand the sources of difficulty for Québec society to integrate immigrant minority groups. They pointed to an anxiety about identity very much linked to the debate over sovereignty versus federalism: those of "French-Canadian ancestry are still not at ease with their twofold status as a majority in Québec and

---

[133] Marie Lavigne, "Accommodating Profound Social Change," in Malette and Chalouh, *The Montreal Massacre*, p. 125.

[134] Nicole Brossard, "December 6, 1989 among the Centuries," in Malette and Chalouh, *The Montreal Massacre*, p. 98.

[135] More promising was a conference held at the Université du Québec à Montréal in December 2009 to commemorate the events, "La tuerie de l'École Polytechnique 20 ans plus tard: Les violences masculines contre les femmes et les féministes." The various comments are available to hear online at www.creum.umontreal.ca/spip.php?article1139.

[136] Marie De Koninck and Diane Lamoureux, "That They Not Be Forgotten ... ," in Malette and Chalouh, *The Montreal Massacre*, p. 118.

a minority in Canada and North America," and they were particularly worried about their cultural distinctiveness being overwhelmed by multicultural diversity.[137] Bouchard and Taylor sought areas of compromise between the majority population and immigrant minority groups, whose linguistic and religious practices, among others, differ from those traditional to Québec. In doing so, the authors identified as core values of Québec society the French language and *gender equality*. So, for example, while proposing a range of "reasonable accommodations" to minority beliefs and practices, the authors averred that "adjustment requests that infringe gender equality would have little chance of being granted, since such equality is a core value in our society."[138] That is good news for those concerned about gender equality, even if it does not resolve the sovereignty question.

Some explorations of feminism and nationalism in Québec by leading feminist scholars have expressed ambivalence about the traditional approach to sovereignty. Consider the analysis of Diane Lamoureux, for example: "I am dubious about the possibilities for arriving at independence by the referendum route," she writes, given the complexity of Québec society, its tendency to political and social fragmentation, and its foundation on democratic individualism. "Is it realistic," she wonders, "to think to be able to reunite a majority of the population around a project whose relevance is fading?"[139] The question is all the more pertinent the more diverse Québec society becomes, especially as immigration strengthens its multicultural character.

In public opinion surveys conducted before the 1995 referendum many supporters of "sovereignty," for example, still wanted to remain Canadian. In one poll, 31 percent of respondents mistakenly believed that a sovereign Québec "would still be part of Canada," and 14 percent did not know. Twenty percent expected that voters in a sovereign Québec "would still elect members of Parliament to Ottawa." A quarter of respondents who *favored* sovereignty expressed, in response to another

---

[137] Gérard Bouchard and Charles Taylor, *Building the Future: A Time for Reconciliation*, The Consultation Commission on Accommodation Practices Related to Cultural Difference, 2008, p. 19, available at www.accommodements.qc.ca/index-en.html. For a suggestive comparative study of such anxieties about identity, see Uriel Abulof, "'Small Peoples': The Existential Uncertainty of Ethnonational Communities," *International Studies Quarterly*, 53, 1 (2009), pp. 227–248.

[138] Bouchard and Taylor, *Building the Future*, p. 21.

[139] Diane Lamoureux, *L'Amère Patrie – Féminisme et nationalisme dans le Québec contemporain* (Montréal: Editions du Remue-Ménage, 2001). The conclusion was published in *Le Devoir*, March 8, 2001, and is available at www.vigile.net/01–3/lamoureux-patrie.html. The title is a play on words. It means "bitter country," but sounds the same as "motherland" (*La Mère Patrie*).

question, their desire for Québec "to remain a province of Canada" rather than "to become an independent country."[140]

The growing segment of Québec society that is multilingual and multi-cultural seems particularly unwilling or uninterested to choose between allegiance to Québec and allegiance to Canada, especially when such a choice would put at risk their personal advancement. It could be that even the genuine *Québécois de souche* are coming around to that position. In 1998, as Robert Lepage's *Nô* was having its premier at the Montréal Film Festival, the province was holding an election campaign. Lucien Bouchard, the Parti Québécois candidate, was running on a platform promising to hold yet another referendum on Québec sovereignty, and was in the lead. His opponents in the Liberal Party were perplexed. "The polls show most people don't want any more referendums, and yet Bouchard is still popu-lar," one of them complained. "What can we do?" Indeed, the PQ won the election, but held off on scheduling a referendum until "winning condi-tions" (*conditions gagnantes*) could be established.[141]

Bouchard resigned his position as premier in January 2001, as a result of a crisis in the Parti Québécois that revealed a deep schism. A seventy-year-old PQ politician named Yves Michaud, running in a by-election, had made comments considered anti-Semitic in a radio inter-view. Bouchard denounced Michaud and demanded that he apologize. Michaud refused, and received the backing of hundreds of party mem-bers who signed a full-page advertisement in his support in *Le Devoir*. They represented what has been called the "ethnic nationalist" wing of the party that favors the *Québécois de souche*, as opposed to the more inclusive wing that stresses the French language as the basis of Québec nationalism. Lacking adequate support within his own party, Bouchard stepped down.[142] The PQ was voted out of office in spring 2003, without having put sovereignty to another vote.

As Lysiane Gagnon, a columnist for the federalist-oriented *La Presse*, suggested, "it's not clear that Quebeckers really want to get rid of ambi-guity. Most francophones have grown used to living with sovereignty's sword of Damocles hanging over their heads... It's been talked about for 30 years and it never happens, so what's the problem?"[143] Sovereigntists might respond with the words from Jackson Browne's song "Late for the

---

[140] Maurice Pinard, "The Secessionist Option and Quebec Public Opinion, 1988–1993," *Opinion*, 2, 3 (June 1994), p. 3, quoted in Delisle, *Myths, Memories and Lies*, p. 236.

[141] Associated Press, "Separatists Lead Vote Despite Doubt," *New York Times*, November 22, 1998.

[142] James Brooke, "Resignation in Quebec Reflects Split in Nationalism," *New York Times*, January 13, 2001.

[143] Associated Press, "Separatists Lead Vote."

Sky": *Don't think it won't happen just because it hasn't happened yet.* Or, more likely, with reference to the late Québécois poet and sovereigntist Gaston Miron whose words grace the website of Intellectuels pour la Souveraineté: *Tant que l'indépendance n'est pas faite, elle reste à faire* [Until independence is achieved, it remains to be achieved]. They would point out that there has been considerable movement in popular opinion on sovereignty in thirty years, with increasingly larger proportions of the Québec population favoring it over time, at least through the 1990s.

In 2003, the Parti Québécois, in seeming acknowledgment of the population's ambivalence about independence, launched its "season of ideas" to discuss issues concerning Québec's relationship to Canada. Bernard Landry, the party leader, staked the success of the sovereigntist movement on the young:

For Québec to become sovereign will require a firm commitment on the part of young people. They are the ones who hold the key to a happy ending to the national question. In 1980, the sovereigntist project was mainly carried by those less than 35 years old. In 1995, those less than 55 years old overwhelmingly supported the "yes." At the turn of the next decade, a new generation of voters will add its voice to the national debate. And I am convinced that this alliance between youth and women activists and first-time activists, between sovereigntists of 1980 who are now grandparents, their children who voted "yes" in 1995, and their grandchildren who will in a few years, will allow Québec to finish its patient and calm march towards becoming a Country.[144]

Landry's intuition that young people are the key to a "happy ending" seems right. During *l'Affaire Michaud* in 2001, it was young party members who responded to the old guard's support of Michaud's position by rejecting ethnic nationalism. Fourteen self-identified sovereigntists, all under thirty-five years old and apparently PQ members, issued a manifesto denouncing Michaud's remarks as "opposite to the Québec in which we want to live, based on respect, inclusion and openness." More than a thousand people signed the statement, which was published as an advertisement in *Le Devoir*: "We reject all nationalisms that promote an identity founded upon ethnicity. We are all Quebeckers [tous Québécoises et Québécois] and we share the same patrimony of rights and responsibilities. We affirm our wish to live together in a Quebec where the French language, democracy and solidarity are at the heart of the whole political project."[145]

---

[144] Bernard Landry, "Parti québécois – La saison des idées," *Le Devoir*, October 18–19, 2003.

[145] Brooke, "Resignation in Quebec." For the statement, published in *Le Devoir*, January 16, 2001, see http://faculty.marianopolis.edu/c.belanger/quebechistory/docs/michaud/34.htm.

In 2006, a new movement called Québec Solidaire was formed in Montréal, as the union of several progressive organizations. It embraced a broad platform of "policies to promote equality, environmental integrity, civil liberties, solidarity, justice, and peace" in a Québec "modern, diverse, pluralist, inclusive," and sovereign. The organization is nonhierarchical, a point emphasized by its eschewing of the title "leader" in favor of *porte-parole* or spokesperson. Its two most prominent spokespersons are Françoise David, a social worker who was elected president of the Fédération des femmes du Québec in 1994 and spokesperson for the feminist group Option Citoyenne ten years later, before it merged into Québec Solidaire; and Amir Khadir, a doctor of Iranian descent with wide international experience, and a former member of the Bloc Québécois. With roots in the feminist and sovereigntist movements, Québec Solidaire promotes "social change adapted to family-positive lifestyles, and responsible governance for a healthier living environment."[146]

Yet despite the language of "solidarity," Québec's population is decidedly split – internally and in relation to the rest of Canada. In the spring of 2010 the Bloc Québécois, in collaboration with the Intellectuels pour la Souveraineté, conducted a poll of people living in Québec and people living in Canada outside Québec.[147] It was transparently designed to show a wide gulf on core issues – in the PowerPoint version many slides were entitled *Les deux solitudes* – and it succeeded. Whereas, for example, 73 percent of those polled in Québec want the Canadian constitution to recognize their province as a nation, 83 percent of those outside the province disagree; 82 percent of Québécois want their provincial government to devote more resources to protect French language and culture, whereas 69 percent of Canadians do not; 62 percent of Québécois believe their province has the right to secede from Canada, whereas 70 percent of Canadians outside believe it does not; and so forth.

Curiously, the Bloc and the Intellectuels were not curious enough to find out the answer to the most straightforward question – whether their respondents in 2010 supported Québec sovereignty or not. Nevertheless their poll yielded some unsettling results for the separatist cause. They asked, for example, whether "it will be possible some day to reform Canadian federalism in a way to satisfy both Québec and the rest of Canada." Seventy-eight percent of Québécois believed that it would indeed be possible to reform federalism in that way (73 percent of the

---

146 Www.quebecsolidaire.net. Thanks to Olivier Barsalou for calling this organization to my attention.
147 Bloc Québécois et Les Intellectuels pour la Souveraineté, *Opinion publique Québec-Canada, Faits saillants*, April 2010, available as a .pdf or PowerPoint file at www.blocquebecois.org/dossiers/colloque-20-ans-apres-Meech/sondage.aspx.

rest of Canada thought so too), rendering formal independence unnecessary. Moreover, 55 percent of Québécois do not believe that the program
of the sovereigntists is achievable anyhow. Forty-seven percent do not
believe that a simple majority (50 percent plus one vote) should be suf-
ficient for a referendum to decide Québec's sovereignty. Thus, a close
victory for "*Oui*" on sovereignty – say, reversing the results of the 1995
referendum – would be perceived as illegitimate by 47 percent of the
population.

A poll conducted at about the same time (May 2010) on behalf of an
evidently federalist organization (a Québec thinktank called The Federal
Idea) yielded mixed results. The headlines of the federalist press seized
on the finding that 58 percent of respondents considered the question
of sovereignty no longer relevant (*dépassé*). Critics immediately claimed
bias on the part of the polling organization.[148] The most striking finding,
however, was the lack of commitment by respondents to either of the
two main axes in the debate between federalism and sovereignty. Asked
if they considered themselves federalist or sovereigntist, 22 per cent said
federalist and 24 per cent sovereigntist (up from 20 percent six years
earlier). Twenty-two percent said they were somewhere in between and
25 per cent declared themselves to be neither. Pollster Alain Giguère
drew the conclusion that people in Québec "in general have become
less interested in politics," and have grown cynical towards politics and
politicians – a finding consistent with other polls. "This is quite new
from a socio-political point of view. The political scene doesn't rouse
the level of passion we've seen in the past. People are more focused on
careers, families and their personal lives" – much like Lepage's Sophie
and Michel.[149]

Robert Lepage's characters Sophie and Michel found hope in the
prospect of raising children to compensate for their disappointment
in the project of Québec sovereignty. The Parti Québécois found hope
for the project of Québec sovereignty in the raising of children – echoes
of the pro-natalist policies of traditional nationalist movements. Its platform at the beginning of the twenty-first century promised to serve the
interests of women, affect a "conciliation between family and work,"
and achieve economic progress "in light of the contemporary realities
of globalization."[150] Its younger members, at least – as well as kindred

---

[148] The thinktank's website is http://ideefederale.ca. For a typical headline, Hubert Bauch,
"Quebec Sovereignty is Irrelevant, Says Poll," *The Gazette* (Montréal), May 18, 2010;
for criticism of the poll, as reported on television and radio, Robert Barberis-Gervais,
"N'importe quoi sur la souveraineté," *Tribune libre de Vigile*, April 7, 2010, www.vigile.net.
[149] Bauch, "Quebec Sovereignty is Irrelevant," unpaginated.
[150] Landry, "Parti québécois," unpaginated.

organizations such as Québec Solidaire – embrace diversity and tolerance along with respect for French language and culture. It is an open question whether those goals can best be achieved by an independent Québec in close cooperation with Canada or a Québec participating in a reformed Canadian federation. Given the other cases we have explored in this book, the main task must be to avoid a violent confrontation with the central government of Canada. That task depends as much on the nature of Canadian nationalism and the policies of the Canadian government as on the actions of the women and men of Québec.

6 "To live to see better times": gender, nationalism, sovereignty, equality

Until now History has been made by men, exclusively. Considering what the men have made of History, we don't see why women shouldn't concern themselves with it a bit.

Frère Untel (Jean-Paul Desbiens), Montréal, 1960[1]

In the eyes of history our men will be heroes. No one will remember us, because our goal, as women, is much more primitive and no one will write about us in the history books. Our goal is to live to see better times. And that is terribly ordinary.

Liza Ibragimova, Grozny, 2000[2]

"How in your opinion are we to prevent war?" That question, posed to Virginia Woolf by the (male) head of a British peace organization, set in motion the deep reflection that resulted in *Three Guineas*. It led Woolf to consider a seemingly wide range of factors that she linked to the prospects for peace: the role of women in the economy and the professions, the prospects for women's higher education, and what stake women have in the prevailing order. Considering women's subordinate position in society, Woolf put forward the claim that they would not be inclined to support the violent defense of that society: "As a woman I have no country." Yet she also considered the possibility that women would embrace war as a means to improve their relative standing – and she cited the example of women's suffrage and the widespread view that women had earned the right to vote because of their support for the Great War.

When Virginia Woolf offered competing hypotheses about the relationship between gender and war, she did not seem troubled by an inability to decide which was the most plausible one, or to identify what social scientists now call the "scope conditions" for determining when one hypothesis rather than another might apply. She had a policy prescription that would seem to serve, regardless of which hypotheses proved

---

[1] *Les insolences du Frère Untel* (Montréal: Les Éditions de l'Homme, 1960).
[2] Quoted in Petra Procházková, *The Aluminum Queen: The Russian–Chechen War Through the Eyes of Women*, trans. by Gerald Turner (Prague: Lidové noviny, 2002; originally: *Aluminiová královna: rusko-čečenská válka očima žen*), p. 112.

most valid: equality for women. She coined the term "equal pay for equal work" and was far ahead of her time (of our time, as well) in proposing that women receive wages from the state for their work as mothers. She put forward a claim that many feminists would endorse today, that "the public and the private worlds are inseparably connected; that the tyrannies and servilities of the one are the tyrannies and servilities of the other." She ultimately decided that the cause of peace and the cause of women's equality "are the same and inseparable."[3]

Yet Woolf did not want women to seek equality though integration into traditionally male institutions, such as the universities and the professions. She feared that women would become socialized into the competitive and status-seeking behaviors associated with those institutions – behaviors that Woolf identified with the propensity to war. She did not, for example, want women to attend traditional male colleges, where, she claimed, they would be taught "the arts of dominating other people," "the arts of ruling, of killing, of acquiring land and capital."[4]

Woolf's solution to wars inspired by the power-hungry, competitive male world was to have women form an "Outsiders' Society," to refuse to engage in any activities that would support war and to foster an alternative culture of peace and cooperation. The audience to which she addressed this appeal consisted of "daughters of educated men," women denied an education of their own outside the home because of their gender, because of *patriarchy* – the word she chose.[5] She averred that the daughters of educated men were weaker than the women of the working class because the former, unlike the latter, could not exert any influence on warmaking by withholding their labor. Numerous observers have claimed that Woolf's approach was rather elitist, that she understood little of the circumstances of women outside her own class. The author became aware of that criticism within weeks of publishing her book, as she received a number of articulate letters from working women who read it. As one wrote: "You say glibly that the working woman could refuse to nurse and to make munitions and so stop the war. A working woman who refuses to work will starve – and there is nothing like stark hunger for blasting ideals."[6] Woolf took this criticism seriously. She responded to this letter and continued a correspondence with its author for the rest of her life, although unfortunately none of it, except the first letter, has survived.

---

[3] Virginia Woolf, *Three Guineas* (New York: Harcourt, Brace, 1966 [1938]), pp. 142–144.
[4] Ibid., p. 34.   [5] Ibid., p. 65.
[6] Letter, M. Agnes Smith to Virginia Woolf, November 7, 1938, reprinted in *Woolf Studies Annual*, 6 (2000), p. 99.

This concluding chapter revisits some of the key issues raised by Woolf in her consideration of how to prevent war: the relationship between women's status in society and their willingness to fight; the impact of women's education on the prospects for peace; and the importance of gender identity – particularly what it means that dominance and warfare are so closely associated with masculinity. It summarizes what we have learned in the four cases examined in the book – Algeria, Yugoslavia, Chechnya, and Québec – and the insights that films about those cases have offered.

Nationalism

As the first chapter of this book pointed out, in *Three Guineas* Woolf revealed a certain blind spot, aside from working women of her own country: women in the colonies who might embrace nationalism and war to overthrow foreign rule. Although Woolf was herself critical of imperialism and colonial domination, she did not anticipate the extent to which women would be drawn to national liberation movements – including violent ones – as a means to both individual achievement and collective rights. Chapter 2 explored this phenomenon in the context of *The Battle of Algiers* and the Algerian war of independence from France. The discussion in chapter 3 of the violent breakup of Yugoslavia, and its depiction in *Pretty Village, Pretty Flame*, presented a different role for women – they rarely engaged in violence as the *poseuses de bombes* of Algiers did, and more commonly became its victim. At first glance the Yugoslav case seemed closer to Woolf's expectations of militaristic males and pacifistic females. It appeared to embody the archetypes that Jean Bethke Elshtain once characterized (and criticized) as the male "just warrior" and the female "beautiful soul."[7] Yet both the reality of the wars in former Yugoslavia and the portrayals in Srđan Dragojević's film complicate those neat generalizations. Chapter 4 found an equally complicated dynamic at work in Chechnya's efforts to assert autonomy from Russian control, where the range of women's roles on both sides found expression in several major films. Nor were men on the Chechen or Russian side constrained by expectations of masculinity as hard, unfeeling, and militaristic – although there were plenty of male characters who fit the Rambo stereotype.

Québec separatism, discussed in chapter 5 in the context of Robert Lepage's *Nô*, provides a contrasting case to the others in the book. Violence in support of the nationalist cause seemed mainly a male activity, yet it

---

[7] Jean Bethke Elshtain, *Women and War* (New York: Basic Books, 1987).

was short lived, and replaced by the end of the film (and in the reality of Canadian politics) by peaceful methods of struggle. In late twentieth-century Québec women enjoyed considerable advances in education and in the professions – removing a possible source of dissatisfaction with the federal system and a motive to engage in violence to overthrow it. Yet, as the 1989 massacre at Montréal's École Polytechnique suggested, the prospect of violence remained to the extent that certain men, humiliated by women's relative success, would lash out against them.

The case of Algeria addresses both of these elements – women's support of militant nationalism as a means to better their lives during the independence war of the 1950s, and the misogynistic male violence of the 1990s. As chapter 2 described, Algerian women such as Zohra Drif – the real-life figure depicted in *The Battle of Algiers* – expressed a certain pride in their contribution to the violent struggle for independence and the positions of authority they came to enjoy.[8] Their feelings were echoed by women engaged in subsequent liberation struggles, from Vietnam to central America. But whereas Drif came from a relatively privileged background – a "daughter of educated men" who was actually allowed to pursue her own education in law – many of the recruits to later struggles were not so fortunate in their upbringing. For some of them, joining a liberation army provided an opportunity for significant individual advancement. The Vietnamese military historian Nguyen Quoc Dung describes the impact of direct engagement in armed struggle on North Vietnamese women, some 1.5 million of whom served in some capacity in the regular army, militia, or local forces during the war against the United States: "Many women learned to read in the jungle … Most women went home more confident and better educated, for the war liberated them from the bamboo gate of the village." The war opened up possibilities for women in fields where they had never previously been accepted. "No profession – worker, teacher, engineer, or physician – was closed to them now."[9] Women's aspirations for equality were especially prominent in the Sandinista revolution in Nicaragua, even if expectations there were disappointed, as they were earlier in Cuba.[10]

---

[8] Interview with Zohra Drif, in Danièle Djamila Amrane-Minne, *Des femmes dans la guerre d'Algérie* (Paris: Editions Karthala, 1994).

[9] Quoted in Karen Gottschang Turner, with Phan Thanh Hao, *Even the Women Must Fight: Memories of War from North Vietnam* (New York: John Wiley, 1999), pp. 20, 58.

[10] Giaconda Belli, *El país bajo mi piel: memorias de amor y guerra* (New York: Vintage, 2003); Maxine Molyneux, "Mobilization without Emancipation? Women's Interests, the State, and Revolution in Nicaragua," *Feminist Studies*, 11, 2. (Summer 1985), pp. 227–254; and the following studies by Margaret Randall: *Sandino's Daughters: Testimonies of Nicaraguan Women in Struggle* (Vancouver, BC: New Star Books, 1981), *Sandino's Daughters Revisited: Feminism in Nicaragua* (New Brunswick, NJ: Rutgers University Press, 1994),

The women who joined the Zapatista army (Ejército Zapatista de Liberación Nacional or EZLN) in Chiapas, Mexico in the 1990s expressed similar motives for individual advancement. One young woman named Isidora joined the Zapatistas as a teenager when she learned there were other female members: "That gave me the courage to escape because I wanted to be free, free as all the *compañeros* who lived there in that army. I wanted to learn what they knew – to read and write." Maria, like Isidora a member of the Tzeltal ethnic group, explained that before she joined the rebels, "I only knew how to make baskets and clay *comales*. I learned Spanish in the EZLN." Particularly interesting for a movement that was based in part on defense of indigenous rights, including the preservation of language and culture, is the importance that women attached to learning the dominant language as a means of social mobility.[11]

Yet, as the chapters on Algeria and Chechnya described, even the achievement of liberation through armed struggle can leave women facing continued discrimination – or even a backlash if their successes appeared to threaten male dominance. As one study of Vietnamese women put it, "nations that are recovering from war all too often put women's issues on the back burner – despite promises to link women's emancipation with national liberation."[12] Other observers have come to associate the very violence of the liberation movements with the plight of women (and men) in the subsequent period of independence. Ranjana Khanna posed the question in the context of the Algerian case: "If the revolutionary desire for national sovereignty ends with exceptional violence as the norm, how is it possible to think of the postcolonial project as anything other than a lost cause in which a military-backed state of exception can be declared at any time and without much need for rationalization?" She wonders "how to maintain hope when state politics seems to have been reduced to war ... ?"[13]

As in many respects, the Algerian case finds parallels in Chechnya, where the violence of both the successful first war against Russia and the disastrous second war bred cynicism about the motives of those fighting. Films such as Rogozhkin's *Checkpoint* and Balabanov's *War*, discussed in

and *Gathering Rage: The Failure of 20th Century Revolutions to Develop a Feminist Agenda* (New York: Monthly Review Press, 1992).

[11] Ellen Katzenberger, ed., *First World, Ha Ha Ha! The Zapatista Challenge* (San Francisco: City Lights Books, 1995), pp. 36–37, 136; see also Mariana Mora, "Zapatismo: Gender, Power, and Social Transformation," in Lois Ann Lorentzen and Jennifer E. Turpin, eds., *The Women and War Reader* (New York University Press, 1998), pp. 164–176.

[12] Gottschang Turner, *Even the Women Must Fight*, p. 186.

[13] Ranjana Khanna, *Algeria Cuts: Women and Representation, 1830 to the Present* (Stanford University Press, 2008), pp. 26–27.

chapter 4, effectively portrayed the self-serving nature of such "new wars."
Interviews with female victims of the conflict reinforced the point:

Those fat, bald men sitting in their ministerial and presidential offices are full
of complexes and making heaps of money out of the war and all they know of
the actual bombing is what they see on the TV screen. It's a war about money,
we all know that. Even our Chechen bigwigs are mixed up in it. During the
first war I still supported our men because most of them really went to the front
with some romantic notions about freedom and independence. Now I don't
believe either side. They sacrificed us, the ordinary people, to line their own
pockets or they went around shooting like street urchins and playing at real
war. Let them die if they like but they have no right to force people like me to
do heroic deeds. I don't want to be a hero. I want to die in old age from 'flu and
not from a bullet in my head.[14]

In retrospect, many women doubted whether pursuing Chechen independence by violence was worth the consequences – even if the Russian
authorities were responsible for most of the destruction: "It would have
been far better to put up with what we had than to die for some slogans
and end up in a situation where 80 percent of the nation goes hungry,
hundreds of thousands have died and we all have a mental trauma that
will never go away ... Many's the time I said, 'If everyone stayed home
and took care of their families there wouldn't be any war.'"[15]

The discussion in chapter 3 suggests that women in the republics of
the Yugoslav federation were perhaps more prescient than those in places,
such as Algeria and Chechnya, where female support for independence
was stronger. Yugoslav women were not the main supporters of violent
nationalist organizations, recognizing that the misogynistic campaigns the
extremists conducted against rival ethnic groups boded ill for treatment
of their "own" women as well. Instead, the most active members of the
peace movement were women – as the film, *Pretty Village, Pretty Flame*,
hints, even while mocking them. Women also served as the symbols of
cross-national comity – remember the film's depiction of the Serb school
teacher Mirjana and her romance with the Muslim postman, Nazim –
but they suffered accordingly as nationalists took their revenge.

The insights of Ranjana Khanna on the Algerian case suggest that
it is not nationalism per se, but the pursuit of nationalist goals by violent means that puts in jeopardy women's equality and even survival –
when democracy and sovereignty become equated with war. As chapter
5 suggested, this is one of the messages conveyed by Lepage's *Nô*. His
Québécois "national liberation" warriors are all men. And even though

---

[14] Interview with Elza Duguyevova, in Procházková, *Aluminum Queen*, p. 31.
[15] Interview with Kalimat, in ibid., pp. 43, 47.

the film portrays them as a comic gang that couldn't shoot straight, their violent activities led to the loss of life – Sophie's miscarriage following her rough treatment by the police parallels the real-life murder of Pierre Laporte following his kidnapping by the Front de Libération du Québec. The film's concluding scene, ten years after the violence of October 1970, offers a vision of domesticity and tolerance as an alternative to nationalist violence. Sophie and Michel remain sovereigntists in their political sympathies, but they are willing to pursue their goals, however unsuccessfully, through the ballot box.

Both Robert Lepage and Srđan Dragojević, however different their filmmaking styles, draw similar conclusions on the consequences for women of violent nationalist movements. The harrowing image of Mirjana, stumbling into the tunnel, seemingly "pregnant" with a bomb, contrasts with Sophie's glowing face as she and Michel tease each other about plans to have children. The disregard for Mirjana's humanity recalls the mass-rape campaigns of the Yugoslav conflict and the misogynistic violence "at home" that continued in their wake. The scene of domestic tranquility in a Montréal apartment promises a better life for women in Québec, even if the province remains within the Canadian federation.

Sovereignty

Sovereignty was the stated goal of all of the nationalist movements discussed in this book and portrayed in the films. In three of the cases groups that considered themselves distinct nations or peoples sought greater autonomy from a dominant central power – Algeria from France, Chechnya from Russia, Québec from Canada. In Algeria, peaceful efforts at achieving sovereignty met with violent responses from the French authorities, most dramatically in the massacres that followed the Sétif incident of May 1945. *The Battle of Algiers* takes up the story as the Algerian rebels seek to bring the violence home to the European residents of the capital city – relying on women to carry out bombings of civilian areas. In the case of Chechnya, local appeals for greater autonomy in the context of a disintegrating Soviet Union met resistance from leaders in Moscow who claimed to fear the breakup of the Russian federation. An armed Chechen resistance achieved de facto sovereignty in 1996 after a brutal two-year war, only to lose it again when Russian forces returned three years later to wreak indiscriminate violence against civilians. Targets included villages, as depicted in *Prisoner of the Mountains*, and hospitals, as shown in *House of Fools*. One result was a new phenomenon for Chechnya – desperate and vengeful female suicide bombers. The case of

Québec is unusual in that the violent campaign for sovereignty by the Front de Libération du Québec was cut short by Pierre Trudeau's decision to call out the army. The result, as Lepage's *Nô* portrayed, was a shift to peaceful contestation over the goal of Québec's status in the Canadian federation. Finally, in the Yugoslav case, nationalist groups emerged in several republics, seeking secession from the federation and engaging in violent "ethnic cleansing" to create contiguous and homogeneous political units. Sometimes local nationalists provoked the violence, at other times the central authorities in Belgrade relied on the Yugoslav army and militia forces to enflame conflict. The resulting conflagration – depicted so effectively in *Pretty Village, Pretty Flame* – appeared spontaneous or inevitable, the product of "ancient hatreds" exploding the "Balkan powder keg." In fact much of the violence was highly calculated, including its distinctive misogynistic elements.

What is this vaunted sovereignty that inspired so much death and destruction? The sad irony is that the ordinary people who got caught up in the wars for sovereignty had something far different in mind than what their nationalist leaders were pursuing. For the leaders, sovereignty meant control of territory and resources, defended by force of arms. That is not what it meant for the followers. Sovereignty for many of them meant simply the means to live better lives, with some control over their destiny. It did not necessarily mean severing ties with the dominant political entity – be it France, Russia, federal Yugoslavia, or Canada – let alone engaging in war against them. Indeed in the three cases that resulted in war it was the violence itself – especially the brutal response from the central authorities – that turned sovereignty from a vague notion allowing for a continued relationship with the center to a demand for full and unequivocal independence.

Consider the evidence from the cases we have discussed. As mentioned in chapter 3, many citizens of Yugoslavia were not ready to give up their connections to the rest of the country or their Yugoslav identity in order to pursue outright independence for their republic. They did not associate notions of "sovereignty" with the traditional model of a nation-state, defended militarily from its neighbors. The more flexible, nuanced view was reflected in public opinion polls, such as the one taken in Bosnia in May 1990. It revealed that 94 percent of respondents favored "a sovereign Bosnia-Herzegovina with existing external and internal borders, within the framework of Yugoslavia."[16] In effect, for the majority of Bosnians "sovereignty" meant simply an improvement on their current

---

[16] V. P. Gagnon, Jr., *The Myth of Ethnic War: Serbia and Croatia in the 1990s* (Ithaca: Cornell University Press, 2004), p. 43.

situation, not a dramatic break. A similar view came through in interviews conducted by the Russian ethnologist Valerii Tishkov regarding
Chechen attitudes towards sovereignty. One interlocutor named Timur
told him, "Now I am for sovereignty, though, frankly, like most other
Chechens, I don't really know what it is. But when I recall what torture Chechens were subjected to in the filtration camps, how they were
dropped alive from helicopters, I do not want Chechnya to remain part
of Russia."[17] In other words, it was Russia's brutal response to the aspirations for a better life on the part of residents of Chechnya – the poorest
region in the federation – that turned the goal of sovereignty into one of
complete separation. The irony is that having largely defeated the separatists through mass destruction of the Chechen republic, Vladimir Putin's
government then granted the loyal successor regime of Ramzan Kadyrov
more autonomy, through the policy of "Chechenization," than the early
proponents of sovereignty had ever imagined. Chapter 4, and the films
discussed there, explore the consequences for ordinary people, especially
single women and their families, of the decision to settle Chechnya's
conflict with Russia by force.

That such a legacy of violent conflict over sovereignty can last for decades is evident from the Algerian case. In Algeria, reformists on both
sides sought to work out a *modus vivendi* that would grant greater autonomy to the indigenous people without severing all ties to France. Lack
of good will on the French side doomed the efforts of such figures as
Ahmed Ben Messali Hadj, a moderate nationalist, or Mouloud Feraoun,
the Kabyl writer and friend of Albert Camus. Recall the response of
Interior Minister François Mitterrand to Algerian offers by the Front
de Libération Nationale (FLN) to negotiate a new relationship: "The
only possible negotiation is war."[18] Efforts at improving the situation of
indigenous Algerians, such as the half-hearted Constantine Plan, were
too little and too late. The FLN, in turn, became increasingly rigid, as it
sought to eliminate its rivals in the Algerian nationalist movement and
impose its own violent solution to the conflict. Already by 1957, as *The
Battle of Algiers* graphically depicts, the FLN was bombing civilians as
the French forces were torturing and murdering suspects and blowing
up apartment buildings.

In post-independence Algeria, Ranjana Khanna argues that the commitment to violence and the glorification of the independence war on the

---

[17] Valery Tishkov, *Chechnya: Life in a War-Torn Society* (Berkeley, CA: University of
California Press, 2003), p. 102.
[18] Alistair Horne, *A Savage War of Peace, Algeria 1954–1962* (New York: Viking, 1977),
p. 99.

part of the FLN came to replace the revolution's original goals of democracy and sovereignty. She cites as an example the Makam Al-Shahid, a huge "Martyrs' Monument" that the Algerian government erected in the early 1980s as a memorial to the war of independence and as a distraction from its political and economic failures. For her, it represents "the burial of the idea of sovereignty as self-determination of the people. In its place, and in this combination of commemoration and celebration, it is the very disposability of bodies that is celebrated. The extraordinarily different accounts of how many died – between 800 thousand and 1.5 million – registers indeed that bodies do not count, that they are born and die with no account or census to mark the nationalist agenda."[19]

As chapter 5 (and the film *Nô*) demonstrates, Québec's movement for greater sovereignty escaped the spiral into violence that the events of October 1970 threatened. I suggested there that popular attitudes towards sovereignty in Québec seem flexible enough to encompass a continuing peaceful relationship with the rest of Canada, even as particular grievances are addressed through democratic procedures. Recall the evidence from the 1995 surveys, conducted shortly before the referendum on sovereignty. A quarter of respondents who advocated "sovereignty" (and presumably planned to vote for it in the referendum) also wanted Québec "to remain a province of Canada" rather than "to become an independent country." Twenty percent expected that voters in a sovereign Québec "would still elect members of Parliament to Ottawa," and 31 percent thought that a sovereign Québec "would still be part of Canada."[20]

The issue of "sovereignty" raises the question of whether it is indeed possible to reconcile allegiances that traditionally have been considered in competition with each other. Everyone experiences multiple identities which sometimes function simultaneously, sometimes in a kind of hierarchy, or sometimes in conflict. One can be a daughter and a mother, a son and a father, the resident of a local community, a member of a profession, a fan of a sports team, a citizen of a particular country, or adherent to a supranational entity – be it the European Union, or a community of speakers of a given language (*la Francophonie* or *Russko-iazychnye*). The identities and allegiances that typically result in conflict, sometimes violent, pit ethnic groups with aspirations to be represented as "sovereign," against existing nation-states. But even such identities, which appear mutually exclusive, need not lead to violence. The example of Québec is

---

[19] Khanna, *Algeria Cuts*, pp. 18–19, 27.
[20] Maurice Pinard, "The Secessionist Option and Quebec Public Opinion, 1988–1993," *Opinion*, 2, 3 (June 1994), p. 3, quoted in Esther Delisle, *Myths, Memory and Lies: Quebec's Intelligentsia and the Fascist Temptation, 1939–1960*, trans. by Madeleine Hébert (Westmount, Québec: Robert Davies Multimedia, 1998), p. 236.

not an isolated one. Lucio Caracciolo described the case of people living in a German-speaking region of Italy known as Südtirol (South Tirol) in German or Alto Adige in Italian. The region for centuries was part of the Austro-Hungarian Empire, but came under Italian control after World War I. Caracciolo describes the case of Silvius Magnano, a prominent political figure from the region, who described his experience of multiple allegiances by referring to three national-political entities which he expressed in German: *Vaterland*, or Fatherland; *Heimat*, the homeland of one's birth, or Motherland; and *Staat*, or State. Magnano spoke of Austria as his *Vaterland*, the South Tirol as his *Heimat*, and Italy as his *Staat*. As Caracciolo comments, "to hold together these three belongings (*appartenenze*) in a multiethnic context is a miracle that has so far been successful in the Südtirol/Alto Adige. Elsewhere this mixture can explode."[21]

How to keep such mixtures from exploding into violence has been an underlying theme of our examination of films about nationalist conflict. In looking at the cases of Algeria, Chechnya, and Yugoslavia, we identified elements that appeared to contribute to violence. A common syndrome involved economic decline's effect on masculine humiliation. Underemployed or unemployed men could no longer meet their society's traditional expectations of manhood – and often turned to alternative means to bolster it by joining armies. In some cases – most strikingly during the Yugoslav wars of secession in the 1990s and post-independence Algeria of roughly the same time – they turned their violence against women as scapegoats for their humiliated masculinity.

The Battle of Algiers provided a hint of this potential violence even in its hero, Ali la Pointe. Escaping from the police, who seek to arrest him for illegal gambling, Ali is tripped by a young, well-dressed European man, possibly a student. Ali, unemployed and illiterate, glances at the man's mocking expression and launches a powerful punch as revenge for his humiliation. As chapter 2 described, a later generation of unemployed Algerian men – Ali's heirs, in effect – would enact their vengeful violence not so much against European men as against Algerian women.

Equality

In thinking about war and peace, Virginia Woolf was drawn to the question of education as a means for women to achieve equality with men. She resented the fact that in England, as in most of the world at the time,

---

[21] Lucio Caracciolo, "Sei il mondo globale non cancella le patrie," *La Repubblica*, May 21, 2009, p. 46.

"daughters of educated men" were not allowed to receive educations themselves, at least not at the institutions of higher learning where their male relatives studied. They were poorly represented in the professions and in politics – partly as a result of lack of education, but also out of sheer discrimination. Woolf argued that the path to peace lay in increasing women's access to education so that they could play a more prominent role in their countries' affairs. At the same time, she recognized a risk that women themselves could become socialized in the hierarchical, competitive, and warlike ways of men and thereby fail to bring about peaceful change. Her proposal for an Outsiders' Society sought to forestall that risk.

Some social scientists working on issues of gender and war have followed Woolf's lead in identifying women's education, and more broadly women's equality, as factors influencing states' propensity to engage in war. In a large statistical study, Erik Melander, for example, has found that whereas the presence of a woman as head of state or government does not affect the degree of a country's involvement in warfare, the proportion of women in higher education and in the legislature does. The higher that proportion the less likely a country is to fight. Melander associates increased female presence in higher education and representative institutions of government with a rejection of traditional gender roles. "These traditional gender roles not only prescribe male violence as a means of establishing domination and protecting honor but also legitimate the subordination of women. What is more, these roles are also highly consistent with chauvinism and imposing behavior toward other groups besides women who are similarly defined as inferior, for example, sexual and ethnic minorities, and political opponents."[22] From there one can see a link between chauvinistic and domineering behavior at home and relationships to foreign Others and foreign countries. This relationship is supported in the work of Mary Caprioli, who identifies a link between gender inequality within a country and the likelihood that the country would initiative armed conflict in an international dispute: the greater the inequality, the more likely the first use of force. Caprioli also finds that the higher the level of gender inequality the more likely a country is to experience internal armed conflict.[23]

---

[22] Erik Melander, "Gender Equality and Interstate Armed Conflict," *International Studies Quarterly*, 49 (2005), pp. 695–714, at p. 698.

[23] Mary Caprioli, "Gender Equality and State Aggression: The Impact of Domestic Gender Equality on State First Use of Force," *International Interactions*, 29, 3 (July–September 2003), pp. 195–214. On the link between internal conflict and gender inequality, she writes: "The higher the level of gender inequality within a state, the greater the likelihood such a state will experience internal conflict. In short, states characterized by gender discrimination and structural hierarchy are permeated with norms of violence that

In some of the cases considered in this book, we have seen the impact of education on improving women's lives and their relations with men. Commenting on the legacy of the Soviet educational system and its encouragement of female education, Liza Ibragimova of Chechnya remarked that "in the more educated sections of society, for instance, where women have the same or even better education than their husbands, their partners treat them a bit differently [i.e., better] now."[24] Another Chechen woman, named Zoya Viziginova, concurred: "The very harsh traditions that treated women something like donkeys applied in the old days, before I was born." During the Soviet era, "lots of things changed. Children started to attend Russian schools, where they only spoke Russian. Little girls started to learn to read and write and find out about Russian culture, so they stopped being so dimwitted. Girls started to study even in Russia and got to know a different way of life. An educated woman will never be downtrodden."[25]

Women's education is now widely recognized as an important contributor to economic development, to the "demographic transition" that moves societies to a higher standard of living while limiting population growth, and apparently to peace.[26] Yet we should acknowledge what the evidence of some of our cases suggests: although increasing women's equality is a valid goal independently of its contribution to peace, under certain circumstances it is also linked to violence. In particular, successful strides towards equality for women can provoke a backlash among men who resent or feel threatened by their progress – especially if they themselves are experiencing "downward mobility."

Virginia Woolf recognized this risk in *Three Guineas* when she described how male students of Cambridge University – women were not allowed to take regular classes there – objected to women who passed the same exams being allowed to put BA after their names to enhance their employment prospects. She cites the British government (Whitehall), which discriminated against women in hiring and salary for the civil service, despite their excellent performance on examinations:

It is quite possible that the name "Miss" transmits through the board or division some vibration which is not registered in the examination room. "Miss" transmits sex, and sex may carry with it an aroma … "Miss," however delicious

make internal conflict more likely." Mary Caprioli, "Primed for Violence: The Role of Gender Inequality in Predicting Internal Conflict," *International Studies Quarterly*, 49, 2 (June 2005), pp. 161–178, at pp. 171–172.

[24] Procházková, *Aluminum Queen*, p. 116.   [25] Ibid., p. 168.

[26] For a popular account of this view, with many examples, see Nicholas Kristoff and Sheryl Wu-Dunn, *Half the Sky: Turning Oppression into Opportunity for Women Worldwide* (New York: Knopf, 2009).

its scent in the private house, has a certain odour attached to it in Whitehall which is disagreeable to the noses on the other side of the partition … As for "Mrs.," it is a contaminated word; an obscene word. The less said about that word the better. Such is the smell of it, so rank does it stink in the nostrils of Whitehall, that Whitehall excludes it entirely.[27]

Woolf suggested that men were afraid of losing jobs to women and were intent on keeping them at home so that they not threaten the traditional male role as family provider. Among other evidence, she quotes then British Prime Minister Stanley Baldwin:

I am certain I voice the opinion of thousands of young men when I say that if men were doing the work that thousands of young women are now doing the men would be able to keep those same women in decent homes. Homes are the real places of the women who are now compelling men to be idle.[28]

Woolf goes on to quote a similar sentiment, expressed by Adolf Hitler, and comments, "One is written in English, the other in German. But where is the difference?"[29] Such provocations on Woolf's part, combined with her claim that there was nothing worth defending in England ("As a woman, I have no country"), earned the author many enemies.

The increased presence of women in fields traditionally reserved for men has sometimes led certain men to express strong resentment – a practice hardly limited to Woolf's era. In some cases those resentments have burst forth as acts of isolated violence, as with the example of the Montréal massacre, discussed in chapter 5. In others, they can have more widespread effects, producing a reaction that can contribute to militarized nationalism with attendant violence against women in the war zones and on the "home front." Learning from the cases of 1990s Algeria and Yugoslavia about how many males reacted to the humiliation of unemployment by attacking women, we might give Woolf credit for a certain prescience in identifying the phenomenon with fascism. As Cynthia Enloe suggested, masculine humiliation in times of economic crisis appeared to be a factor in the genesis of the Yugoslav conflict. It is an important element of Chris Dolan's "proliferation of small men" thesis, which he applied to Uganda and we have seen as relevant to Algeria too.

In the wake of the economic recession of 2007, male unemployment hit a postwar high in the United States, outpacing female unemployment by several percentage points. Young people in the 16–24-year-old age cohort were employed at the lowest rate recorded – about 46 percent – since the

---

[27] Woolf, *Three Guineas*, pp. 50, 52.   [28] Ibid., p. 51.
[29] Ibid., p. 53.

United States began tracking such figures in 1948.[30] Statistics revealed a similarly dire situation in the United Kingdom.[31] We recall from the discussion of Yugoslavia in chapter 3, how a 50 percent unemployment rate for men in Belgrade in the late 1980s, and worse in the countryside, provided ready recruits for the nationalist militia forces that helped tear the country apart.

A 2008 study of changes in income for the 25–34-year-old age cohort in the United States demonstrates striking differences by gender. For the period 1975–2005, the only category in the age group that saw an improvement in its income was women with a bachelor's degree or higher, who enjoyed a 10 percent increase (in 2004 dollars). Men with less than a high school education saw a drop in median income of 34 percent from the generation of 1975 to that of 2005; men with no more than a high school diploma saw a decline of 29 percent; men with some college education, a decline of 21 percent; men with a bachelor's degree or higher, a 2 percent drop. Women still earned less than men overall, but the disparity in earning power between educated women and uneducated men is particularly stark.[32] As chapter 2 discussed, such disparities in job prospects and income between young men and women helped fuel the misogynistic violence of the 1990s in Algeria.

Could such a volatile mix of gender-based inequality and male resentment spark violence in the United States? The discussion of Québec in chapter 5 might provide some comfort, given that the Montréal massacre did not appear to represent a widespread phenomenon in a country that prides itself on egalitarianism and tolerance. But the United States increasingly diverges from its northern neighbor on those qualities, and many others. There are, in fact, a number of high-profile cases where US murderers have explained their behavior in terms of masculine failure and humiliation, and presumably many lesser-known ones that go unreported. Anecdotal evidence abounds: Susan Faludi quotes one of the young men who brutally raped and murdered a professional woman jogging in New York's Central Park in 1989 as seeking to compensate for his feeling "like a midget, a mouse, something less than a man." She

---

[30] Ayşegül Şahin, Joseph Song, and Bart Hobijn, "The Unemployment Gender Gap during the 2007 Recession," *Current Issues in Economics and Finance*, 16, 2 (February 2010), Federal Reserve Bank of New York; US Bureau of Labor Statistics, *Economic News Release*, June 4, 2010, Table A-6: Employment status of the civilian population by sex, age, and disability status, not seasonally adjusted; Peter Coy, "The Lost Generation," *Business Week*, October 8, 2009.

[31] Larry Elliot, "Unemployment among 16 to 24 Age Group Heads Above One Million Barrier," *The Observer*, October 11, 2009.

[32] Tamara Draut, *The Economic State of Young America* (New York: Dēmos, 2008), pp. 5–6. Figures are rounded to the nearest whole number.

describes the 1990 case of "Charles Stuart, the struggling fur salesman in Boston who murdered his pregnant wife, a lawyer, because he feared that she – better educated, more successful – was gaining the 'upper hand.'"[33] Similar motives appear in cases of mass murder of women by men, such as the man who invaded an Amish schoolhouse in Pennsylvania in 2006, separated the girls from the boys and shot ten girls, killing five; or the one who opened fire in an aerobics class in 2009, wounding the pregnant instructor and killing three women. "What I've concluded from decades of working with murderers and rapists and every kind of violent criminal," reported one Massachusetts psychiatrist in regard to such cases, "is that an underlying factor that is virtually always present to one degree or another is a feeling that one has to prove one's manhood, and that the way to do that, to gain the respect that has been lost, is to commit a violent act."[34]

Unfortunately there is also systematic evidence supporting a connection in the United States between relative economic decline and male resentment and violence against women. The US Department of Health and Human Services, as Faludi reports, identified homicide as "the leading cause of workplace death in many cities hit by downsizing in the eighties, and the second-largest cause of workplace fatalities nationwide by the nineties." Particularly striking was the gender difference. Murder accounted for 12 percent of men's fatalities, but 42 percent of women's.[35] Given that sexual harassment by men of women increased during the same period, in many instances as women were retaining their (lower-paid) jobs in the same factories where men were losing theirs, one infers a misogynistic motive for many of these murders.[36]

Finally, it is not too much of a stretch to make the further connection between economic decline, misogynistic violence, and nationalism – the core relationship identified in this book – even for the United States. In this case, the nationalism takes the form of anti-immigrant sentiment. The evidence is episodic, but nonetheless suggestive: the leader of an extremist militia group in San Diego verbally attacked female immigration activists as sluts and prostitutes and claimed that they were motivated by desire for sex with dark-skinned foreigners (this is a paraphrase of something much cruder); an online video game called "Border Patrol"

[33] Susan Faludi, *Backlash: The Undeclared War against American Women* (New York: Three Rivers Press, 2006; originally published in 1991), p. 81.
[34] James Gilligan, quoted in Bob Herbert, "Women at Risk," *New York Times*, August 7, 2009.
[35] Susan Faludi, *Stiffed: The Betrayal of the American Man* (New York: Perennial, 2003; originally published in 1999), p. 60.
[36] Ibid., p. 88.

has been circulating through the internet since 2002, prompting players to kill Mexicans seeking to cross the US border, including pregnant women ("breeders"); in 2009 an elected city official in Georgia resigned from office and faced a lawsuit for racial harassment when it became known that he had forwarded the game to colleagues with his endorsement.[37] Meanwhile, across the border in Ciudad Juárez an epidemic of misogynistic murders has raged since the 1990s – linked to the US-backed "war on drugs" and the dislocation and inequality associated with the North American Free Trade Agreement.[38] The cases of Algeria, Chechnya, and Yugoslavia revealed the impact on vulnerable economies of the austerity programs and free-trade regimes associated with neoliberal reforms of the 1990s, and the role economic decline played in creating conditions for the violence that devastated those countries. Although the connections between economic dislocation, misogynistic violence, and extremism may not be so evident in the United States, they are worth watching.

Sequel: gender and nationalist violence on film

In my introductory chapter, I identified the association of males and masculinity with war not only as a key theme of Virginia Woolf's *Three Guineas*, but also as one addressed more recently by political scientists and public intellectuals such as Joshua Goldstein and Francis Fukuyama. Woolf's prescription of women's equality as a guarantor of peace met a range of responses when it appeared in 1938. One of her friends, Shena Simon, commented on the role that children's upbringing played in socializing boys into warriors – a theme that appears prominently in Goldstein's *War and Gender* as an explanation for warfare as a mostly male activity. As Simon wrote:

from the beginning, boys are brought up to hit back if they are attacked – little girls are scolded for doing the same. A fight between boys is considered

[37] Alex DiBranco, "Minutemen Leader Sued for Calling Activist Slut, Prostitute," *Immigrant Rights*, March 9, 2010, http://immigration.change.org/blog/category/antiimmigrant_hate_crimes; Jonathan Silverstein, "Racist Video Game Incites Anger: Internet Game Lets Players Take Shots at Immigrants," ABC News, May 1, 2006, http://abcnews.go.com/Technology/story?id=1910119&page=1; Kay Powell, "Kennesaw to Hold Special Election to Replace Dowdy: Councilman Resigned after Being Named in Racial Harassment Suit," *The Atlanta Journal-Constitution*, March 17, 2009.
[38] Charles Bowden, *Murder City: Ciudad Juárez and the Global Economy's New Killing Fields* (New York: Nation Books, 2010); on the impact of NAFTA on income inequality in Mexico, see Marcela González Rivas, "The Effects of Trade Openness on Regional Inequality in Mexico," *The Annals of Regional Science*, 41, 3 (September 2007), pp. 545–561.

'natural' and 'manly' – a quarrel between girls which develops into a fight is considered disgraceful. Are men afraid of the effect of encouraging physical courage in girls, or is it merely that they want boys later on to be ready to fight, and girls later on merely to weep?[39]

Simon complemented Woolf's proposal for enhancing the rights and education of girls and women by focusing on the education of boys. "I am more and more convinced that we shall never abolish war until the so-called 'Womanly Virtues' are inculcated in boys all through their school life and I would begin by insisting that all boys should be taught by women teachers – provided the women would treat them as if they were girls."[40]

This proposal – for the "feminization" of boys – was addressed by both Goldstein and Fukuyama. We recall from chapter 1 that their explanations for the predominance of men in warfare differed substantially – with Fukuyama emphasizing the impact of biology and genetics, and Goldstein social and cultural influences. Surprisingly their assessments of the "feminization" solution were remarkably similar. Fukuyama observes a gradual feminization of politics among advanced industrial democracies, especially in Europe, but he sees it as a dangerous development, if states elsewhere continue to raise boys to become fighters. His recommendation is that the United States and its European allies persist in promoting militarism as a manly virtue: "In a system of competitive states, the best regimes adopt the practices of the worst in order to survive."[41] Goldstein also considers the value of raising boys to be more sensitive and cooperative, less inclined to resort to violence. Yet, he cautions, "societies would still face an additional dilemma in raising boys: if they raise boys who are not warriors, they could someday be overrun by other societies that keep raising warriors."[42]

Shena Simon was aware of this concern already in 1938, but did not find it convincing: "Of course, it will be said that this would result in a race unwilling and unable to fight if necessary. But I do not think the combative spirit and certainly not the defensive spirit is so easily quelled."[43] The heirs of Virginia Woolf and Shena Simon might go a step further. They would stress the opportunities for cooperative solutions to potential international conflicts, inculcating the values that

---

[39] Letter, Shena D. Simon to Virginia Woolf, January 8, 1940, reprinted in *Woolf Studies Annual*, vol. 6 (2000), p. 161.

[40] Ibid.

[41] Francis Fukuyama, "Women and the Evolution of World Politics," *Foreign Affairs*, 77, 5 (September/October 1998), p. 36.

[42] Joshua S. Goldstein, *War and Gender: How Gender Shapes the War System and Vice Versa* (Cambridge University Press, 2001), p. 413.

[43] Letter, Simon to Woolf, p. 161.

Woolf thought could best be expressed in the Society of Outsiders. They might insist that efforts at socialization focus on men, in order that they come to accept women as equals, and in many cases superiors – that society cease to associate masculinity with dominance. In that spirit, feminist writers such as Margaret Randall have advocated a "feminization of power" within society as a whole.[44] Susan Faludi has suggested replacing "the male paradigm of confrontation, in which an enemy could be identified, contested, and defeated," with a "new paradigm for human progress that will open doors for both sexes."[45] Cynthia Enloe argued that if feminists played a more significant role in articulating national aspirations, "if more nation-states grew out of feminist nationalists' ideas and experiences, community identities within the international political system might be tempered by cross-national identities."[46]

Some of the films discussed in this book, such as *Aleksandra* and *House of Fools*, reflect the promise of shared, cross-national identities as an alternative to discrimination and violence. Others, such as *Pretty Village, Pretty Flame* or *War*, remind us how far we have to go. In any case, as I hope this book has demonstrated, cinema – like literature – provides important insights into such social and political dynamics and can serve as a generator of and complement to conventional social-science research. Many of the most profound insights about gender and war came from the pen of the novelist Virginia Woolf, writing in the late 1930s. In subsequent decades, particularly starting in the 1980s, feminist scholars writing at the intersection of the humanities and social sciences developed Woolf's insights and applied them to nationalist conflict. At the turn of the new millennium, social scientists such as Joshua Goldstein, Erik Melander, and Mary Caprioli have sought systematically to explore the relationship between gender, ethnicity, and conflict. Studying these topics through the movies provides additional benefits. Cinema offers insight into what popular audiences see and accept as natural or take for granted. This is especially so when a film does not explicitly address the topic at hand – such as gender in many of the ones discussed here. Watching movies through our "gender lenses" reveals relationships that may not otherwise be apparent, but can be matters of life and death.

---

[44] Randall, *Gathering Rage*, pp. 50, 61–62.
[45] Faludi, *Stiffed*, pp. 604, 608.
[46] Cynthia Enloe, *Bananas, Beaches and Bases: Making Feminist Sense of International Politics* (Berkeley, CA: University of California Press, 1990), p. 64.

Index

Abbas, Ferhat, 36, 37
Abdul Murat (character in *Prisoner of the Mountains*), 173
Abkhazia, 173
abortion, 15, 100, 128, 226, 233, 234, 237, 243
Aboud, Hichem, 68
Abu Ghraib prison, 2
Abuzaidova, Tamara, 169
Adams, Bryan, 196
adat (traditional system of justice in Chechnya), 160, 164
Afghanistan, 160
Akhmed (character in *House of Fools*), 197
al Jazeera television network, 158
al Qaeda terrorist network, 158
Albright, Madeleine, 106
alcohol and alcoholism
   Algerian Islamist campaign against, 68
   FLN campaign against, 41
   and Islam in Bosnia, 87
   result of unemployment and male humiliation, 14, 91, 195
Aleksandr I, Tsar, 143
Aleksandra, 10, 23, 143, 199–202, 271
Aleksandra (character in *Aleksandra*), 200
Algeria, 3, 11, 15, 21
   after independence, 63–79
   Black October riots, 69, 75, 153
   civil war in 1990s, 15, 21, 66
   Constitution of 1976, 67, 69, 71, 152
   Constitution of 1989, 70, 76, 153
   economic crisis of 1980s–1990s, 65
   Family Code of 1981, 69, 152
   Family Code of 1984, 69, 71, 74, 76, 153
   French colonial rule, 27–33
   gender and French colonialism, 35
   immigration from Europe, 29–30
   National Assembly, 64
      women's representation, 67
   natural gas as key export, 65
   similarities to Chechnya, 27, 141

   status of Muslims under colonial rule, 32
"Algeria Unveiled" (Fanon), 13, 33, 52, 53
Algerian army, 67, 68, 70, 71, 75, 77
   battles Islamist forces, 65
   role in independent Algeria, 64
Algerian government, 41, 61, 75, 77, 262
   imposes discriminatory election law, 71, 153
Algerian war of independence (1954–1962), 9, 22, 255
   origins, 27, 35–39
Algérie Française, 144, 223
Algiers, 28, 41, 42, 44, 45, 49, 56, 57, 58, 60, 69, 79
   Casbah, 42, 59
   European quarter, 39, 42
Algiers (French *département*), 29
Algiers, Battle of (January–October 1957), 41, 42, 44, 60, 67, 78, 184, 192, 223
Ali la Pointe (character in *The Battle of Algiers*), 25, 41, 42, 54, 60, 263
Aliev, Geidar, 182
Alisa (character in *Checkpoint*), 179
Alive, 195
"All the Men are in the Militias, All the Women are Victims," 81, 103, 137
"All Yugoslavia Dances to Rock 'n' Roll" (*Igra rokenrol cela Jugoslavija*), 121–122
Allen, Beverly, 111, 116, 136
allophones (Québec), 239
Alsace-Lorraine, 29
Alto Adige, 263
Aluminum Queen, The, 160
Amara, Ali (Ali la Pointe), 41
Amrane-Minne, Danièle Djamila, 47, 115
ancient hatreds
   as explanation for conflict in Yugoslavia, 81, 89, 260
Anderson, Benedict, 2
anglophones, 207, 209, 218, 231, 237
   as owners of businesses in Québec, 217

Anna (character in *Caucasian Roulette*), 189
anticolonialism, 9, 13, 26
Anti-Fascist Front of Women (Yugoslavia), 98
Anya (granddaughter of Zhenya), 161, 164
Apocalypse Now, 131, 177
Arkan. *See* Raznatović, Zeljko
Armstrong, Louis, 174
Arnaud, Bernadette (character in *The Battle of Algiers*), 43
Arnaud, Henri (character in *The Battle of Algiers*), 42
Aslan (character in *Caucasian Roulette*), 189
Aussaresses, Paul, 60, 61, 64
Austro-Hungarian Empire, 81, 82, 101, 263
Azerbaijan, 182

Babel, Isaac, 2
backlash by men against women's achievements, 15, 257, 265
  in 1990s Algeria, 72–75
  in Québec, 244
  in Yugoslavia, 80, 92
Bagreev, Roman, 166
Baker, Peter, 157
Balabanov, Aleksei, 23, 142, 181, 184, 185, 186, 187, 195, 257
Baldwin, Alec, 16
Baldwin, Stanley, 266
Balkan wars (1912–1913), 96
Ballad of a Soldier, 181
Banja Luka, 87, 125
Baraev, Arbi, 183
Barberousse prison, 42, 54
Basaev, Shamil', 151, 154, 155, 164, 181
  criticized by Chechen women, 154
Bashkortostan, 140, 151
Battle of Algiers, The, 9, 22, 26–27, 39–63, 184, 192, 255, 256, 259, 261, 263
  historical accuracy, 58–63
  problems screening it in France, 62
  soundtrack, 47, 51, 172
Battle of the Plains of Abraham, 204
Baymuradova, Shakhidat, 188
Bela (character in *Hero of Our Time*), 166
Belarus, 150
Belgrade, 24, 81, 86, 91, 94, 99, 101, 103, 105, 107, 115, 118, 120, 121, 128, 131
Belhadj, Ali, 76
Ben Bouali, Hassiba, 49
Ben M'hidi, Larbi, 25, 45, 63, 64
Bendjedid, Chadli, 64, 69, 70
  declares martial law, 71, 153
  voids election, 71, 153
Bendjedid, Halima, 70
Berbers. *See* Imazighen
Berezovskii, Boris, 182, 183, 184
Beslan, 156, 157, 158, 164
Bigeard, Marcel, 59
Bijeljina, 105
biology, 5, 6, 9, 270
Bjelogrlić, Dragan, 119
Black Widows (female suicide bombers), 191–192
Blake (character in *Glengarry Glen Ross*), 16
Bloc Québécois, 250
blood feud (*krovnaia mest'*) in Chechnya, 164, 169, 176, 193
Bodrov, Sergei, 10, 23, 170, 173, 177
Bodrov, Sergei, Jr., 172, 181
Bolsheviks, 26
bombing
  by Algerian women, 27, 39, 46, 49–52, 53, 55, 259
  by Chechen women, 141, 259
  by Chechens in Russia, 156
  directed by Saadi Yacef in Algiers, 41
  by the FLQ in Québec, 219, 220, 224, 226, 227, 228
  by French in Algeria, 36, 45, 261
  of Grozny, 153, 160
  of Hiroshima, 232
  of Kijevo by Yugoslav army, 86
  by the OAS in Algeria, 58
  on Rue de Thèbes. *See* Rue de Thèbes massacre
  of Russian apartment buildings in 1999, 141, 153, 154
  by Russians in Chechnya, 37, 141, 154, 155, 157, 162, 194, 197, 258
  suicide. *See* suicide bombers
  of Yugoslavia by Nazi forces, 101
  of Yugoslavia by US forces, 101
Bosnia and Herzegovina, 21, 24, 34, 81, 83, 84, 86, 87, 88, 93, 94, 131
  1990s war, 81, 86
  collective presidency, 105
  cuisine, 87
  customs, 87
  declares independence, April 1992, 85, 153
  interethnic relations, 86–90
  language, 86
  as partisan base during World War II, 82
  women as producers of cultural difference and interethnic comity, 104

Bosnian army, 106
Bosnian Serb army, 86
Bouchard, Gérard, 246, 247
Bouchard, Lucien, 239, 240, 248
Bouhired, Djamila, 49, 67
Boumediène, Houari, 64, 67, 68, 70
Boupacha, Djamila, 62
Bourassa, Henri, 211
    opposes women's political rights and
        democracy, 211
Bourassa, Robert, 217, 222
Bourdieu, Pierre, 31
Boyce-Thompson Institute, 106
Brezhnev, Leonid, 190
British Empire, 9
British Parliament, 205, 210
British Petroleum, 182
Brother, 195
Brother II, 195
brotherhood and unity (Yugoslav
    ideology), 12, 133, 134, 136
Brown, Julie, 14
Browne, Jackson, 248
Browning, Christopher, 135
Broz, Josip. *See* Tito
Brzi (Speedy) (character in *Pretty Village,
    Pretty Flame*), 126
Buchanan (character in *Nô*), 232
Budanov, Iurii, 166–168, 186
Budennovsk, 151, 152, 160
Bulić, Vanja, 115

Cambridge University, 8, 265
Ćamil (character in *Pretty Village, Pretty
    Flame*), 130
Camus, Albert, 64, 261
Canada, 21
    Act of Union 1840, 142, 206
    British North America Act of 1867, 143,
        207, 208
    Constitution 1867, 143, 208
    Constitutional Act 1791, 138, 206, 209
    House of Commons, 209
    peaceful evolution contrasted to United
        States, 207
    Supreme Court, 226
Canadian army, 219, 222, 242,
    246, 260
Canadian federal government, 203
Canadian federation, 11, 208, 252,
    259, 260
Canadian Multiculturalism Act, 153,
    239
Caprioli, Mary, 264, 271
captivity narratives, 170–171, 172–173
Caracciolo, Lucio, 263

Carey, Scott (character in *The Incredible
    Shrinking Man*), 16
Carr, Camilla, 182, 183, 187
Cartier, Jacques, 204
Casbah, 28, 40, 41, 42, 44, 45, 48, 54,
    59, 78
Caucasian Roulette, 142, 189–191, 200, 202
Caucasus, 27, 28, 163, 170, 171, 172, 184,
    196
Ceca. *See* Ražnatović, Svetlana
central America, 256
central Asia, 26, 34
Chartrand, Michel, 222
Che Guevaras in Turbans, 117
Chechen identity
    forged in response to Russian offensives,
        144
Chechen Republic of Ichkeriia, 146
Chechenization, 22, 156, 200, 261
Checheno-Ingush Autonomous Soviet
    Socialist Republic, 145
Chechens
    mass deportation in 1940s, 145
    return from exile in 1950s, 145
    romantic image from Russian literature,
        146
Chechentsy, 195
Chechnya, 3, 10, 11, 21
    first war (1994), 10, 21, 22, 23
    gender relations, 159–165
    second war (1999), 22, 23
    similarities to Algeria, 27, 159
    in Soviet cinema, 169–170
Checkpoint (Blokpost), 23, 142, 177–181,
    187, 188, 191, 257
checkpoints
    between Casbah and European quarter
        of Algiers, 42, 44, 48, 53
    in Chechnya, 177, 194
Chekhov, Anton, 1
Cherkasov, Aleksandr, 150
Chernomyrdin, Viktor, 151, 152
Chetniks (Četnici), 82, 83, 111, 124, 128,
    131, 133, 134, 135
Chiapas, 257
Chukhrai, Grigorii, 181
Cimino, Michael, 191
cinéma direct, 226, 233
cinema of the intelligentsia (*intelligentskoe
    kino*), 180
cinéma vérité, 22
Cité Libre (Montréal), 213
Ciudad Juárez, 269
civilians
    defined to include only women and
        children, 113

as deliberate targets of violence in
  Bosnia and Croatia, 104
indiscriminately targeted by Russians in
  Chechnya, 151, 259
as main victims of Algerian, Chechen,
  and Yugoslav wars, 38
massacred at Philippeville, August 1955,
  38
massacred at Samashki, 151
Serbs targeted for Nazi collective
  punishment, 82
as targets of Algerian women bombers,
  39, 259
as targets of Chechen suicide bombers,
  159
as targets of Rue de Thèbes bombing, 44
as targets of violence in Algeria, 22, 44,
  45, 261
used as human shields by Russian
  troops, 152
as victims of French aerial
  bombardment in Algeria, 45
victims of Grozny bombing, 153
as victims of Russian violence in
  Chechnya, 186
class, 8, 12
  subproletariat, 31
Cockburn, Cynthia, 7, 98–100, 104, 113
Cocteau, Jean, 232
Cohen, Leonard, 203
collective punishment
  French policy in Algeria, 30, 45
  Nazi policy in Yugoslavia, 82
collective theater (Québec), 230
colonialism, 9, 41, 255
Comfort, Alex, 138
Commission on Accommodation Practices
  Related to Cultural Difference
  (Québec), 246–247
Committee of Soldiers' Mothers, 153, 172,
  190, 196, 201
Commonwealth of Independent States
  (CIS), 183
Communist Party of the Soviet Union
  (CPSU), 143
communists
  in Bosnia, 94
  in Chechnya, 149
  in Croatia, 124
  in Serbia, 84, 94
  in Slovenia, 85
  in Yugoslavia, 83
Condee, Nancy, 202
Constantine (French département), 29,
  30, 38
Constantine Plan, 31, 261

contraceptives, 15, 225
Cooper, Gary, 18, 20
Coppola, Francis Ford, 131
Cossette-Trudel, Jacques, 223
Crimean war, 30
Croatia, 13, 83, 84, 96, 113
  declares independence, June 1991, 85
  as Nazi puppet state, 82
Cronauer, Adrian, 131
Cross, James, 220, 222, 223
Cuba, 256
culture, 5, 7, 127, 177
  biological effects of, 7
Czech Republic, 12
Czechoslovakia, 12

Dagestan, 23, 28, 141, 145, 152, 153, 154,
  155, 171, 184, 188
daughters of educated men (Virginia
  Woolf), 8, 57, 254, 264
David, Françoise, 250
Dayton Plan, 106
de Broca, Philippe, 142
de Gaulle, Charles, 27, 232
de Jonge, Alex, 1
death estimates
  in Algerian war of independence, 38,
    262
  during Battle of Algiers, 61
  in Bosnian war of 1990s, 86
  from pieds noirs violence at end of
    Algerian war, 42, 58
  of Russian assault on Grozny, August
    1996, 153
  in Sétif massacre, 36
  of Yugoslav women in anti-Nazi
    resistance, 98
  of Yugoslavs killed in World War II, 83
decolonization, 9, 26, 37
Dedić, Milan, 110
Deeb, Mary-Jane, 31, 57, 69
Deer Hunter, The, 191
Delacroix, Eugène, 33
democracy
  and ambivalence of English-Canadian
    political elite, 208
  as challenge to communist rule in
    Yugoslavia, 99
  as inspiration for Algerian revolution,
    40, 262
  of masculine gender in eastern Europe,
    101
  in Québec, 22
  vs. self-government in French Canada,
    208
  and women's suffrage in Québec, 211

demographic transition, 265
  in Québec,1950s–1960s, 212
demographics, 4, 14
  conditions in Algeria, 32, 65, 76
  and ethnic intermarriage in Bosnia, 88
Denis (character in *Aleksandra*), 200
Derluguian, Georgi, 117, 147, 148, 168
Desbiens, Jean Paul, 222; *See also* Frère
  Untel
Déserteurs de l'Armée Française (DAF),
  67–68
Devils (1872), 2
Devoir, Le (Montréal), 211, 215, 221, 238,
  248, 249
Dien Bien Phu, 37
Dilberović, Suada, 104
Dina (character in *Prisoner of the
  Mountains*), 172
disappearances
  in Chechnya, 141, 155, 164, 192, 200
  during Battle of Algiers, 61
Djamila (character in *The Battle of Algiers*),
  42
documentary film, 21, 22, 39, 58, 96, 114,
  118, 172, 185, 186, 226
Dolan, Chris, 14, 16, 66, 91, 108, 138, 266
domestic violence, 98
  in Québec, 242
  in Yugoslavia, 102; *See also* SOS Hotline
  (Belgrade)
Dostoevskii, Fedor, 1, 2, 7
Dragojević, Srđan, 10, 22, 81, 114, 117,
  125, 132, 133, 134, 136, 196, 198,
  255, 259
Drakulić, Slavenka, 80, 99, 101
Drif, Zohra, 47, 49, 53, 56, 57, 78, 256
  in independent Algeria, 66, 69
  leadership role in Algiers, 54
Dubrovka Theater hostage crisis, 156, 157,
  158
Dubrovnik, 104
Dudaev, Dzhokhar, 140, 146, 148, 149,
  150, 151, 182
  killed by Russian forces, 152
Duguyevova, Elza, 166, 194, 195
Dundjerovic, Aleksandar, 230, 233
Dunlop, John, 143
Duplessis, Maurice, 213
Dupuis-Déri, Francis, 208, 211
Duras, Marguerite, 232
Duvivier, Julien, 59

eastern Europe, 10, 80, 83, 101
École Polytechnique of Montréal, 244, 256
economic conditions and recruitment of
  soldiers, 15

economic decline, 65
  impact on women in Yugoslavia, 101
  and masculine humiliation, 263, 268
economic discrimination
  against Muslims in colonial Algeria,
  30–32
economic emasculation, 15
economic factors contributing to violence,
  4, 14, 15, 147, 268, 269
education, 8
  French discriminatory policies in
  colonial Algeria, 30–32
  and gender equality in Soviet Union,
  265
  and gender in Yugoslavia, 99
  proportion of women associated with
  peace, 264
  religious schools in precolonial Algeria,
  31
  role of female teachers in Québec, 215
  women's, as source of resentment for
  men, 15
Eisenstein, Sergei, 59, 170
Eisenstein, Zillah, 110
Ejército Zapatista de Liberación
  Nacional(EZLN), 257
El Kader, Fusia, 51
Električni orgazam, 122
Elshtain, Jean Bethke, 255
England, 8
Enloe, Cynthia, 7, 11, 12, 15, 39, 53, 57,
  80, 103, 137, 138, 266, 271
equality, 263–269
Equipes Médico-sociales Itinérantes
  (EMSI), 34
Ermolov, Aleksei, 143, 165
Estonia, 149, 188
ethnic cleansing
  in Chechnya, 139
  in Yugoslavia, 80, 89, 97, 104, 105, 110,
  137, 260
ethnic scapegoating, 17, 80, 92
Evans, J. A. S., 240
Evans, Martin, 36, 67, 70, 76, 77
Évian Accords, 58, 64
Expo '70, 224, 225

Faludi, Susan, 16, 267, 268, 271
families, 5, 13
  in colonial Algeria, 34
  focus of Islamist politics in Algeria, 76
  in precolonial Algeria, 32
Fanon, Frantz, 13, 33, 34, 52, 53, 56, 219
Fathia (character in *The Battle of Algiers*),
  39
Fatima (accused Chechen sniper), 188

Fatma (character in *The Battle of Algiers*), 43
feminine attributes, 6
feminine identity, 18
Feminine Mystique, The, 16
feminism and feminist scholarship, 4, 7,
    133, 158, 175
  essentialist approaches, 41, 103
  maternalist approaches, 52
feminists, 254, 271
  in Algeria, 66, 69, 70
  in Québec, 237, 244
  in Yugoslavia, 99, 100
feminization of enemies, 6, 7
Feraoun, Mouloud, 25, 63, 261
Feydeau, Georges, 231
film noir, 59, 226
flash-backs, 22, 118, 124, 128, 171
flash-forwards, 121, 122
Foley, James, 16
Foreign Affairs, 4, 5
Foreign Legion. *See* French army
Fork (character in *Pretty Village, Pretty*
    Flame), 125
Forman, Milos, 142
Fowler, Amy (character in *High Noon*),
    18, 19
fragmented narrative style, 22, 171
France, 58, 61, 63
François-Xavier (character in *Nô*), 227
francophones
  vs. Arabic speakers in Algeria, 68, 76
  in Canada, 209
  as employees in Québec, 217
  media in Québec, 220, 221, 222, 245
  in Québec, 207, 212, 217, 220, 222,
    231, 239, 248
  women in Algeria, 76
  women in Québec, 237
Franco-Prussian war, 29
French air force, 36, 45
French army, 28, 33, 34, 36, 38, 58, 64,
    67, 144
  Foreign Legion, 36, 59
  paratroopers, 36, 59, 79
French colonialism, 9
French Foreign Legion. *See* French army
French government, 29, 31, 34, 62
French language
  laws in Québec, 217–218
French New Wave, 227
French paratroopers. *See* French army
French settlers in Canada, 22
Frère Untel (Jean-Paul Desbiens), 215,
    218, 224, 230, 253
Freud, Sigmund, 88
Friedan, Betty, 16

Front de Libération du Québec (FLQ),
    218, 260
  and the October Crisis, 218–223
  political manifesto, 220, 222, 228
Front de Libération Nationale (FLN), 33,
    71, 261
  accommodates Islamist demands on
    women, 68, 69
  appeal to Islam, 40
  assassinates suspected traitors, 61
  asserts civil authority in Algiers, 39–40,
    41
  and attacks against civilians, 44
  campaign to eradicate prostitution, drug
    abuse, and alcoholism, 40
  contributes to rise of Islamism and FIS,
    71
  economic policies in independent
    Algeria, 64, 66
  as francophone elite, 76
  governing independent Algeria, 66
  impact on Algerian family, 34
  influence of military wing from 1960s,
    68
  internecine conflict, 37, 39, 64, 261
  launches insurrection, 36
  liberalizes economy and politics in
    1980s, 70
  offers of negotiation refused, 37
  orders massacre at Philippeville, 38
  political manifesto, 36
  and violence against women, 61
Front Islamique du Salut (FIS), 71
  challenges FLN, wins 1991 election, 72
Fukuyama, Francis, 4, 5, 6, 7, 8, 9, 269,
    270
Full Metal Jacket, 131

Gabin, Jean, 59
Gagnon, Charles, 220
Gagnon, Lysiane, 248
Gagnon, V. P., Jr., 81, 84, 86, 88, 89, 90,
    92, 96, 97, 107, 123
Gandhi, Indira, 105
gangs
  basis of Ramzan Kadyrov's rule, 147,
    156
  in Chechnya, 195
  in colonial Algeria, 38
  in independent Algeria, 66, 72
  and new wars, 22
  and organized crime in Chechnya, 169
  in Yugoslavia, 91, 137
Garanger, Marc, 34, 35, 79
Garne, Mohamed, 62
Gasheeva, Zainap, 157

Gelaev, Ruslan, 188
gender discrimination, 7, 9, 25
gender equality, 8, 15, 263–269
  advocated by Virginia Woolf, 254
  as a core value in Québec society, 247
  fostered by Soviet educational system,
    265
gender identity, 1, 6
gender inequality, 13
  in Yugoslav workforce, 98
gender norms, 14, 24
  challenged in *House of Fools*, 197
  and female soldiers in Yugoslavia, 106
  reinforced in *Aleksandra*, 199
  and the Srebrenica massacre, 113
  and Yugoslav male draft resisters, 107
gender relations
  in Chechnya, 159–165
gender roles, 9, 76
  in Algerian war of independence, 61
  challenged by women's
    education, 264
  challenged by women's political
    participation, 264
  in colonial Algeria, 27, 32–35, 53
  in *Prisoner of the Mountains*, 175
  reversal in Chechnya, 192–199
  in warfare, 39
gender segregation, 6
gender stereotypes, 3, 18, 23, 26, 39, 185
  challenged in Chechnya, 192–199
  challenged in *House of Fools*, 199
  subversion of, 23
  subversion of, in *The Battle of Algiers*,
    27, 39
gender, definitions, 5
gendercide, 112
  in Bosnia, 112–113
  against Muslim men in Bosnia, 113
Gendercide Watch, 112, 245
gender-differentiated play styles, 6
Geneva Conventions, 172
genocide
  charge against Zeljko Raznatović, 105
Georgia, Kingdom of, 143
Georgia, Republic of, 145, 173, 181
German language, 126, 127, 134, 263, 266
Germany
  Nazi, 11, 35, 82
    collective punishment in Serbia, 82
    Gestapo, 59
    invasion and occupation of Yugoslavia,
      82, 83, 98
    soldiers as members of French
      Foreign Legion, 36, 59

support for Croatian and Slovenian
    independence, 91
  Weimar, 96
  and Yugoslav guestworkers, 124, 135,
    136, 148
Giguère, Alain, 251
Gilligan, Carol, 234
"Give Peace a Chance," 132
Glengarry Glen Ross, 16
globalization, 65, 251
Godard, Jean-Luc, 227
Gogol, Nikolai, 2, 7
Goldstein, Joshua, 5, 6, 7, 8, 9, 12, 25,
    269, 270, 271
Good Morning, Vietnam!, 131
Gorbachev, Mikhail, 149, 150
Goscilo, Helen, 190
Grant, Bruce, 163
Grbavica, 104
Grbavica (film), 116
Greater Serbia, 85, 99, 241
Gregg, Herbert, 184
Grozny, 143, 145, 147, 149, 150, 151, 153,
    160, 165, 168, 182, 200
Guevara, Ernesto Che, 146, 147, 197
Gulf war (1991), 6
Gutman, Roy, 112

Hacène (character in *The Battle of Algiers*),
    41
Hadji Murat, 170, 177
Hague, The, 86, 105, 106
Halil (character in *Pretty Village, Pretty
    Flame*), 115, 118, 120
Halimi, Gisèle, 62
Halimi, Jean-Yves, 62
Halligan, Benjamin, 117
Hamlet, 181
Hanako (character in *Nô*), 225
Hasan (character in *Prisoner of the
    Mountains*), 174
Hassiba (character in *The Battle of Algiers*),
    49–52, 60
Hébert, Patricia (character in *Nô*), 228
Hero of Our Time, 165
High Noon, 18, 20, 108
Hiroshima, 232
Hiroshima Mon Amour, 232
Hitler, Adolf, 96, 129, 266
hittistes, 76
Hokanson, Katya, 171
Hollywood, 227
homosexuality, 6, 226
Horton, Andrew James, 115, 117
hostage-taking. *See* Beslan, Dubrovka
    Theater hostage crisis, kidnapping

House of Commons
  British, 9
  Canadian, 209
House of Fools, 23, 142, 196–199, 259, 271
Hunt, Swanee, 104, 105, 107
hypotheses on gender, nationalism, and war, 4, 11–17, 57, 98, 190, 253

Iandarbiev, Zelimkhan, 152
Ibragimova, Liza, 162, 193, 195, 265
identity, 14
  See also specific types (e.g., gender, masculine, Yugoslav)
ideology, 5, 243
Ighilhariz, Malika, 53, 54, 57
Illyichenko, Alla, 157
Imazighen (Berbers), 28, 70
imperialism, 9, 255
Incredible Shrinking Man, The, 16
Ingush, 145, 147, 148, 162, 163
Ingushetiia, 162, 163
Insolences du Frère Untel, Les, 214–218
Intellectuels pour la souveraineté, Les, 241, 249, 250
International Criminal Tribunal for the Former Yugoslavia, 105, 124
International Monetary Fund, 65, 75, 90
Iordanova, Dina, 116
Iraq war (2003), 6
Isidora (Tzeltal member of Zapatista army), 257
Islam
  political Islam in Algeria, 67–69
  and the FLN, 36, 40, 41
  and opposition to gender equality in Algeria, 66
  in Bosnia, 87
  in colonial Algeria, 29
  as source of identity in Chechnya, 141
  and women's violence in Chechnya, 156–159
Islamic law, 160
Islamicization
  of Chechen resistance movement, 23, 140, 154, 181
Islamist campaign against women's rights in Algeria, 66–70, 76–77
Islamist violence against women in 1990s Algeria, 34, 66, 67, 72, 77–78
Italian neorealist cinema, 22, 59
Italy, 263
  support for Croatian and Slovenian independence, 91
Ivanov, Sergei, 168
Izetbegović, Alija, 112

Jaffar, El-hadi (character in *The Battle of Algiers*), 41, 45, 47, 54
James, Jon, 182, 183, 187
JNA (Jugoslovenska narodna armija).
  See Yugoslav army
John (character in *War*), 185
Johnson, Barbara, 234
Jones, Adam, 112, 245
joual, 215, 216, 217
Joy of Sex, 138
Jugoslovenska narodna armija (JNA).
  See Yugoslav army
Jurado, Katy, 20

Kabylie, 30, 64
Kadyrov, Akhmat, 156
Kadyrov, Ramzan, 146, 156, 164, 192, 261
  endorses polygamy, 161
Kadyrovtsy, 156, 169
Kaldor, Mary, 22
Kalimat (café owner in Grozny), 139, 161, 162, 168, 194
Kandiyoti, Deniz, 13
Kane, Will (character in *High Noon*), 18, 19
Karadžić, Radovan, 87, 105
Karaulac, Miroslav, 81
Katsav, Moshe, 168
Kazakhstan, 149, 161
Kazi Mullah, 146
Kelly, Grace, 18
Kertes, Mihajl, 110
Kessler, Ronald, 16
Khadir, Amir, 250
Khanbiev, Magamed, 164
Khanna, Ranjana, 35, 62, 63, 69, 257, 258, 261
Khasaviurt Accord, 153, 182
Khattab, Emir (Samir Saleh Abdullah Al-Suwailem), 154, 155, 188
Kheira (Algerian rape victim), 62–63
Khrushchev, Nikita, 145, 170, 181
kidnapping
  of brides in Chechnya and Ingushetiia, 163
  in Chechnya, 163–164, 172–173, 181
  of families, 164
  of James Cross, 220, 222, 223
  of Jon James and Camilla Carr, 181–183
  and murder of Pierre Laporte, 221
  for ransom, 163
  of Valentin Vlasov, 183
  of women, 78
Kidnapping Caucasian Style, 163, 170
Kijevo, 85

King of Hearts, 142
Kirkland-Casgrain, Claire, 210
Kizliar, 152
Konchalovskii, Andrei, 23, 142, 196, 198, 199
Kosovar Albanians, 84
Kosovo, 83, 84, 86, 91, 92, 93, 96, 99, 100
Kouaouci, Ali, 32, 73, 74, 75
Kovačević, Ivan, 132–133
Krajina, 84, 85, 86, 89, 92, 93, 96, 107
Krstić, Igor, 117, 130
Kubrick, Stanley, 131
Kuleshov effect, 50
kum (in Serbian culture), 132–133
Kungaeva, Elza, 166–167, 186
Kutsenko, Viktor, 150
Kyōgen, 233

Lacoste, Robert, 67, 78
Lakhdari, Samia, 56
Lanctôt, Jacques, 223
Lanctôt, Louise, 223
Landry, Bernard, 249
language, 1
    conflict between Arabic- and French-speaking Algerians, 76
    militarized, 136
    sexualized, 17
    as source of Québec nationalism, 204–205, 214–218, 220, 228, 241, 248, 249
    violent misogyny in Yugoslav swears, 117, 127–128, 130, 137, 138
Lapointe, Walter (character in *Nô*), 228
Laporte, Pierre, 221, 222, 259
"Late for the Sky," 249
Latvia, 149, 188
Laurendeau, André, 215
Lavrentiev, Sergei, 185, 187
Laza (character in *Pretty Village, Pretty Flame*), 124
Lazreg, Marnia, 34, 79
Lebed', Aleksandr, 153
LeClerc, Patrice, 211, 237
legislature
    proportion of women in Algerian, 67
    proportion of women associated with peace, 264
Lennon, John, 108, 132
Lepage, Robert, 10, 23, 203, 214, 217, 218, 223, 232, 242, 248, 251, 255, 259
Lépine, Marc, 244, 245
Lermontov, Mikhail, 146, 165, 170, 171, 177
"Let My People Go," 174

Lévesque, René, 213, 218, 221, 223, 238
Levi, Pavle, 82
Levinson, Barry, 131
Liberal Party (Canada), 213, 219, 220, 221, 238, 245, 248
    Claude Ryan leads Québec branch, 238
    governs Québec, early 1960s, 213
    governs Québec in 1970s, passes language law, 217
Lidové noviny, 160
Life and Opinions of Tristram Shandy, The, 233
Linell, Liza (character in *Pretty Village, Pretty Flame*), 125
Lithuania, 149, 188
Little, Allan, 104
Ljubljana, 99
Ljujić-Mijatović, Tanja, 96
Lokshina, Tanya, 160
Los Angeles, 16, 17
Louis XIV, King (France), 204
Louise (character in *The Incredible Shrinking Man*), 16

Maass, Peter, 87, 95, 97, 108, 109, 125
Macedonia, 83
MacKinnon, Catherine, 109
magical realism, 22, 23, 114, 115, 117
Magnano, Silvius, 263
Mahmud (character in *The Battle of Algiers*), 39
Makam Al-Shahid Martyrs' Monument, 262
Makanin, Vladimir, 170
Makavejev, Dušan, 22, 114
Makhachkala, 184
Maksimović, Gvozden (character in *Pretty Village, Pretty Flame*), 123
Malashenko, Igor', 183
male competition for status, 3, 4, 8, 18, 25, 254
male humiliation, 16, 17, 131
    in Algeria, 70, 263
    in Chechnya, 194
    and murder in the USA, 267–268
Malika (character in *Aleksandra*), 200
Mamet, David, 16
Manitoba, 208
maquis
    in Algerian civil war of 1990s, 77
    in Algerian war of independence, 39, 47, 188
March of the Slav Woman, 196, 200, 202
Margaret (character in *War*), 185
Maria (character in *Caucasian Roulette*), 189

Maria (Tzeltal member of Zapatista army), 257
Mark (character in *High Noon*), 18
Marko (character in *Pretty Village, Pretty Flame*), 131
Marković, Mirjana, 105
marriage
  in Algerian Islamic tradition, 32, 34
  ceremony in *The Battle of Algiers*, 39
  ceremony in *High Noon*, 18
  contracts under the *Coutume de Paris* in French Canada, 210
  contracts under Québec Civil Code of 1866, 210
  depends on men's employment, 17, 72, 73, 74, 76
  forced in 1990s Algeria, 165
  forced in Chechnya, 163
  intermarriage in Bosnia, 88, 106
  intermarriage with native peoples in French Canada, 208, 224
  intermarriage in Yugoslavia, 93
  and polygamy in Chechnya, 159, 161, 162
  in post-independence Algeria, 73, 74
  proposal in *House of Fools*, 198
  as sole source of wealth for women in Virginia Woolf's England, 8
Marseilles, 59
Martin, Jean, 59
masculine attributes, 6
masculine identity, 15, 18, 19
masculinity, 17
  and armed defense of the nation, 39
  associated with employment, attracting a wife, supporting a family, 14, 17
  associated with violence, 12, 18, 39
  associated with willingness to fight, 6, 56, 169, 193
  crisis in 1990s Algeria, 68
  in independent Algeria, 67
  linked to armed defense of women, 11, 108
  threatened by women's success, 15–16
Masha (character in *Checkpoint*), 178
Maskhadov, Aslan, 140, 151, 152, 153, 154, 156, 164, 181, 182, 183, 184, 185
Maslov (character in *Prisoner of the Mountains*), 173
Massu, Jacques, 59, 79
Mathieu, Colonel Philippe (character in *The Battle of Algiers*), 45, 59, 60
Mathieu, Rhéal, 220
matriarchy
  in Algeria, 33

in French Canada, 22
in North America, 216
in Québec, 203, 216, 224, 230, 242
Medvedev (character in *War*), 185
Meech Lake Accord (1987), 239
Mekhralieva, Susanna, 173
Melander, Erik, 264, 271
Mellen, Joan, 59
Memorial (Russian human rights organization), 160
Messali Hadj, Ahmed Ben, 37, 261
métis, 208
Michaels, Paula, 173, 177
Michaud, Yves, 248, 249
Michel (character in *Nô*), 224, 259
Middleton, Henry, 205
Midnight's Children, 233
Milan (character in *Pretty Village, Pretty Flame*), 118, 120
Milićević, Aleksandra Sasha, 107, 111
militarization of nationalist conflict, 11, 23, 91
militarized masculine stereotype, 6, 137
Miller, Frank (character in *High Noon*), 18
Miloš (character in *Pretty Village, Pretty Flame*), 135
Milošević, Slobodan, 81, 93, 94, 95, 96, 99, 100, 105, 107, 115, 117, 118, 120, 133, 241
  consolidation of power, 84–85
  and destruction of Yugoslavia, 85–86
Mirjana (character in *Pretty Village, Pretty Flame*), 134, 258
Miron, Gaston, 249
Mishima, Yukio, 225, 232
misogynistic violence, 10, 22
  in Algeria, 15, 21, 34, 66, 267
  in Chechnya, 185, 194
  in Québec, 245–246
  in Yugoslavia, 21
misogyny, 14
  of Algerian *hittistes*, 76
  of Belgrade police, 103
  part of military training, 6
  in Serbo-Croatian language, 116
  in Yugoslav culture, 133
Mitterrand, François, 37, 261
Mladić, Ratko, 86
modernization, 26, 213
montage, 22, 122, 129, 232
Montenegro, 83, 85, 106
Montesquieu, Charles-Louis de Secondat, baron de, 205
Montréal, 23, 215, 217, 218, 222, 224, 225, 226, 227, 231, 233, 239, 243, 248, 250

Montréal (*cont.*)
anglophone Jewish population, 209
site of first Canadian school for girls,
124, 209
Montréal massacre (1989), 244–246, 256,
266, 267
Morocco, 33, 67, 73, 75
Moscow, 105, 140
Moscow Times, 167
mothers and motherhood, 1, 3, 5, 6, 10, 52
in Chechen wars, 153
in Chechnya, 168
contradictory role in Yugoslav antiwar
activism, 114
in Russia, 188, 196
in Yugoslav wars, 114
Mouvement National Algérien, 37
Mouvement Souveraineté-Association, 214
Mozzhukhin, Ivan, 50
music
in *The Battle of Algiers*, 47, 51, 60
common among ethnic groups in
Bosnia, 87
in *House of Fools*, 197
in *Pretty Village, Pretty Flame*, 122, 129,
132, 133
in *Prisoner of the Mountains*, 172, 174
turbo-folk and Serbian nationalism, 122
Yugoslav rock as symbol of
cosmopolitanism, 122
Muslimović (character in *Pretty Village,
Pretty Flame*), 132
Muslims
in Bosnia, 83, 86–89, 97
in Bosnia as victims of genocide,
113
committed to evolutionary change in
Algeria, 36
discrimination against in colonial
Algeria, 29, 30
in Kosovo, 84
as the Other in colonial Algeria, 40
in Sarajevo, 105
subject of Serb propaganda, 97–98
as victims of collective punishment in
colonial Algeria, 30
victims of FLN violence, 39,
See also Islam

Nagel, Joane, 7, 11
Napoleon III, 29
narcissism of minor differences, 88
national liberation movements, 9, 10, 22,
25, 26
nationalism, 255–259
Sleeping Beauty theory, 89, 119, 136

as a source of improving women's status,
13
as a source of violence, 12,
See also specific types (*e.g.*, Québec;
Serb)
nationalist mobilization, 13
native populations
in Canada, 22, 204, 208, 224
in North America, 224
in Québec, 239
Nazim (character in *Pretty Village, Pretty
Flame*), 120, 258, 259
Nelson, Robert, 210
Nevzorov, Aleksandr, 142, 188, 189, 198,
199
new wars (Mary Kaldor), 22, 258
Newsday, 112
Nicaragua, 256
Nivat, Anne, 160, 192
Niven, Charles, 171
Nô, 10, 23, 214, 223–236, 248, 255, 258,
260, 262
Noh (or *Nō*) Japanese theater, 224, 225,
227, 233
nonviolence, 9, 18
and abortion, 234
and Canada's political evolution, 207
and the Parti Québécois, 218
as a strategy for Algerian independence,
36
and women during Yugoslav wars of
1990s, 98
North American Free Trade Agreement
(NAFTA), 214, 269
North Caucasus, 24, 140, 141, 144, 145,
155, 163, 165, 169, 196
North Ossetiia, 145
North Vietnamese army, 256
nouveau théâtre Québécois, 217
Nouvelle France, 204
Novi Sad, 99, 116
nuclear weapons, 16, 38

O'Brien, Tim, 137
October, 59
October Crisis, 1970 (Québec), 218–223,
227
oil
in Chechnya, 37, 147, 182, 184
discovered in the Sahara, 37
effect of price drop in the 1980s, 65, 75
effect of price rise in the 1970s, 90
effect of price rise from 1999, 153, 155
and gas as key Algerian exports, 64
nationalization of the industry in
Algeria, 68

Ol'ia (character in *March of the Slav Woman*), 196
Olmert, Ehud, 168
"On the Rainy River," 137
One Flew over the Cuckoo's Nest, 142
Ontario, 207, 212
Open City (Roma, città aperta), 59, 60
Operation Fatima, 192
Oran (French *département*), 29
Organisation de l'Armée Secrète (OAS), 58, 64
Organization of Petroleum Exporting Countries (OPEC), 68
Organization for Security and Cooperation in Europe (OSCE), 179
organized crime
    and new wars, 22
Orthodox Christianity
    in Bosnia, 87, 88
Osaka, Japan, 23, 224, 225, 228, 232, 233
OSCE. *See* Organization for Security and Cooperation in Europe
Oslobodenje (Liberation), 120
Ottawa, 221, 237, 240, 243, 247
Ottoman Empire, 27, 81, 82, 88, 143, 144
Outsiders' Society, 18, 25, 108, 202, 254, 264, 271
"Overcoat, The" (1842), 2, 7
Oxford University, 8

Paisan (Paisà), 59
Pajić, Zoran, 84
Pale, 96
Papineau, Louis-Joseph, 210, 211, 219
    hostility to women's political rights, 210
paratroopers. *See* French army
Paris, 34, 53, 64, 230
Parizeau, Jacques, 240
Parti Patriote, 206, 210
Parti Québécois, 214, 218, 221, 223, 237, 238, 243, 244, 248, 249, 251
patriarchy, 5, 13, 22, 102, 159, 203, 230, 254
    in precolonial Algeria, 32
    in rural Algeria, 67
patrilineal tradition
    in Algeria, 32, 33
    in Serbia, 111
Patriot, 170
Payette, Lise, 238, 240
peace
    related to gender equality, 15
peace activists
    in Yugoslavia, 107, 114, 131–132

Pechorin (character in *Hero of Our Time*), 166, 167
Peckinpah, Sam, 131
Pelletier, Gérard, 213
Penavin, Olga (Borsy), 116
Pépé le Moko, 59
Pervomaiskoe, 152
Petar, the professor (character in *Pretty Village, Pretty Flame*), 125
Petit Omar (character in *The Battle of Algiers*), 60
Philippeville massacre, 38, 44
Phillips, John, 36, 67, 70, 76, 77
Piankova, Natal'ia, 196
pieds noirs, 27, 30, 38, 42, 58
Plavšić, Biljana, 105–106, 111, 137
Politkovskaia, Anna, 160, 167
polls. *See* popular opinion
polygamy
    in Chechnya, 160, 161
Polytechnique, 246
Pontecorvo, Gillo, 9, 22, 25, 26, 40, 42, 47, 53, 62, 79, 173
    use of crowd as collective actor, 59
Popov, Fedor, 142, 189, 191
popular opinion
    in Algeria, 75
    in Bosnia, 260
    manipulated in Yugoslavia, 81, 95
    in Québec, 222, 243, 247, 249, 250–251
    in Russia, 14, 22, 167, 177
    of Russians on second Chechen war, 155
    surveys on ethnic relations in Bosnia, 88, 123
    surveys on ethnic relations in Yugoslavia, 90, 92–94
    survey on ethnic and religious affiliation in Bosnia, 87
Potemkin, 59
Presse, La (Montréal), 222, 243, 248
Pretty Village, Pretty Flame, vii, ix, 10, 22, 81–82, 114, 115, 116, 118, 119, 121, 123, 138, 186, 196, 198, 255, 258, 260, 271
    Hollywood influences, 131
    montages, 122
    soundtrack, 118, 119, 122, 131
primatology, 4
"Prisoner of the Caucasus" (1822), 170, 176
"Prisoner of the Caucasus" (1872), 170, 173
Prisoner of the Mountains, 10, 23, 142, 170–177, 178, 180, 187, 199, 200, 202, 259
    soundtrack, 172

Procházková, Petra, 160, 161, 162, 164, 166, 169, 178, 193, 194, 195, 200
proliferation of small men, 4, 14, 15, 16, 22, 66, 91, 138, 266
    in Algeria, 67–69
    in Yugoslavia, 91
pro-natalist policies, 13, 15
    in Québec, 238, 240, 251
    in Yugoslavia, 100
prostitution
    as allegory for female FLN members, 48
    in Chechnya, 177, 179
    FLN campaign against, 40, 41
    forced in Bosnia, 110
    involvement of UN forces in Bosnia, 111
public opinion. *See* popular opinion
Pudovkin, Vsevolod, 50
Pulikovskii, Konstantin, 153
Purgatory, 142, 188, 191, 198
Pushkin, Aleksandr, 146, 170, 176, 177
Putin, Vladimir, 27, 141, 147, 155, 156, 158, 166, 168, 185, 261
    praises rapist, 168

Québec, 3, 11, 15, 21, 22
    Commission on Accommodation Practices Related to Cultural Difference, 246–247
    comparison with Yugoslavia, 240–242
    emigration to the United States, 207
    federalists vs. sovereigntists, 213, 238, 246, 251
    immigrants, 206, 217, 239, 240, 246, 247
    industrialization and urbanization after World War II, 212
    multiculturalism, 239, 241, 243, 247, 248
    National Assembly, 210
    nationalism, 10, 248
        origins, 204–209
    October Crisis (1970), 218–223
    Rebellion of 1837–1838, 206, 207, 209–210, 219, 223
    referendum of 1980, 224, 234, 239
    referendum of 1995, 239
    rejection of ethnic nationalism, 249
    women and the early nationalist movement, 209–212
    women's attitudes towards sovereignty, 242–244
Quebec Act of 1774, 137, 205
Québec City, 23, 204, 238
Québec solidaire, 250, 252

Québécois de souche, 241, 242, 248
Québec-Presse, 220
Quiet Revolution (*Révolution tranquille*), 212–214
Quoc Dung, Nguyen, 256
Qur'an, 31, 40, 41, 97, 165

racism
    charged in 1995 Québec referendum, 240
    in Russian attiudes towards Chechens, 142, 181
    in US attitudes towards immigrants, 268–269
Radomirović, Zoran Švaba, 122
Raduev, Salman, 152, 181, 183
Ram Plan (1991), 94, 110
Ram, Harsha, 146
Rambo, 117, 146, 173, 197, 255
Ramet, Sabrina, 116
Randall, Margaret, 271
rape
    in 1990s Algeria, 78
    exaggerated claims about Albanian Kosovars in 1980s, 100
    and enslavement of women in Russian conquest of the Caucasus, 165
    of FLN women, 61
    and forced marriage in Algeria, 77–78
    and forced marriage in Chechnya, 163–165
    and forced pregnancy in Bosnia, 110, 111–112
    by French soldiers in Kabylie, 64
    mass rape in Algeria, 21
    mass rape in Bosnian war, explanations for, 109–114
    mass rape by French troops in Algerian villages, 61
    mass rape in former Yugoslavia, 13, 21, 34, 80, 137
    of men, 6
    and murder of Elza Kungaeva, 167
    and murder of women in 1990s Algeria, 66
    as part of Yugoslav army's Ram Plan, 110
    rape camps in Bosnia, 109, 110, 117
    rape camps in colonial Algeria, 62
    rape camps in independent Algeria, 78
    as source of shame in Chechnya, 166, 178
    threatened by FLN to extort money, 61
ratissages. *See* sweep operations
Ravarino, Mauro, 118
Ražnatović (née Veličković), Svetlana, 122

Raznatović, Zeljko (Arkan), 105, 122
redemption, 23, 199
referendum
    on Algerian independence (1962), 58
    on Bosnian independence (1992), 94
    on Québec sovereignty (1980), 223, 234,
        236–239, 240, 242
    on Québec sovereignty (1995), 239, 240,
        247, 251, 262
refugees
    from Algeria emigrate to France, 58
    from Alsace-Lorraine settle in Algeria, 29
    from Bosnia, 86
    from Bosnia and Croatia, 89
    from Chechnya, 140
    from Grozny, 153
    Serbs from Bosnia and Croatia, 86
    Serbs from Slovenia, 85
    suffer abuse in Serbia, 102
religion, 1
    and citizenship in Algeria, 29
    relevance to Algerian war of
        independence, 40, 41
    in rural Algeria, 77
    as source of identity in Bosnia, 86–88
    as source of identity in Québec, 204 ,
    See also specific religions (Islam,
        Orthodox Christianity, Roman
        Catholicism)
René (character in *Nô*), 228
reproductive rights, 13, 15
    in Yugoslavia, 100
Republika Srpska, 94, 125
resistance movements
    anti-Nazi, 26, 82–83, 98
    French, 26
    gender identity in, 26
    Greek, 26
    Italian, 26
    role of women, 26, 98
    Yugoslav, 82–83, 98
Resnais, Alain, 62, 232
revenge
    motive for violence in Algeria, 45, 65,
        70, 263
    motive for violence in Chechnya, 177,
        181, 187, 193,
    See also blood feud
    and women's violence in Bosnia, 107
    and women's violence in Chechnya, 158,
        191
Riel, Louis, 208
Roberts, Hugh, 64, 70
Rogozhkin, Aleksandr, 23, 142, 177, 178,
        179, 187, 257
Rolling Stones, 129

Roman Catholicism
    in Bosnia, 87, 88
    cause of discrimination in Canada, 205
    and domination of health and education
        in Québec, 213, 215
    influence on Québec's political life, 208,
        213, 215
    in Nouvelle France, 204
    officially recognized in Quebec Act of
        1774, 205
    and opposition to women's suffrage in
        Québec, 211
    as source of Québécois swears, 117, 232
Rossellini, Roberto, 59
rough-and-tumble play, 6
Rue de Thèbes massacre, 42, 44, 45, 46
Ruedy, John, 29
Rushdie, Salman, 233
Russia, 10, 21
Russian army, 140, 151, 152, 153, 154,
        157, 166, 169, 172, 177, 187, 189,
        196, 200, 202
Russian Empire, 27, 82, 143
Russian Federation, 139, 151, 195, 259
Russian government, 105
Russian literature, 1, 2, 142, 165, 171, 173,
    source of images of Chechens, 146
Ryan, Claude, 221, 238
Ryan, Madeleine, 238
Rybkin, Ivan, 182

Sadek (character in *The Battle of Algiers*), 60
Sakha (Iakutia), 140
Samary, Catherine, 83
Samashki, 151, 160, 165
Sandinista revolution, 256
Sarajevo, 86, 88, 89, 96, 97, 99, 104, 109,
        128
    Serb plan for partition, 105
Sarajevo University, 96, 106
Sarkisova, Oksana, 163, 170, 173, 180,
        185, 200
Sasha (character in *March of the Slav
        Woman*), 196
Sasha (character in *Prisoner of the
        Mountains*), 172
secession
    of Bosnia-Herzegovina, April 1992, 85
    of Chechnya, 139, 149–156
    of Croatia, June 1991, 85, 102, 107
    inherent in structure of Yugoslav
        Federation, 85
    of Québec, 233, 242, 250
    risk in Russian Federation, 140
    of Slovenia, June 1991, 85, 91, 102
    and violence, 13, 260

Seferdjeli, Ryme, 34
Seierstad, Åsne, 160
Seifert, Ruth, 109
Serb army, 110
Serb identity, 118, 130, 132
Serbia, 13, 83, 89
Serbian Academy of Sciences and Arts, 99,
    125, 241
Serbian nationalism, 85, 92, 132
Sesar, Rada, 96
Šešelj, Vojislav, 85
Sétif, 35, 36, 259
sex, as a biological category, 5
sexual violence, 7, 10, 167
    against men in Yugoslav wars, 109, 131,
        136
    in Algerian civil war of 1990s, 78
    in Algerian war of independence, 61, 62,
        79, 116
    in Chechnya, 165–169
    in Russian conquest of the Caucasus,
        165
    in Yugoslav culture, 117
sexualization of war, 6
Seymour, Michel, 240
Shakespeare, William, 181
shakhidki (female martyrs in Chechnya),
    157
Shamil', 146
Shane, 20
shari'ia, 160
Shelley (character in Glengarry Glen Ross),
    17
Shteyngart, Gary, 170
Silber, Laura, 104
Simon, Shena, 269, 270
Slapsak, Svetlana, 99
Sloba (character in Pretty Village, Pretty
    Flame), 120
Slovakia, 12
Slovenia, 83, 91
    declares independence, June 1991, 85
Smith, Anna Marie, 223
Smith, M. Agnes, 254
snipers
    in Chechnya, 142, 159, 167, 177, 188,
        189, 191, 198; See also White
        Stockings
socialization, 6, 12, 271
Society of Outsiders. See Outsiders'
    Society
Sokurov, Aleksandr, 10, 23, 143, 199
Solidarity trade union movement (Poland),
    83
Solinas, Franco, 47, 53, 62
Solzhenitsyn, Aleksandr, 175

Sophie (character in Nô), 224, 259
SOS Hotline (Belgrade), 102, 103, 117,
    131, 133
South Ossetiia, 145
sovereigntists (souverainistes), 10, 24, 249,
    250, 251
sovereignty, 259–263
    advantages and disadvantages for
        women, 257–258
    advocated for Québec, 213, 214, 223,
        234, 237, 239, 240, 241, 242, 247,
        248, 251
    associated with war in Algeria,
        Chechnya, and Yugoslavia, 257–258
    contradictory definitions, 248, 259–263
Soviet Union, 10, 12, 26, 82, 163, 183
    communist ideology favors gender
        equality, 159
    disintegration, 139, 145, 148, 189, 259
    impact of reforms on Yugoslavia, 83
    modernization contributes to ethnic
        assimilation, 144
    nationalities policy, 144
    women's education fostered equality,
        265
Spain
    civil war in, 11
Speedy (character in Pretty Village, Pretty
    Flame), 126
Srebrenica, 113
St. Petersburg (Russia), 140
Stalin, Iosif, 58, 123, 144, 145, 174
    orders mass deportation of Chechens,
        144
Stallone, Sylvester, 117, 173
Stambolić, Ivan, 84, 133
Stanford University, 5, 82
Sterne, Laurence, 233
Stiglmayer, Alexandra, 112
Stojanović, Slavica, 101–102
Strike, 59
structural adjustment
    comparison to colonial Algeria, 30
    impact on independent Algeria, 65
    impact on Soviet Union, 30
    impact on Yugoslavia, 30
Stuart, Charles, 268
subordination of women, 6, 264
    in Chechnya, 160, 162
Südtirol, 263
suicide bombers, 2, 141
    in Russia, 10, 141, 156, 158, 159, 191,
        259; See also Black Widows
Šumadinac (character in Pretty Village,
    Pretty Flame), 130
Suny, Ronald, 89, 119

surrealism, 22, 117
surveys. *See* popular opinion
Svetlana (character in *March of the Slav Woman*), 196
swearing
  in Québec French, 117, 231–232
  in Russian, 116
  in Serbo-Croatian, 116–117
sweep operations, 36
  in Algerian war of independence, 36, 172
  in Chechnya, 37, 172, 192
  in US war in Iraq, 172
"Sympathy for the Devil," 129

Tamara (Chechen refugee in Czech Republic), 139
Tatarstan, 140, 151, 152
television
  and censorship in Russia, 159
  inciting ethnic violence in Yugoslavia, 95–98, 100, 102, 124, 125, 129
terrorism, 2, 10
  in 1990s Algeria, 70
  in Algerian war of independence, 21, 26, 35, 45
  changing attitudes towards, 192
  Chechen reaction to Russian brutality, 152
  counterterrorism in Algeria, 42
  in first Chechen war, 151–152, 154
  and Islamism in Chechnya, 158
  by *pieds noirs* extremists in Algeria, 42, 58
  and Québec separatism, 223
  in Russian films on Chechnya, 186
  in second Chechen war, 156
  as a weapon of the weak, 45
Testament of Orpheus, 232
Thatcher, Margaret, 105
The Wild Bunch, 131
This Was Not Our War, 80
Three Guineas, 2–4, 7, 9, 11, 18, 23, 25, 98, 253, 255, 265, 269
Tickner, J. Ann, 13
Timur (interviewed by Valerii Tishkov), 261
Tishkov, Valerii, 147, 148, 150, 160, 165, 188, 193, 261
Tito (Josip Broz), 82, 89, 120, 124, 130, 136
Tolstoi, Lev, 1, 2, 28, 146, 170, 173, 177
torture
  at Abu Ghraib prison, 2
  in Alain Resnais' *Muriel*, 62
  in Algerian civil war of 1990s, 70, 77
  in *The Battle of Algiers*, 59, 60, 115, 184

  in Chechnya, 195, 261
  by French troops in Algerian war of independence, 37, 57, 60, 61
  in *Open City*, 59
  in *Pretty Village, Pretty Flame*, 131
  in Québec (hoax), 222
  of women in Algerian war of independence, 61, 62–63, 116, 191
  of women in Chechnya, 158, 166
  in Yugoslav wars of 1990s, 109
Torture and the Twilight of Empire, 79
Toth, Anthony, 27, 29, 38, 58, 65, 68
Traynor, Ian, 96
Treaty of Paris 1763, 135, 204
Tremblay, Michel, 203, 217
Trgovčević, Ljubinka, 133
Trollope, Anthony, 2
Trudeau, Pierre Elliott, 208, 213, 219, 220, 221, 222, 223, 226, 234, 238, 239, 260
Truffaut, François, 227
Tuđman, Franjo, 84, 96
Tunisia, 67, 75
Tunnel of Brotherhood and Unity (*Tunel Bratsvo i Jedinstvo*), 118
Tunnel of Peace, 137
Turgenev, Ivan, 1, 7
Turkey, 161
Tuzla, 106, 120
Twain, Mark, 215

Udugov, Movladi, 183
Uganda, 14, 91, 266
Ukraine, 150
Umarov, Doku, 164
unemployment, 14, 15, 17, 65
  in Algeria, 1980s–1990s, 65, 66, 76
  in Chechnya, 148
  disproportionately affects uneducated men in the USA, 266
  resulting from discrimination in Chechnya, 147
  source of male humiliation, 266
  structural, in Chechnya, 147
  in Yugoslavia, 1980s–1990s, 90, 91
Union nationale, 213
United Nations Protection Force (UNPROFOR), 111, 113, 128, 133
United States, 15, 95, 96, 206, 207, 210, 214, 270
  gender differences in income, 267
  male humiliation
    and murder, 267–268
  potential for misogynistic violence, 267–269
  unemployment, 266

University of Michigan, 16
UNPROFOR. *See* United Nations
    Protection Force
Urus-Martan, 183
Ustashe (*Ustaše*), 83, 92

Vallières, Pierre, 220, 222
Vance-Owen Plan, 95
Vancouver Sun, 222
veil, the
    as disguise for Algerian men, 54
    in central Asia, 26
    in Chechnya, 158
    in colonial Algeria, 33, 35, 53
    in independent Algeria, 67
    as an instrument of colonialism and
        resistance, 26, 33, 35, 53, 54, 55
Veledinskii, Aleksandr, 195
Velja (character in *Pretty Village, Pretty
    Flame*), 124, 149
Vidal-Naquet, Pierre, 62
Vietnam, 22, 37, 137, 256
Vietnam war films, 117, 131
Vika (character in *House of Fools*), 197
Viljuška, the Fork (character in *Pretty
    Village, Pretty Flame*), 125
Villeneuve, Denis, 246
Višegrad, 115
Vishnevskaia, Galina, 200
Viziginova, Zoya, 265
Vlasov, Valentin, 183, 184
Vojvodina, 83, 85, 99, 116

Wahhabis, 158, 159, 188
Walzer, Michael, 44
War (Voina), 23, 142, 184–187
War and Gender, 5, 25, 269
War and Peace (1869), 2
war as a mostly male activity, 4–8, 25, 41,
    153, 269
war crimes
    in former Yugoslavia, 86, 102, 106
    in Russia, 166, 167, 179, 186
War Measures Act (Québec), 221, 223,
    225, 226, 234
war on terror, US, 2
War (Voina), 257, 271
Warren, Mary Ann, 112
Washington, Ned, 19
Way We Live Now, The (1875), 2
Wayne, John, 20
Weir, Fred, 157
West, Lois, 211, 237
West, the
    gendered as female or effeminate, 186,
        187

Western, the (film genre), 4, 17, 20, 131,
    163, 186
White Stockings (female snipers),
    187–191, 198
Wild, Daniel, 190
Williams, Grant, 16
Williams, Robin, 131
women
    attitudes towards Québec sovereignty,
        242–244
    as boundary markers, 1, 104
    and nonviolence, 9, 18
    in North Vietnamese army, 256, 257
    as peacemakers in Chechnya, 169
    and rejection of war, 18
    as sexual container for impregnation, 63,
        111–112, 136
    as soldiers, 6
    as targets of colonial policies, 34
    as targets of Islamist violence in 1990s
        Algeria, 34, 72
    as targets of male resentment in 1990s
        Algeria, 72–75
    and types of violent resistance in Algeria,
        39, 47
    in Yugoslav anti-Nazi resistance, 98
    in Zapatista army, 257
"Women and the Evolution of World
    Politics," 4
"Women of Algiers," 33
women's suffrage
    in Canada, 211
    opposed by (male) Québec nationalists,
        210, 211
    result of World War I, 253
Wood, Elisabeth, 137
Woodward, Susan, 80
Woolf, Virginia, 2–4, 7, 8–10, 11, 18, 21,
        23, 25, 57, 80, 98, 101, 107, 108,
        130, 143, 153, 158, 190, 202, 246,
        253–255, 269, 270, 271
    on education, equality, and peace,
        263–269
    on male resentment of working women,
        265–266
World Bank, 65, 75, 90
World War I, 8, 263
    Québécois opposition to Canada's
        participation, 209
    and women's suffrage, 253
World War II, 8, 9, 21, 26, 33, 35, 82, 89,
        96, 101, 113, 149, 170, 211
    and changes for Canadian women, 211
    changes in Québec, 212
    Québécois opposition to Canada's
        participation, 209

World's Fair (Expo '70), 225, 231, 232

Yacef, Saadi, 41, 45, 46, 47, 53, 54, 55, 56,
    57, 63, 64
Yeltsin, Boris, 140, 141, 149, 150, 151,
    152, 153, 155, 182, 183, 184, 185
youth bulge, 14
    in Algeria, late 1940s–1950s, 15, 32
    in Algeria, late 1980s, 65, 75, 79
Yugoslav army, 85, 86, 94, 107, 108, 113,
    123, 125, 128, 132, 133, 135, 241,
    260
    deserters and draft resisters, 107, 108
    volunteers, 108
Yugoslav cinema, 22, 114
Yugoslav federation, 21, 83, 85, 95, 139
Yugoslav identity, 92, 101, 123, 124, 260
Yugoslav partisans, 82, 83, 105, 123
Yugoslavia, 3, 10, 11, 12, 15, 21
    historical overview, 82–86
Yvette phenomenon, 237, 238, 244

Zaccaria, Giuseppe, 110, 111
zachistki. See sweep operations
Zagreb, 81, 99, 101, 118
zaouedj el moutaa. See marriage, forced
Zapatista army, 257
Žbanić, Jasmila, 116
Zelimkhan, 170
Zhanna (character in House of Fools),
    196
Zhenya (interviewed by Procházková),
    161, 164, 165
Zhenya (sister of Anya, granddaughter of
    Zhenya), 164
Zhilin, Ivan (Vanya) (character in Prisoner
    of the Mountains), 172
Zinnemann, Fred, 17
Živojinović, Velimir Bata, 123
Zone Autonome d'Alger, 39
Zoya (interviewed by Procházková), 161
Zvereva, Galina, 181, 186
Zvigeskaia, Irina, 169